Mother Tongues and Other Tongues

China Studies

PUBLISHED FOR THE INSTITUTE FOR CHINESE
STUDIES, UNIVERSITY OF OXFORD

Series Editor

Rana Mitter, *Harvard Kennedy School*

VOLUME 53

The titles published in this series are listed at *brill.com/chs*

Mother Tongues and Other Tongues

Creating and Translating Sinophone Poetry

Edited by

Simona Gallo
Martina Codeluppi

BRILL

LEIDEN | BOSTON

The editors would like to thank the Department of Languages, Literatures, Cultures and Mediations of the University of Milan for underwriting the copyediting of this book.

Cover illustration: "天平 Balance" (acrylic on canvas, 50 × 70 cm) by Yo Yo 友友 (pen name of Liu Youhong 劉友紅)

The Library of Congress Cataloging-in-Publication Data is available online at https://catalog.loc.gov
LC record available at https://lccn.loc.gov/2024031720

Typeface for the Latin, Greek, and Cyrillic scripts: "Brill". See and download: brill.com/brill-typeface.

ISSN 1570-1344
ISBN 978-90-04-71159-4 (hardback)
ISBN 978-90-04-71160-0 (e-book)
DOI 10.1163/9789004711600

Copyright 2024 by Simona Gallo and Martina Codeluppi. Published by Koninklijke Brill BV, Leiden, The Netherlands.
Koninklijke Brill BV incorporates the imprints Brill, Brill Nijhoff, Brill Schöningh, Brill Fink, Brill mentis, Brill Wageningen Academic, Vandenhoeck & Ruprecht, Böhlau and V&R unipress.
Koninklijke Brill BV reserves the right to protect this publication against unauthorized use. Requests for re-use and/or translations must be addressed to Koninklijke Brill BV via brill.com or copyright.com.

This book is printed on acid-free paper and produced in a sustainable manner.

Contents

Acknowledgments   VII
Conventions   VIII
List of Figures   IX
About the Contributors   X

Introduction: Sinophone Poetry as an Interlingual Space   1
  Simona Gallo and Martina Codeluppi

PART 1
Thinking, Writing, and Translating the Sinophone

1   "My Country of Origin Has Something to Do with It I Suppose"
  Sinophone Poetry, Global English, and Translational Poetics   11
    Lucas Klein

2   Hong Kong Poetry and Diaspora
  The Wang Tao Mode and the Sinophone   34
    Chris Song

3   "It Can't Be All in One Language"
  Poetry in the Diverse Language   50
    Cosima Bruno

4   Translingual Poetry and the Poetics of Translingualism
  Sinophone verses, Thirdspaces and "Thirdlanguagings"   66
    Simona Gallo

PART 2
Translation, Contamination, and Foreign-Language Writing

5   Translingual Poetic Experiments by Amang, Tsai Wan-Shuen,
  and Jami Proctor-Xu   95
    Justyna Jaguscik

VI   CONTENTS

6   Speaking from "In-Between"
     Jennifer Wong and the Translation of the Self   111
         Martina Codeluppi

7   Saying More by Writing Less
     Sinophone Small Poetry from Thailand   125
         Rebecca M. Ehrenwirth

8   Poetry in Motion
     Transnational Sinophone Poets across Italy and China   143
         Valentina Pedone

9   Borderless Creation
     Ming Di's World of Poetry between Translation, Self-Translation and Co-Translation   162
         Nicoletta Pesaro

10   Epistolary Translation
     Daryl Lim Wei Jie's Correspondence with Bai Juyi   190
         Joanna Krenz

PART 3
Experiences from the Sinophone

11   A Matter of Survival   217
         Ying Chen 应晨

12   The Other Mother Tongues and Minority Writing in China   224
         Ming Di 明迪

13   Why Do I Translate Myself?   256
         Mai Mang 麥芒

     Index   279

Acknowledgments

We wish to express our deepest gratitude to all the contributors to this book, whose dedication to our project made *Mother Tongues and Other Tongues: Creating and Translating Sinophone Poetry* possible.

We sincerely thank the editors at Brill, Qin Higley and Stephanie Carta, for expertly guiding the publication process. Their patience and enthusiasm were invaluable.

We are also grateful to Yo Yo 友友, Gao Xingjian 高行健, Hsia Yü 夏宇, Li Hui 李輝, Robert Wilson, and Zhang Huan 張洹, for permission to use some pictures, and to Steve Bradbury and Manuela Lietti for their kind mediation.

The editors also wish to thank the Department of Languages, Literatures, Cultures and Mediations of the University of Milan for funding the final copyediting of each part of the book, as well as the copyeditor Mark D. Mathias.

Last but not least, we would like to express our gratitude and appreciation to our peer reviewers for truly constructive criticism. This book would have been much poorer without their wisdom and insight.

Conventions

Chinese characters are transcribed in *pinyin* and reproduced full-form, as *fantizi* 繁體字. For consistency, we use full-form even when texts were first published in simplified characters, and when citing names or passages in Wade-Giles or other romanization systems.

Chinese texts are reproduced especially when treated as primary sources, accompanied by translations. Relevant names and terms under discussion can be found in the finding index at the end, which includes Chinese characters and provides suggested translations.

Figures

0.1 Zhang Huan 張洹. 2001. "Family Tree" 家譜 (1/9). Chromogenic print. Courtesy of Zhang Huan 張洹   8

0.2 Wilson, Robert. 2005. "Gao Xingjian". In *Robert Wilson Video Portraits*. Courtesy of Robert Wilson and Gao Xingjian 高行健   8

4.1 Hsia Yü 夏宇. 2016. *First Person* 第一人稱, translated by Steve Bradbury. A line from chapter n. 22. Taipei: self-published. Courtesy of Hsia Yü 夏宇 and Steve Bradbury   79

4.2 Hsia Yü 夏宇. 2016. *First Person* 第一人稱, translated by Steve Bradbury. Lines 4 and 5 from chapter n. 27. Taipei: self-published. Courtesy of Hsia Yü 夏宇 and Steve Bradbury   82

12.1 Administrative Map of China. Public domain   229

12.2 Recurring symbols and compounds on Dônđäc Floral Belts   248

About the Contributors

Cosima Bruno

is Reader in Chinese Literature at the School of Oriental and African Studies University of London. Her publications include *Between the Lines: Yang Lian's Poetry through Translation* (Brill, 2012), translations, and articles in *Concentric*, *Translation and Literature*, JMLC, *Life Writing*, *Target*, *Intervention*, *Shi tansuo*, *Black Mountain Review*, *In forma di parole*, and in the collected volumes *Prismatic Translation* (Legenda, 2019), *Translating Chinese Art and Literature* (Routledge, 2019), *China and Its Others* (Rodopi, 2012), *Made in China* (Mondadori, 2008) and *Translating Others* (St Jerome, 2006). Her main research interests are in contemporary Chinese, Sinophone and bilingual poetry, poetry performativity and the theoretical issues related to its translation; visual and sound poetry; language art.

Martina Codeluppi

is Associate Professor of Chinese Studies at the Alma Mater Studiorum – University of Bologna. She holds a PhD in contemporary Chinese literature from Ca' Foscari University of Venice and Sorbonne Nouvelle University – Paris 3. She specializes in contemporary Chinese literature from a comparative perspective and her main publications deal with migrant literature, self-translation, and literary theory. She is the author of the book *Fictional Memories: Contemporary Chinese Literature and Transnationality*, published in 2020 by L'Harmattan, and the translator of fiction by contemporary Chinese authors such as An Yu, Shi Yifeng, Hao Jingfang, Wei Wei, and Yan Ge.

Rebecca M. Ehrenwirth

received her PhD in Sinology from Ludwig-Maximilians-University Munich in 2017. In 2019 she joined the University of Applied Sciences/SDI Munich as an Assistant Professor for Translation. She is a founding member and the current Secretary-Treasurer of the Society of Sinophone Studies. Her main research fields include Sinophone Studies, Postcolonial Literature, Contemporary Art and Translation Studies. Her article on Intertextuality in Contemporary Sinophone Literature in Thailand has been published with the journal *Modern Chinese Literature and Culture* (MCLC).

Simona Gallo

is Associate Professor of Chinese Studies at the University of Milan. Specializing in contemporary Chinese and Sinophone Literature, she combines her literary research with Translation and Cultural Studies. She edited and translated a collection of essays of the Sinophone Nobel laureate Gao Xingjian and authored a monograph about his critical thinking (*Per un nuovo Rinascimento*, 2020). She has published several papers on the topics of cultural translation, intertextuality, as well as self-translation and contemporary Sinophone poetry, which currently stand as her main research interests.

Justyna Jaguscik
holds a joint doctorate in Chinese Studies from the University of Zurich and the University of Warsaw and additionally, an MA degree in Sociology from the University of Warsaw. Currently, she is teaching modern Chinese language and developing a new study program dedicated to modern Chinese language and the history and culture of Chinese-speaking regions. Her main research interests are modern and contemporary Chinese-language literature and culture, Chinese-language poetry, transnational feminism, ecocriticism and nonconfrontational cultural activism. Since 2011 she has coorganized a number of international workshops dedicated to a broad range of topics, such as Chinese responses to the Anthropocene (2015), Chinese utopianism (2018) and the newest trends in contemporary Chinese and Sinophone poetry (2022). She is also an active member of the academic community and serve as Board Member and Vice Secretary of the European Association for Chinese Studies.

Lucas Klein
(PhD Yale) is a father, writer, translator, and Associate Professor of Chinese at Arizona State University. He is executive editor of the *Hsu-Tang Library of Classical Chinese Literature* (Oxford), author of *The Organization of Distance* (Brill, 2018), co-editor of *Chinese Poetry and Translation* (Amsterdam, 2019), and translator of Mang Ke (Zephyr, 2018), Li Shangyin (NYRB, 2018), Duo Duo (Yale, 2021), and Xi Chuan (New Directions, 2012, 2022).

Joanna Krenz
(PhD Leiden) is an Assistant Professor at the Institute of Oriental Studies of Adam Mickiewicz University in Poznań, Poland. Her research focuses on contemporary literature in a comparative perspective, in particular literature's connections with science, technology, and philosophy. She is the author of *In Search of Singularity: Poetry in Poland and China Since 1989* (2022) and an active translator of Chinese poetry and prose into Polish, her recent translations include Yan Lianke's novels *Heart Sutra* (*Sutra Serca*, 2023), *The Day the Sun Died* (*Dzień, w którym umarło słońce*, 2022), *Dream of Ding Village* (*Sen wioski Ding*, 2019) and *Explosion Chronicles* (*Kroniki Eksplozji*, 2019).

Mai Mang 麥芒 (*Yibing Huang*)

is an award-winning poet, critic, curator, and translator writing in both Chinese and English. He is the author of *Contemporary Chinese Literature: From the Cultural Revolution to the Future* (2007). In 2016, he was nominated for a Pushcart Prize by *World Literature Today* for two of his poems, "About Freedom" and "Do Not Write Poetry with Your Heart," which he translated into English himself. He has curated a series of contemporary Chinese art exhibitions and written on a wide range of subjects related to Chinese literature and art. He is currently Professor of Chinese and Curator of the Chu-Griffis Asian Art Collection at Connecticut College.

Ming Di 明迪

is a poet and translator from China, author of seven books of poetry in Chinese and one in collaborative translation: *River Merchant's Wife* (Marick Press, 2012). She is co-founder and editor of *PoetryEastWest* and editor of the *China domain of Poetry International Web*. She co-translated four books of poetry from Chinese into English including Empty Chairs – Poems by Liu Xia (Graywolf Press, 2015) which was a finalist of the Best Translated Book Award 2016 and won a translation prize from Poetry Foundation. She translated six books of poetry into Chinese including Marianne Moore's *Observations* (Sichuan Wenyi, 2018). She received the Lishan Poetry Award (translation) and the Best Ten Translator Award 2021 in China. She was guest co-editor of three issues of *Mānoa: A Pacific Journal of International Writing.* She has edited and co-translated *New Cathay – Contemporary Chinese Poetry* (Tupelo Press, 2013) and *New Poetry from China 1917–2017* (Black Square Editions, 2019) and compiled six other anthologies including *Mujeres poetas de China contemporánea* (Vaso Roto, 2021) and *Geografía de la poesía china del siglo XXI* (Sonámbulos Ediciones, 2022). Her new anthology *Indigenous-Minority Voices from China* is forthcoming.

Valentina Pedone

is Associate Professor of Chinese language and literature at the University of Florence, Italy. Her research focuses on Chinese mobility to Italy with special attention on cultural issues. She is the co-editor of the peer-reviewed book series on Chinese and Japanese Studies titled Florientalia. In 2013 she published the book *A Journey to the West: Observations on the Chinese Migration to Italy* (Firenze University Press). In 2021 she won the Canada Italy Innovation Award for *VulCa2021*, a project aimed at producing an artistic documentary about COVID-triggered Sinophobia in Canada and Italy.

ABOUT THE CONTRIBUTORS

Nicoletta Pesaro

is Professor of Chinese language and literature at Ca' Foscari University of Venice, where she coordinates the PhD program on Asian and African Studies. Her research interests include modern and contemporary Chinese literature, theory of narrative and Translation Studies. She wrote several articles on Chinese literature and literary translation, and translated various novels, among which *Huozhe* (To live) by Yu Hua and *Xiao tuanyuan* (Little Reunions) by Zhang Ailing. The Italian publisher Sellerio published her new Italian translation of Lu Xun's first two collections of short stories (*Nahan* and *Panghuang*). She edited *The Ways of Translation. Constraints and Liberties of Translating Chines* (2013) and a collection of essays on globalized Chinese literature: *Littérature chinoise et globalisation: enjeux linguistiques, traductologiques et génériques* (2017). She is the author of a book on modern Chinese fiction *Narrativa cinese del Novecento. Autori, opere, correnti* (Twentieth-Century Chinese Fiction: Authors, works and schools, Carocci, 2019) co-authored with M. Pirazzoli. She is the director of the book series *Translating Wor(l)ds.*

Chris Song

is Assistant Professor at the Department of Language Studies (UTSC) with a graduate cross-appointment at the Department of East Asian Studies (UTSG) of the University of Toronto. His research falls at the intersection of Translation Studies, modern poetry in Chinese, and Hong Kong culture, with a focus on Chinese anthologies of American poetry. He is appointed by the International Federation of Translators as the managing editor of *Babel: Revue internationale de la traduction / International Journal of Translation* (John Benjamins).

Ying Chen 应晨

is a Chinese Canadian author. She writes mostly in French and also translates her own works into Chinese and English. Ying Chen's novels include *La mémoire de l'eau, Les lettres chinoises, L'ingratitude* (which won the Prix Québec-Paris, and was published in the US as "Ingratitude," translated by Carol Volk, and published in China as "再见妈妈", self-translated), *Immobile* (which won the Prix Alfred-DesRochers), *Le champ dans la mer* (published in China as "V 家花园", self-translated), *Querelle d'un squelette avec son double* (self-translated and published on Amazon as "Skeleton and its double"), "Le Mangeur", "Un Enfant à ma porte", "Espèces", "La Rive est loin". She wrote two books of essays: "Quatre mille marches" and "La Lenteur des montagnes" She practices a lean, polished and deceptively simple writing style, free of flourishes and excess verbiage. As a child, one of her schoolteachers once told her "the most simple is the most beautiful", and she has retained this idea.

Introduction: Sinophone Poetry as an Interlingual Space

Simona Gallo and *Martina Codeluppi*

The title of this book encapsulates not only the key concepts that have inspired and steered our work – "Sinophone poetry," "mother/other tongues," "creation," and "translation" – but also some foundational questions on our agenda, starting with a crucial one: "What is Sinophone poetry?" We believe that dwelling on some preliminary observations about the core elements at play is the most suitable way to introduce this edited volume.

Originally conceived by Shu-mei Shih as the "study of Sinitic-language cultures and communities on the margins of China and Chineseness" (Shih 2004), the concept of the Sinophone has been described as underscoring "issues and controversies pertaining to multiple identities, ethnicities, languages, and cultures" (Tsai in Shih, Tsai, Bernards 2013, 17) on the margins of China and Chineseness (Shih 2004). Their polyphonic, place-based, and multifarious nature can be investigated through a wide range of academic discourses and across a variety of fields (Shih 2011). Despite its ideal openness, this theoretical framework, along with its boundaries, has been subject to discussion and revision, in an effort to eschew an ideological posture that may engender new forms of hegemony and new ethnocentrisms, for the sake of a more inclusive outlook – especially when it comes to literature. Sinophone literature, primarily envisioned as the literature written by Sinitic-language writers outside China and across the world (Shih 2004), has also been approached by scholars from multiple perspectives, by either emphasizing its multilingual and polyscriptic nature (Zhang 2014, 13), and cultural hybridity, or else avoiding the exclusivity of the ethnographic, linguistic, and political connotation (Tsu and Wang 2010; Tsu 2010; Chiu and Zhang 2022).

With all this in mind, we have decided to adopt a translational and transcultural attitude toward the Sinophone and the Sinosphere, envisaging the latter as a kaleidoscope of linguistic and cultural articulations. Our purpose is twofold: on the one hand, we wish to shed light on some of the manifold translingual phenomena (see Kellman 2000; 2019) that are taking place in the Sinophone literary world, and which are often triggered by creativity; on the other hand, we aim to contribute to de-marginalizing the translational field, which still appears rather peripheral in the already prosperous nexus of methodological stances.

© SIMONA GALLO AND MARTINA CODELUPPI, 2024 | DOI:10.1163/9789004711600_002

Speaking of the "margins" of critical discourse, what certainly comes to the fore is contemporary Sinophone poetry. While contemporary Sinophone literature has been widely surveyed over the last decade, most research has concentrated on fiction, whereas poetry – especially in its creative and translational dimension – has not yet been investigated thoroughly and thus deserves further scrutiny. In this book, Sinophone poetry admittedly constitutes a genre encompassing hybrid, polyphonic, and polymorphic literary practices inherently bound to translingualism[1] and, therefore, to translation. Accordingly, Sinophone writers can be described as translingual writers juggling between a metalingual consciousness and a "postmonolingual identity" (Yildiz 2012), and as subjects attempting to traverse borders (national, cultural, and linguistic) by means of literary creation.

But how do contemporary Sinophone poets deal with multilingual creativity? To whom are they speaking? How does a translator of poetry identify this unique form of expression and recode the intertext? The literary practices of negotiation between the self and the Other(s), between native and foreign, and between first tongues and second tongues, along with the poetic renderings of such transactions, ultimately designate the core issues of this edited book.

Mother Tongues and Other Tongues: Creating and Translating Sinophone Poetry discusses the creative process and product of poetic translation both as the translingual author's reaffirmation and as the interlingual translator's empowerment. It aims to spark a dialogue on the complex yet stimulating binomial of poetic "creation and translation," against the background of cross-culturality, in the domain of the contemporary Sinosphere. Drawing attention to authors either writing from outside Mainland China – in Chinese or in other languages – or based in the PRC but belonging to cultural minorities, as well as authors living in "in-between" and sensitive areas, this book encompasses a multiplicity of aspects concerning a wide range of issues in the creation and translation of Sinophone poetry. Starting from a view of Sinophone poetry as an interlingual space, it investigates theoretical and methodological perspectives, the field of translingual practices, and accounts of first-hand experiences. It is organized into three interlaced parts, introduced below along with the thirteen chapters.

Part 1, titled "Thinking, Writing, and Translating the Sinophone," introduces Sinophone poetry and its translational implications from a theoretical point

---

1 The charismatic and influential notion of translingualism, offered by Steven Kellman (2000; 2019) in the context of World literature, condenses a multiplicity of experiences across languages and identifies that are both the product and the underlying process of negotiation.

INTRODUCTION 3

of view. It begins (**Chapter 1**) with Lucas Klein's critical review of two main shortcomings in the field of Sinophone Studies: the lack of attention towards poetry written in Sinophone areas and the challenges of its translation. He adopts a Sinophone Studies-informed perspective and substantiates his discussion by surveying the translational poetics of four anglophone poets from the Sinophone region – Chris Song, Tammy Lai-Ming Ho, Joshua Ip, and Wong May – as well as their engagement with issues of locality, translationality, and Chinese traditions. He then probes Shu-mei Shih's vision of diaspora and its "expiration date," by asking whether Sinophone poets' translational poetics can represent a sense that they are at such an expiration date or not. **Chapter 2** contains Chris Song's reflections on the theoretical borders of the Sinophone and its diaspora, with a specific focus on the case of Hong Kong poetry. To present "Sinophone Hong Kong literature," and especially the "southbound writers" (*Nan lai zuojia* 南來作家), Song reads Hong Kong poet Wong Man's 黃雯 autobiographical poems alongside his migration route. He historicizes this poet's writings in political contexts and studies his bilingual practice through the lens of "biliterate modality." This is an influential approach through which to read Sinophone Hong Kong writers' bilingual poetry and explore their links with issues of cultural identity and cultural hybridity in multifarious historical contexts of Hong Kong, as opposed to the traditional emphasis on nostalgia. Cosima Bruno, in **Chapter 3**, offers another shift in perspective: she explores the concept of "one language" in relation to translation, to review some theoretical and practical propositions offered by scholars, poets, and translators who deal with heteroglossic texts. Bruno scrutinizes the ways in which linguistic bordering has intersected with and affected political and social bordering, and vice versa, by looking at multilingual Sinophone poetic texts, and especially at the ways migrant poets dramatize difference among languages, so as to understand the kind of difference at stake between the languages employed, their hierarchy and status. Her essay therefore undertakes an analysis of the aesthetics defined by lyrical works that pursue the tensions inherent in the monolingual paradigm and the mother tongue. Echoing the previous chapters' theoretical discussions about positioning and describing Sinophone poetry through the lenses of language diversity, translation, and self-translation, in **Chapter 4** Simona Gallo contributes to the debate on the relationship between multilingualism and the lyrical Sinosphere, envisaged as an intrinsically translingual and translational domain. By assuming that Sinophone poetry epitomizes individual practices and constitutes a site of creative construction of selves, Gallo introduces the concept of "thirdlanguaging" as a paradigm of subjective re-location through language. She draws upon three case studies covering different contexts, and dissimilar relationships between mother tongues and other tongues, to illustrate how this "thirdlanguaging" shapes various manifestations of the (Sinophone) poetics of creation and translation.

Part 2, "Translation, Contamination, and Foreign-language Writing," contains four chapters that continue the exploration of Sinophone poetry by scrutinizing its multilingual practices, along with the issue of translation. It opens with Justyna Jaguscik's investigation of the poetics of translingualism in the context of Sinophone lyrical writing (**Chapter 5**). Her discussion draws upon three contemporary female voices from the literary Sinosphere that express postmonolingual lyrical subjectivities and advocate inclusive paradigms: texts written by Amang and Tsai Wan-Shuen, who grew up in multilingual Taiwan, and by the US-based author Jami Proctor-Xu, are read in an attempt to reveal the creative potential of the negotiation of multiple linguistic affiliations, which is fulfilled through translation, disruption, and a ("transgressive") freedom to live across one's mother tongue and other tongues. In **Chapter 6**, Martina Codeluppi engages in a close reading of 回家 *Letters Home*: a bilingual collection of poems by Jennifer Wong – an author born in Hong Kong and currently based in the UK – which employs the metaphor of homecoming to represent in-betweenness. Her discussion further brings into focus the issue of composite cultural identities connected with a new linguistic dimension. As a synecdoche for the Sinophone diaspora in the Western Anglophone world, Wong's poetry – Codeluppi contends – represents a journey through mother/other tongues that goes back to a non-dimensional limbo, where places and languages are translated, hybridized, and thus recreated. In **Chapter 7**, Rebecca Ehrenwirth also questions traditional ideas of cultures as ethnically closed areas and spotlights another diasporic context, located in Southeast Asia, namely Sinophone literature in Thailand. After sketching the main developments and current trends in Sinophone Thai literature, the chapter sheds light on a contemporary form written in Chinese by the Sinophone community in Thailand, namely "small poetry" (*xiaoshi* 小詩). Ehrenwirth illustrates how "small poetry," with its limited number of characters, condenses in miniature form the in-betweenness of these writers: an ambivalent condition, well embodied by a translingual and transcultural poetics, that mirrors both an act of resistance against the loss of roots and the pitfall of a ceaseless non-belonging. In **Chapter 8**, Valentina Pedone shifts the discussion to Europe by considering some amateur Sinophone authors who are active across Italy and China. Relying on a framework of Mobility Studies and Sinophone Studies, Pedone scrutinizes the translingual and transnational textual practices of these Sino-Italian writers who publish their works in both countries, as well as online, performing their hyphenated identities in accordance with their place-based readerships. Pedone gives an account of the lyrical quandary emerging from

INTRODUCTION

the conflict between nostalgia for the mother(land) and "obsession" with the other, engendered by the fear of exclusion. Another relevant debt owed to self-translation and collaborative translation comes to the fore in **Chapter 9**, where Nicoletta Pesaro undertakes an in-depth analysis of the case of Ming Di 明迪, a "cosmopolitan Chinese poet" based in Los Angeles, and closely connected to her mother tongue and homeland, who locates herself within "World literature," thereby avoiding both a politicized approach and the narrowness of a purely linguistic or geographic perspective of the Sinophone paradigm. Ming Di continuously blends lyrical creation and translation, embodying the role of a prominent mediator between the Sinophone and Anglophone literary worlds. Her theories and practices of co-translating and self-translating her own works are discussed from sociological and linguistic perspectives, and introduced by Pesaro as a valuable paradigm of trans-creation, not to mention an opportunity for Ming Di to make her multiple identities visible through lyrical writing and to recognize her Others. With **Chapter 10**, Joanna Krenz steers the volume away from a synchronic conceptual framework and broadens the spectrum of Sinophone poetry and translation, by focusing on the interaction between the Tang dynasty poet Bai Juyi 白居易 and Daryl Lim Wei Jie. Born in Singapore to a family of mainland-Chinese immigrants, but raised and educated in an Anglophone environment, Lim considers English his mother tongue, while trying to connect to Chinese and its lyrical legacy. Against the backdrop of a translingual, transcultural, and trans-epochal correspondence, Krenz examines Lim's experimental translation of several poems by Bai Juyi. She then examines the process of identity construction undertaken by this contemporary Sinophone poet-translator by bridging remote spatiotemporal realities, as well as his dehegemonization and dehomogenization of the Chinese-language cultural heritage through creative translation.

"Experiences from the Sinophone," the third and conclusive Part of this book (**3**), brings forward authentic first-hand experiences in the field of writing and translating Sinophone poems. In **Chapter 11**, Ying Chen, a Chinese-Canadian author who dwells among Chinese, English, and French, describes her creative efforts to build a "cultural mosaic" through poetry devoted to a cosmopolitan society of migrants. By means of a "hybridized" language, she portrays this experience as a medium for looking into Chinese ethnicity and otherness, but also as an endeavor to carefully preserve a valuable cultural and linguistic ecosystem that appears much broader than "simple" bilinguality, and to promote translingual and transcultural communication also by means of translation. Next, in **Chapter 12**, Ming Di addresses the topic of minority language poetry from the People's Republic of China as a new poetry scene she has been documenting as part of an experimental project. In an attempt to answer questions like "What makes a minority poet a minority poet?" and "Do minority poets write the same Chinese or a new Chinese?", she tackles the issues of an in-betweenness stemming from a "double" mother tongue, and of what is gained or lost through translation. With such issues in mind, she provides a conspicuous number of case studies, organized according to an anthropological approach, to investigate the interaction between diglossia and (self-)translation and creativity. The thorny relationship between foreignness and rootedness is pursued in the closing **Chapter 13**, in which the scholar and poet Mai Mang describes his own experience of self-translation from a twofold perspective: as a way to explore, penetrate, and bring to the fore the multiple identities of the self, along with its polyphonies, but also as a tool to prove the worth of a kind of poetry that crosses linguistic and cultural boundaries, be it in the East or the West, in contrast to a hegemonic, Western-centric "World literature." The author's discourse on the epiphanic encounter with the unseen other(s) thus coalesces in a discussion about the universal language of poetry, with all its different voices and silences.

The thirteen chapters, like the book itself, spring from the need to answer a number of questions concerning the Sinophone poetic field – questions evidently revolving around the relationship between different tongues, cultures, and practices of translation and creation. Even though these chapters draw multiple trajectories and proceed along different routes, they do not lose themselves in a centrifugal disarray or cacophony of voices. On the contrary, their interwoven coordinates compose a harmonious symphony based on recurring notes, which include issues like heteroglossia and (un)translatability, translingual or transcultural creolization, borders and border-crossing, subjectivity and otherness, ethnicity and roots, migration and routes, localization and displacement, center(s) and peripheries, identity and difference(s), along with many others. The multifariousness of arguments, underpinned by a heterogeneous collection of case studies, further corroborates our preliminary assumption, that is to say, the lyrical Sinophone is not a monolingual space, and should rather be conceived as a galaxy where a wide range of interlinked phenomena take place. Hence, it deserves to come out of the margins.

This book attempts to tackle the issue of marginality surrounding Sinophone poetry and its translational gist by pursuing a twofold strategy, namely by drawing attention to authors whose work, for a number of different reasons, has not yet attracted significant scholarly or commercial attention, and by engaging in multiple approaches to properly represent the countless manifestations defining the lyrical Sinophone. All this considered, we hope that *Mother Tongues and Other Tongues* will help to further enrich the critical, multidisciplinary discourse on contemporary Sinophone poetry.

Works Cited

Bernards, Brian and Chien-hsin Tsai. 2013. "PART III. Introduction." In *Sinophone Studies: A Critical Reader*, edited by Shu-mei Shih, Chien-hsin Tsai and Brian Bernards, 183–190. New York: Columbia University Press.

Chiu, Kuei-fen, and Zhang Yingjin. 2022. *The Making of Chinese-Sinophone Literatures as World Literature*. Hong Kong: Hong Kong University Press.

Kellman, Steven G. 2019. "Literary Translingualism: What and Why?" *Polylinguality and Transcultural Practices* 16 (3): 337–346.

Kellman, Steven G. 2000. *The Translingual Imagination*. Lincoln: University of Nebraska Press.

Shih, Shu-mei. 2004. "Global Literature and the Technologies of Recognition." *PMLA* 119 (1): 16–30.

Shih, Shu-mei. 2011. "The Concept of the Sinophone." *PMLA* 126 (3): 709–718.

Shih, Shu-mei, Chien-hsin Tsai, and Brian Bernards, eds. 2013. *Sinophone Studies: A Critical Reader*. New York: Columbia University Press.

Tsai, Chien-hsin. 2013. "Part I. Issues and controversies." In *Sinophone Studies: A Critical Reader*, edited by Shu-mei Shih, Chien-hsin Tsai and Brian Bernards, 17–24. New York: Columbia University Press.

Tsu, Jing. 2010. *Sound and Script in Chinese Diaspora*. Cambridge, MA: Harvard University Press.

Tsu, Jing, and David Der-wei Wang, eds. 2010. *Global Chinese Literature*. Leiden – Boston: Brill.

Yildiz, Yasemin. 2012. *Beyond the Mother Tongue: The Postmonolingual Condition*. New York: Fordham University Press.

Zhang, Yinde. 2014. "Transnational Chinese Literature and the Sinopolyphone Perspective." *Diogène* 246–247 (2–3): 222–234.

FIGURE 0.1
Zhang Huan 張洹. 2001. "Family Tree" 家譜 (1/9).
Chromogenic print.
COURTESY OF ZHANG HUAN

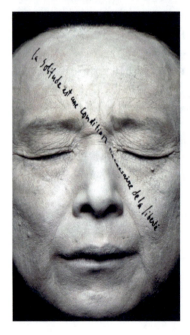

FIGURE 0.2
Wilson, Robert. 2005. "Gao Xingjian". In
Robert Wilson Video Portraits.
COURTESY OF ROBERT WILSON AND
GAO XINGJIAN

PART 1

Thinking, Writing, and Translating the Sinophone

CHAPTER 1

"My Country of Origin Has Something to Do with It I Suppose"

Sinophone Poetry, Global English, and Translational Poetics

Lucas Klein
Arizona State University

"Diaspora," says Shu-mei Shih, *"has an end date"* (italics hers). But how does anyone know if the end date is here? Trying to support her statement, Shih spends most of her time explaining why diasporic populations might not want to see that end date reached quite yet:

> When the (im)migrants settle and become localized, many choose to end their state of diaspora by the second or third generation. The so-called "nostalgia" for the ancestral land is often an indication or displacement of difficulties of localization, voluntary or involuntary. Racism and other hostile conditions can force immigrants to find escape and solace in the past, while the cultural or other superiority complexes can estrange immigrants from the locals. Emphasizing that diaspora has an end date is therefore to insist that cultural and political practice is always place-based. Everyone should be given a chance to become a local. (2013a, 37)

I agree that cultural and political practices are place-based, that everyone should be given a chance to be treated as a local. But I wonder how her assertions are supported by the sentences that follow the statement that second- or third-generation immigrants often stop looking to their ancestral homelands. Even as she argues against diaspora, Shih herself has a hard time extricating herself from its pull. Likewise, while I agree that diaspora has an end date, the question I will ask of the texts I'll be reading in this chapter is the following: do they suggest that they have reached it yet?

Regardless of which version of Sinophone Studies we follow – that of defining Sinophone like "Anglophone," where the various English-speaking countries mix and contend in presumed inclusivity, or rather like "Francophone," where the language and literature of the metropole is not welcomed as part of postcolonial *mélange* – one of the aims of the Sinophone is to decenter China from the consideration of literature in Chinese (or, if you prefer, in Sinitic).

© LUCAS KLEIN, 2024 | DOI:10.1163/9789004711600_003

This is as true of David Der-wei Wang's formulation of having the literature of Mainland China "included without" (*baokuo zaiwai* 包括在外) in Sinophone Studies (Wang 2006) as it is of Shih's definition of the Sinophone as pertaining to "*the Sinitic-language communities and cultures outside China as well as ethnic minority communities and cultures within China where Mandarin is adopted or imposed*" (Shih 2013, 11; italics hers).[1] It is very difficult, however, to decenter knowledge without recentering it somewhere else.[2]

For this reason, the new conceptualization of the Sinophone that motivates *Mother Tongues and Other Tongues* – with, I take it, an inclusive *and* – is better than either Shih's or Wang's definition of the Sinophone, as it focuses on the issue of language and the irreducibly hybrid, polyphonic, and polymorphic literary practices through which translingual Sinophone writers transgress national, cultural, and linguistic borders. As Martina Codeluppi has written, one of the intrinsic characteristics of a globalized Chinese literature is a "plurality in terms of the languages used by its authors," particularly in the "the heteroglossia composing the mosaic of Sinitic languages that shatters the illusion of a standardized Mandarin" (Codeluppi 2020, 19–20) – which, if taken to its logical conclusions, could potentially include all works generated within and beyond the borders of Mainland China, in Chinese or in other languages.[3] I had long wondered how Sinophone Studies might involve translation, as translation into other languages can very easily obscure differences between languages such as Cantonese and Mandarin (or even nonstandard or regional uses of Mandarin). By defining the Sinophone on a decentralized and definitionally translational translingualism, though, this new definition improves on the others not only by defining literature on interplays of always centerless languages (rather than on geopolitical wills to power), but also by showing that Sinophone literary creation can in fact be understood as always emmeshed in acts of translation.

Not, of course, that everything will fall into place just by saying multilingual decentrality, over geopolitical wills to power. The difficulty of decentering without recentering is on display in Sinophone Studies in at least two areas: that of English, and that of fiction. It is against these potential recenterings that I will discuss acts of translation in Anglophone poems by poets originally from the Sinophone or Chinese-speaking region – Chris Song 宋子江, Tammy Lai-Ming Ho 何麗明, Joshua Ip 小葉子, and Wong May 黃梅 – themselves

---

1 This is a straightforward point that has been made too many times for me to cite them all, but for one of my favorites, see Hayot (2010).

2 For a sharp critique of Sinophone studies *vis-à-vis* the issue of centrism, see Shi (2021).

3 See also Gallo 2020, and Zhang 2014 on "Sinopolyphony."

native speakers of Chinese, whether Mandarin or Cantonese or other. Can they help recenter poetry in the discussions of Sinophone literature, while interrogating the centering of Anglophone's global power in the choice to write in English? And what is the role of translation in their work and its potential?

A look at the tables of contents of *Global Chinese Literature: Critical Essays* and *Sinophone Studies: A Critical Reader* should be enough to demonstrate the discourse's gravitational pull toward fiction and English.[4] Not only do the main Sinophone Studies discussions take place in English (as happens with much academic work around the world), the *Reader* also features Ha Jin's 哈金 "Exiled to English" (2013) – which deserves particular consideration in light of Shih's arguments against diaspora. As for the centrality of fiction to Sinophone Studies, of the fifty-one chapters (including the introductions) by an array of scholars in the two *Critical* books, I count only chapters by Rey Chow (2010 and 2013) on Leung Ping-kwan 梁秉鈞 (a/k/a, P.K. Leung or Yesi 也斯), and one by Te-hsing Shan (2013) on the Angel Island poems, that focus on Sinophone poetry.[5] And poetry was once so central to Chinese cultural identity that China has called itself a "nation of poetry" (*shi de guodu* 詩的國度 or *shi de minzu* 詩的民族; Yeh 2008, 13, and Inwood 2014, 3)!

Or is that the point, that if *China* is a *nation* of poetry, then the primary literary genre of that nation's borderlands must be something else? Such a position would require taking Shih's definition of the Sinophone, rather than Wang's – a question I think is best left unresolved (see Klein 2018). Certainly, Sinophone Studies has done wonderfully in promoting deserving fiction writers, such as Chang Kuei-hsing 張貴興, Li Yung-p'ing 李永平, and Ng Kim-chew 黃錦樹. But there is indeed Sinophone poetry beyond Mainland China, not only by mainland poets in exile or in Taiwan and Hong Kong, but in Malaysia, Indonesia, the Philippines … (for the latter, see Stenberg 2017 and 2021) – much more than suggested by the contents of these two compendia. So, where is the poetry in Sinophone Studies?

One answer is: in English. Many poets from the Sinophone region write in English. This makes Sinophone Studies' discursive recentering on English at once more understandable, even as its missing category of poetry becomes all but inexplicable. More pertinently, it draws our conversation into the realm of Global Englishes – which of course has its own centrisms and power dynamics to negotiate (what is the relationship between English as a world language and

---

4   See Tsu and Wang 2010 and Shih, Tsai, and Bernards 2013. These books are over a decade old, but no new collections have replaced them yet. See also Klein 2014.

5   Edmond 2013 gets an honorable mention for its discussion of Yang Lian 楊煉 and Gu Cheng 顧城, as well.

the history of English colonialism and the geopolitical dominance of the US? To what extent do the norms of the Anglophone metropole define or determine standards of English for non-native speakers and writers? And so on).[6] But whereas the writing in English appears, at least on the surface, to represent a turning away from China and the centripetal force of Chineseness, close readings of certain poems might complicate this picture. As Karen Van Dyck writes, "the translational hinges on hybridity as a given of linguistic communication rather than as the communicative failure of monolingualism" (Van Dyck 2021, 472). At any rate, the fact of Sinophone poets writing in English, and how their work might embody translation – and what such embodiment of translation means for the notion of the Sinophone – is the focus of this paper.

I will address writings by Song, Ho, Ip, and Wong, and how those works embody translation and what such translations have to say about Sinophone diaspora and centrism, in turn.

1   "Don't Burn the Zither"

Since P.K. Leung has already been mentioned as one of the most written-about of non-mainland Sinophone poets, let me start this discussion about Anglophone/Sinophone poetry translation with Chris Song – as Song in many ways apprenticed himself to Leung. Raised outside Guangzhou and educated in Shenzhen and Macau, Song enrolled in a PhD program in translation at Lingnan University in Hong Kong in part to be under Leung's poetic tutelage. After Leung's death in 2013 Song continued his apprenticeship with Bei Dao 北島, but aesthetically he has remained closer to Leung's style and what Song has described in academic articles as Leung's "true to life" (*shenghuo hua / saangwut faa* 生活化) poetics (see Song 2019 and 2023) – and with reference

---

6 These questions can drill far into the bull's horn: in his relevantly titled *Diaspora Poetics*, Timothy Yu looks at poets of East Asian heritage in the US, Australia, and Canada to argue that whereas "it has sometimes seemed that Asian Americanists much choose between diaspora and cultural nationalism," diaspora differently conceived can remind us that the concept "can be used to describe not just the opposition between the national and the global, but also the relationship between the two" (Yu 2021, 2–3). His intellectual heritage is the rejection of Asian American Studies' "cultural nationalism and of the patriarchal and culturally absolutist implications of that nationalism," and he wants to offer "a model of transnationalism that focuses less on the role of origins and destinations than on the way the circulation of bodies, cultures, and identities [...] can connect disparate national spaces" (3), but in focusing on "Anglophone white settler colonies," is he centering global literary production on terms most appropriate to the US? I do not have an answer to this, but my paper here offers a supplement to his project by looking at English-language poems by poets writing in Chinese-language dominant spaces.

to Chow's 2010 article about Leung, "Thinking with Food, Writing off Center," I will mention that many of Song's poems are also, like Leung's, about food. But Song's inheritance of Leung that I will discuss here is less in the content of the poetry than in the form – and in particular, the translational form, by which I mean the bilingual publication of the poems in Chinese and English translation, in response to Hong Kong's multilingualism.

Consistent with his standing as Hong Kong's most renowned poet during his lifetime, Leung was, and remains, the most widely translated of Hong Kong poets. His books in English include such titles as *Binfaa dik bin'gaai* [*Bianhua de bianjie*] 變化的邊界 (*Shifting Borders*; 2009) and *Jingtau jyu niuzaau* [*Yingtou yu niaozhao*] 蠅頭與鳥爪 (*Fly Heads and Bird Claws*; 2012a), with translations by such respected poets and translators as John Minford, Brian Holton, Michelle Yeh, Afaa Weaver, Jennifer Feeley, Martha Cheung, and Kit Kelen, as well as Chris Song, not to mention Leung himself – but the volume that may be most important in terms of forming the habit of publishing Hong Kong poetry in bilingual English and Chinese editions is *Jingzoeng Heonggggong* [*Xingxiang Xianggang*] 形象香港 (*City at the End of Time*; Leung 1992; reis. 2012b).[7] Co-translated with Gordon T. Osing, an American poet on a Fulbright at the University of Hong Kong while Leung was on faculty there, the publication of *City* was, as Martha Cheung explains in her introduction to the reprint, "a landmark event in the development of Comparative Literature as well as Postcolonial and Cross-cultural Studies in Hong Kong" (Cheung 2012, 10–11). It was also a landmark event in Hong Kong poetry, and in the integration of the otherwise separate Chinese- and English-language poetry communities in the city: to my knowledge, *City* is the first major collection of Chinese-language Hong Kong poetry to be published as a book in English, and the fact that it was published in Hong Kong set a precedent for other Hong Kong poets (especially Chinese-language Hong Kong poets) to consider publishing their work bilingually, as well.[8] And Chris Song follows in this historical trajectory.

That the translations in *City* are not very good has not hindered the impact of its bilingualism. Osing was interested in classical Chinese poetry (as many American poets have been, since Ezra Pound and Kenneth Rexroth), but he did not know Chinese, and as Cheung points out, "Some bilingual readers

---

7   For other book-length collections of Hong Kong poets translated into English, see Eleanor Goodman's translation of Lok Fung 洛楓 2018, and James Shea and Dorothy Tse's translation of Yam Gong 飲江 2022.

8   I say "the first major collection of Chinese-language Hong Kong poetry" to be published bilingually, but what is "major"? Chris Song tells me some precursors to Leung's *City* were self-translated poetry publications by Wong Man 黃雯 in the 1950s, as well as bilingual books by Shu Hong-sing 舒巷城 (S.C. Wong 王深泉) in the seventies. But these books did not exert the influence of Leung's.

have found Osing's translations very different in tone and style from Leung's original" – though of course "Others say that the English translation augments the Chinese original, aiding their understanding of Leung's poems," and "in the ensuing creative process the intensity of cross-cultural communication became more important than any strict issues of fidelity" (Cheung 2012, 11). Such defenses are often made of poetry in translation (see Zhang and Chen 2007; Sherry and Sun 2017 ...), but can we not put such arguments to use in support of good translation? Chris Song's publishing of his own poems with *en face* English translations, many by himself, then, not only descends from, but just as importantly *improves upon* the tradition inaugurated by Leung.

Consider Song's poem *Zi guzaang* [*Zhi guzheng*] 致古箏 ("To the Zither"), in his bilingual *Gaakmat camjan* [*Gewu xunren*] 格物尋人 (*Whisky Effusions*; 2018). Some poems in the book were translated by others (including by the author of this paper), but this one is a self-translation.

致古箏

他們不許你入閘，不許你彈奏
逼你讀港鐵條例。你要醒目
不要入閘，也不要當他唱歌。因為

他們會再耍詭計，測量你立起的
高度。一旦發出反對的聲音
就會被列入黑名單。一旦不幸

入閘，你要學會隱藏自己
學會無間道，躲在背包客背後
水貨客身邊。被發現也不要驚慌

不要做焚琴的浪子，要懂得變通
微明時舉火記得找施政報告
返學遲到記得說信號故障

在課堂上要有耐心，學習數學
和樂理，將來把致命的音樂
彈入權力的耳朵，讓他流出

可加可減的血
      SONG 2018, 二〇 – 二一

To the Zither

They don't let you swipe your card. They don't let you play.
They force you to read the MTR by-laws. You shall play
smart. Don't do it. Say boo. Don't fall into their trap.

Because they'll set you up again and measure
your vertical height. Once you speak,
you'll be blacklisted. Once, unfortunately

you're in the train, you shall take cover, hide among
travel grey backpacks, grey good traders' luggage,
learn the art of infernal affairs. Once caught

don't panicked. Don't burn the zither. Be pliable.
Expediently. Burn the policy address to make breakfast;
Late for school, say there was signal failure.

In the class, you shall be patient, do the math
study music theory. One day you shall play
lethal notes into the ear of power and make it bleed

fare adjusted formulaically.

SONG 2018, 17

As an example of how the intensity of cross-cultural communication can become more important than any strict issue of fidelity, the poem/translation bears interesting moments: "swipe your card" for *ruzha* (*japzaap*) 入閘 or 'enter the gate'; and a phrase I might at first glance render as 'blood that can increase or decrease' 可加可減的血 given clearer explanation as "fare adjusted formulaically." Other linguistic infelicities include "vertical height" (what other kinds of height are there?) and "don't panicked" (though that may just be a typo). But if, as Simona Gallo has written, the poetics of self-translation constitute a "polyphony of one" (*polifonia individuale*) (Gallo 2020, 102), wherein the "mimetic function of translation is [...] enclosed by the pursuit of other poetic selves" (Gallo 2022, 13), then Song's poem/translation ends up, paradoxically, many-voiced and contrapuntal.

The contrapuntal aspect of "To the Zither" is what is worth focusing on here. Why did Song translate this poem on his own, when he asked others to translate other poems? As I read it, "To the Zither," a poem about a Chinese instrument, is to some degree a poem about Chineseness, about Chinese cultural identity. In this case, the Chinese cultural identity in the shape of the zither comes up against the regulations of Hong Kong's public transportation system – regulations that, in the context of Hong Kong *c.*2018, between the Umbrella Movement of 2014 and the Anti-Extradition Law protests of 2019–2020, read as an indication of the city's mainlandization and tightening restriction of individual liberties. The fact that Chinese cultural identity is framed *against* mainland draconianism is an interesting irony that Sinophone Studies discourse is well-poised to analyze, but I will gap that discussion and conclude only about the translation into English: even, or especially, in English, the poem is not only *about* Chinese cultural identity but an assertion of Chinese cultural identity struggling against Chinese political realities. To translate – and self-translate, no less – the poem into English then expands the possibilities of what English-language poetry can be expected to do, by linking it back to a Chinese context. The reader of the poem in English must confront this point-counterpoint, and while the poem has the right to "become a local," in Shih's phrase, it also has the right not to be local to English, the right to remain foreign, focused on its ancestral land and the difficulties of localization, wondering about escape and the solace of the past. Translated into English, it nevertheless pulls back with diasporic themes.

2 "Rivers of When, Why, and What"

Where Chris Song's Anglophone poetry is translation, Tammy Lai-Ming Ho's poems can contain translation – often in hiding. On surface her career as a poet in the realm of Global Englishes seems closer to diaspora's end date, more centered on the metropole: raised in UK-governed Hong Kong before the 1997 handover to PRC rule, she later earned a PhD in English at King's College London and is an expert on Victorian and neo-Victorian literature – which is to say, the literature of the high point of the British empire and nostalgia for that era of empire. But she returned to Hong Kong after her PhD, where she taught for a decade before relocating to Europe in 2022. Perhaps the best indicator of her in-between position in literature is her editorship of *Cha: An Asian Literary Journal*: an English-language journal, it is nevertheless, as its title says, Asian-oriented, which is to say that it features writing in English from and about (or translated from the languages of) Asia, occupying a diasporic position.

If Ho's poetry is diasporic, it is not because it deals with the pull of China as such (though this happens occasionally, as in "Beijing Standard Time": "People so often discuss / how Chinese characters / were simplified by Mao. / Do they know time, too, // was simplified? / Five zones reduced to one" (Ho 2018, 54)), but rather because her poetry so well encapsulates questions of Hong Kong and its multicultural, multilingual tensions, born and borne in that borderland both part of China and not.

Translation, too, is part of that encapsulation. Here is a poem titled "Poem with Cantonese Sight-Rhymes":

> How not to weave knowledge
> into sheer hatred?
> To be lenient about bad situations
> with pure sentiments?
> To slowly make the worst possibilities
> disappear and to once again enjoy
> the sun in open spaces,
>
> hoping and pretending we're
> memorialising? Are we remembered?
> I'm afraid of the faint beating
> of the heart of home, now loud
> only in our vivid memory. Those calligraphied
> banners wielded by marchers
> are now objects of terror. We touch
>
> many walls: walls of neglect
> and indifference, to exchange
> for rivers of when, why, and what?
> Still steely, despite our frustrations
> but graveyards of emotions will open
> this lunar month and again.
> We've created many angry ghosts
>
>   HO 2024, 84-85

On first read, it looks like a poem about Hong Kong's protests – the Anti-Extradition of 2019–2020 and perhaps also the Umbrella Movement / Occupy Central of 2014 – mentioning "calligraphied / banners wielded by marchers," wondering how to "make the worst possibilities / disappear and to once again enjoy / the sun in open spaces." And that remains, even as the title's hint that the poem employs "Cantonese sight-rhymes" sinks in: the poem is structured around associations made because of an underlying Chinese text.

This makes the poem in some ways a translation. In the first line, "weave knowledge" comes from Chinese *zhi* 織 (Cant. *zik*; 'to weave') and *shi* 識 (Cant. *sik*; 'knowledge'). Later, "hoping and pretending" are from *pan* 盼 (Cant. *paan*; 'to look forward to') and *ban* 扮 (Cant. *baan*; 'to play a role'); the words of "memorializing? Are we remembered?" are from *ji* 紀 (Cant. *gei*; 'to commemorate'), *ji* 記 (Cant. *gei*; 'to remember'), and *ji* 己 (Cant. *gei*; 'self'); "banners" and "terror" come from *bu* 布 (Cant. *bou*; 'cloth') and *bu* 怖 (Cant. *bou*; 'fear'); and at the end of the poem "graveyards" and "angry ghosts" is from *fen* 墳 (Cant. *fan*; 'grave') and *fen* 憤 (Cant. *fan*; 'to be angry'). She calls them "Cantonese sight-rhymes," but this is not quite accurate: the Chinese character set is basically the same regardless of which version of Chinese (Cantonese, Mandarin, Hakka, etc.) it is pronounced in, and the lexicon under Ho's English here does not contain particularly Cantonese vocabulary (which is why my transcriptions before the character are in *pinyin*, with *jyutping* in parentheses after). Sometimes they are indeed sight-rhymes, or as close as Chinese can come to such a phenomenon, relying on characters that have the same radicals or constituent parts; at other times she will rely on two-character compounds that share a character. For instance, "lenient," "bad situations," and "pure sentiments" come from *huai* 懷 (Cant. *waai*; 'to cherish') and *huai* 壞 (Cant. *waai*; 'bad'), alongside *qingkuang* 情況 (Cant. *cingfong*; 'situations') and *ganqing* 感情 (Cant. *gamcing*; 'feelings'). Perhaps the most poetically intricate of these sight-rhymes is in the line "rivers of when, why, and what?" where *he* 河 (Cant. *ho*) is 'river' but *he* 何 is not only 'what' and a component of words *weihe* 為何 (Cant. *waiho*; 'why') and *heshi* 何時 (Cant. *hosi*; 'when'), it is also the poet's own surname. As she questions, she has written herself into the layers of this poem about Hong Kong's protest movements and its multilingual mechanisms, bringing to mind Salman Rushdie's famous statement, "Having been borne across the world, we are translated men" (1982).

The diaspora is made up of women and men living in translation, and in bringing this fact into the English of her poem, Ho has written a poem that is at once Anglophone and Sinophone.

3 "Thoughts Shade between the Lines"

Joshua Ip's *Translations to the Tanglish* (2021) is also a work that is at once Anglophone and Sinophone, likewise because of its engagement with translation – though here we must ask more about the term "translation." Where Esther

Cheung noted the differences "in tone and style" of Osing and Leung's translations of Leung's poems, and countered that "the English translation augments the Chinese original" and in the "creative process" of translation "the intensity of cross-cultural communication" is "more important than any strict issues of fidelity," with Ip's work we have the same ingredients – differences of tone and style, English augmenting Chinese poetry, and questions of cross-cultural communication overriding fidelity – but get to see them mixed very differently.

Are Ip's *Translations to the Tanglish* even translations, or should they rather be called versions, adaptations, imitations, rewritings, or some other synonym? I do not find this a pertinent question. There are times for such considerations, yes, but here, the point is how the poems are translation*al*, which is to say, how they interact with translation as more conventionally defined (along the lines of *saying or writing the meaning of a text in one language in another language*), and in the process tweak or even challenge that definition. Here is a poem titled "Ellipsis":

> no new texts in the group chat
> but someone's status: "typing ..."
> thoughts shade between the lines
> and moss your face with evening.
>
> IP 2021, 37

A curious poem, which I believe would leave most monolingual readers scratching their proverbial heads, what makes the text interesting is what comes across the gutter:

> 空山不見人
> 但聞人語響
> 返景入深林
> 復照青苔上
>
> IP 2021, 36

This is the text of a poem (though in Ip's book it is printed in simplified characters, as used in Singapore, and punctuated) by Tang poet Wang Wei 王維 (699–759), one of the most renowned poets in his day and one of the most canonical of classical poets in the Chinese-speaking world now. The English text is a response to Wang's poem *Lu zhai* 鹿柴, and though Ip's book is full of many such reactions, this particular poem happens to be one of the most important Chinese poems in the field of translation studies, thanks to its being featured in Eliot Weinberger's *Nineteen Ways of Looking at Wang Wei* (1987; reis. 2016). I will quote two of my favorite of the many translations Weinberger assembled for his exhibit. By Gary Snyder (1978):

> Empty mountains:
>   no one to be seen.
> Yet — hear —
>   human sounds and echoes.
> Returning sunlight
>   enters the dark woods;
> Again shining
>   on the green moss, above.
>   in WEINBERGER 2016, 45

And by Burton Watson (1971):

> **Deer Fence**
>
> Empty hills, no one in sight,
> only the sound of someone talking;
> late sunlight enters the deep wood,
> shining over the green moss again.
>   in WEINBERGER 2016, 27

It is Watson's rhythm and presentation of "English-as-Chinese" (Kern 1996), not Snyder's, that Ip is modeling – but of course Ip is also responding to Wang's poem, translating it not into English but "Tanglish" (whatever that might be).

What, then, does Ip's "Ellipsis" have to do with Wang Wei's poem? What can we say of his echo? I quoted Esther Cheung, above, about cross-cultural communication being more important than fidelity, but here the emphasis is more cross-temporal than -cultural, and the *cross*-cultural element is a more active crisscrossing back and forth than that term might always imply. "But what if these two cultures were not separated by distance, but instead by time?" (Ip 2021, 121), writes Ip in his "Afterword." And in the translator's note that begins the book he explains the temporal and spatial context more directly:

> in my latest hot take on some of the Tang and Song Dynasties' top hits, I have happily shoved these poems through (a) several thousand years of technological modernization, (b) several thousand miles of migration to sunny Singapore (which as we all know is a southern province of China), (c) and a huge dollop of COVID-19 (which is probably more Chinese than I am anyway). (2021, 18)

"MY COUNTRY OF ORIGIN HAS SOMETHING TO DO WITH IT I SUPPOSE"   23

I admit to not seeing how the Covid pandemic (or the swipe, which for US-based readers will come off as borderline slur, at its Chineseness) has to do with his responses to classical Chinese poems. But the assertion that Singapore remains in China's orbit even as "several [sic] thousand years of technologi-cal modernization" have transpired demonstrates the tension Ip is testing in *Tanglish*. The book is not aimed at English-language readers to inform them about Chinese poetry, but rather at readers of a Chinese cultural background. The book even opens in what English readers would think of as the back, and the pages are numbered right to left, counter-current to Anglophone books, the way Chinese books used to be. "I deliberately chose pieces that are more well-known" to Chinese Singaporeans, he explains:

> Many of these are poems that Chinese schoolchildren can (or should be able to) recite by heart. The reader that would take away the most from this is ostensibly bilingual – I would love for them to know the original Chinese piece, and have it play in the background of their mind while they read the English, as if a backing polyphonic track or an interlin-ear gloss. I want the experience of the poem to exist in that Third Space (Homi Bhabha!), with as much bilingual, bicultural, bigenerational code-switching in a moment as is necessary to live as a Chinese person in an English-speaking world. (Ip 2021, 125)

Meanwhile, the reader who does not know Chinese poetry is only an after-thought: "will my non-Chinese-speaking friends hear the anguished bone-rattlings of a foreign fossil animated by a wanton puppeteer, or marvel, as I do, at the earth-shaking, time-traveling roar of a spectral dinosaur?" (Ip 2021, 126).[9] Written in English, the poems nevertheless do not adhere to the expected direction of translational carrying-over, let alone the presumed centrism of Anglophone power and its monolingual readers.

Ip's mention of "Third Space" (see Bhabha 1994) gives a postcolonial tinge to his global Anglophone project, on which he elaborates with reference to "Brazilian translator and poet Haroldo de Campos' idea of transcreation as modern cannibalism – appropriating the European distaste of anthropophagy for the use of a postcolonial uprising where [a] former servant ingests the mas-ter and/or his tools on its own terms" (see Vieira 1999). With respect to his project, however, he explains that

---

9   An afterthought that has nevertheless prompted considerable work: "I have provided a web-site worth of notes and 'actual' translations, separated from the text by the modern-day bag of holding that is a QR code, but I also wonder, to allude to the Chinese, if I am adding feet to a snake or dotting a dragon's eye" (Ip 2021, 126).

the source text is not the domain of a colonial master, but that of a distant ancestor who still wields a unique and significant source of cultural and historical power, relative to a displaced ethnically-Chinese Singaporean who thinks and dreams in English rather than their government-mandated "mother tongue." (Ip 2021, 127)

The postcolonial critique, then, also takes on a local political valence. In this way, Shih's call for literature such as this to have a chance to be read as local means that it also must be read as engaging with the fact of Singapore having made Mandarin compulsory for ethnic Chinese schoolchildren (and Malay compulsory for Malays, and Tamil compulsory for South Indians). Chinese centrism is no longer viable, but neither can Chinese cultural dominance just be ignored. The poems' decentering of Chineseness even as they wrestle with being diasporic is what makes them Sinophone cultural productions, despite their being in English.

These are some of the thoughts that shade between the lines. These are the points that are left unspoken in "Ellipsis," but which, I think, can be inferred from context – in the word's literal meaning as referring to the accompanying text, in this case Wang Wei's poem on the facing leaf. And whereas another translator might want to suppress their self (Weinberger 2016, 20: "translation is dependent on the dissolution of the translator's ego: an absolute humility toward the text"), I notice that Ip inserts his last name right in the middle of "Ellipsis." This means that not only is the context of *Translations from the Tanglish* Sinophone, but the text of the poem, too, places the poet directly in its diasporic meditations and mediations.

4   "Aglimmer the Remains"

The *Tanglish* of Ip's title is a portmanteau of *English* and *Tang*, the latter referring to the dynasty (618–907) but also metonymically to Chinese culture as a whole (Chinatowns around the world are often called "Tang people's streets," *Tangrenjie* 唐人街, and in certain versions of Chinese the language is called "Tang speech," *Tang hua* 唐話, etc.), because the dynasty is considered to have been a golden age, particularly in terms of its poetry. Interestingly, the Tang is also known as one of Chinese history's most cosmopolitan dynasties, so just as the Tang signifies "China," it also signifies a China in full engagement with the rest of the world. Chongqing-born Singaporean Anglophone poet now resident in Dublin Wong May's presentation, in *In the Same Light: 200 Tang Poems for Our Century* (2022), of her translations of Tang poetry, then, also demonstrates diasporic tensions, representing a kind of "'nostalgia' for the ancestral land," in Shih's words, even if it does not try "to find escape and solace in the past."

In many ways Wong's looking back toward China with translations of Tang poetry is a surprise. The title of her previous collection, *Picasso's Tears* (2014) – her first since 1978, and the one most helpful in earning her the 2022 Windham-Campbell Prize in poetry – suggests a fully westernized aesthetic by a poet not interested in wrestling with questions of immigration or cultural identity. And yet, even within a style, sensibility, and reading list that comes from European and North American modernism, certain links to China remain, perhaps not in what she has read but in an awareness of how she has been read. One of her "Two English Postcards" is titled "Paul Celan Drowned in the Seine":

> In Oxford at Blackwell's
> > I asked for a book of your poems
> & was directed to the Arts & Crafts
> > for "porcelain".
> My Country of Origin has something to do with it
> > > I suppose.
> You're not entirely
> To blame.
> > WONG 2014, 20

When I first read the poem, I thought it was simply about her accent, how her pronunciation of "Paul Celan" had been misunderstood as "porcelain." But on further reading, I realized that the mishearing of the accent probably has to with an association based on Wong's race, as well: not only that a Chinese woman could not be interested in a modernist Germanophone poet, but that she must be interested in something Chinese – "porcelain" being another word, of course, for "china."[10] That the misunderstanding took place in Blackwell's in Oxford, a storied academic bookstore located at the capital of Anglophone knowledge production, only adds to the poem's drawing out of the tension between Chinese and Global English identities.

As for the translations of *In the Same Light*, here is her version of the poem Ip handled, above, made famous in Translation Studies by Weinberger's *Nineteen Ways*:

---

10   For an account of the importance of translating Celan's work to contemporary Chinese poetry, see Krenz (2019).

Deer Grove

> Empty Mountains
> no one about
> but
> sounds
> Sounds speaking of humans
> whilst
> back
> In the deep wood
> a glimmer
> On the green moss
> Aglimmer
> the
> remains
> Of the day

WONG 2022, 102

The translation is good, for me, but could be better. "Sounds speaking of humans" is a deft way to handle Wang Wei's positioning of himself as simultaneously present and absent from the scene of the poem (a lingering concern in Weinberger's commentaries), but replacing the specifics of the returning sunlight at sunset with a *cliché* that calls to mind Kazuo Ishiguro does not demonstrate a deep understanding of the Chinese poem. Poetically in English it is effective – and affective – but it does little that Snyder's version forty-four years earlier did not do already, breaking up the field of composition in a Projective Verse-inspired extension of form and content.[11]

Of course there are many poems in *In the Same Light* that have not been translated by Snyder or other poets with similar aesthetics, but what really sets her book apart is the afterword, nearly 100 pages long, titled – as if in allusion to where she was sent to look for Celan – "The Numbered Passages of a Rhinoceros in the China Shop." Reviewer Noah Warren describes it as "shape-shifting": "Wong and a magical rhinoceros, who sounds suspiciously like her classical

---

11   My allusions here are to Charles Olson and Robert Creeley, but the relevance to modernist anglophone poetry's approach to Asian poetry is in Olson's extension of Ezra Pound's poetics and his mentioning of Ernest Fenollosa in "Projective Verse" (see Olson 1997). For more on international ripples of this influence, see Weinberger on Octavio Paz after his exposure to Japan and Japanese poetry in the 1950s: "from there, the almost inevitable move is toward an adaptation of Pound's 'ideogrammic method': the stepped lines, the free-floating images forming configurations of meaning, the simultaneity ..." (1992, 33).

Chinese poetry-writing mother, enter the Tang chat" (Warren 2022).[12] This is where the "for our Century" of the subtitle changes from implying that the book contains primarily contemporary updates of medieval poems to intimating that it is rather a meditation on the work we have to do in our language and epoch to understand the very different milieu of Tang China, and the power of poetry in that age. Two excerpts of many I highlighted:

> What was it like to be a human being in Tang China?
> *Twenty-one families together entered Shu, only one man came back from Camel Pass.*
> The undocumented with no papers, the refugees with no camps, in the Tang Dynasty they have poetry. (Wong 2022, 266–67)

And:

> Poetry was a set subject in the civil service exam, with an importance nowadays according to maths & science. A couplet could win you an influential post, an inept word in a verse could doom you. Such was the dictate of Poetry. The country's civil service was run for hundreds of years like a poetry workshop; multifarious court-intrigues helped with the running. You couldn't be a governor if you couldn't come up, after hard drinking, with a faultless quatrain. Talents of the Land were honored: John Ashbery in Kabul holding peace talks with the Taliban? Louise Glück as Secretary of State? Interesting. Would that change the world? More pertinent – impertinently, Secretary Glück, will it change the way you write? Poets were acknowledged legislators in China. (279)

Wong's afterword is not scholarly, but it does leave "the writer in peace as much as possible and moves the reader toward him," as scholarship does, rather than leave "the reader in peace" to move "the writer toward him" (Schleiermacher 2012, 49). That the direction of this movement is at the hands

---

12 The reference to a rhinoceros comes from Li Shangyin's 李商隱 (813–858) famous line (心有靈犀一點通) from one of his "Untitled" (*Wuti* 無題) poems. Wong translates this as "But the heart / The heart, set / On the point of / A rhino's horn, / What will it not transmit or disclose?" (118). Sabina Knight (2022) writes that a "less fluent but more faithful translation would be, 'The body hasn't the coloured phoenix's pair of flying wings, [but] the heart understands [as keenly] as the point of the rhino's sensitive horns,'" and adds: "Many interpret the poem as a love poem, for the rhino's horn was thought to have telepathic powers, a sensitivity that enabled it instantaneously to pass stimuli from its tip straight to the brain.".

of a writer born in China and raised in Singapore makes it diasporic, even as she writes in English – but does this also mean that her project is therefore Sinocentric? Her country of origin has something to do with it, I suppose, but no, her words have none of the reverence or veneration for Tang poetry familiar from those educated in an atmosphere of mainland cultural nationalism.[13] She is not presenting Chinese poetry as a center of gravity she expects her readers to orbit, she is instead presenting Tang poetry as a near land in a distant time that has something to say to us, if it can speak the right way and if we know how to listen. In *In the Same Light*, then, we have a work of literary translation proper by a diasporic poet that complicates the expectations of how diasporic subjects will represent their countries of origin, just as Wong's Anglophone poetry complicates its categories by also being Sinophone.

5 Conclusion: the Polyphony of the Anglophone-Sinophone

In addition to Sinophone Studies being fiction- and English-centered, it also has some blind spots – translation among them. A combination of the many versions of Chinese (often called dialects) opened up by a Sinophone approach, and the fact that such distinctions are often flattened in translation, have conspired to leave translation generally undiscussed in Sinophone Studies.[14] Contributing to Sinophone Studies by filling this gap is, as I understand it, one of the goals of this volume (even though the other side of contribution is critique).

In this chapter I have considered the question of the end date of diaspora – one of Sinophone Studies' many provocative points – by looking at the residual centrism of Sinophone Studies in juxtaposition against Global English, to ask if translation can help resolve these discourses' potential centrisms, while also restoring poetry to the center of the problematic. My argument has been that the way these poets' writings in English refer back or relate to China indicates that for them, they have not reached the end point of diaspora – but this does not mean that their writing is Sinocentric. Such a conclusion would be reductive; nevertheless, I acknowledge that a skeptical reframing of my question would be, *Do you really expect that poetry in English could help resolve the Anglocentrism of Sinophone Studies? Why would writing in English be* less *Anglocentric than writing in Sinitic or Chinese?* And yet, I think the answer

---

13   For an example of a mainland Chinese poetic-scholarly take on Tang poetry similarly free of such veneration, see Xi Chuan 2018 (on which, see Klein 2021).

14   To my knowledge, Bachner (2014) comes closest to discussing translation from the perspective of Sinophone Studies.

is: it can be. Because of English-language audiences and publishing venues throughout the world, English literature ends up looking much more diffuse than literature in Chinese. Not to mention, in its embodiment and incorporation of translation, Global English and diasporic texts work to bring literatures from other languages into English, against the normative delimitations of Greenwich Mean Time or American Standard.

Not only can poetry in English from the Sinophone regions help the Sinophone break out of the Anglocentric orbit, it can do so without reverting to a Sinocentric epistemic frame. As the examples above show, the translational as an element of Anglophone poetry from Sinophone regions often pits its poetry against a Sinocentric world view and its limitations. For all that translation might contain its own latent centrisms (reiterating one national literature's received canonicity, for instance, even as it challenges another's), translation is also very good at disrupting the centripetal pull of any grand tradition by virtue of its multivocality, its polyphony. In looking at the different ways Song, Ho, Ip, and Wong manifest translation in their poetry, it is clear that translation is not a monolith, but rather a shapeshifting, liquid thing. If this quality can also saturate the Sinophone Studies perspective, even as it comes from writing in English, then perhaps translation and translationality can resolve, and dissolve, the centric opposition between Sinophone and Anglophone, and bring them both into a decentered polyphony.

Works Cited

Bachner, Andrea. 2014. *Beyond Sinology: Chinese Writing and the Scripts of Culture*. New York: Columbia University Press.

Bhabha, Homi K. 1994. *The Location of Culture*. London: Routledge.

Cheung, Esther M.K. 2012. "Introduction to the New Edition: New Ends in a City of Transition." In *City at the End of Time*, by Ping-kwan Leung, 1–19. Rpt. with New Introduction. Hong Kong: Hong Kong University Press.

Chow, Rey. 2010. "Thinking with Food, Writing off Center: Notes on Two Hong Kong Authors." In *Global Chinese Literature: Critical Essays*, edited by Jing Tsu and David Der-wei Wang, 133–55. Leiden: Brill.

Chow, Rey. 2013. "Things, Common/Places, Passages of the Port City: On Hong Kong and Hong Kong Author Leung Ping-Kwan." In *Sinophone Studies: A Critical Reader*, edited by Shu-mei Shih, Chien-hsin Tsai, and Brian Bernards, 207–26. New York: Columbia University Press.

Codeluppi, Martina. 2020. *Fictional Memories: Contemporary Chinese Literature and Transnationality*. Paris and Turin: Harmattan Italia.

Edmond, Jacob. 2013. "Inverted Islands: Sinophone New Zealand Literature." In *Sinophone Studies: A Critical Reader*, edited by Shu-mei Shih, Chien-hsin Tsai, and Brian Bernards, 339–52. New York: Columbia University Press.

Gallo, Simona. 2020. "Attraversare il *Wen* 文: Quattro Traiettorie Autotraduttive Nella Letteratura Sinofona" [Crisscrossing *Wen* 文: Four Trajectories of Self-Translation in Sinophone Literature]. In *Autotraduzione: Pratiche, Teorie, Storie / Autotraduction: Pratiques, Théories, Histoires*, edited by Fabio Regattin, 93–116. Universitariae 39. Città di Castello: I libri di Emil.

Gallo, Simona. 2022. "The Prism of Self-Translation: *Poiesis* and Poetics of Yu Guang-zhong's Bilingual Poetry." *The Translator*, December, 1–16. https://doi.org/10.1080/13556509.2022.2140623.

Ha Jin. 2013. "Exiled to English." In *Sinophone Studies: A Critical Reader*, edited by Shu-mei Shih, Chien-hsin Tsai, and Brian Bernards, 117–24. New York: Columbia University Press.

Hayot, Eric. 2010. "Commentary: On the 'Sainifeng 賽呢風' as a Global Literary Practice." In *Global Chinese Literature: Critical Essays*, edited by Jing Tsu and David Der-wei Wang, 219–28. Leiden: Brill.

Ho, Tammy Lai-Ming. *If I Do Not Reply*. Exeter: Shearsman Books, 2024.

Ho, Tammy Lai-Ming. 2018. *Too Too Too Too*. Singapore: Math Paper Press.

Inwood, Heather. 2014. *Verse Going Viral: China's New Media Scenes*. China Program Book. Seattle: University of Washington Press.

Ip, Joshua. 2021. *Translations to the Tanglish*. Singapore: Math Paper Press.

Kern, Robert. 1996. *Orientalism, Modernism, and the American Poem*. Cambridge Studies in American Literature and Culture 97. New York: Cambridge University Press.

Klein, Lucas. 2014. Review of *Sinophone Studies: A Critical Reader*, by Shu-mei Shih, Chien-hsin Tsai, and Brian Bernards. *Chinese Literature: Essays, Articles, Reviews* 36 (December): 216–19.

Klein, Lucas. 2018. "One Part in Concert, and One Part Repellence: Liu Wai-tong, Cao Shuying, and the Question of Hong Kong and Mainland Chinese Sinophones." *Modern Chinese Literature and Culture* 30 (2): 141–72.

Klein, Lucas. 2021. "What Does Tang Poetry Mean to Contemporary Chinese Writers? Li Bai and the Canonicity of Tang Poetry in Liu Liduo, Ha Jin, Yi Sha, and Xi Chuan." *Prism: Theory and Modern Chinese Literature* 18 (1): 138–69.

Knight, Sabina. 2022. "Sculpted Time." *Mekong Review* 7 (28). https://mekongreview.com/sculpted-time/.

Krenz, Joanna. 2019. "Celan's 'Deathfugue' in Chinese: A Polemic about Translation and Everything Else." In *Chinese Poetry and Translation: Rights and Wrongs*, edited by Maghiel van Crevel and Lucas Klein, 287–308. Amsterdam: Amsterdam University Press.

Leung, Ping-kwan 梁秉鈞. 1992. *City at the End of Time*. Translated by Gordon T. Osing and Ping-kwan Leung. Hong Kong: Twilight Books.

Leung, Ping-kwan 梁秉鈞. 2009. *Shifting Borders: Poems of Leung Ping-Kwan*. Translated by Ping-kwan Leung, Chris Song, Kit Kelen, and Debby Vai Keng Sou. Macau: Association of Stories in Macao.

Leung, Ping-kwan 梁秉鈞. 2012a. *Fly Heads and Bird Claws*. Translated by Brian Holton, Afaa M. Weaver, Luo Hui, John Minford, Michelle Yeh, Glen Steinman, Jennifer Feeley, Martha Cheung, Jonathan Chaves, and Helen Leung. Hong Kong: MCCM Creations.

Leung, Ping-kwan 梁秉鈞. 2012b. *City at the End of Time*. Edited by Esther M.K. Cheung. Translated by Gordon T. Osing and Ping-kwan Leung. Rpt. with New Introduction. Hong Kong: Hong Kong University Press.

Lok Fung 洛楓. 2018. *Days When I Hide My Corpse in a Cardboard Box: Selected Poems of Natalia Chan*. Translated by Eleanor Goodman. Bilingual edition. Brookline, MA: Zephyr Press.

Olson, Charles. 1997. "Projective Verse." In *Collected Prose*, edited by Donald Allen and Benjamin Friedlander, 239–49. Berkeley: University of California Press.

Rushdie, Salman. 1982. "Imaginary Homelands." *London Review of Books*, October 7, 1982. https://www.lrb.co.uk/the-paper/v04/n18/salman-rushdie/imaginary-homelands.

Schleiermacher, Friedrich. 2012. "On the Different Methods of Translating." In *The Translation Studies Reader*, edited by Lawrence Venuti, translated by Susan Bernofsky, 3rd ed., 43–63. New York: Routledge.

Shan, Te-hsing. 2013. "At the Threshold of the Gold Mountain: Reading Angel Island Poetry." In *Sinophone Studies: A Critical Reader*, edited by Shu-mei Shih, Chien-hsin Tsai, and Brian Bernards, 207–26. New York: Columbia University Press.

Sherry, James and Sun Dong 孙冬, eds. 2017. *The Reciprocal Translation Project*. New York: Roof Books.

Shi, Flair Donglai. 2021. "Reconsidering Sinophone Studies: The Chinese Cold War, Multiple Sinocentrisms, and Theoretical Generalisation." *International Journal of Taiwan Studies* 4 (2): 311–44. https://doi.org/10.1163/24688800-20201156.

Shih, Shu-mei, Chien-hsin Tsai, and Brian Bernards, eds. 2013. *Sinophone Studies: A Critical Reader*. New York: Columbia University Press.

Shih, Shu-mei. 2013a. "Against Diaspora: The Sinophone as Places of Cultural Production." In *Sinophone Studies: A Critical Reader*, edited by Shu-mei Shih, Chien-hsin Tsai, and Brian Bernards, 25–42. New York: Columbia University Press.

Shih, Shu-mei. 2013b. "Introduction: What Is Sinophone Studies?" In *Sinophone Studies: A Critical Reader*, edited by Shu-mei Shih, Chien-hsin Tsai, and Brian Bernards, 1–16. New York: Columbia University Press.

Song, Chris 宋子江. 2018. *Whisky Effusions*. Translated by Lucas Klein, Tammy Lai-Ming Ho, and others. Hong Kong: Musical Stone.

Song, Chris 宋子江. 2019. "Ronald Mar and the Trope of Life: The Translation of Western Modernist Poetry in Hong Kong." In *Chinese Poetry and Translation: Rights and Wrongs*, edited by Maghiel van Crevel and Lucas Klein, 249–63. Amsterdam: Amsterdam University Press.

Song, Chris 宋子江. 2023. "The Trope of Life in Hong Kong Poetry: Realism, Survival, and Shenghuohua." *Writing Chinese: A Journal of Contemporary Sinophone Literature*, 2 (1): 88–105. DOI: http://doi.org/10.22599/wcj.45

Stenberg, Josh. 2017. "The Lost Keychain? Contemporary Chinese-Language Writing in Indonesia." *Sojourn: Journal of Social Issues in Southeast Asia* 32 (3): 634–68.

Stenberg, Josh. 2021. "Diverse Fragility, Fragile Diversity: Sinophone Writing in the Philippines and Indonesia." *Asian Ethnicity*, September, 1–19. https://doi.org/10.1080/14631369.2021.1951598.

Tsu, Jing and David Der-wei Wang, eds. 2010. *Global Chinese Literature: Critical Essays*. Leiden: Brill.

Van Dyck, Karen. 2021. "Migration, Translingualism, Translation." In *The Translation Studies Reader*, edited by Lawrence Venuti, 4th ed., 466–85. New York: Routledge.

Vieira, Else Ribeiro Pires. 1999. "Liberating Calibans: Readings of Antropfagia and Haroldo de Campos' Poetics of Transcreation." In *Post-Colonial Translation: Theory and Practice*, edited by Susan Bassnett and Harish Trivedi, 95–113. Translation Studies. London: Routledge.

Wang, David Der-wei 王德威. 2006. "Wenxue lüxing yu shijie xiangxiang" 文學旅行與世界想象 [Literary Trajectories and the Global Imagination]. *United Daily News*, July 8, 2006, sec. Literary supplement.

Warren, Noah. 2022. "Enter the Tang Chat." *Astra*, September 20, 2022. https://astra-mag.com/articles/enter-the-tang-chat/.

Weinberger, Eliot. 1992. "Paz in Asia." In *Outside Stories, 1987–1991*, 17–45. New York: New Directions.

Weinberger, Eliot. 2016. *Nineteen Ways of Looking at Wang Wei (with More Ways)*. New York: New Directions.

Weinberger, Eliot, and Octavio Paz. 1987. *Nineteen Ways of Looking at Wang Wei: How a Chinese Poem Is Translated*. Kingston, RI: Moyer Bell Limited.

Wong, May. 2014. *Picasso's Tears: Poems, 1978–2013*. Portland: Octopus Books.

Wong, May. 2022. *In the Same Light: 200 Tang Poems for Our Century*. Manchester: Carcanet.

Xi Chuan 西川. 2018. *Tangshi de dufa* 唐詩的讀法 [*Reading Tang Poetry*]. Hong Kong: The Chinese University Press.

Yam Gong 飲江. 2022. *Moving a Stone: Bilingual in Chinese and English*. Translated by James Shea and Dorothy Tse. Bilingual edition. Brookline: Zephyr Press.

Yeh, Michelle. 2008. "'There Are No Camels in the Koran': What Is Modern about Modern Chinese Poetry?" In *New Perspectives on Contemporary Chinese Poetry*, edited by Christopher Lupke, 9–26. New York: Palgrave Macmillan.

Yu, Timothy. 2021. *Diasporic Poetics: Asian Writing in the United States, Canada, and Australia*. Global Asias. New York: Oxford University Press.

Zhang Er 张耳 and Chen Dongdong 陈东东, eds. 2007. *Another Kind of Nation: An Anthology of Contemporary Chinese Poetry*. Jersey City: Talisman House.

Zhang, Yinde. 2014. "La littérature chinoise transnationale et la sinopolyphonie." Translated by Nicole G. Albert. *Diogène* 246–247 (2–3): 222–34. https://doi.org/10.3917/dio.246.0222.

CHAPTER 2

Hong Kong Poetry and Diaspora

The Wang Tao Mode and the Sinophone

Chris Song
University of Toronto

1 Introduction

Diaspora has been one of the core concerns in the Chinese-language scholarship of Hong Kong literature. Specifically, the so-called southbound writers *Nan lai zuojia* 南來作家, who migrated from the mainland southward to Hong Kong in the twentieth century, have contributed a significant bulk of literary works to the mass of Sinophone Hong Kong literature. Some mainland sojourners moved northward back to the mainland; others emigrated further away from the Sinosphere. More gradually settled in Hong Kong with a local literary identity recognized as "Hong Kong writers." The precursor studies on southbound writers (e.g., Lo 1987), more archival than analytical, have inspired abundant writerly research that contextualizes their migrations, writings and ties to their places of origin. This mode of southbound writers' migration characterized by a diasporic nostalgia with a China-centric Central-Plain mentality is known in the field as the "Wang Tao mode" (*Wang Tao moshi* 王韜模式; Wong 2005). Lawrence Wang-chi Wong summarizes the five elements of the Wang Tao mode:

> 一、因政治因素被迫離開中國大陸，南來香港；二、以中原心態觀照香港文化的邊緣位置；三、在香港收到西方文化的衝擊；四、利用香港的特殊空間從事各種各樣的文化活動，以尖銳的言詞及其他形式向祖國「喊話」；五、仍然希望「落葉歸根」，返回故鄉。

> 1. [The southbound writers] were forced to leave Mainland China due to political reasons and came southward to Hong Kong; 2. [They] viewed Hong Kong culture in the marginal position with a Central-Plain mentality; 3. [They] were influenced by Western culture in Hong Kong; 4. [They] undertook various cultural activities and called out to the motherland via pungent comments or in other forms; 5, [They] still hope to return to their homeland – "leaves fall back to the roots."
>
> WONG 2005, 75; my translation

© CHRIS SONG, 2024 | DOI:10.1163/9789004711600_004

The Wang Tao mode, however, appears insufficient when addressing writers with complicated migration routes, such as Wong Man's 黃雯 (1896–1963). This chapter reads this under-researched poet's autobiographical poems alongside his migration route and historicizes his works in political contexts. The chapter then studies Wong Man's bilingual practice by engaging Elaine Yee Ling Ho's idea of "biliterate modality" with Shu-mei Shih's concept of the Sinophone. The chapter ends with a discussion of the weaknesses of the Wang Tao mode in light of Shih's critique of the diaspora and reconsiders the relationship between diaspora and the study of Hong Kong poetry.

2   Wong Man's Life and Writing

Wong Man published an English-Chinese parallel bilingual volume entitled *Between Two Worlds* 在兩個世界之間 in 1956 in Hong Kong, which collects his poems written since at least the 1940s. Wong's poetic craftsmanship is paraded through the collection's wide range of topics and styles, from Christianity to scientific imagination of the future, from short lyrical poems to long autobiographical records, and from realist depictions of the poor to critical reflections of social agency. Elaine Yee Lin Ho observes,

> there is an integrative dynamic at work in Wong's identification of a common social project for the poet and poetry beyond cultural and national boundaries or the historical conflict that divides England and China. What is at stake for Wong is the prerogative of action to further this project, and as the young student is replaced by the more mature considerations of the doctor in the later poems, social agency is intellectualized so that the integrative dynamic is rechannelled towards ... abstract cultural concerns. (2003, 16)

When read alongside his diasporic routes, Wong Man's autobiographical poems reflect his inclination to embrace Chineseness.[1] Wong's grandfather was a Danish sea captain named Carl Frederik Vang (1848–1887), and his grandmother was Chinese with the family name Wu 吳. They gave birth to Wong Kam-fuk 黃金福 (1870–1931) in the northeastern port city of Dalian. Vang brought the family to Hong Kong but left them behind when he returned to

---

1   The biographical account about Wong Man in this paper is corroborated with the footnotes in *Between Two Worlds* as well as a few sources scattered here and there, including Yu (1963), Wong (1966), Guangzhou Chronicle Editorial Committee (1996, 251–252), Chang (2018), and Chen (2020, 647–650).

Denmark. His son Wong Kam Fuk later became one of the most successful compradors in Hong Kong and founded the Kowloon Wharf (Chang 2018).[2] The Eurasian comprador was married to Robert Hotung Bosman's 何東 (1862–1956) half-sister Ho Sui-ting 何瑞婷 (1868–1942) and had four children. Wong Man, originally named Wong Sik-man 黃錫文, was their third son. Ho brought their children to England for education, and Wong Man received training at the University of Cambridge to become a medical doctor.

During this time, Wong's Chinese patriotic consciousness burgeoned, as he wrote in what seems to be his biographical poem "A Chinese Student's Love Story 一個中國留學生的戀愛故事":

> 他決心不讓任何東西，包括求愛在內，
> 延阻他委身祖國：
> 對於中國學生，還有很多時代吧，
> 青春不是一個求愛時期；
>
> For him nothing, including love, should intervene
> In the dedication of his talents to his land:
> For the Chinese student, many generations yet
> At least to come, youth was not the time for love;
>
> WONG 1956a, 62–63

In the early twentieth century, many Chinese male writers had or imagined such melodrama. It was ended by their perceived duty of returning to help modernize the homeland and their lovers' refusal to leave for China with them. While the breakup represents the cliché motif of the East-West cultural gap, it betrays their frustrated wish to attain an equivalent to Western masculinity, and the inferiority felt when romantically involved with Western females. Their return to China is not a choice but precisely a lack of choices. It appears to be a cover-up for the failure in the interplay of gender, race, and power in a relationship. It is a self-pitied miniature of China's overall failure in the encounter with Western powers since the mid-nineteenth century. The poem shows that Wong shared the same sensibility with many such modern Chinese writers. The stanza ends with the speaker parting ways with his British lover, contrasting the former's progressive politics with the latter's conservatism:

---

2 Some records show Vang was Norwegian. However, Chang's research on Vang's official documents shows that he was Danish.

She the conservative fair rose of England
He the earnest builder of a modern China

她是典型英國保守派的玫瑰花朵
他是熱烈的新中國的建設者

WONG 1956a, 62–63

After graduation, Wong went to Guangzhou to teach medicine, followed by a short appointment as Hong Kong's first Chinese president of Tung Wah Hospital. Wong appeared to have practiced medicine in Shanghai and organized medical aid to Chinese casualties in the Shanghai Incident (January 28th–March 3rd 1932) in collaboration with politicians such as Soong Ching-ling 宋慶齡 (1893–1981) and Ho Hsiang-ning 何香凝 (1878–1972). This relationship possibly helped him establish the Dr. Sun Yat-sen Medical College in 1935. Wong's experience in Shanghai inspired him to participate in the anti-Japanese national salvation on the side of the Chinese Republican government during the second Sino-Japanese War (1937–1945). While appointed by the Republican government to lead the Provincial Department of Health of Guangdong, Wong was also elected president of the Red Cross in Guangzhou and worked among the poor in the rural areas in Guangdong and Hunan, just as he wrote in the poem "The Poet 詩人":

回到中國他用不變的信心
立言立志，離開了都市；
年復一年他嚐嘗土地的滋味，
直至鋼鐵深入了他的筋絡，
和人民一起工作，從頭學起
如何使人類可生活到饜足的狀況，
充份利用他的科學智識，
從事值得一個有高尚目的者花時間的工作
任何一個愛國者都會這樣做。

Back in China, with steadfastness he pursued
His resolves, turning a back to the cities;
Long years he tasted naked earth
Until steel entered also his sinews,
Working with real people, learning
Anew of human living in satiety,
Utilising knowledge to the utmost,
Doings worthwhile to men of high endeavour
As any lover of his country should.

WONG 1956a, 66–67

"People" here is rendered as *renmin* 人民, an ambivalent translation in a contextual reading. On the one hand, socialist realism prevailed in Mainland China in the 1950s and naturalizing the translation as *renmin* seems to resonate with the poetic and political sensibilities up north. On the other hand, it is reasonable to speculate that, at the time of writing, the 1940s, "people" in the English poem was meant to echo Sun Yat-sen's loose definition of it as "any unified and organized body of men" with certain political agency in his political philosophy *San Min Zhu I* 三民主義 (Three Principles of the People; Sun 1927, 151). In 1942, Wong famously published a long essay, "*San Min Zhu I* and Medicine." What appeared as a natural Chinese translation of "people" covertly washed the political overtone of the original English poem. It might also signify Wong's shift of political inclination from *San Min Zhu I* to Maoism. As a result, the Chinese translation reads akin to a socialist realist poem, which was the prevalent literary style in Mainland China and was influential in the leftist fraction of Hong Kong's Chinese poetry scene in the 1950s.

On the Victory in Europe Day, Wong worked on an obscured little hill called Tai-Che 大拓 in Guangdong and wrote about his lament that true peace was not yet achieved in China (1956a, 30–31). Wong was appointed director of Guangzhou city's Department of Health in 1946 and only remained there for a year. He founded the Hua Ying Hospital during China's civil war. Besides, he edited two bilingual periodicals, *World Forum* 世界論壇 and *China Tribune* 中國報. In 1949, Wong finally settled back in his birthplace until he died in London on September 21st, 1963. The biographical records about his time in Hong Kong were primarily about his medical work. Not much about his literary endeavors is known, except that he published an English collection of his translations of classical Chinese poetry, *Poems from China* 唐詩宋詞選 in 1950, and a volume of his own poems, *Between Two Worlds* 在兩個世界之間 in 1956. His poems and translations also appeared in *Wen Wei Po* 文匯報, one of the leftist newspapers in Hong Kong controlled by the Chinese Communist Party (see Wong 1956b; 1957; 1958). His English translations of Mao Zedong's 毛澤東 (1893–1976) poetry were posthumously published as a volume by Hong Kong's Eastern Horizon Press in 1966.

From Wong, back to Hong Kong where "East Meets West" 東方相遇西方 was "With love, / At ease: / The home return" 仁愛為懷 / 衷心自如：/ 回到家裏 (1956a, 70–73). Whereas "East Meets West" presents a utopia of total comfort, "Indulgence" 縱任自己 contrasts the local, peaceful, bourgeois life "in the freedom of Hong Kong" 在香港的自由生活中 (1956a, 16–19) with the distant blood-shedding revolution and the building of the New China up north. While "East Meets West" registers a profound, emotional identification with Hong Kong, "Indulgence" indicates his political allegiance with the New China.

As conflicting as it seems in the identity politics of today's Hong Kong, local Chinese nationalism was not uncommon during Cold War (see Law 2009, chapters 5–6), when Wong had often been recognized as a "patriotic doctor" (*aiguo yisheng* 愛國醫生) in CCP-backed leftist newspapers (e.g., Tian 1983).

3   Ambiguous Translatorship and Biliteracy

As the translators are not credited in Wong Man's *Between Two Worlds*, Elaine Yee Lin Ho argues that "it is impossible to tell which is the source and which the target language" (Ho 2009b, 94). Whether Wong authored the poems in both languages is also ambiguous. In a 1957 review of *Between Two Worlds*, leftist poet He Da 何達 (1915–1994) asked Wong which was the original, and Wong answered, "very difficult to know" (*hao nan zhi* 好難知) (He 1957). However, Wong's close friend Chan Kwan-po's 陳君葆 letter to his third son on December 7th, 1956 reveals,

> 黃雯醫生的詩是先用英文寫成，然後由北京人民出版社譯為中文替他
> 出版
>
> Dr. Wong Man wrote his poems in English first, and then the People's Press in Beijing translated and published them for him.
>
> CHAN 2018, 166; my translation

The ambiguous translatorship warrants a brief reading of Wong's poems in *Between Two Worlds* with English as the original text and Chinese as the translation. Wong might be the translator or working with other translators of his poems. There is no way to verify this now. The translationese of the Europeanized Chinese syntax on the verso pages stands in sharp contrast against the ease of English verses on the recto pages. For example:

> 漠然于任何優越感或驕矜
> 卑恭而怕羞地
> 把自己的詩獻以世上
> （一些思想科學方面仍沒敢下斷論），
> 全出自集中周身精力，
> 一生每刻的衝動，
> 結果只是濾過的或傳遞的
> 一些天賦贈品或甄士披里純
> 來自內，外，過去和現在，

或偶爾被發見是有果實的東西：
因為那會一副腦筋孕育出十全十美的東西呢？
或者詩人亦將會被尊崇
列在一群
用腦力工作的專家中
在偉大的新世界裏面呢？

Unconscious of superiority or pride,
Humbly and diffidently
He submits his poems to the world,
(Thoughts that science as yet dares not say),
Out of a harnessing of total energies,
Pulsating minutes of a whole existence,
In the end what but filtering or passing on
Of gifts or inspirations from the many
Within, without, before and present,
Perchance they be found as fruitful: for
How can one brain concoct perfection?
Perchance the poet also shall be honoured
Into the company
Of specialist workers with the brain
In the great new world?

WONG 1956a, 176–177

The stiff and awkward Chinese syntax is typically caused by difficulty translating a winding sentence that wriggles through a few lines. Moreover, *yanshi pili chun* 煙士披里純, an olden transliteration for "inspiration," is particularly odd. Liang Qichao's 梁啟超 (1873–1929) late-Qing invention became popular during the May Fourth Movement and was famously used by Xu Zhimo 徐志摩 (1897-1931) in his poetry two decades later.[3] However, by the 1950s, this transliteration had become a stereotypical mockery of bad Chinese writing. It is difficult to imagine Wong mocking poets' role in a poem that affirms the value of their contribution to building "the great new world." Throughout the book, numerous incongruous word choices are present in the Chinese versions. In addition to the offbeat Chinese verses viewed from the linguistic perspective, some of the poems discussed above also show how the versioning was affected by ideological factors.

---

3 See Liang ([1901] 1999); Xu ([1921] 2019).

Drawing on translation theories emphasizing cultural hybridity, Elaine Yee Ling Ho delineates the connection between biliteracy and cultural identity in Hong Kong. She illustrates her idea of "biliterate modality" with Leung Ping-kwan's 梁秉鈞 (1949–2013), Wong Man's, and Tammy Lai-Ming Ho's 何麗明 (b.?) poems published as parallel texts (Ho 2010). In Wong's "Indulgence" 縱任自己 as in the other two poets' poems, "Chinese English *simultaneity* ... the subject of the poem as utterance ... must be posited as necessarily in two languages – with no self-other, hierarchical, core-peripheral or primary-secondary discrimination" (68).

What Ho calls "biliterate modality" fills the gap in the research on Hong Kong literature in Shu-mei Shih's Sinophone framework. Shih's concept of the Sinophone refers to "Sinitic-language cultures and communities outside China as well as those ethnic communities in China where Sinitic languages are either forcefully imposed or willingly adopted" (Shih 2010, 36). Although Shih acknowledges that "Hong Kong literature has always been a multilingual literature, including Anglophone and Sinophone writings" (Shih 2008, 15), Hong Kong Sinophone poets' Anglophone writings have rarely been read with depth in or against this framework. Deviating from the approach of translation criticism or translatorly research, Ho looks not at the published texts but at the situated practices of publishing these texts in the bilingual, parallel format. In so doing, Ho's "biliterate modality" provides a powerful methodology of reading many Sinophone Hong Kong writers' bilingual publications and exploring their links to the issues of cultural identity and cultural hybridity in multifarious historical contexts of Hong Kong. In addition to Leung Ping-kwan and Tammy Ho mentioned above, the translational practices of Hong Kong writers such as Shu Hong-sing 舒巷城 (1921–1999), Wan Kin-lau 溫健騮 (1944–1976), Chris Song 宋子江, Florence Ng 吳智欣 and many more may receive critical attention in the framework of Ho's "biliterate modality."

4   From Chinese Diaspora to Hong Kong Diaspora

Wong Man's migration route was complicated yet common in the twentieth century. He was born in Hong Kong and was educated in Britain when and where he may be considered Chinese diaspora. He returned to help modernize the homeland. He worked in cities like Guangzhou and Shanghai and in many villages in southern China. He appeared to travel frequently between Mainland China and Hong Kong in the 1940s before finally settling back in his birthplace in 1949. His migration route is similar to many Chinese overseas students in the early twentieth century, many writers who traveled between Hong Kong and Guangzhou, and many postwar southbound writers in Hong Kong. More importantly, as discussed above, his poetry shared sensibility with those writers in different chronotopes and to different degrees.

With Wong's complicated migration route comes his complicated diaspora statuses. When he was educated in Britain, was he Chinese diaspora and/or Hong Kong diaspora? How do we consider his time in Mainland China from the perspective of the Hong Kong diaspora? The same questions can be asked when studying the writers who frequently traveled between Guangzhou and Hong Kong in the early twentieth century. For example, Outer Out 鷗外鷗 (1911–1995), born in Hong Kong and educated in Guangzhou, commuted throughout his early years. He left the Pearl River Delta and fled to Guilin upon the Japanese army's 1941 seizure of Hong Kong. After the war, he settled in Guangzhou until his passing.

The Wang Tao mode cannot be used to study writers with such complicated migration routes, not just because the two writers discussed here were born in Hong Kong, but because of this mode's inherent limitation, which fixes China to the southbound writers' place of origin and Hong Kong their diasporic destination. Therefore, the Wang Tao mode is insufficient to address the writings that fall outside this diasporic pattern, less so when encountering Wong Man's poems that record his transnational and transregional moves and his diasporic or homeland experiences in various chronotopes. Similar to the Wang Tao mode in Literary Studies, earlier research from other disciplines also invariably considers Hong Kong a destination, at least a sojourning one, for Chinese refugees, exiles, and emigrants when explicating the relationship between Hong Kong and the concept of diaspora.[4]

The Cultural Revolution from 1966 to 1976, the Sino-British Joint Declaration in 1984, the June Fourth incident in 1989, the Handover in 1997, the Umbrella Movement in 2014, and most recently, the Anti-Extradition Law Amendment Bill Movement (anti-ELAB movement) in 2019–2020, and the enactment of the National Security Law (NSL) in 2020, the series of political events are a premonition of the PRC's authoritarian domination over Hong Kong. In these historical episodes, the city witnessed a considerable population exodus, forming the basis for what is known today as the "Hong Kong diaspora." For many, Hong Kong is the place of origin. Over the past two decades, scholarly literature from various disciplines has seen Hong Kong as the place of origin for its diaspora in Australia, Canada, the United Kingdom, the United States and Africa.[5]

---

4 For example, Sinn (1997); Lin (2002); Sinn (2011).
5 For example, Tam (2002) on Hong Kong diaspora in Australia; Kobayashi, Preston, and Murnaghan (2011) in Canada; Cheung and Gomez (2012) in the United Kingdom; Tang (2014) in the United States; Wen and Raja (2022) in Africa.

Moreover, the research focusing on the relationship between the anti-ELAB movement and Hong Kong diasporic communities scattered to various world ends, including the Netherlands and Sweden, reveals that they are politically and emotionally connected to the catastrophic turbulence back home.[6]

In Hong Kong Studies research, Hong Kong has been positioned as a destination for the Chinese diaspora first and then as the origin for the Hong Kong diaspora recently. The observable shift warrants reconsidering diaspora in the study of Hong Kong literature, in which the Wang Tao mode that has been fruitfully applied to studying southbound writers appears outmoded when examining contemporary diaspora phenomena of Hong Kong literature.

In fact, the topic of the Hong Kong diaspora has been, by and large, under-discussed in the research on Hong Kong literature, despite the high-profile post-NSL publication of English-language anthologies such as *Looking Back at Hong Kong* (Wong 2022). To borrow Shu-mei Shih's critique, the research on the southbound writers in the Wang Tao mode considering Hong Kong a destination for the Chinese diaspora is symptomatic of an "inability to see beyond Chineseness as an organizing principle" (2010, 35). The same could be said on previous theorizations of the relationships between diaspora and Hong Kong. Positioning herself as "a diasporic person in diaspora, a Hong Kong person in North America" (1993, 23), Rey Chow's study of Hong Kong citizens' "diasporic consciousness" that shows the contradiction between the forces of Sinicization inspired by an awakened sense of Chineseness in Hong Kong and "Hong Kong's historical difference from China … as the most uncompromisable opposition to the mainland" (1993, 24). Elaine Yee Lin Ho's critiques in conceptualizing "diasporized nation" and "nation-in-diaspora" also pivot around "how China and Chineseness have been conceived, negotiated, and deconstructed" (2009a, 5).

In her seminal essay, "Against Diaspora," Shu-mei Shih insists that,

> *Diaspora has an end date.* When the (im)migrants settle and become localized, many choose to end their state of diaspora by the second or third generation. The so-called nostalgia for the ancestral land is often an indication or displacement of difficulties of localization, voluntary or involuntary. Racism and other hostile conditions can force immigrants to find escape and solace in the past, while cultural or other superiority complexes can estrange them from the locals. To emphasize that diaspora has an end date is therefore to insist that cultural and political practice

---

6 For example, Wong (2021); Fong 2022; Lee 2022. See also Bergsten (2020) on Hong Kong diaspora in the Netherlands; Vane (2021) in Sweden.

is always place-based. Everyone should be given a chance to become a local. (2010, 45; original emphasis)

However, Shih's critique also appears unable to see beyond its target – the Chinese diaspora – and becomes problematic in engaging with the Hong Kong diaspora within the Sinophone purview, especially in the post-NSL era. Before their diasporas end in "the second or third generation," while cultural and political practice is "place-based," does the political and emotional connection to one's homeland only indicate "displacement of difficulties of localization"? Is writing about the place of origin in the local or homeland's language always only meaningful in terms of the writer's current localization? Does becoming a local contradict concerns or nostalgia for one's homeland?

In the post-NSL era, many Hong Kong writers emigrated to other Sinophone communities in and out of the Sinosphere. For example, Chan Wai 陳慧, Chan Chi-tak 陳智德, Liu Wai-tong 廖偉棠 and many more have moved to Taiwan; Chris Song to Canada; Ng Mei-kwan 吳美筠 to Australia; Tammy Lai-Ming Ho to France; Tim Tim Cheng to the UK. However, their writings continue to feed back to Hong Kong's literary scene and endeavor to fortify its cultural identity in dire straits from afar, and so do the works of earlier Hong Kong diaspora such as Jennifer Wong, Mary Jean Chan, Eric Yip, and many others.

After winning UK's National Poetry Competition with "Fricatives" which departs from the issue of language and enters issues of colonialism, race, and diaspora, Eric Yip commented in an interview that he "wanted to examine the transformation of my city, as well as accompanying sentiments of anger, frustration, and diasporic guilt" (quoted in Chan 2022). Hong Kong diaspora poets have always been keen to explore the complicated status of one's mother tongue in the diasporic situation. Mary Jean Chan writes in "Written in a Historically White Space (1)"

> The reader stares at my 皮膚 and asks: why don't you write in 中文? I reply: 殖民主義 meant that I was brought up in your image. Let us be honest. Had I not learnt 英文 and come to your shores, you wouldn't be reading this poem at all. Did you think it was an accident that I learnt your 語言 for decades, until I knew it better than the 母語 I dreamt in? (2019, 43)

Such exploration has found echoes from biliterate poets based in Hong Kong today, such as in Florence Ng's "My Tongue 我嘅母語" in her bilingual volume *Wild Boar in Victoria Harbour* 維多利亞港的野豬:

佢把九聲零舍刁鑽
佢揸槌鬼殺咁嘈

成日俾官話　住又迫住戴括號
正經公文永冇佢份

國歌唔到佢唱
人民嘅大禮堂冇佢講嘢

佢係雜草乜風吹都生
由意志孵化並生養八千萬人

生命力強過小強同感冒菌
將來同我必喺天堂一同復活

佢係
我
嘅
母
語——

tongue that baffles with nine tones
and snaps and shouts and swears all the time

tongue that must be shackled
in brackets or banned from the official

tongue that can't sing to the raised flag
or voice in the great hall of the people

tongue as weeds blazed by winds
hatches by its will and has begotten 80 million

with life tougher than cockroaches and flu
which I will carry and rise in heaven with

my
tongue –

2019, 30–33

5 Conclusion

To borrow Elaine Yee Ling Ho's conclusion for her paper on biliterate modality: "as tropes of cultural identity, these biliterate language acts speak of encounters with forces that shape individuals and communities and connect them with others globally" (2010, 73). Hong Kong writers now based in and out of this city connect through their shared concern for their mother tongue's survival in translational language acts. This connection has become increasingly important for Hong Kong's endangered cultural identity today. Diaspora writers should be allowed to actualize themselves locally as much as devote their cultural practices to fortifying the cultural identity back home. The post-NSL Hong Kong diaspora is tied to Hongkongeseness, precisely because the recent political oppression at home was derived from Chineseness. In the early phase of diaspora, emphasizing its "end date" might discourage building a crucial connection to the home city, not to mention that it is emotionally impossible to imagine.

Works Cited

Bergsten, Mattias. 2020. "Supporting Hong Kong from a Distance: An Interview Study of the Hong Kong Diaspora in Sweden on Their Transnational Engagement towards the Hong Kong Protest Movement of 2019–2022." MA diss., University of Gothenburg.

Business Tales of Hong Kong 商城雜記. 2021. "Maiban shijia zhi Jiulong cang Huang jia" 買辦世家之九龍倉黃家 [Comprador families: The Wong family of the Kowloon Wharf]. Facebook, December 4. https://bit.ly/3V1ESJj.

Chan, Ginny 陳淑霞. 2022. "Shijiusui Gangchan Jianqiao sheng zuopin tansuo yimin lisan qinggan. Duo Yingshi guojia bisai zui nianqing guanjun" 19歲港產劍橋生作品探索移民離散情感。奪英詩國家比賽最年輕冠軍 [Nineteen-year-old Hong Kong student in Cambridge's work explores migrants' diasporic feelings and becomes the youngest winner of UK's National Poetry Competition]. *HK01* 香港01, 1 April. https://bit.ly/3GzM4XJ.

Chan, Kwan-po 陳君葆. *Chen Junbao quanji: Shuxin ji* 陳君葆全集：書信集 [Collected works of Chan Kwan-po: Letters], edited by Liu Xiulian 劉秀蓮 and Xie Ronggun 謝榮滾. Guangzhou: Guangdong renmin chubanshe.

Chan, Mary Jean. 2019. *Flèche*. London: Faber & Faber.

Chang, Michael. 2018. "Svar: Carl Frederik Vang, b1848, Aalborg." *Danish Family Search*. 28 August. https://www.danishfamilysearch.dk/forum/message7452.

Chen, Xiaoka 陳小卡, ed. 2020. *Xifang yixue chuanru zhongguo shi* 西方醫學傳入中國史 [History of Western medicine entering China]. Guangzhou: Zhongshan daxue chubanshe.

Cheung, Gordon C.K., and Edmund Terence Gomez. 2012. "Hong Kong's Diaspora, Networks, and Family Business in the United Kingdom: A History of the Chinese 'Food Chain' and the Case of W. Wing Yip Group." *The China Review* 12 (1): 45–71.

Chow, Rey. 1993. *Writing Diaspora: Tactics of Intervention in Contemporary Cultural Studies*. Bloomington: Indiana University Press.

Fong, Brian C.H. 2022. "Diaspora Formation and Mobilisation: The Emerging Hong Kong Diaspora in the Anti-Extradition Bill Movement." *Nations and Nationalism* 28 (3): 1061–1079. https://doi.org/10.1111/nana.12804.

Guangzhou Chronicle Editorial Committee 廣州地方誌編纂委員會, ed. 1996. *Guangzhou shi zhi juan shijiu renwu zhi* 廣州市誌卷19人物誌 [Guangzhou chronicle, volume 19, biographies]. Guangzhou: Guangzhou chubanshe.

He Da 何達. 1957. "Huang Wen yisheng de shi" 黃雯醫生的詩 [Dr. Wong Man's poetry]. *Wen Wei Po* 文匯報, 5 January.

He Da 何達. 1966. "Du Huang Wen yi *Mao Zedong shi ci*" 讀黃雯譯《毛澤東詩詞》 [Reading Wong Man's translation of *Mao Zedong's Poetry*]. *Wen Wei Po* 文匯報, 1 June.

Ho, Elaine Yee Lin. 2003. "Connecting Cultures: Hong Kong Literature in English, the 1950s." *New Zealand Journal of Asian Studies* 5 (2): 5–25.

Ho, Elaine Yee Lin. 2009a. "China Abroad: Nation and Diaspora in a Chinese Frame." In *China Abroad: Travels, Subjects, Spaces*, edited by Elaine Yee Lin Ho and Julia Kuehn, 3–22. Hong Kong: Hong Kong University Press. https://doi.org/10.5790/hongkong/9789622099456.001.0001.

Ho, Elaine Yee Lin. 2009b. "Nationalism, Internationalism, the Cold War: Crossing Literary-Cultural Boundaries in 1950s Hong Kong." In *China Abroad: Travels, Subjects, Spaces*, edited by Elaine Yee Lin Ho and Julia Kuehn, 85–103. Hong Kong: Hong Kong University Press. https://doi.org/10.5790/hongkong/9789622099456.001.0001.

Ho, Elaine Yee Lin. "Chinese English, English Chinese: Biliteracy and Translation." In *Hong Kong Culture: Word and Image*, edited by Kam Louie, 55–73. Hong Kong: Hong Kong University Press. https://doi.org/10.5790/hongkong/9789888028412.003.0005.

Kobayashi, Audrey, Valerie Preston, and Ann Marie Murnaghan. 2011. "Place, Affect, and Transnationalism through the Voices of Hong Kong Immigrants to Canada." *Social and Cultural Geography* 12 (8): 871–888. https://doi.org/10.1080/14649365.2011.624191.

Lan, Shanshan. 2012. "Negotiating Multiple Boundaries: Diasporic Hong Kong Identities in the United States." *Identities* 19 (6): 708–724. https://doi.org/10.1080/1070289X.2012.752370.

Law, Wing-sang. 2009. *Collaborative Colonial Power: The Making of Hong Kong Chinese*. Hong Kong: Hong Kong University Press.

Lee, Francis L.F. 2022. "Proactive Internationalization and Diaspora Mobilization in a Networked Movement: The Case of Hong Kong's Anti-Extradition Bill Protests."

Social Movement Studies. Advance publication. https://doi.org/10.1080/14742837.2022.2031957.

Liang, Qichao 梁啟超. (1901) 1999. "Yanshi pili chun" 煙士披里純 [Inspiration]. In *Liang Qichao quanji yi* 梁啟超全集 1 [Collected works of Liang Qichao 1], 375–376. Beijing: Beijing chubanshe.

Lin, George C.S. 2002. "Hong Kong and the Globalisation of the Chinese Diaspora: A Geographical Perspective." *Asia Pacific Viewpoint* 43: 63–91. https://doi.org/10.1111/1467-8373.00158.

Lo Wai-luen 盧瑋鑾. 1987. *Xianggang wenzong: Neidi zuojia nanlai ji qi wenhua huodong* 香港文縱：內地作家南來及其文化活動 [Tracks of Hong Kong literature: Southbound Mainland writers' cultural activities]. Hong Kong: Huahan wenhua.

Shih, Shu-mei. 2008. "Hong Kong Literature as Sinophone Literature." *Journal of Modern Literature in Chinese* 8 (2)–9 (1): 12–18.

Shih, Shu-mei. 2010. "Against Diaspora: The Sinophone as Places of Cultural Production." In *Global Chinese Literature*, edited by Jing Tsu and David Der-wei Wang, 29–48. Leiden and Boston: Brill. https://doi.org/10.1163/9789004186910_004.

Sinn, Elizabeth. 1997. "Xin xin guxiang: A Study of Regional Associations as a Bonding Mechanism in the Chinese Diaspora: The Hong Kong Experience." *Modern Asian Studies* 31 (2): 375–397. https://doi.org/10.1017/S0026749X00014347.

Sinn, Elizabeth. 2011. "Hong Kong as an In-Between Place in the Chinese Diaspora, 1849–1939." In *Connecting Seas and Connected Ocean Rims*, edited by Donna R. Gabaccía and Dirk Hoerder, 225–247. Leiden: Brill. https://doi.org/10.1163/ej.9789004193161.i-552.60.

Sun, Yat-sen. 1927. *San Min Chu I: The Three Principles of the People*, translated by Frank W. Price, edited by L.T. Chen. Shanghai: China Committee, Institute of Pacific Relations.

Tam, Siumi Maria. 2004. "Heunggongyan Forever: Immigrant Life and Hong Kong Style Yumcha in Australia." In *The Globalization of Chinese Food*, edited by, 131–151. New York: Routledge.

Tang, Winnie. 2014. "(Re)imagings of Hong Kong: Voices from the Hong Kong Diaspora and Their Children." *Journal of Chinese Overseas* 10 (1): 91–108. https://doi.org/10.1163/17932548-12341275.

Tian, Xinping 田心坪. 1983. "Aiguo yisheng Huang Wen de shi" 愛國醫生黃雯的詩 [Patriotic doctor Wong Man's poetry]. *Xin wan bao* 新晚報 [New evening post], 9 October.

Vane, Esmeralda. 2021. "When Authoritarianism and Democracy Meet: Resistance and Submission of Members of the Hong Kong Diaspora in the Netherlands to Chinese Authoritarian Repression and Securitization." MA diss., Utrecht University.

Wen, Guozhu, and Rameez Raja. 2022. "The Historical Trajectory and Diaspora of Hong Kong Immigrants in Africa." *Asian Journal of Social Science* 50 (1): 35–43. https://doi.org/10.1016/j.ajss.2021.10.003.

Wong, Kenney Chi-Pan. 2021. "From Helmets to Face Masks: How Collective Emotions Sustain Diaspora Mobilization from Homeland Uprising to Global Pandemic among the Hong Kongers." *Social Transformations in Chinese Societies* 17 (2): 117–126. https://doi.org/10.1108/STICS-10-2020-0028.

Wong, Lawrence Wang-chi. 2005. "Nanlai wenhua ren: Wang Tao moshi" 南來文化人：王韜模式 [Southbound intellectuals: The Wang Tao mode]. *Ershiyi shiji* 二十一世紀 [Twenty-first century] 91: 69–77. https://www.cuhk.edu.hk/ics/21c/media/articles/c091-200503080.pdf.

Wong, Man 黃雯. 1942. "Sanmin zhuyi yu yixue" 三民主義與醫學 [Three Principles of the People and medicine]. *Guangdong weisheng* 廣東衛生 [Guangdong health] 37–39: 1–7.

Wong, Man 黃雯. 1956a. *Between Two Worlds* 在兩個世界之間. Hong Kong: The Student Book Store.

Wong, Man 黃雯. 1956b. "Shamian waitan" 沙面外灘 [Shamian island]. *Wen Wei Po* 文匯報, 1 December.

Wong, Man 黃雯, trans. 1957. "Mao zhuxi shici yingyi—Changzheng" 毛主席詩詞英譯——長征 [Chairman Mao's poem in English translation – The Great March]. *Wen Wei Po* 文匯報, 29 June.

Wong, Man 黃雯, trans. 1958. "Mao zhuxi xinci yingyi—Dielianhua" 毛主席新詞英譯——蝶戀花 [Chairman Mao's new poem in English translation – Butterflies in love with flowers]. *Wen Wei Po* 文匯報, 25 January.

Wong, Man 黃雯, trans. and annot. 1966. *Poems of Mao Tse-Tung*. Hong Kong: Eastern Horizon Press.

Wong, Nicolette, ed. 2022. *Looking Back at Hong Kong: An Anthology of Writing and Art*. Hong Kong: Cart Noodle Press.

Xu, Zhimo 徐志摩. (1921) 2019. *Xu Zhimo shixuan* 徐志摩詩選 [Selected poems of Xu Zhimo]. Beijing: Minzhu yu jianshe chubanshe.

Yu, Dingguo 余定國. 1963. "Zhengqi haocun yidai shibiao—Jinian yixueyuan laoshi Huang Wen boshi" 正氣浩存一代師表——紀念醫學院老師黃雯博士 [A righteous spirit, an outstanding teacher – In memory of a teacher in the medical school, Dr. Wong Man]. *Lingnan tongxun* 嶺南通訊 [Lingnan newsletter], 14 November.

CHAPTER 3

"It Can't Be All in One Language"

Poetry in the Diverse Language

Cosima Bruno
SOAS *University of London*

1   Premise

In this chapter I aim at exploring multilingual works by poets of Chinese descent, whose experience, and actual use of language urge us to reconsider the concept of language as unitary and of translation exclusively as an object. The idea is to verify notions of language diversity, translation, nontranslation, antitranslation, self-translation, which inevitably impact our understanding of Chinese, Sinophone, and hyphenated literatures.

On the background of a nationalist agenda – be it from the PRC or the UK – I will first outline the monolingual paradigm which treats a writer's native language as a solid indication of their nationality, and the writers themselves as members of one language community only.

With reference to contemporary multilingual poetry by writers such as Mary Jean Chan, Sarah Howe, Theophilus Kwek, Laura Jane Lee, Cynthia Miller, Jay Gao, Victor Yip (and many more in mind), I will then try to detail how multilingual poetry specifically pursues the tensions inherent in the monolingual paradigm, undermining it through a certain use of languages.

I will discuss two main issues. Firstly, I will look at the multilingual poem as a way to clarify hierarchies and power relationships among the languages employed. Secondly, I will explore some of these poems as ensuing a new aesthetics that stimulates certain reactions from the reader. I will argue that the multilingual aesthetics defined by some of these texts can be compared with the modernist aesthetics that employs (an)other language(s) to "make it new"; while some other texts have a different motivation, aiming at highlighting and also work across difference in language, gender, race, identity and place. Drawing from theoretical propositions indicated by Jan Blommaert, Naoki Sakai, and Yasemin Yildiz, I will study how this new aesthetics defines a multiple linguistic entity that is impossible to homogenize, demanding translation as its reading framework.

© COSIMA BRUNO, 2024 | DOI:10.1163/9789004711600_005

2 Multilingual Poetry and the National Language

Languages – plural – divide. Hence the need for translation. While many theorists take as an implicit starting point the fact that national languages are unitary, well-defined by an outer border, and therefore liable to be exchanged through translation, I wish to challenge this assumption here, by looking at the work of poets of Chinese descent who write in more than one language at once.

In her 2012 book *Beyond the Mother Tongue: The Postmonolingual Condition*, Yasemin Yildiz argues that monolingualism is no longer a sustainable condition. It relates to European nation building in the eighteenth century, when it had the aim of fixing a cultural identity to serve the purpose of the modern nation. We currently live in postmonolingual times, she argues. On a similar line, Naoki Sakai asks: "Is language a countable, just like an apple and an orange and unlike water? Is it not possible to think of language, for example, in terms of those grammars in which the distinction of the singular and the plural is irrelevant?" (Sakai 2009, 73). Jan Blommaert argues that multilingualism – by which he means that repertoire of language varieties, accents, registers, genres, etc., needs to be studied as a matter of capital importance, it "should not be seen as a collection of 'languages' that a speaker controls, but rather as a complex of specific semiotic resources" (Blommaert 2010, 102), defining "stakes for language in society," "social barriers and gateways for social mobility," and regulating through language (138).

Most of us agree that Chinese, as all national languages, is constitutively multiple and heterogenous,[1] and that the question of monolingualism (as its opposite multilingualism) can be thought of as an artificial construct. Yet it

---

1 Historically, "modern Chinese" was officialized in 1932, following the fall of the Qing dynasty, the establishment of the Republic of China in 1912, and the numerous attempts to unify the diversity of spoken and written languages and speeches that were thought of as unintelligible to each other. As Lau Kin-chi, Hui Po-keung and Chan Shun-hing remind us, "the so-called Standard Modern Chinese normalized the incorporation of Europeanized syntax and diction and other hybrid elements in the contending discourses of the building of a national identity, the quest for modernization, and the promotion of class struggle and revolution" (Lau, Hui and Chan 2001, 254). Modern Chinese was therefore thought of as a tool to produce transpersonal intelligibility, since linguistic multiplicity breaks the connection between sound and sense. In the historical contingency of the imagined community of the Chinese nation, among other nations, language diversity was to be rejected, because context-bound, and thus representing an obstacle to citizens' integration, and flawless knowledge in that community. In the mid-20th century, Mandarin Chinese was chosen as the official language of the People's Republic of China, through a process of compulsory education in the whole

is under the scheme of the exclusive partitioning of the national language, and its discriminatory border, that multilingual aesthetics developed by poets of Chinese descent is usually discussed. To be sure, an increasing number of scholars recognizes the difference between a work written in one language and a multilingual work. Notably, Rebecca Walkowitz argues that some contemporary works are "born translated" and should not be analyzed under one single linguistic category (2015). Steven Kellman, working on translingualism, asks the important question of what difference it makes to the writer and the reader to write in more than one language (2020, 5). Nevertheless, when exploring the works of poets of Chinese descent, their multilingualism is often somewhat minimized, prioritizing one language over another. Yulia Dreyzis attributes this attitude to the "enclosed, self-centered system" of Chinese poetic tradition, for which "it seems impossible to imagine a bilingual poet working simultaneously with two languages." Dreyzis refers to Rey Chow, according to whom "the habitual obsession with 'Chineseness'" is a "reaction to the West" and to "past victimization" (Dreyzis 2020, 491–492). While noticing a recurrent attitude, and proposing an agreeable argument, Dreyzis, however, inadvertently emphasizes the Chinese element of multilingual poetry, entitling her essay "The Quest for Bilingual *Chinese* Poetry: Poetic Tradition and Modernity" (italic added).

I will look at the ways migrant poets from the (ex) colonies of Hong Kong, Malaysia, and Singapore dramatize difference among languages, so as to understand the kind of difference at issue between the languages employed, their hierarchy and status, and thus scrutinize the ways linguistic bordering intersected with and intervened into political and social bordering, and vice versa.

The key issue of course is not so much how many languages are present in a multilingual poem, but the relationship between them. In particular, whether a language is considered as standard, and another as a minority language; whether standard languages are seen as dynamic fields or are denied historical contingencies, whether one language is acquired in the family, and another in the classroom, whether migration results in a change of language and what that entails at the level of affects, etc. Along the way, I hope to plant some pointers to go beyond such an important recognition of the power relationship among languages and look at some of these poems as statements to the reader.

Chinese State. For a fascinating discussion of the essential role played by the foreign in the production of national languages, see Berman (1984).

"IT CAN'T BE ALL IN ONE LANGUAGE" 53

"Scrupulous Travesty" is a poem from the collection *Travesty58*, by Jay Gao.[2] Gao here uses procedural digital-language techniques in order to rewrite the ancient Chinese book of divination *Yijing* 易經. The exagramme *dui* 兌 in the poem generates unfit, highly opaque translations, something that dislocates English and seems to confirm untranslatability, while also portraying a culture of spam:

> The time allocated for running scripts has expired
>
> d* duì
> 兌
>
> "Open"
>
> Other variations include opening "the joyous, lake" up and "usurpation"
> Both its inner and outer trigrams are
> The time allocated
> for running scripts has
> expired.
>
> duì) open = (The time allocated
> for running scripts is
> now.) marshland.
>
> …
>
> Gao 2022

Gao's multilingualism includes machine language of technological maloperation, as well as *pinyin*, Chinese characters, foreignizing English, and Wade-Giles, his writing showing translation as ineffective and full of gaps, exacerbated by the incongruous layout. Gao seems to indicate that in a multilingual community, whether or not a language prospers or decays depends on the social habits of its speakers, and on whether or not proficiency in a particular language implies socioeconomic benefits.

Cynthia Miller's "Glitch Honorifics"[3] appears like a three-dimensional poem, in which the poet explains Chinese honorifics, as in a glossary formed by a series of boxes, slightly overlapping each other, without compromising

---

2 Gao is a poet, fiction writer, critic and translator based in Edinburgh. His debut poetry pamphlet is *Wedding Beasts* (2019), followed by *Katabasis* (2020), *Travesty58* (2022), Imperium (2022), and *Bark, Archive, Splinter* (2024).

3 Cynthia Miller is a well-reputed Malay-American poet, whose poem "Glitch Honorifics" appeared in her 2021 debut poetry collection *Honorifics*.

legibility. The honorifics in question are given first in a non-standard transliteration (presumably to mark it as Hokkien) and then in non-simplified Chinese characters. To that, follows a personal explanation of the terms, which draws from the poet's personal and familial background. In a note appended to the poem, Miller explains:

> Like Heptapod B from the film *Arrival*, I wanted to visualise the entirety of a concept, past and present at once. Central to the plot is Sapir-Whorf hypothesis, a theory of linguistic relativity that asserts language literally shapes how you see the world ... The Hokkien that my family speaks is a Southern Chinese language, originally from Fujian, that incorporates Bahasa, English, Mandarin, and a smattering of other dialects like Teochow and Hakka. It's a local Rojak dialect, from a colloquial Malay phrase meaning 'mixed', and would probably be incomprehensible to someone from the mainland. The unease lurking behind both 'Honorifics' and 'Dream Opera' is a frustration that I can understand a little but not speak, and therefore find no entry into that world. Easier to exist in an uprooted 'elsewhere.' (Miller 2020)

Similarly, Hong Kong poet Laura Jane Lee[4] uses Chinese characters and transliterations, as in the poem "爹 deh" (father):

> you gave me my name:
> *chu ching,*
> *clear pearl*
> which in your heavy farmer's accent
> sounded like
> *suu ching*
> *lost-it-all*
>> LEE 2020

Such a multilingual strategy that conflates Chinese characters, translated, for the benefit of the monolingual reader, both into *pinyin* and into English, by apposition, creates a visible internal tension. These trilingual texts point in two

---

4   Laura Jane Lee was born in 1998 in Hong Kong and currently lives in Singapore. She writes in English and Cantonese. Miller is also the founder of KongPoWriMo and Subtle Asian Poetry Collective, and the author of the pamphlets *flinch & air* (2021), and *chengyu: chinoiserie* (2020), published under her former name Rachel Ka Yin Leung.

directions: on the one side they wish to legitimize the language of privacy and on the other side they avoid relegating it into absolute difference, through the use of translation into English. These single words constitute brief exchanges of a Chinese and a Chinese deviant pronunciation, simulating cultural verisimilitude, soon disrupted by the translation into English.

Are the Chinese characters in these poems sufficient to call them Chinese, or, better still, to call them Sinophone poems? What does the use of italic imply?

The persona in Laura Jane Lee's poem receives her name from her father, an identity that she not only needs to translate, but that she also sees as misinterpreted by the standard language. The Sinophone transliterations distinguish the characters in their not standard usage. Standard Chinese and mother tongue develop pidgin and creole languages, world Englishes, code-switching and code-mixing, borrowing, interference, etc. But in Laura Jane Lee's poem, standard Chinese is brought into the poem's linguistic repertoire through the misinterpretation of the father's minor language, while the transliteration of the characters remains non-standard. The evocative, affective quality of the name Clear Pearl is disrupted by the inaccurate and diminishing translation of standard Chinese. Without even physically being in the text, standard Chinese is however the language of authority, it is official and normative.

Theophilus Kwek's poem "Dead Man Savings Won't Go to Wife"[5] portrays strangeness by a defamiliarizing translation of Chinese idiomatic segments given in italic: *yijianrugu* 一见如故 (*your first glance was that of an old lover's*); *biyishuangfei* 比翼双飞 (*wings touching as we flew*); qianjinmaixiao 千金买笑 (*for my smile*); aiwujiwu 爱屋及乌 (*I loved the house and the crows that nested there*); *zhiyinnanmi* 知音难觅 (*one who knows my voice is hard to find*). At the end of the poem, we learn that these segments are given as "loose translations of Chinese idioms for love."

I see this kind of multilingualism as working in a modernist fashion, that is "to make it new," a challenging practice of linguistic defamiliarization, borne out by the aim of revolutionizing literary language. We can find this defamiliarizing use of multilingualism in Pound's poetry, and more generally in modernism's literary theory. For the modernist writer, multilingualism consists

---

5   Theophilus Kwek, "Dead Man Savings Won't Go to Wife," in *Moving House* (2020, 15–16). Kwek is a writer and editor based in Singapore. He has been shortlisted twice for the Singapore Literature Prize and won the New Poets' Prize for his pamphlet *The First Five Storms*, published in 2017. He is also the author of many essays on migration and citizenship.

of several artistic languages (e.g. plastic and sonorous), and different forms of expression and linguistic approaches; it is aimed at counterbalancing the inaptitude of verbal language to match and change the world. Pound deliberated that no single language is quite enough and that "it can't be all in one language" (Pound 1975, 583), hence the need for different languages and for different modes of expression to be used comprehensively, so as to achieve a more thorough understanding of reality. Thus, the modernists' use of translation and multilingualism had the specific aim of innovating literary language.

Whether they use italics or not, these poets write in a multilingual format. Where do we draw a line with the foreignness of a language? How can we resolve to call this writing just "Sinophone," or "English," or "Chinese"? Sakai's words keep lurking into my mind: "the unity of a language is represented always in relation to another unity. It is never given in itself, but in relation to another," "nothing starts until we come across the foreign" (Sakai 2009, 83).

3 Nontranslation

The relatively recent experimental practice of leaving words untranslated and unexplained in literature creates a multilingual aesthetics that was defined by Apter (2003) as "nontranslation" and that can work as a form of resistance to or accommodation of alterity.[6]

The poetry collection *Flèche* (2019), by Mary Jean Chan,[7] has its title and those of the sections in French. The title in French could induce the readers to think that the book is in that language, but when they open the book, they will

---

6 As Emily Apter discusses in relation to Spitzer's multilingual writing, the multilingual text is a nontranslation that "is not an argument against translation per se but, rather, a bid to make language acquisition a category imperative of *translatio studii*. A profound respect for foreignness as the sign of that which is beyond assimilation within language itself." Emily Apter (2003, 278).

7 Mary Jean Chan were born and raised in Hong Kong and currently live in Oxford, where they also work as senior lecturer in creative writing at Oxford Brookes University. Their collection *Flèche* (London: Faber & Faber, 2019) won the 2019 Costa Book Award for Poetry, and was shortlisted in 2020 for the International Dylan Thomas Prize, the John Pollard Foundation International Poetry Prize, the Jhalak Prize and the Seamus Heaney Centre First Collection Poetry Prize. In 2021, *Flèche* was a Lambda Literary Award Finalist. Chan's poems have been translated into multiple languages, including Italian, Chinese, Japanese, Arabic, Galician, Greek and Romanian. Part of the observations made on Chan and Howe, below, are also published in another essay of mine: Cosima Bruno (2024, 319-331).

"IT CAN'T BE ALL IN ONE LANGUAGE"

soon recognize that the language used is mainly English, with some Chinese. The poet early on explains the use of English as due to the postcolonial condition of the persona. In the "Preface," we find a footnote, in which the poet refers to the 1842 Treaty of Nanjing, which stipulated the cession of Hong Kong to the British Empire as a Crown colony, in the aftermath of the First Opium War. Further down the volume, at a glance, we can see a few Chinese characters embedded in English sentences, like in "Written in a Historically White Space (1)":

> The reader stares at my 皮膚 and asks: why don't you write in 中文? I reply: 殖民主義 meant that I was brought up in your image. Let us be honest. Had I not learnt 英文 and come to your shores, you wouldn't be reading this poem at all. Did you think it was an accident that I learnt your 語言 for decades, until I knew it better than the 母語I dreamt in? (Chan 2019, 43)

Through a more minute reading, we can notice that while the English here functions as basis, morphologically, syntactically, and grammatically coherent, the Chinese characters have all specific meanings of otherization, that is a collision between the subject and the intended monolingual reader: "skin" (皮膚), "Chinese" (中文), "colonialism" (殖民主義), "English" (英文), "language" (語言), "mother tongue" (母語). Similarly, the title of the collection, as well as of its three sections – "parry," "riposte" and "corps-à-corps" – are all French terms used in fencing to indicate dueling techniques. As general framework of the collection, fencing sets a text world in which two persons of the same sex synchronically duel with one another, providing a consonant setting for both the theme of queer lovemaking (further emphasized by the *double entendre* created by the homophony between *flèche* and *flesh*), and that one of the intercultural translational battle, where the body is site of the border and boundary between I and you, Chinese, English, French, mother tongue and language of Empire.

We can conclude that the French and the Chinese words in *Flèche* do not have the purpose of just marking different languages for the sake of portraying a multilingual context – which could be done by using any Chinese character or French word. For Chan, multilingualism is there to mark a differential identity. Writing in English is the result of a power relationship, where the colonized uses the language of the colonizer. But English is not just a matter of necessity; it is the medium to build her struggle and talk back to the colonizer:

> Let us be honest. Had I not learnt 英文 and come to your shores, you
> wouldn't be reading this poem at all. (Chan 2019, 43)

What is Chan's mother tongue? In postmonolingual fashion, and under the guidance of Blommaert, Chan's multilingual battle can be considered as having no mother tongue, even though they state they dreamt in their mother tongue. All languages used are languages of translation, in relation to which the subject is positioned further out. The co-presence of these languages marks the untranslatable space between the states of being of the persona, and grounds their critique of differential power relations. French, English, and Chinese can mediate or be illegible according to the linguistic proficiencies of the readers; for both reader and writer, however, language becomes cause of slippage and instability. Language is the token that gives access to or shuts the body out of "conditional spaces" (Chan 2019, 63). Chan's cartographies, like those of their Shanghainese mother who migrated to Hong Kong, are invariably marked with social, political and racial alterity:

> Your spot given
> To a *worker's child*
> CHAN 2019, 51

The heteroglossia of the fragment "worker's child," marked with italic to indicate they are voiced, subvocalized fragments, from the "foreign" language of Maoist speech, emphasizes alterity. This is the native language from which Chan also departs. Chan's native language is not their mother's Shanghainese. Their native language, the language to which they were exposed since childhood may be Cantonese, or the equally colonizing standard Chinese and English. To borrow Yildiz's words, we can state that Chan's collection situates itself in the "postmonolingual condition," "writing beyond the concept of the mother tongue." At the same time, Chan also engenders a "postmonolingual mode of reading" which is "a mode of reading that is attentive to both multilingual practices and the monolingual paradigm" (Yildiz 2012, 21).

Chan transposes the friction among colonizers' languages in their border-crossing poems. They use English as a language acquired by birth into a colonial social setting, marked by a dynamic of economic and/or cultural power relationship. English is not the mother tongue, but it is learned through education, migration, and travel. Their poetry not only reflects a certain social condition that is multilingual (the migrant author happens to be writing and living in the translingual environment of a multilingual city), it also entertains a one-to-one discussion with the reader.

"IT CAN'T BE ALL IN ONE LANGUAGE"

In a colonial context, the desire for language possession, for close-to-native proficiency of English, places the premium language as capital, in Bourdieu's terminology. This is visible in Eric Yip's "Fricatives,"[8] which reveals a different type of multilingualism, operating by absence:

> To speak English properly, Mrs Lee said, you must learn
> the difference between *three* and *free.*

Yip construes alterity within a monolingual text, while also playing with the word "free," which may be read as bearing extra meaning from the perspective of a colonial language.

From her mixed cultural background, Sarah Howe[9] plays with orientalism in her collection *Loop of Jade* (2015), which takes Jorge Luis Borges' 1942 essay "The Analytical Language of John Wilkins" as its interface. John Wilkins was a seventeenth-century philosopher, who attempted to devise a universal scientific language, based, according to Borges, on an ancient Chinese taxonomy of animals, entitled *Celestial Emporium of Benevolent Knowledge.* Borges lists 14 taxonomical categories allegedly discovered by the translator Franz Kuhn and concludes that all attempts at describing the universe through one language are arbitrary and futile. Howe adopts the same 14-category structure as allegedly the *Emporium* had, presenting autobiographical yet fantastical poems full of orientalist images that define a liminal incantatory world of real and imagination, as childhood memories and transmitted family stories usually do. In the poem "Crossing from Guangdong," for example, translational processes overlap generations, places and worlds, where the Whitehall and the Cenotaph are found in the streets of China.

Howe's is a multi-layered meaning in constant flux, continuously translated, with no path connecting the particular to the universal, the known to the unknown. Her Cantonese mother's tongue and her Shanghainese grandmother's tongue entangle with each other. The Cantonese in:

---

8 Hong Kong poet Eric Yip speaks Cantonese and Mandarin, and writes in English. He was the youngest National Poetry Competition at 19, as the author of "Fricatives," written while studying at the University of Cambridge. Eric Yip, "Fricatives," *Varsity* 21 April (2022), https://www.varsity.co.uk/arts/23534.

9 Howe was born in Hong Kong in 1983 to an English father and a Chinese mother, who migrated to the UK when Sarah was seven years old.

> *Yut, ye, sam, sei. ...*
> ... I hear
> again your voice ...
>> HOWE 2015, 3

and an old woman met by chance on a bus in Datong could have well been her grandmother, who she never met, speaking in a dialect she does not understand.

Languages, texts and places are continuously crossed and translated, without pretense of an exchange, or an orderly resolution. This is effectively articulated in the poem "(l) Others," which starts with a quotation from *Genesis* and carries on reflecting on the matter of genetic inheritance:

> I think about the meaning of *blood*, which is (simply) a metaphor
> and *race*, which has been a terrible pun.
>> *
>
> From *castus* to *chaste*, with a detour for *caste*.
> *English*, 廣東話, *Français d'Egypte*, מאַמע־לשון: our future children's
> skeins, carded.
>> *
>
> ...
> The spiralling path from *Γένεσις* to *genetics*. Language revolves like a ream
> of stars.
>> HOWE 2015, 46

The poem further refers to Gregor Mendel's universalistic theories of inheritance, which immediately evokes the risk of Mischlinge Laws, while "ream of stars" is a luminous image describing language as emanating in somewhat parallel ways – an apt figure for the simultaneous, multiple national and linguistic identity portrayed in multilingual writing.

Written mainly in English, the poems are liberally inclusive of many languages, repeatedly repositioning the reader as inadequate and outsider, generating a critical distance from dominant ideas and truth claims about culture and language, nation, history. Howe seems to remark that personal experience and affect are impossible to convey, they cannot translate into a language of truth, instead they can only lead to the classification of stereotypes. Her use of multilingualism here is ontological, ethical and aesthetic. It works as a continuous, viral, defamiliarizing, and yet essential translation. She borrows and refutes texts (Borges, Chinese songs, Pound), showing that cultural difference can become commodified in a late-capitalist system in which these discourses circulate.

I consider the aesthetics defined by these latter texts as having a slightly different purpose from that one encountered in Kwek, Lee, Miller, and Gao. I find these texts bearing a stronger ethical weight towards changing, updating, and upgrading the monolingual reader.

4 Final Remarks

I contend that we must continue to define these works as "multilingual," without prioritizing any of the languages used. I also contend that we can use translation as our reading model.

Calling these texts "Sinophone" only mitigates the problem of the monolingual paradigm and of the unitary national language, because the Sinophone still looks for an identifiable language in relation to nationality, regional or cultural origin. So, despite the opening up to linguistic diversity in the notion of Sinophone, multilingual poetry does not belong to a single system and needs to be considered on a broader linguistic scale, which recognizes languages as operating in relation (often in discordance) with each other, and not in isolation from each other.

The dynamic alternating national languages in multilingual poetry are usually not examined as acts of translation from one language into another.[10] But if not translation, what does the switch from one language to another entail?

Translation begins from an attitude of perceptiveness and responsiveness to something that addresses us and cannot be ignored. As Susanne Klinger states in relation to post-colonial writing, "source and target language come into contact – and often merge with one another – not only in the process of creating the text but also in the reality portrayed in this text, as this reality itself constitutes an arena of past and ongoing translation" (Klinger 2013, 113). This act of translation reaches beyond the model of an exchange between two monolingual systems of two unitary languages. It involves forms of transposition within a linguistic system, or between idiolects as well as between languages. This model of translation foregrounds the presence of one language within another, not to smooth over its differences but to emphasize both its particularity and its ability to engender new stories and new readings.

---

10   In fact, Reine Meylaerts laments the fact that multilingual writing constitutes a blind spot in Translation Studies (2010, 227–30).

The excerpts above are from multilingual poems because from the start the poets present different proportions of languages in the same textual space. They complicate the global hegemony of the dominant language, by way of a translative act that accounts for their different proportions of languages. If monolingual translation can be thought of as a bridge that takes a national language or national culture to another in temporal and spatial sequence, the multilingual text cannot be thought of as a bridge, but as a translation that continuously switches between one or more linguistic nations, alternating themselves in the same textual space, at the same time. In precisely their linguistic asymmetry and inequality, these multilingual poems can convey the irreducible heterogeneity of linguistic and cultural situations, in which translation can never simply be communication between equals. Although still expressing a desire for the capital of English, translation in the multilingual text demystifies, rather than mystifies the dominant language.

Multilingual poetry does not signal exhaustive translatability or transparency, as we would find in monolingual translations, rather it conveys partial opacity or illegibility of writing in multiple languages. The reader of the multilingual text either knows the languages the text is written in or knows one language and not the other. For the latter kind of reader, the multilingual text may feel defamiliarizing, but, I argue, not necessarily alienating. To such defamiliarizing text the reader may react with curiosity towards the portion of text he or she does not understand, or may succumb to ignorance. In each of these cases, however, reading the multilingual poem is for the reader a moment of realization, in the cognitive comparative processing of different languages, which we may call "translation."[11] As Blumczynski (2016, 40) reminds us, quoting Berman: "It is the drive to translate that makes the translator a translator ... This drive may arise of its own or be awakened by another person" (Berman 2009, 58).

In the multilingual text, we find not a relationship between a multilingual translator and a monolingual reader, but something, instead, like the multilingual writer and reader as translators.

These multilingual poems show a kind of linguistic relativism that enables us to see others and, within some limits, to communicate with them. In this way it reassesses our ethnocentrism, by adding (rather than substituting) more than one culture, more than one material structure, as well as emotional sphere, in other words, more than one symbolic system. Even if the English-language persona superimposes itself on all the others, or if we cannot retrieve an *original* unitary persona, in the multilingual poem there are the

---

11   Brian Lennon argues in favor of this understanding of the reader of what he calls "strong bilingual or plurilingual text" (2010, 75).

"IT CAN'T BE ALL IN ONE LANGUAGE" 63

seeds of other languages, idioms that are private and public, forms of experience that present not one but two, three, four personae.

The multilingual poem thus discredits the authoritarian impersonal truth of a national language in its claimed accessibility to all, posing the question: how do those who do not share the same language declinate and communicate their own experience? It is through a language that shows the relation to other languages, that is in a multilingual language.

In the cracks of multiple language-worlds, we find not the transparency of the monolingual translation, but multilingualism *in translation*. As Lennon considers, in the multilingual text "translation is already, and in advance, denied – but also, in an important way, already performed" (2010, 74).

Multilingual poetry ensues from complicated relations of proximity to and distance from the writing languages. From the perspective of the writer, multilingual poetry is often produced by migrants and exiles, with a translingual experience and actual multilingual use of language. Performing multiple speeches, rubbing deviant against standard idioms, these multilingual poems constitute a dynamic form of cultural porosity that communicates at the elusive point of discontinuity (Sakai 2009, 72), mistranslation, and incompatibility. These multilingual poems mark cultural difference, incorporating a variety of languages, they represent different centers of power, including forms of vernacular, familial, standard and vehicular languages, as well as translation and transposition of literary references and myths, single words, sentences, or brief segments of dialogues.

I have started by looking at the kind of multilingualism used in these poems: what languages (French, English, machine language, Mandarin, Chinese familial vernacular, Hokkien, Hebrew, Cantonese, Maospeak); what kind of markers (italic, in-text translation, *pinyin*); what kind of words; what status, what accent and form? Along the way, I have distinguished two kinds of aesthetic use of multilingualism, to conclude that these texts radically change the way the reader shares and develops knowledge. Here we are not in the presence of a specific decoding of a message contained in a visible text and reformulated in another language. We are instead in the presence of a process that complicates and facilitates intercultural relations and the transmission of knowledge.

Thus, translation in this chapter has been conceived as a practice of writing and reading with many implications for views of culture, and personal and collective identity.[12] In all of these works we can recognize similar thematic

---

12   Readers less familiar with this conception of translation and wishing to find out more can consult comprehensive studies on this by Ricoeur, Blumczynski, Hermans, Tymoczko, Geertz, Gentzler and more.

preoccupations arising from a multilingual consciousness in the intercultural space of migration. These writers live in translation, as their multilingual life experience is embedded in their writing, and their crossing national languages is emotionally involved in a form of self-transformation.

Language is translational, and translation is not just a text but also a necessary process of the diverse society that generates interpersonal relations with who is not us, and for whom we may feel fascination, suspicion, conflict, hostility.

These poems are multilingual in their internal linguistic diversity. Reading them together makes them doubly multilingual, because they enact the differences between Chineses, as well as their individual differences from the standardized national English language.

Works Cited

Apter, Emily. 2003. "Global Translation: The 'Invention' of Comparative Literature, Istanbul, 1933." *Critical Inquiry* 29 (2): 253–81.

Berman, Antoine. 1984. *The Experience of the Foreign.* Translated by Stefan Heyvaert. Albany: SUNY Press.

Berman, Antoine. 2009. *Toward a Translation Criticism: John Donne.* Translated by Françoise Massardier-Kennedy. Kent, Ohio: Kent State University Press.

Blommaert, Jan. 2010. *The Sociolinguistics of Globalization.* Cambridge: Cambridge University Press.

Blumczynski, Piotr. 2016. *Ubiquitous Translation.* London and New York: Routledge.

Bruno, Cosima. 2024. "Translation in a Multilingual Context: Six Authors Writing the City." In *The Bloomsbury Handbook of Modern Chinese Literature in Translation,* edited by Cosima Bruno, Lucas Klein, and Chris Song, 319-331. London: Bloomsbury.

Chan, Mary Jean. 2019. *Flèche.* London: Faber & Faber.

Dreyzis, Yulia. 2020. "The Quest for Bilingual Chinese Poetry: Poetic Tradition and Modernity". In *Literary Translation, Reception, and Transfer,* edited by Norbert Bachleitner, vol. 2, 491–501. https://doi.org/10.1515/9783110641998-039.

Gao, Jay. 2024. *Bark, Archive, Splinter.* London: Outspoken Press.

Gao, Jay. 2022. *Imperium.* Manchester: Carcanet.

Gao, Jay. 2020. *Katabasis.* Sheffield: The Poetry Business.

Gao, Jay. 2022. *Travesty58: Lake Poems.* Glasgow and London: SPAM Press.

Gao, Jay. 2019. *Wedding Beasts.* London: Bitter Melon 苦瓜.

Geertz, Clifford. 2000 [1973]. *The Interpretation of Cultures.* New York: Basic Books.

Gentzler, Edwin. 2016. *Translation and Rewriting in the Age of Post-Translation Studies.* London: Routledge.

Hermans, Theo. 2019. *Translation in Systems: Descriptive and Systemic Approaches Explained.* London: Routledge.

Howe, Sarah. 2015. *Loop of Jade.* London: Chatto & Windus.

Kellman, Steven G. 2020. *Nimble Tongues: Studies in Literary Translingualism.* Indiana: Purdue University Press.

Klinger, Susanne. 2013. "Translated otherness, self-translated in-betweenness: Hybridity as medium versus hybridity as object in Anglophone African Writing." In *Self-Translation. Brokering Originality in Hybrid Culture*, edited by Anthony Cordingley, 113–126. London and New York: Bloomsbury Academic.

Kwek, Theophilus. 2020. *Moving House.* Manchester: Carcanet Press.

Kwek, Theophilus. 2017. *The First Five Storms.* Sheffield: The Poetry Business.

Lau, Kin-chi, Hui Po-keung, and Chan Shun-hing. 2001. "The Politics of Translation and Accountability." In *Specters of the West and the Politics of Translation*, edited by Naoki Sakai and Yukiko Hanawa, 241–268. Hong Kong: Hong Kong University Press.

Lee, Laura Jane. 2021. *flinch & air.* London: Out-Spoken Press.

Lennon, Brian. 2010. *Babel's Shadow: Multilingual Literatures, Monolingual States.* Minneapolis: University of Minnesota Press.

Leung, Rachel Ka Yin. 2020. "爹 deh" (father), *Mekong Review* 5 (18).

Leung, Rachel Ka Yin. 2020. *chengyu: chinoiserie*, Clevedon: Hedgehog Poetry Press.

Meylaerts, Reine. 2010. "Multilingualism and Translation." In *Handbook of Translation Studies*, edited by Yves Gambier and Luc van Doorslaer, vol. 2, 227–30. Amsterdam and Philadelphia: John Benjamins.

Miller, Cynthia. 2021. *Honorifics.* Leicester: Nine Arches Press.

Miller, Cynthia. 2020. "Three Poems and a Note." *Poetry Birmingham*, no. 5 (2020). Available online: https://poetrybirmingham.com/cynthia-miller-three-poems-and -note. Accessed March 23, 2023.

Pound, Ezra. 1975 [1934]. *The Cantos of Ezra Pound.* London: Faber and Faber.

Ricoeur, Paul. 2006. *On Translation.* London and New York: Routledge.

Sakai, Naoki. 2009. "How do we count a language? Translation and discontinuity." *Translation Studies* 2 (1): 71–88.

Tymoczko, Maria. 2007. *Enlarging Translation, Empowering Translators.* Manchester: St Jerome.

Walkowitz, L. Rebecca. 2015. *Born Translated. The Contemporary novel in an Age of World Literature.* New York: Columbia University Press. Available online: https:// warwick.ac.uk/fac/cross_fac/g19c/activities/displacements/readingnovelswork shop/walkowitz_born_translated.pdf. Accessed March 23, 2023.

Yildiz, Yasemin. 2012. *Beyond the Mother Tongue: The Postmonolingual Condition.* New York: Fordham University Press.

Yip, Eric. 2022. "Fricatives." *Varsity* (21 April). Available online: https://www.varsity.co .uk/arts/23534. Accessed March 23, 2023.

CHAPTER 4

Translingual Poetry and the Poetics of Translingualism

Sinophone verses, Thirdspaces and "Thirdlanguagings"

Simona Gallo
University of Milan

1 Introduction

Defined as the "phenomenon of writers who create texts in more than one language or in a language other than their primary one" (Kellman 2019, 337), translingualism acts as a *mise en abyme* of literary multilingualism, encompassing a plethora of approaches and practices related to domains of Sociology, Cultural Studies, Translation Studies and, of course, Literary Studies. It optimizes a varied multidisciplinary vocabulary and offers a comprehensive descriptive device for phenomena that nonetheless need to be closely investigated in context.

What happens in the Sinophone literary context, then? To be more specific, what is the relationship between translingualism and Sinophone literature, especially in the less explored field of poetry? In this chapter, I will try to sustain a threefold thesis, condensed as follows: the first part argues that the literary Sinosphere is intrinsically translingual and translational, and that Sinophone poetry is the genre that epitomizes translingual and translational writing as an individual practice; the second part centers on Sinophone poetry as a site of creative construction of languages, or what I will refer to as "thirdlanguaging"; the third and last part substantiates this phenomenon through three case studies, which diverge not only because they symbolize three different contexts of the Sinosphere – in terms of space and the dissimilar relationships between mother tongues and other tongues – but also in illustrating various manifestations of the poetics of creation and translation.

© SIMONA GALLO, 2024 | DOI:10.1163/9789004711600_006

2 Translingual and Translational, That Is, Sinophone Poetry

The literary Sinosphere – that is, that universe of cultural production inhabited by a wide variety of tongues, cultures, and ideologies[1] – can be conceived a multifarious galaxy of literary phenomena, bound by the gravitational force of translingualism. Translingualism echoes different social conditions, aesthetic strategies, ideological stances, and even commercial needs. For instance, the societal bilingualism of minority language writers does not necessarily overlap with the individual bilingualism (or "bilinguality") of the migrant or exiled writer (Hamers and Blanc 2004), nor can their respective literary manifestations be labelled equally (Grutman 2009, 183). In point of fact, in many sites of the Sinophone, self-determination and linguistic freedom gain paramount importance (Bernards and Tsai 2013, 188), and to be more precise, the issues of Sinitic-language writers from non-dominant cultures in the People's Republic of China, Taiwan, Hong Kong, and Southeast Asia might differ from the ones experienced by the "China-born" Sinophone authors in the West, in that the *ethos* of the translingual practices and their manifestations follow separate trajectories.[2] The literary Sinosphere, then, embraces a number of practices, from code-switching to multilingual creativity, but they can all be understood as ways of transforming identity through the appropriation, revision, and rewriting of languages.

Literary writing represents here a kind of aesthetic research, while still embodying a quest for an individual *locus* of language and cultural mediation – as language from a philosophical perspective is an instrument for the progressive construct of individuality, in its thoughts, its emotions, its feelings, its inner world (Cheng 2002, 10). To that end, the various literary articulations shape different orbits of the Sinophone and its identities where translanguaging and self-translation reveal a diversity of approaches to each language of the "self," intended as a poetics of the individual. Drawing upon a vast array of

---

1   As Tee Kim Tong puts it, "Each Sinophone literature works in its own field/system within various environments that differ in geographical zone, dominant language, ethnic combination, mainstream ideology, and literary as well as cultural traditions." (Tong 2010, 83).

2   In this respect, the decision to take shelter in one of the two or more languages dominated by an author appears particularly relevant or even emblematic in literary writing, especially when the choice entails the abdication to literary bilinguality in favor of a new monolingualism. This is the case of a number of well-known writers who have taken root in the West, such as the anglophone Ha Jin 哈金, who has defined himself as "exiled to English" (2013), and the francophone Dai Sijie 戴思傑, safely harbored in French, but also of the complex multilingualism of Ying Chen 應晨 as well as the individual stance of Yang Lian 楊煉, describing himself as "a poet writing in Yanglish" (Bruno 2017, 7).

possibilities and phenomena provided by such an inherently heterogeneous and multilingual space (Shih, Tsai and Bernards 2013), this chapter attempts to shed light on three different contexts where translingualism occurs in poetry, since lyrical writing stands as the privileged domain of linguistic creativity, driven by translingual and translational practices. That might be explained by the fact that poetry stands as an unconventional language – even challenging the explanatory possibilities at the disposal of analytical philosophy (Blackburn 2015), in that, for instance, creativity cannot be rationalized or expounded. Poetry can also be understood as a language *of* and *for othering*, as it engenders a further, individual, realm or an atmosphere in which an author occasionally dwells, creating an*other* language. According to Emanuela Nanni, this peculiar feature is what binds poetry to multilingualism, since poetry, by its definition, is a foreign language or a distanced territory from our everyday world (2007, 71).

Poetry also constitutes an arena in which the unrest of a translingual mind can be productively reinterpreted, to give birth to works that both picture and annihilate the process of negotiation between multiple selves. A second, pragmatic response might simply come from logical deduction: if we agree that Sinophone literature is grounded on translinguality, shouldn't Sinophone poetry be considered an occurrence of translingualism? At any rate, this is the claim I am making here: that poetry is a space for creative re-location through language.

3 Space, Bilingualism and Thirdlanguaging

Amidst a spectrum of conceptual configurations and approaches, I draw upon the domain of space, since it allows for an observation of the boundaries between languages proffered by the text through the author's conscious negotiation with his own languages. In the first place, the image of the "boundary" immediately pictures at least two facets: on the one hand, the presence of two differing albeit bordering elements; on the other, the possibility of the encounter, through the movement of traversing or trespassing in either direction. In *The Location of Culture*, Homi Bhabha (1994) elucidates the interaction between the threshold and what stays "beyond,"[3] and in his discussion of

---

3 "'Beyond' signifies spatial distance, marks progress, promises the future; [...] The imaginary of spatial distance – to live somehow beyond the border of our times – throws into relief the temporal, social differences that interrupt our collusive sense of cultural contemporaneity." (Bhabha 1994, 4).

"in-betweenness" he postulates the impulse of overstepping liminality as well as hierarchies. Metaphorically speaking, going beyond gives access to an*other* space, which becomes a field of "strategic possibilities," in Foucault's words (1972, 37). In this respect, many Sinophone translingual authors who juggle with their hyphenated identities become translators and often self-translators, straddling the frontier between two linguistic territories.

This is especially true for migrant writers, as well as for minority writers,[4] but can also be true for those Sinophone writers who find themselves engaged in the challenge of transcending borders through their diverse linguistic experiences. As mentioned above, some even manage to portray the passage through the interliminal space of difference with their aesthetics, thus originating a production of culturally translingual meaning, or what Bhabha calls the "Third space" (1994). As a site of hybridity, Bhabha's Third Space enables the subject to "elude the politics of polarity" (38–9) and to destroy "this mirror of representation in which cultural knowledge is customarily revealed as an integrated, open, expanding code" (37), though Edward Soja's "Thirdspace" (1996b) reconstructs the binarism in its referring to spaces defined by border-crossing, to interstices where the individual can produce a counternarrative, and in which subjectivity can reckon with otherness through a "thirding-as-Othering" (2009, 50), a process that reveals the hidden dimensions and creates a flow of articulations carried out by the individual. "Basically what the strategy suggests," Soja explains, "is that when faced with a strict binary choice, with either/or option, one should reject the imposed binary, deconstruct and disorder it, and force it open to a multiplicity of alternative choices" (1996a, 1421). The genetic composition of the concept also refers to George Steiner's "third language," or what he calls "a medium of communicative energy which somehow reconciles both [source and target] languages [in a translation] in a tongue deeper, more comprehensive than either" (1970, 29; see also Lefebvre 1991, and van Crevel and Klein 2016).

Against this background, acknowledging that "in translingual writing the process of negotiating assumptions about language is more important than the product" (Matsuda, quoted by Gramling 2016, 104–105), the very effort to eclipse the cultural and linguistic boundaries through literary creation shapes my idea of the process of "thirdlanguaging." Rather than limit my parameters to translation, however, I want to make the claim that thirdlanguaging can even describe the poetics of creation. In fact, what I refer to as thirdlanguaging depicts the prominence of the subject's *ethos*, and hence translates the

---

4 In such regard, refer to Ming Di's chapter in this book.

forces beneath literary performance: it depicts a way of disidentifying with two (or more) languages in order to shape a unique literary language materialized through the text.[5] Moreover, it reconciles with Evangelista's "voice speaking from an in-between space, where one is allowed to go deeper, to find something new" (2013, 185). Be it an entrenched poetics or an occasional experimentation, thirdlanguaging identifies a literary practice, namely the disidentification with the condition of linguistic in-betweenness, trapped in an alternate monologism, asserting a unique aesthetic narrative of the self. It is spurred by a yearning to flee paradigms of dominance and approach spaces wherein the subject is entitled to design a subjective pattern: ergo, it enhances self-determination, supporting individual creativity.

In lieu of defining a collective stance, thirdlanguaging portrays a subjective gesture that is eventually substantiated by means of a literary work, hence originating a "thirdlanguaged" text, whose privileged scope is poetry – too often overlooked by Sinophone Studies[6] – by virtue of its exceptional relationship with creativity. Three examples follow.

4   Thirdlanguagings: Three Fields and Poetics, to Begin with

4.1   *The Unrest of Sounds and Scripts: Ouyang Yu*
My first example of a translanguaging Sinophone poet is Ouyang Yu 歐陽昱 (b. 1955). Ouyang is a contemporary Chinese-Australian poet and accomplished artist who straddles the border between two countries and (cultural-linguistic) identities. Born in Huangzhou, Hubei, he migrated to Australia in the 1990s.[7] More recently, he has been going back and forth between Melbourne and Shanghai (at least until the pandemic), taking roles as a scholar and Professor in China and a writer and translator in Australia. Since the poet exhibits

---

5   Despite it sharing the intention of going beyond, my idea of thirdlanguaging differs from Gramling's concept of "supralingualism" (2019, 11; 2020, 129). Another touchpoint for my thinking is that of Haroldo de Campos on transcreation (see Vieira 1999).

6   In this connection, see Lucas Klein's chapter in this book.

7   As with many other Chinese artists and intellectuals, he decided to leave his motherland and to move to the West after the 1989 Tiananmen square massacre. Before he left, he completed a Master's degree in Australian and English Literature at the East China Normal University in Shanghai, where he had earlier graduated with a degree in English and American Literature. Then, two years later, in 1991, Ouyang moved to Melbourne to undertake a doctorate at La Trobe University. He is now a prolific and versatile writer, who has authored more than one hundred books in both Chinese and in English, as a critic, scholar, translator, essayist, novelist, and poet.

his disenchantment with reality and declares the sense of loss and refusal from both China and Australia, his experimental works verbalize a sarcastic defiance[8] of fixed linguistic paradigms and emancipation from canonical bilingualism, while trying to mold a personal poetic language that he can eventually inhabit but not necessarily share.

All this is fully unveiled by his *Flag of Permanent Defeat* (2019), a collection gathering 213 experimental pieces, composed since 1982, where the condition of the bilingual writer struggling to gain a space of recognition and empowerment is on display. A close reading of the poems allows us to observe that the writer's thirdlanguaging articulates signifying principles in two major directions, namely allographic otherings and semiotic otherings. The latter, semantic patterning, is shaped by concurrently obstructing and reinventing the graphic properties of language:

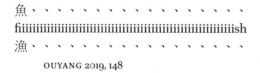

OUYANG 2019, 148

Against both Western theories of signification and Sinocentric discourse on the Chinese script as inviolable sign of cultural identity, the poet triggers the pictographic potential of sinograms and reinvests punctuation with other signifying energy, even as he mocks the flatness of alphabetic language. In fact, the radical indicating water composed of four traits resembling drops, in the lower part of the non-simplified characters of *yu* 魚 (fish) and *yu* 漁 (to fish/fisherman) is used as a figurative element that thereby becomes part of the discourse. Gliding through other signifying functions, the Chinese script is transfigured into a dynamic medium, as if in a contemporary Sinophone *tuxiang shi* 圖像詩 (picture-image poetry), or visual poetry, that plays with the pictographic quality of the Chinese script to create new architectures of meaning.[9]

---

8 As declared in the back cover of the book: "Ouyang Yu is still alive and writing. This is his most posthum(or)ous work" (Ouyang 2019).

9 This experiment also echoes the unreadability of the Malaysian-Chinese writer Kim-chew Ng 黃錦樹 and his "crypto-Chinese" work, but resounds even more with the Taiwanese author Wuhe's 舞鶴 exploitation of punctuation as a concrete signifier (Bachner 2014). it likewise recalls the piece *Er mifeng ye dui ni gechang* 而蜜蜂也對你歌唱 (And the Bees are Singing to You Too) by the prolific Taiwanese poet Chen Li 陳黎, whereby the interaction between the typographical shape and signifying strategies produces a multilingualism (Lee 2015, 74–75).

Polyvalence is indeed a key feature of Ouyang Yu's poetics of thirdlanguaging, depicted by the practice of allographic otherings wherein the manipulation of sounds arbitrarily creates phonic ambiguity through the interpenetration of two languages. A straightforward example is provided by the poem "Or," through which the poet explores the latent morphological possibilities of writing and reading juxtaposed languages by gambling on renderings of the word *jiandan* 簡單 (simple):

Jan 單
Or
簡 dan

Jan 談
Or
減 dane

Jian 膽
Or
劍 damn

Janne 誕
Or
尖 den

Jann 彈
Or
賤 done

Johanne 耽
Or
簡 damn

OUYANG 2019, 138–9

This fetishization of intrusion constitutes a disruptive approach, renegotiating the boundaries of speech and writing, disallowing one language to be framed against, or in terms of, the other. This is also at work in "Miss Takes taken," where the influence of internet sociolects further impacts linguistic clarity:

Don't be 累 zy   [*lei* 累: tiring]
Or 雷 zy   [*lei* 雷: thunder]

番人 ners never learn	[*fanren* 番人: foreigner]
they really are 煩人 ner	[*fanren* 煩人: annoying]

Some like to play skytrue	
Which is, of course, not my 菲 vourites	[*fei* 菲: for "favourites"]

Shakespeare sai: Chinese students doo
two much
ho me work bcaus they want2 bcom
confucious

If you 做 that	[*zuo* 做: do]
My you live in intriguing time	

But I know 瓦特 that is:	[*wate* 瓦特: for "what"] Rather be a 太平 dog, 不做亂世 woman [*taiping* 太平: peace; *bu* *zuo luan shi* 不做亂世: not causing turmoil[10]]

Yellow long gone	
Memory still a 賴夫	[*lai fu* 賴夫: for "life"]

190–91

The fictive confusion is a literary strategy adopted by the poet "for the purpose of ridicule and criticism" (Ouyang 2020), a practice enhancing the sense of liminality and lameness of the individual, polemically expressed by Ouyang Yu (2013; 2016).

To the extent that the link between the signifier and the signified is broken and the linguistic or script tradition is disavowed, the poet speculates both on transitivity and homophonic features to produce ambiguity of sound and meaning. Such *modus operandi* is a blueprint of the new media scenes, but unlike these works, Ouyang Yu's scoffing dismantling of both languages demeans the hegemony of a doubled monolingualism, so much so that neither one of the two languages exists *per se*, since meaning is reached through an

---

10   The poet deliberately misquotes a classical Chinese saying *Ning wei taiping gou, mo zuo liluan ren* 甯為太平狗，莫作離亂人, often attributed to the first Ming emperor Zhu Yuanzhang 朱元璋 (1328–1398), meaning: "Better to be a dog of peace than a person of chaos."

artificial, desecrating collusion of phonetic and semantic features. The contrast to the signifying *status quo* relates to alterity, untranslatability and, ultimately, the author's self-referentiality.

The maelstrom of signifiers is underpinned by the presence of different transcription systems: not only the *pinyin* and its erratic idiosyncrasy, but also a fictitious elaboration of English morphemes based on a Chinese framework. With the poem "a more," such technique reaches an apotheosis, his words metamorphosizing into an uncanny, untranslatable, even unreadable language:

你需要 i   [*Ni xuyao i* / you need (romance)]
情   [*(ai)qing*[11] / romance]
你又，得 no 到   [*ni you, de* no *dao*]
age 的 mountain   [age *de* mountain]
比 ocean 還 g   [bi ocean hai(g)]
ao   [*(g)ao*[12] / high]
as cuddly as a s
pikes
此時，it's r   [*cishi*, it's r / this moment, it's r]
kisses, curses, 抗 s   [kisses, curses, *kang*s / kisses, curses, fights]

伸出去的 hands   [*shen chuqu de* hands /extended hands]

離 horizon   [*li* horizon / from the horizon]
只差 one mi   [*zhicha* one mi / just one mi]
ll   [(llimi) /]
i
米
yu 宙 is an   [*yuzhou* is an / the universe is an]
other
wave 費的 par   [par(ellel) / parallel]
elle
l

OUYANG 2019, 34–5

In this excerpt from the long poem "Words 文字 wenzi," the poet asserts an anti-exotic yet anti-Western hostility:

---

11   As of *aiqing* 愛情, that is "romantic love."

12   The author plays on the affinity of sound and meaning of *hai* 還 *gao* 高, "higher," and *hai* 還 g for "high," that preceded by *bi* 此 [...] also reads "higher."

I
詩 T
therefore
I
aM

119

To be read as "I shit therefore I am," the lines ultimately epitomize the author's rebuttal, not only in the aberration of the well-known Cartesian aphorism, but also in the iconoclastic use of the monosyllabic word *shi* 詩, "poetry."

Ouyang's poetics safeguard a subjective cultural-linguistic specificity of multilingual practice, what Emily Apter calls the "right to untranslatability" (2013), inasmuch as it upholds the irreproducibility of the individual imagination. As Ouyang has stated:

> Honestly, I like my mistake better [...]. Who wants grammar if it is only meant to hamper creativity and innovation? But how can one be totally correct if not born into the language and why can't one claim it as one's own if one works hard enough to learn and has the intelligence to achieve the ownership in one's own way? (2020)

The poet's thirdlanguaging takes the shape of a declared irreverence that dismantles Chinese and English, as his first and acquired languages, to build an identity and a practice, while asking for attention and respect to be paid to the practice he 'owns'.

4.2 Re-reading the Unreadable: Hsia Yü's Uncanny Thirdlanguagings

A more venturesome stance has been developed by the Taiwanese poet Hsia Yü 夏宇 (b. 1956), pen name of Huang Qingqi 黃慶綺. Called by Tong King Lee "one of the most transgressive avant-garde poets in the Chinese literary world" (2015, 21), she dwells between Taiwanese Chinese, French and English, plus other languages,[13] and though her rich corpus of audaciously creative poetry has been anthologized, translated, and researched, and is, as Michelle Yeh points out, "a towering figure on the poetry scene, first in Taiwan, then in Hong

---

13   Hsia Yü graduated in film and drama from the National Art College in Taiwan and specialized in creative writing. After spending many years in France, the USA, and Taiwan, she returned to Taipei, "where she continues to be a productive and influential writer in and beyond Taiwan" (Bruno 2019, 176).

Kong, and increasingly in Mainland China and around the world" (2023, 81), she is still something of a cult writer, rather than a mainstream one.

Much scholarly attention has been put on the investigation of her pioneering feminist poetics, as well as on her innovative trans-semiotic creativity and its challenging of the relationships between writing and translating, between human and technology skills, and the roles of author and reader, at once. Her best-known collection, *Pink noise* 粉紅色噪音 (2007), stands at the borders of both natural language and poetic aesthetics. Yeh describes it as "a supremely executed expression of the poetics of noise" (2008, 177), and while much has been written about the "noisy" displacement enacted by her provocative visual and multilingual metalanguage, something more can still be said about the configuration of her unconventional translingualism, whereby creative writing and translation conflate. In fact, whereas a rhetoric of deconstruction, desecration, and dismantling is typically adopted in approaching Hsia Yü's work,[14] I suggest a contrapuntal perspective grounded on a logic of *pro*-duction, that is, a production of a dialectic space consisting of a protean relationship with tongues and languages – made possible by poetry. If we look at her poetry as a negotiation, rather than negation, of the expressive potential of languages, we might be able to cross into her Thirdspace.

Hsia Yü's production of dialectic space begins early. In a piece composed in 1985, "Yarmidiso Language Family" (*Yi'ermidisuo yuxi* 伊爾米弟索語系),[15] the poet confesses a desire to grasp an unknown language, to let her thoughts and emotion find expression:

> （行走在陌生的語言的邊緣。
>   像一件試穿過的新娘禮服
>   突然失蹤了在婚禮的
>   前一個晚上。）
>   突然想用一种完全不懂的语言
>   表達自己而且是深刻的表達並
>   用及所有偏僻危險的字眼好譬如就是
>   伊爾米弟索語系
>   他們也用伊爾米弟索語辦報紙編纂
>   學童課本發行旅行指南發明填字遊戲等等

14   Let us just quote, by way of example, Lee's perceptive statement: "She enacts the death of her role as author-poet by adopting a literary procedure that unravels the intertextual network within which language is embedded and meaning disseminated" (2015, 33).

15   Recently defined by Yeh as "a manifesto declaring the poet's 'carnal love' for language" (2023, 85).

TRANSLINGUAL POETRY AND THE POETICS OF TRANSLINGUALISM

我應該下定決心花10年時間懂得怎樣
用伊爾米弟索語系示愛跟隨公園種的
大提琴手回家用彼此的母语教对方
一些成語和繞口令
如果你會燉我的燉凍豆腐你就燉我的
燉凍豆腐如果你不會燉我的燉凍
豆腐你就不要
燉壞了我的燉凍豆腐——
豆腐　完全不可自拔的
豆腐且用草繩拴著——
再花10年的時間學會辯論　準確
而不經意地涉及各種生猛的字眼
如同某些蟹類
無法藏匿牠們的螯
又花10年可以写诗了当滑膩的
音節逼近喉嚨通過舌尖
引發出純粹感官感官感官　的
愉悅（發現對字的肉慾的愛）：
搜索尋覓　使用
一切暱稱　擲筆　微笑
嘆息　為了那人性中還未曾被
任何語系穿透的部分
即使是已如此親愛
如此嫻熟的
伊爾米弟索語

(Walking on the margins of a strange language
like a wedding dress that had been tried on
suddenly disappearing on the eve
of the wedding)
Suddenly I'd like to use a language I don't understand at all
to express myself furthermore it's a profound expression and also
useful for any obscure and dangerous terminology
[...]
Spend another ten years' time learning how to debate with
precision
and without effort, insert all manner of unexpected terminology
like certain kinds of crustaceans
that can't conceal their claws
Spend yet another ten years and then be able to write poetry &

when oleaginous
syllables press near my throat pass over the tip of my tongue
producing a pure sensory sensory sensory
joy (discover the carnal love of words):
exploring searching to use
every endearment throw away the pen smile
sigh for the part of human nature that still hasn't been
penetrated by any language
even this beloved
this polished and refined
Yarmidisoese

trans. by ANDREA LINGENFELTER, in YEH and MALMQVIST 2000, 407–408

Hsia Yü named one of her collections *Friction · Indescribable* (*Moca · Wuyimingzhuang* 摩擦·無以名狀; Hsia 1995): what if such "friction" stems from her insight into the inadequacy of monologism, rather than from a narcissistic eccentricity? A multi-layered heteroglossia can be detected in her poetry, such as within the explicatory glosses, the body of the poems, and even their titles. As an example, the well-known collection *Salsa* (Hsia 1999) shows a number of multilingual "intrusions" not only in its title, but proceeding into the table of contents, as well, where "Fusion Kitsch," "To be Elsewhere," "Bad Trip," "Tango," "Salsa," "Swing," "Somehow" and "Soul" are erratically indexed among Chinese titles. This ostensible duet is itself interrupted by poems that unveil echoes of yet other languages, like Spanish and, especially, French. The latter appears in the form of intertextual or inter-discursive echoes, made explicit by allograph translation,[16] but also of direct quotes.[17]

Going beyond this first interpretation of the de-territorialization of languages, which brings translingualism to the fore, the dialogic (re)imagination of languages she performs through her versification acts as a quest for polyphony. From this perspective, we can re-read *Pink Noise* as what Bakhtin would call a "carnivalesque" literary space, where different semiotic languages are stratified, intertwined, questioned, translated and reinvented.

---

16   I am referring to Bradbury's renderings into English collected in *Fusion Kitsch* (2001), where the translator's notes also unravel the many hidden references absorbed in the originals.

17   I have in mind the "schmilblick avance" in "Tango" – as well as footnotes, like "cêpe" in the poem "Meihao xie'e wangri" 美好邪惡往日 ("This Gloriously Sinful Days of Old"). Worthy of note is the self-translated piece "Chenshui ru yishuang muxie" 沉睡如一雙木鞋, where Chinese and French confront each other, thereby sharing an in-betweenness with the reader.

FIGURE 4.1 Hsia Yü 夏宇. 2016. *First Person* 第一人稱, translated by Steve Bradbury.
A LINE FROM CHAPTER N. 22. TAIPEI: SELF-PUBLISHED. COURTESY OF HSIA YÜ 夏宇 AND STEVE BRADBURY

With the illusion of "ventriloquism," the poet seems to aim at a three-dimensional kind of glossolalia produced by natural and artificial tongues, formed by words and voids, signs and pictures.

The result of such a complex and yet uncanny *poiesis*, in my understanding, is her performance of thirdlanguaging. Her thirdlanguaging also takes place in her recent *First Person* 第一人稱 (Hsia 2016), a bilingual visual poetry collection (a *yingxiang shiji* 影像詩集, then) in which 400 blurry pictures taken in Paris by the poet, covering the 520 pages of the volume, accompany single lines in Chinese followed by their English translation by Steve Bradbury.[18] It features 43 seven-line verses, which can be read as a long 301-line poem divided into 43 chapters, its rhythm enhanced by consistent metrics and regular rhymes. What is "cinematic" about *First Person* 第一人稱 is straightforward: not only does the

---

18 Whom I once again thank for providing me with a hardcopy of the book.

design of the volume intentionally emulate an "arthouse devoted to vintage films," in the author's words (Hsia 2016), but the poetic lines superimposed on the pictures give the illusion of subtitles, as well.

By way of example, chapter no. 22 reads:

永不再見不失為一個好概念

To never meet again is a pretty good idea

做為一個概念也就夠了實踐屬於另外一個象限

A good idea is quite enough, but putting it into practice belongs to a whole other sphere

此等美好概念促生詩發現情境主義發明蒸餾法

A beautiful idea like this will give an impetus to poetry, the discovery of situationalism and the invention of distillation

讓三四個人在酒館門外分享一根大麻

Allows three or four people to share a joint outside a bistro

重重走私的菸草終於顯得詩之為物稍稍具體

A bag of smuggled weed finally renders poetry's materiality a little more concrete

我的意思是非常非常好的詩否則一切白費

The trouble is this poetry has got to be better than the very best weed

比較麻煩的是必須是好詩更超過好的菸草

What I mean is it must be awfully good poetry or it's all a total waste

The closing couplet provides an insightful clue of the author's attitude: Hsia Yü shows no concern at all for the quality of her pictures, as repeatedly declared throughout the pages and explicitly by chapter no. 27, but rather wants the words to stay in the foreground:

許多照片將被輕易唾棄我深深同情觀看者的失望

That so many photos will be so lightly cast aside, I deeply sympathize
    with the
disappointment of viewers

如貓尋覓陰涼處午睡彼處賜予貓的滿意相對於牠的午睡

Like a cat in search of a cool and shady place to take a nap who finds a
    place satisfying to its nap

此等照片並不提供彼等舒適之觀看對應觀者期待之眼

Such photos don't pretend to offer viewers the sort of comforting imagery
    that gratifies
their expectations

She thus establishes a "fluid" relationship between words and images, a kind of transmedial aesthetic that stirs several questions within the reader: is this poetics stemming from an anxiety toward a monolingual paradigm? Does it reflect Hsia Yü's need to re-invent a language for poetry, that is, a translingual paradigm where languages are not confined to tongues? Whose language is this, anyway?

A tentative answer is provided by the rest of the poem, where the poet introduces a metaphor for death (see Fig. 4.2) which may be interpreted as the end of the communicative potential of language:

死亡以象之形藏匿以便成熟壯大就像任何無動於衷之物

Death in the form of an elephant hides itself away in order to mature and
    grow strong like
any aloof and indifferent thing

我不知睡者是否為語言之再不容棲居乃於大雪之夜逝去

I do not know if the sleeper passed away on a snowy evening because
    language is no
longer inhabitable

Despite the fact that the author introduces her work as "a book of stills taken from a movie yet to be made [...] to encourage discussion of strangers and

FIGURE 4.2 Hsia Yü 夏宇. 2016. *First Person* 第一人稱, translated by Steve Bradbury.
LINES 4 AND 5 FROM CHAPTER N. 27. TAIPEI: SELF-PUBLISHED. COURTESY OF HSIA YÜ 夏宇 AND STEVE BRADBURY

poetry and drifting and crappy photography," *First Person* 第一人稱 remains a book about poetry and its language(s). This reveals Hsia Yü's attitude. As poetry here materializes through the blending of images and phrases, poetry appears as a variable and even fickle phenomenon, and should be understood as not only a language itself, but in particular as a sensory kind of language to be experienced in a polyphonic, multidimensional way. Thus, by disrupting the readers' expectations and habits of thinking (Liao 2020), Hsia Yü once again[19] asserts her own self – her *first person* – as a creator and interpreter of what poetry means, even as she institutionalizes her lyrical Thirdspace and thirdlanguaging.

4.3 Making the 'Thirdspace' Visible: the Ultimate Challenge of the Translator

As has been discussed so far, thirdlanguaging constitutes a specific articulation of translingualism that can exemplify a paradoxical, paroxysmal, and even iconoclastic structure of the multilingual self – as a need to pit difference

---

19 This is also demonstrated by her most recent collection, *Ji zhui zhi zhou* 脊椎之軸 (The Axis of Spine), self-published in Taipei in 2020. The 33 brief pieces composing the whole white body, like the vertebrae of the human spinal column, reveal the plasticity and the strength of poetry as a structural need of the self, which requires the full cooperation of a mother tongue with other tongues, in order to transcend the border of finiteness. The inkless lines superimposed on white paper do not produce noise, yet they are not silenced. On the contrary, a euphonic reverberation of thoughts is tuned through the touch of words.

against sameness, autonomy against hegemony. It unfetters the author from the obsession with duality (expressed through affixes such as *bi-* or *cross-*), which implies an alienating seclusion between two poles. But can such literary practice be decoded and recoded? In other words, does the translation of a translingual text necessarily reduce the acts of poetic code-mixing into one, or can a translator comply with poetic thirdlanguaging to make the author's Thirdspace visible? While I do not suppose that there exists a unidimensional solution to this quandary, I would like to attempt to elaborate a first response, which is: by performing strategies that enact both cultural and linguistic hybridity, a translator might become a trans/creator of thirdlanguaged texts (see de Campos 1992).

My assumption orbits around a particular locus, namely the rich, heterogeneous, and heteroglossic sphere of the so-called Sinophone "minority poetry," a domain of "minority literature" – or *shaoshu minzu wenxue* 少數民族文學 in Chinese, identifying "a literature written by an author belonging to a Chinese ethnic minority" (Rojas 2010, 118). So far, however, the much-needed interest in the field seems to be led by an anthropological approach, inherently driven by the strong ethnographic nature of many texts and the declared *ethos* of many poets; this undoubtedly takes into account the polyphonic and polyscriptic nature of such works, but it still tends to sublimate them under other extra-textual aspects. Central to the heuristic of my study, though, is the translatological point of view, an engagement with the *poiesis* of a "Third-spaced language" that is often tied to the activity of self-translation (Gallo 2022a; 2002b).

Thirdlanguaging and self-translation are common for diglossic subjects, particularly "minority writers," who confront themselves with the choice of "re-territorializing"[20] one of their cultures, though not necessarily at the cost of blurring or annihilating their *other* one. As pointed out by Rainier Grutman, for a diglossic subject, the choice of a composing language is never neutral, in that languages are not simple tools for communication, but rather symbolic representations charged with values. Therefore, by selecting a composing language, diglossic subjects select their own weapons (2005, 7).

As it happens, a number of bilingual Sinophone writers of the diaspora or from ethnic minorities succeed in de-centering and re-centering both their tongues at once, therefore shaping a unique Thirdspace. As a case in point, Carlos Rojas describes Alai's work as not only "the product of a 'translation' of local subject matter into written Chinese but [as works that] also consistently draw attention to this process of translation itself" (2010, 117–118). In addition,

---

20 As Deleuze and Guattari put it, when defining the concept of "minor literature" (1986).

Duncan Poupard introduces the Naxi author Sha Li 沙蠡 (1953–2008) as a writer whose "Sinophone work goes beyond simply transcribing the odd word or sentence in his native language of Naxi, and begins, ludically, to shift the norms of Chinese usage," in order to create a unique "variation of Chinese, a Naxi-Chinese interlanguage," as a tangible testimony of both cultures (2022, 50–51). Given that poetry, as argued above, is the privileged site of thirdlanguaging's creative construction – even as it is often called "untranslatable" – it is worth looking at the translation of poetry and its extension of minority poetry's performance of linguistic hybridity. Such distinctive territory can be the result of a creative interaction between standard Chinese and one "minor" Sinitic language, which indeed often makes the text hardly accessible to most readers, therefore enclosing many valuable cultural productions to a peripheral area. This is when allographic translation comes into play: the challenge to translators posed by thirdlanguaged texts written by diglossic poets is that of unveiling both their polyphony and their processes of "thirding-as-Othering."

The case of Mark Bender and his poetics of translation is an instructive one, in that he enacts several strategies to give voice to the bilingualism of the poet, across what the well-known Yi poet Aku Wuwu 阿庫烏霧 has termed his "first mother tongue" and "second mother tongue." Aku both values the "cultural hybrid" (*wenhua hunxue* 文化混血) (Aku 2001, 57–58) and advocates a "mother tongue literature" (*muyu wenxue* 母語文學), engaging in creating texts by means of either Chinese or the Nuosu language (the northern dialect of Yi) through a reformed Northern Yi script (created on the basis of traditional Yi scripts). "Mother tongue" to him, explains Bender,

> means not only the level of language, but the ways of thinking and cultural perceptions that are inherent in language use. [...] Even in his works in Chinese, it is important to him to utilize Nuosu folk ideas and patterns of thinking. On the other hand, Chinese as a medium of poetic expression is enriched by voices from outside the linguistic and cultural mainstream. (2016, 502)

Particularly relevant is a long poem entitled "Axlu yyr kut" ("Calling Back the Soul of Zhyge Alu"), that – as Bender himself highlights – "has been translated into English (and thus made available to Anglophone readers globally) utilizing many Nuosu words and phrases" (2011, 84).

> According to legend,
> You changed, it is said,

Into the *apu yoqo* bird,
The tiny, black *apu yoqo* bird
Flitting here and there
Around the house.
Is the fireplace that you flew through in the sky
Still burning?
Do you remember still the secrets of mankind?
[…]
You change it is said,
Into the ritual *yyrx yyr* grass.
The rich green grass grows
Forever on the rocky hillsides.
The history of the *yyrx yyr* grass
Is indeed like a head of flowing tresses.
The story of the *yyr yyr* grass must include
The smooth river stones.
[…]
If you changed into a *ssep ziet* ghost,
The moment you go against your family has come.
Come, like a ferocious storm fast as lightning,
Come, like a landslide in a jumble of trees and rock.

The rice Abbo and Amo have prepared is steaming –
The rising steam has no soul.
In the four directions all is sunlit –
The sun's rays have become icicles.
Every heart is becoming a wooden compote
Searching in every direction: east, west, north, south.
Screaming,
   Crying,
   Shouting –
Calling back the soul.
O la, come back!
O la, come back!
Whether in the Yi areas,
Come back!
Whether in the Han areas,
Come back!

BENDER 2011, 93–94

The Anglophone version attempts to maintain the polyscriptic nature of the original to produce a tangible dialogue between languages that recreates the author's cultural in-betweenness,[21] both disrupting the expectations of a monolingual tradition and creatively picturing a "thirding-as-Othering."

Another incisive example is offered by Lama Itzot (b. 1987), a proficient translator of Nuosu who is also a young Yi author whose poetics has been influenced by Aku Wuwu. It can be seen in this co-translation with Kaitlin Banfill of a poem by Nuosu writer Jjinuo Dazzi (b. 1985):

> **The Orphan of *Ho Ggux Mop****
> That winter in *Ho Ggux Mop*
> It should have snowed
> But it did not
> […]
> On the way back home
> When a bird pooped on his father's head
> The *bimox* said it was *shufi*
> And surely before long
> His father died
> That winter in *Ho Ggux Mop*
> The snakes should have hibernated
> […]
> That winter in *Ho Ggux Mop*
> Everyone should have gathered together
> To joyously sing *A hat ly* for three days of the New Year
> He knelt by the fire
> Sucking his thumb
> He wanted to go to *shyp mu nge hxat*
> With his parents
> But when he went to hang himself from a tree
> A leaf drifted down
> Bringing poetry into his heart
> The Waxsa spirit said that poetry can give life
> After that year
> His life was indeed better

---

21   In this respect, see also Poupard's investigation on the translation of the identities of Chinese Minority Writers (2017).

TRANSLINGUAL POETRY AND THE POETICS OF TRANSLINGUALISM

Anthologized in *The Borderlands of Asia* (2017, 209–210), the translation is followed by an explanatory gloss, thus delegating to this short metatext the task of unraveling what interpretative doubts might be raised by the thirdlanguaged poetic text.[22] Of note is that both strategies are sometimes adopted for the poems Lama Itzot self-translates into English, further amplifying the powerful relationship between creation and translation. In conclusion, a translator might indeed grasp the momentum that arises from the Sinophone to participate in a translingual practice that at once makes the Thirdspace visible and thirdlanguaging more audible.

5   Concluding Remarks

As Andrea Bachner observes,

> once one's own position within a culture has been questioned by its more authoritative representatives, once the label of the "same" becomes contested grounds, the self finds [it]self in close vicinity to the "other." This other, however, can also never become a supplemental, secondary "same," even as it remains elusive to becoming totally "othered." Frequently, for diasporic Chinese writers, the Chinese writing system is both the inevitable basis for signification and something they cannot lay a total claim to. The resulting in-between position fuels texts that recuperate a hybrid and changing sinograph against both Sinocentric discourses and Western theories of signification. (2014, 134)

The "in-betweenness" also results in a translingual aesthetic, "a complex web of tensions [that has] produced its multilingual dialogue within itself" (Klimkiewicz 2013, 189), taking a concrete shape in a lyrical Thirdspace.

By acknowledging that

> *Everything* comes together in Thirdspace: subjectivity and objectivity, the abstract and the concrete, the real and the imagined, the knowable

---

22   "*Hu Ggux mop* is a place name in the Liangshan Mountains of southern Sichuan. Traditional Yi villages often had a protected forest nearby, where the cutting of wood was strictly controlled. A bird defecating on the head is a sign of coming bad luck, indicating a violation of taboo (*shu fi*). *A hat ly* are folk songs performed at New Year time. The land of the dead is called *Shyp mu nge hxat. Waxsa* is a protector spirit; those of shamans (*sunyit*) are especially powerful." (210)

and the unimaginable, the repetitive and the differential, structure and agency, mind and body, consciousness and the unconscious, the disciplined and the transdisciplinary, everyday life and unending story (Soja 1996b, 56)

we can also infer that translingual creativity is the transcendence of the border, the seizure of a creative space not dominated by binaries, the coexistence of both the real and the imagined. In fact, in a time when the idea of non-binarism is finally recognized as valid, thirdlanguaging intends to offer a more supportive approach towards linguistic hybridity and otherness, as well as linguistic estrangement – with diverse strategies to surpass the pitfalls of monolingualism, to confront difference, and concurrently to overshadow the aporias of duality. Such a poetics expresses a shift from fixed paradigms towards blurred, hybrid, complex patterns that do not shoulder the responsibility of being globally intelligible, but rather demand a subjective relationship with both languages and poetry. This does not mean that thirdlanguaging aims at institutionalizing linguistic chaos, only that it endorses a productive awareness of difference, as a process of translating unsettlement into polyphonic and polyscriptic creativity.

In the case of Ouyang Yu, who by means of bilinguality experiences loss and the refusal of roots and routes at once, thirdlanguaging reflects the hyperbolic quest for individuality, demanding the right to "disinvent and reconstitute languages" (Makoni and Pennycook 2006) as a means of self-affirmation. By instrumentalizing languages, the translingual writer is empowered to create a personal poetics, a creative realm that needs to preserve its openness. Hsia Yü's poetics of thirdlanguaging seems, instead, to be inspired by an urge to seek a lyrical multilingualism that can hint at the complexity of poetry as a part of everyday life, made of perceptions and not only words; her unafraid transcendence of linguistic boundaries, semiotically speaking, produces polyphonic and multi-layered lyrical experiences that magnify the heteroglossia of the Sinosphere. In this variegated realm, where in-betweenness can also represent a situation imposed by birth, as in the case of "ethnic minority writers," the exploration of a Thirdspace through poetry might hybridize mother tongues with other tongues, and thereby complicate supposed subalternities, distances, and differences. It is quite reassuring, then, that allograph translation can also interpret such a process of "thirding-as-Othering," transforming the unsettlement into a literary practice that, amidst the wide horizon of Sinophone multilingual articulations, not only deserves but *claims* its own, third, space.

Works Cited

Aku Wuwu. 2011. *Ling yu ling de duihua—Zhongguo dangdai shaoshu minzu Hanyu shilun* 靈與靈的對話一中國當代少數民族漢語詩論 [Spirit to Spirit – Discussions of Modern Ethnic Minority Poetry in Chinese]. Hong Kong: Tianma.

Apter, Emily. 2013. *Against World Literature: On the Politics of Untranslatability*. New York and London: Verso Books.

Bachner, Andrea. 2014. *Beyond Sinology. Chinese Writing and the Scripts of Culture*. New York: Columbia University Press.

Bender, Mark. 2011. "Ogimawkwe Mitiwaki and 'Axlu yyr kut': Native Tongues in Literatures of Cultural Transition." *Comparative Literature: East & West* 15 (1): 82–103.

Bender, Mark. 2015. "Ethnic Minority Literature." In *A Companion to Modern Chinese Literature*, edited by Zhang Yingjin, 261–275. Chichester: John Wiley & Sons.

Bender, Mark. 2016. "Poet of the Late Summer Corn: Aku Wuwu and Contemporary Yi Poetry." In *The Oxford Handbook of Modern Chinese Literatures*, edited by Carlos Rojas and Andrea Bachner, 498–520. Oxford: Oxford University Press.

Bender, Mark, ed. 2017. *The Borderlands of Asia. Culture, Place, Poetry*. Amherst, New York: Cambria Press.

Bernards, Brian and Chien-hsin Tsai. 2013. "PART III. Introduction." In *Sinophone Studies: A Critical Reader*, edited by Shu-mei Shih, Chien-hsin Tsai and Brian Bernards, 183–190. New York: Columbia University Press.

Bhabha, Homi. 1994. *The Location of Culture*. London: Routledge.

Blackburn, Simon. 2015. "Can an analytic philosopher read poetry?" In *The Philosophy of Poetry*, edited by John Gibson, 111–126. Oxford: Oxford University Press.

Bradbury, Steve. 2000. "The Poetry of Hsia Yü." *Inter-Asia Cultural Studies* 1 (2): 249–50.

Bruno, Cosima. 2017. "Writing in London. Home and Languaging in the Work of London Poets of Chinese Descent." *Life Writing* 14 (1): 37–55.

Bruno, Cosima. 2019. "Translation Poetry: The Poetics of Noise in Hsia Yü's *Pink Noise*". In *Prismatic Translation*, edited by Matthew Reynolds, 173–188. Cambridge: Legenda.

Campos, Haroldo de. 1992. "Translation as Creation and Criticism." In *Metalinguagem e Outras Metas: Ensaios de Teoria e Crítica Literária*. Sao Paulo: Perspectiva.

Cheng, François. 2002. *Le Dialogue: Une passion pour la langue française*. Paris: Desclée.

Crevel, Maghiel van, and Lucas Klein, eds. 2016. "Introduction: The Weird Third Thing." In *Chinese Poetry and Translation. Rights and Wrongs*, 9–17. Amsterdam: Amsterdam University Press.

Deleuze, Gilles, and Félix Guattari. 1986. *Kafka: Towards a minor literature*. Minneapolis: University of Minnesota Press.

Evangelista, Elin-Maria. 2013. "Writing in translation: A new self in a second language." In *Self-Translation. Brokering Originality in Hybrid Culture*, ed. Anthony Cordingley, 177–187. London and New York: Bloomsbury.

Foucault, Michel. 1972. *The Archaeology of Knowledge and the Discourse on Language*. New York: Pantheon Books.

Gallo, Simona. 2022a. "Across Wor(l)ds: Ouyang Yu's Transcultural Journey in Self-Translation." *Nouveaux cahiers de Marge* 6. DOI: 10.35562/marge.531.

Gallo, Simona. 2022b. "The prism of self-translation: *poiesis* and poetics of Yu Guangzhong's bilingual poetry." *The Translator* (December) DOI: 10.1080/13556509. 2022.2140623.

Gramling, David. 2016. *The invention of monolingualism*. London: Bloomsbury.

Gramling, David. 2019. "On reelecting monolingualism: Fortification, fragility, and stamina." *Applied Linguistics Review* 13 (1): 1–18.

Gramling, David. 2020. "Supralingualism and the translatability industry." *Applied Linguistics* 41 (1): 129–147.

Grutman, Rainer. 2009. "Multilingualism." In *Encyclopaedia of Translation Studies*, edited by Mona Baker and Gabriela Saldanha. London and New York: Routledge.

Grutman, Rainer. 2005. "La textualisation de la diglossie dans les littératures francophones." In *Des cultures en contact: visions de l'Amérique du Nord francophone*, edited by Jean Morency, Hélène Destrempes, Denise Merkle, and Martin Pâquet, 201–223. Québec: Nota bene.

Ha Jin. 2013. "Exiled to English." In *Sinophone Studies: A Critical Reader*, edited by Shu-mei Shih, Chien-hsin Tsai, and Brian Bernards, 93–98. New York: Columbia University Press.

Hamers, Josiane, and Michel Blanc, eds. 2004. *Bilinguality and Bilingualism*. Cambridge and New York: Cambridge University Press.

Hsia Yü 夏宇. 1995. *Moca · Wuyimingzhuang* 摩擦·無以名狀 [Friction · Indescribable]. Taipei: *Xiandai shi jikan she* 現代詩季刊社 (*Modern Poetry Quarterly*).

Hsia Yü 夏宇. 1999. *Salsa*. Taipei: Modern Poetry.

Hsia Yü 夏宇. 2001. *Fusion Kitsch*. Trans. By Steve Bradbury. Brookline (Mass.): Zephyr Press.

Hsia Yü 夏宇. 2007. *Pink Noise* 粉紅色噪音. Taipei: Garden City Publishers.

Hsia Yü 夏宇. 2016. *Di yi rencheng* 第一人稱 *First Person*. Taipei: self-published.

Hsia Yü 夏宇. 2020. *Ji zhui zhi zhou* 脊椎之軸 [The Axis of Spine]. Taipei: self-published.

Kellman, Steven G. 2019. "Literary Translingualism: What and Why?" *Polylinguality and Transcultural Practices* 16 (3): 337–346.

Kellman, Steven G. 2000. *The Translingual Imagination*. Lincoln: University of Nebraska Press.

Klimkiewicz, Aurelia. 2013. "Self-translation as broken narrativity: Towards an understanding of the self's multilingual dialogue." In *Self-Translation. Brokering Originality in Hybrid Culture*, edited by Anthony Cordingley, 189–201. London and New York: Bloomsbury.

Lee, Tong King. 2015. *Experimental Chinese Literature. Translation, Technology, Poetics*. Leiden and Boston: Brill.

Lefebvre, Henri. 1991. *The Production of Space*. Oxford and Cambridge: Blackwell.

Liao, Yu-Cheng 廖育正. 2020. "缺席與再現的辯證：論吳俞萱《沒有名字的世界》與夏宇《第一人稱》的攝影及詩" [The Dialectics Between Absence and Representation: A Study on the Photography and Poetry of Wu Yuxuan's *World Without Names* and Xia Yu's *First Person*]. *Taiwan shixue xuekan* 臺灣詩學學刊 (Bulletin of Taiwanese Poetics) 36: 101–141.

Makoni, Sinfree, and Alastair Pennycook. 2006. *Disinventing and reconstituting languages*. Bristol: Multilingual Matters.

Nanni, Emanuela. 2007. "Quelques réflexions sur l'autotraduction poétique: entre poésie comme langue étrangère par excellence et autotraduction poétique interlinéaire." *Atelier de Traduction* 7 (October): 67–78.

Ouyang Yu. 2013. "Twenty-Three Years in Migration, 1989–2012: A Writer's View and Review." In *Diasporic Chineseness after the Rise of China Communities and Cultural Production*, edited by Julia Kuehn, Kam Louie and David M. Pomfret, 32–46. Vancouver: UBC Press.

Ouyang Yu. 2016. "'A bilingual force moving in between': memories of a bilingual animal." *Westerly* 61 (2): 71–81.

Ouyang Yu. 2019. *Flag of Permanent Defeat*. Waratah: Puncher & Wattmann.

Ouyang Yu. "Mistakes make poetry." 13 November 2020. https://overland.org.au/2020/11/mistakes-make-poetry/.

Poupard, Duncan, 2017. "The Translated Identities of Chinese Minority Writers: Sinophone Naxi Authors." *Journal of Modern Literature in Chinese* / 現代中文文學學報 14 (1): 189–208.

Poupard, Duncan, 2022. "Ethnic minority language and Sinophone minority literature in China." *Writing Chinese: A Journal of Contemporary Sinophone Literature* 1 (1): 37–59.

Rojas, Carlos. 2010. "Alai and the Linguistic Politics of Internal Diaspora." In *Global Chinese Literature. Critical Essays*, edited by Jing Tsu and David Der-wei Wang, 115–132. Leiden and Boston: Brill.

Shih, Shu-mei, Chien-hsin Tsai and Brian Bernards, eds. 2013. *Sinophone Studies: A Critical Reader* New York: Columbia University Press.

Soja, Edward. 1996a. "Afterword." *Stanford Law Review* 48 (5): 1421–1429.

Soja, Edward. 1996b. *Thirdspace: Journeys to Los Angeles and Other Real-and-Imagined Places*. Malden: Blackwell.

Soja, Edward. 2009. "Thirdspace: Toward a New Consciousness of Space and Spatiality." In *Communicating in the Third Space*, edited by Karin Ikas and Gerhard Wagner, 49–61. New York: Routledge.

Steiner, George. 1970. "Introduction." In *Poem into Poem. World Poetry in Modern Verse Translation*, edited by George Steiner, 21–35. London: Penguin Books.

Tong, Tee Kim. 2010. "(Re)mapping Sinophone Literature." In *Global Chinese literature: critical essays*, edited by Jing Tsu and David Der-wei Wang, 77–92. Leiden and Boston: Brill.

Vieira, Ribiero Pires Else. 1999. "Liberating Calibans: Readings of Antropofagia and Haroldo de Campos' Poetics of Transcreation." In *Post-Colonial Translation*, edited by Susan Bassnett, and Harish Trivedi, 95–113. London: Routledge.

Yeh, Michelle. 2008. "Toward a Poetics of Noise: From Hu Shi to Hsia Yü." *Chinese Literature: Essays, Articles, Reviews* 30 (December): 167–178.

Yeh, Michelle. 2023. "Xia Yu, the Supreme Stylist." *Taiwan Literature in the 21st Century. A Critical Reader*, edited by Chia-rong Wu and Ming-ju Fan, 81–93. Singapore: Springer.

Yeh, Michelle, and Nils Göran David Malmqvist, eds. 2000. *Frontier Taiwan. An anthology of modern Chinese poetry.* New York: Columbia University Press.

PART 2

Translation, Contamination, and Foreign-Language Writing

∵

CHAPTER 5

Translingual Poetic Experiments by Amang, Tsai Wan-Shuen, and Jami Proctor-Xu

Justyna Jaguscik
University of Bern

This chapter[1] examines the various ways in which translingualism manifests itself in Sinophone poetry. It draws upon texts by contemporary female authors – Amang (b. 1960s), Tsai Wan-Shuen (b. 1978), and Jami Proctor-Xu (b. 1974). Despite writing mainly in standard Chinese, these three poets occasionally apply translingualism as a poetic method. Amang and Tsai Wan-Shuen both grew up in multilingual Taiwan, while the American Proctor-Xu, who also lived in Mainland China for many years, writes verses in a non-native language, Chinese. By providing close readings of two texts by the two Taiwanese poets, followed by one text by the US-based Proctor-Xu, this chapter inquires into the creative potential that lingers in postmonolingual lyrical subjectivity. It approaches translingual poetry from the perspective of Postcolonial Studies that sees languages not as closed and complete but as porous, interactive, always becoming. It is, furthermore, inspired by the conceptual shift proposed by Rey Chow (2014), who argues against the negativity typically associated with languaging as a postcolonial experience. Instead, she speaks of languaging as a kind of "prostheticization" (14) that allows the non-native speaker to overcome the sense of loss through an openness towards the emerging interlingual community.

1 On Not Speaking English …

The poet, video artist and documentary filmmaker Amang was born and raised in Hualian on the east coast of Taiwan. In an intimate conversation with her American translator, Steve Bradbury, Amang recalls the childhood of a neglected tomboy, who was brought up by her grandmother with substantial

---

1 Research on this chapter was supported by 2023 MOFA Taiwan Fellowship.

© JUSTYNA JAGUSCIK, 2024 | DOI:10.1163/9789004711600_007

support from "the mountains and the sea" (Amang 2020, 62–68). Today, despite writing in Chinese, the poet still believes that nature is her mother tongue.

On first glance, Amang's poem "i am hurt by english 及如何對英語復仇" ("i am hurt by english and how to get revenge against it") may look like an example of "ludic translingualism" (Loda and Viselli 2021, 18–30). The content warning (*jinggao* 警告) that precedes the first verse of the poem reads like a mockery of the trend to preemptively manage possible controversies by simultaneously seeming to decline responsibility for the effects a text may have on its audience. In her tongue-in-cheek advisory, Amang addresses linguistic purists who may suffer from side effects from her poem's flawed English and unwomanly Chinese (*buliang* 不良 english + *wuniang Zhongwen* 無娘中文).

The opening stanzas air the poet's frustration with English grammar, its "past tense and all big letters" (Amang 2016, 208). Each of the sixteen stanzas of the text consists of an equal number of lines of English and Chinese verse. The English version comes first, followed by a Chinese text that at first glance looks like a translation of the preceding lines, but under careful scrutiny, it reveals some important shifts in meaning. Amang creates these shifts by using the passive voice differently in both languages. For example, the poet pairs the opening verse "I was hurt by English" with the corresponding Chinese line *wo shanghai le Yingyu* 我傷害了英語 (I hurt English). In an act of poetic revenge through syntactic manipulation, the victim becomes the oppressor. In the second stanza, the poet admits that after English has tortured her for more than twenty years, this identity swap finally brings her some relief: "that's definitely a cure" (Amang 2016, line 11). What follows is a rhythmic enumeration of the many features of the English language that brought the most suffering to the poet:

> hurt by its past tense
> hurt by its future tense
> hurt by its big letters
> hurt by 500 basic sentence patterns
> AMANG 2016, 210

In contrast to the previous one, in this stanza the subsequent Chinese is a literal translation of the preceding English verse. The poet continues the naming of the tortuous grammatical features of the foreign language until she introduces a surprising turn in the sixth stanza. Here, a new strain of thought seems to derail Amang's revenge poem. In a sudden change of poetic mood, the poet compares English with magic. She describes herself as a rabbit that is under the foreign language's spell and, finally, magically disappears. The following two stanzas take up the enumeration of grammatical phenomena that affect the rabbit's well-being – this time, humorously:

> to sum up
> rabbits
> hurt separately and collectively
> hurt conditionally and unconditionally
> hurt literally and figuratively
> to sum up
> ...
> hurt
> magically
>> AMANG 2016, 210–211

In these stanzas, the Chinese, again, creates ambiguity and, consequently, grants more agency to the rabbits, as well as to the poet, who identifies with the animals ("i am one of the rabbits," (Amang 2016, 209)). Amang translates the flawed English directly into Chinese without changing the word order, which reads as follows:

> 兔子
> 傷害單獨和集體
> 傷害有條件和無條件地
> 傷害名副其實地
> 綜上所述
> ...
> 傷害
> 神奇
>> AMANG 2016, 211

> (Rabbits
> hurt individuals and the collective
> hurt conditionally and unconditionally
> hurt genuinely
> ...
> hurt
> magic)

In Chinese grammar, the verb "hurt" (*shanghai* 伤害) usually takes an object that refers to a human or other-than-human agent on which emotional or physical injury was inflicted. Thus, in the Chinese language version, the rabbits become the subject of the sentence and, consequently, the ones that hurt an unknown object since these Chinese verses are, from a grammatical point of view, incomplete. The following short stanza consists of only two lines and four characters. It may be hinting at the identity of the unknown object tortured by the rabbits. In the English version, we read "hurt / magically," but its Chinese counterpart (*shanghai/shenqi* 傷害/神奇) could as well be translated "hurt the magic." The magic is the English language and the poet-rabbit avenges her linguistic suffering in that she breaks linguistic rules. Throughout the first part of the poem, the poet and English remain in a tormented relationship, hurting each other. In the first nine stanzas, Amang creates a translingual game by playfully alternating between correct and distorted grammar and syntax. The poet engages in a linguistic exchange of blows, in the course of which she repays the English language for torturing her by contorting it.

In the tenth stanza the playful mood shifts again into a more serious one. The poet moves to the topic of power relations between different languages and their speakers:

> and i'm less hurt by latin, hebrew, sanskrit
> they are old and weak and sacred
> i am hurt by the young and strong
> AMANG 2016, 211

The following stanzas continue the enumeration of other languages that "hurt" less, because none of them is as influential as English in its role as the global lingua franca. The worldwide spread of English is also a direct consequence of the geopolitical and cultural dominance of the English-speaking first world countries. Amang addresses the inequality inscribed into communication between native and non-native English speakers in the second-to-last stanza, which is the climax of the poem. The previous translingual teasing finally culminates in an angry outburst that is visually signposted by the broad use of capitalization:

> but how can a rabbit do
> when the rabbit hurts?
> i ask english in english
> (it doesn't speak my language after we know each other more
> than 20 years)
> Listen!
> it tells me

TRANSLINGUAL POETIC EXPERIMENTS

> NOT ONLY TO SPEAK,
> BUT ALSO TO THINK, DREAM, ACT, EAT, DRINK, AND
> MAKE LOVE
> IN ENGLISH
> PRACTICE MAKE PERFECT!
> REPEAT AFTER ME!
> READ ALOUD!
>> AMANG 2016, 212–213

English lacks compassion and empathy, as the only answer it gives to the rabbit's suffering is to intensify the language drills and hurt the animal even more. The poet's parenthetical comment makes it clear that the didactic relationship between the language learner and the anthropomorphized English language is hierarchical and, furthermore, based on unilateral transmission. No genuine exchange of views between the master and the pupil will be possible as long as the master does not intend to "unlearn" his privilege (Danius, Jonsson and Spivak 1993). Even if Amang's text begins like a playful language game, nevertheless, in the course of the poem, the lyrical voice gradually strikes more serious tones. The angry outburst in the second-to-last stanza turns the text into a creative intervention in the field of linguistic power relations. Toward the end of the poem, Amang reminds her readers that while, similar to her, many people are forced into multilingualism at school – the institution that forms subjects according to the expectations of the globalized world – in the same highly interconnected world, other people still have the choice to remain monolingual, which nowadays is a luxury and a sign of privilege. Here the poet's intervention follows the trajectory of reasoning similar to an important contribution from Postcolonial Studies, which bares the complicity between language, education, and cultural incorporation. As such, (neo)colonial education goes far beyond merely teaching linguistic norms since it also targets different layers of the pupil's subjectivity. Languages are not equal, and neither are the people who speak them. Around the world, legacies of colonialism, as well as of globalization that brought the domination of English-language culture with it, have been targeted by a countermovement of grassroots multilingualism that demonstrates that language is an important site of minority struggle. In her revenge poem, "i am hurt by english 及如何對英語復仇," Amang creates her own subversive English idiom out of incorrect spelling and grammar mistakes and she uses her creation to "talk back" to the dominant language. In doing so, apart from experiencing emotional relief, the poet simultaneously explores the creative potential of translingual writing. For example, when she writes in Chinese, she continues to use English syntax, which creates the effect of linguistic estrangement.

Given the creative potential hidden in translingual writing, the exposition on the hegemony of the English language no longer posits a mere threat but also engenders transgressions and opens a new realm of poetic freedom, which is also relevant to composition in Chinese, the poet's native language.

Interestingly, Amang reflected on the differences between the two languages in the long conversation with her translator, Steve Bradbury. On this occasion, she recalls her shock when she first encountered the idea of English tenses:

> What horrible ideas! It was like a language had been given the plague of old age, sickness, and death. It was like the fall from Eden, the fall from grace. In Chinese, every verb is immortal, eternal, for all time. Past, present, future – they mean nothing to it. (Amang 2020, 78)

The "fall from grace" of the verb may be the beginning of a new linguistic freedom. A freedom that may indeed seem disturbing to monolingual linguistic purists of all sorts, whom the poet addressed in her warning that precedes the first line of the poem.

2   The Translingual Palimpsest

The visual artist and poet Tsai Wan-Shuen grew up in the Penghu archipelago where the local dialect of Taiwanese Hokkien was the prevailing language. However, after she entered the official education system, her socialization to the official language of the Republic of Taiwan, the National Language, began. According to Tsai, throughout her school years, she gradually lost fluidity in her local language, which was replaced by the foreign, mainland variant of spoken Chinese. Later she studied and lived in France for several years and now is based in Taipei.

After her return to Taiwan from Europe, Tsai has begun to explore her relationship with her local dialect, standard Chinese and writing. Today, the poet often returns to the language of her childhood when she composes and performs poetry in Hokkien that has for long remained buried under layers of school-designed standard Chinese. Her poem "You lu de dao" 有鹿的島 (The Island with Deer) states an example of translingual writing and self-translating. Tsai first wrote this poem in her mother tongue, Taiwanese Hokkien. Later, she translated it into standard Chinese.[2] The original and the Chinese text follow

---

2   The poet shared the standard Chinese version with me in September 2022 when I asked her to contribute to a poetry reading in Zurich. Tsai could not attend the event in person, so she sent a recording of her reading in Hokkien.

the same pattern. Both consist of three stanzas of an unequal number of lines. In every stanza verse are regular, either of eight or nine characters. Between the second and third stanza, the poet inserted a single longer verse in parentheses that reads like a footnote to the previous lines. Tsai wrote this poem for her daughter, thus from the formal point of view, it resembles a nursery rhyme (Tsai Wan-Shuen, e-mail to author, September 28, 2022). Not only the regularities, but also repetitions, enumerations and rhymes are typical for the genre of children's poetry. In the three stanzas with fixed-length lines, the poet describes in simple words the activities of herds of deer that spend their days frolicking in the woods and sleeping peacefully in Deer Valley at night. Nevertheless, the idyllic image of the animals' unrestrained activities depicted in the poem is misleading. The long verse between the second and third stanza breaks abruptly with the bucolic convention. Thus, it disrupts not only the regular structure of the poem, but it undermines the cheerful content as well. The historical truth mentioned as if in passing, in parentheses, suddenly intrudes on the reader's vision:

> (Hunters' huts were small at that time. Deer meat and deerskin were rarely shipped from Deer Harbors)[3]
>
> TSAI 2020, 38

This line makes clear that the landscape depicted in the opening stanzas of the poem belongs to the pre-colonial past of the island. Commercial deer hunting thrived in the seventeenth century, when Taiwan was a Dutch colony. The Dutch East India Company, which monopolized the export of Taiwanese deerskins, competed with Chinese and Japanese hunters for the animals' skin and meat. The growing interest in these marketable goods finally led to overhunting and, consequently, to the eventual extinction of the Formosan sika deer (Koo 2011, 186–187). Today only geographical names, of which many contain the character *lu* 鹿, which means "deer," remind one of the island's lost species.

Tsai incorporated many of these place names into the text of her poem; nevertheless, the double meaning will surely be lost on a reader unfamiliar with Taiwan's geography. That means that Taiwanese readers may easily decipher the Hokkien and Chinese versions. The standard Chinese one has the potential to attract a broader audience located, for example, in Mainland China, as well as non-native Chinese-speakers, however, these foreign readers will not necessary be able to decode its description of the island's colonial past.

---

3 English translation by Andrea Riemenschnitter.

These place names issue an even bigger challenge to the translator in the choice of a translation strategy when translating the poem into a distant language, such as English. One possibility is to simply ignore the ambiguity and translate the verses literally. In this case, the English rendition of the first stanza reads as follows:

> One big deer eats deer tree (鹿樹)
> Two small deer eat deer weed (鹿草)
> Ten deer speed in the deer woods (鹿林)[4]

What is at stake and left to the translator's decision is the question of how to acknowledge the colonial violence and the grief in the face of ecological loss that hides between the lines of Tsai's poem. If one leaves the place names romanized, but untranslated, the opening stanza of the poem will read differently from the literal translation above:

> One big deer chews on the Bodhi tree
> Two small deer chaw on Lók-tshó-hiông[5]
> Ten deer walk in Lu-lin[6]

This translation no longer sounds like a cheerful nursery rhyme. The inclusion of culturally and linguistically foreign elements into the English-language translation results in a reading that is much more arduous from the perspective of Western readers. The accumulation of elements from different traditions invites the foreign reader to a transcultural and translingual encounter with a cosmopolitanism that does not take the familiar Western tradition for its center, but transverses the Asian time-space instead. The "deer tree" is the Chinese popular name for a fig species, *figus religiosa*, which is native to the Indian subcontinent. Due to the widespread belief that Buddha attained enlightenment (Bodhi) when meditating underneath a fig tree, the botanic species gained a religious significance in Buddhism. This sacral context allows the reader to establish an intertextual connection to the perhaps most famous deer poem in Chinese poetic history – "The Deer Fence," a classical quatrain by the Tang

---

4   Unless otherwise indicated translations are mine. The original Taiwanese Hokkien-language version of the first stanza reads as follows:
    一隻大鹿咧食鹿仔樹
    兩隻小鹿咧食鹿仔草
    三隻鹿佇鹿林邊散步
5   A township in southwestern Taiwan.
6   Mount Lu-lin in central Taiwan.

poet Wang Wei (701–761). In his masterpiece, Wang turns a description of a lush mountain forest landscape into a Buddhist allegory. The "Deer Fence" that figures in the title of the poem was a site at Wang Wei's estate at Lantian (Egan 2008, 207). In this text, the Tang poet transforms natural phenomena into vehicles for Buddhist concepts, such as emptiness and enlightenment. This tension between emptiness and presence is a productive way of reading Tsai's poem too. Taiwan, the "island with deer" as it is called in the poem's title, has lost one of its endemic species to colonial environmental exploitation. Thus, the "island with deer," and other geographical names mentioned in the poem that contain the "deer" character have all lost their actual referent. Consequently, these empty signifiers currently point rather to the void left by foreign forces, whose intervention into the island's ecosystem erased one of its inhabitants. In this intertextual reading, the disruptive long line between the second and third stanza not only brings back the memory of colonialization but also provides a painful enlightenment in that it breaks away from the illusion of the "island with deer" that has been relegated to the stuff of children's fairytales.

According to Loda and Viselli, translingual poetry has the ability to create "more inclusive and fluid ideas of the world" and, furthermore, it enables the emergence of more open and "all-embracing poetic subjectivities" (2021, 26–29). This is possible due to, among others, a heightened attentiveness that translingual poetry pays to the more-than-human world. Tsai Wan-Shuen masks her tale of ecological extinction and violence against the other-than-human as a children's rhyme that she originally composed in her childhood idiom. Thus, as a translingual palimpsest, this poem also points to the creative potential of translingualism. The masquerade of bucolic innocence is intentionally flawed since the author of "The Island with Deer" allows the mature adult consciousness to undermine the apparent peace in the nursery rhyme.

Throughout history, the literary language in Taiwan has remained closely tight to geopolitical arrangement, often violent and unjust. Tsai chose to return to her local dialect, even though she notices that her standard Chinese skills are superior. Not only in Taiwan, the local language of the colonized ones was often cultivated in privacy, if at all, and a linguistic coming-of-age was identified with acquiring the official language of the colonizer. Translingualism has not always been a matter of choice, earlier generations of Taiwanese writers were often forced into it, for example, as subjects of the Japanese Empire (see Lin 1985). Many years later, when Tsai absolved her primary school education, Mandarin Chinese, the official language of education and literature, was still an instrument in the Nationalist government's Sinocentric ideology, however, since the 1970s it has been challenged by a counterhegemonic nativist literary movement (Chang 2014, 7). The lifting of martial law in 1987 put an end to the enforced monolingualism of the official culture and poetry written in Hokkien "began to thrive" (Yeh 2001, 40). Since then, linguistic plurality and openness became an important marker of Taiwanese identity.

Tsai's "The Island with Dear" is a milestone in her journey back to the language of her childhood that, according to the poet, began with the birth of her child (personal communication, Taipei, July 2023). The poem takes on important themes addressed by postcolonial discourse – the loss of language and the loss of the natural environment. However, it approaches these two dispossessions with a different attitude. The extension of the endemic Taiwanese deer due to extensive hunting and export of deer skins is met with a feeling of melancholia. In Tsai's poem "The Island" is haunted by its past that is represented in the geographical names that include the "deer" character. Taiwan is no longer an exploited colony, but its current physical environment, as well as its identity are rooted in this historical experience of loss. However, in contrast to the distraction of nature, Tsai's example shows that the loss of language must not be forever. She belongs to the last cohort of Taiwanese that received their primary education under the Nationalist regime. While many of them spoke Hokkien or Hakka at home, at school they were socialized to, in Derrida's words (1998), a "monolingualism of the other." The succession of state-sponsored monolingualisms left not only Tsai with an educated person's command of standard Chinese that is neither hers, nor "foreign" to her (Derrida 1998, 5). Later she mastered the "foreign" French that also occasionally appears in her poetry. Finally, she decided to re-learn her mother tongue and turn it into the poetics means of expression that feels right to her. Tsai's return to Hokkien via the experience of motherhood and with the help of the genre of children's poetry comments on Derrida's and his interpreters' observation (see Chow 2014, Chapter 1) that the monolingualism of the colonizer means that humanistic education and creation was only possible in the hegemonic language. Instead of bemoaning the loss of her mother tongue and now also the loss of an educated person's Chinese, the poet recreates the image of the island from the times prior to colonization in her childhood's idiom that was later displaced by the rigor of monolingual education. Her personal history intermingles with that of the island and the local language becomes the thread that binds three generations – her parents, herself and her child – together. Thus, the local language does not only represent the poet's and the island's past, but also their future. Tsai's translingual writing illuminates Rey Chow's proposal to perceive the postcolonial experience not as mere "deprivation of linguistic autonomy" (2014, 14). Instead of essensializing the loss, Chow proposes that the loss can be treated as a "kind of prosthetics" (17). While Tsai's poem essentializes the ecological loss and meets it with a feeling of injury and melancholia, the poet approaches the issue of postcolonial languaging with a different attitude that gives a chance to the many ways of coming to terms with language.

According to Tsai, writing poetry in her native dialect is a different affective experience from writing in the official national language. The poet describes it as an "intimate" (*qinmigan* 親密感) creative act. Analogically, she speaks of reciting poetry in her mother tongue as of a distinct bodily experience (*shentigan* 身體感). Since, in comparison with Mandarin, Taiwanese Hokkien has a greater variety of tonal patterns and it differentiates between spoken and written pronunciations, Tsai perceives the impact of the Hokkien spoken word as greater than that of Chinese script. Even though the poet perceives her compositional skills in her mother tongue as inferior to those in the standard national language, she still believes that writing in Taiwanese Hokkien broadens her poetic horizons and grants her access to new means of creative expression. For example, when writing in the local language, she can choose to write in Chinese characters, in romanization or in a mix of both writing systems (Tsai Wan-Shuen, e-mail to author, October and November 2022).

Tsai's linguistic openness turns her poetry into an example of the "postcolonial creative languaging domain," for which Rey Chow proposes the name "xenophone" (2014, 59). Chow describes this domain through concepts such as mimicry and adaptation, but at the same time, it is a space of noise and disruption, in which the notion of the dominant language as a closed entity becomes illusory. Chow's concept draws upon Derrida's utopian moment in his "monolingualism of the other" in that he perceives language as "what inherently undoes any attempt at appropriation and ownership."[7] Tsai's personal trajectory shows how her educated monolingualism have finally become disrupted by linguistic multiplicities and "xenophonic memories" (2014, 59). Importantly, the poet remarks on the physicality of the experience of interrogating with her mother tongue, tune in with Chow's writing, in which affects, gestures and habits play an important role. One's relationship with language is always emotionally charged, but it does not have to become haunted by the sense of irreversible loss. In Chow's words "[i]n postcolonial languaging, dispossession is the key that opens unexpected doors" (2014, 60) and translingual poetry speaks in favor of this observation.

---

7   See Rey Chow's discussion of Derrida's "monolingualism of the other" in Chow 2014, 29.

3 Translingual Interpellation

The last example that demonstrates the creative potential of translingual poetry comes from the US poet and translator Jami Proctor-Xu (Xu Zhenmin 徐贞敏), who writes in English and Chinese. In her bilingual poem "Duidian" 对点 (Counterpoint) Proctor-Xu deconstructs the monolingual (Chinese? English?) poem. At the same time, her text raises questions about the notions of originality, translation and authorship. It also forms a counterpoint to the still-widespread belief that poetry is accessible to native speakers only. The opening section of the poem depicts the interpellation of a translingual poetic subjectivity through naming:

> 贞敏 阿敏 jami
> jami 阿敏 贞敏
>
> 徐
> 徐
> 徐
>
> XU 2016, 76

Naming is a powerful tool of cultural control since it provides the terms in which the world may become accessible and shared as a common experience. This text, however, rejects the hegemony of any language to claim the right to describe or create a knowledgeable world. The multilingual impure interpellation in "Counterpoint" points to the endless possibilities of subversion of linguistic hegemony that are inherent to language itself. Significantly, with the growing numbers of foreign Mandarin-learners around the world, those who respond to the multilingual interpellation may be of very different racial and class backgrounds. Amang's English and Proctor-Xu's Chinese are both examples of "xenophone" (Chow 2014) writing that taints a language with foreign sounding elements.

The following section of the poem moves on from the act of creating through calling into being to confirming that everything that exists is real. Every creature in the universe has its own voice – the birds, grass, and an ant – and none of them can be missed:

> 她说每一个声音是必要的
> 每一个声音以自己的方法喊出来
>
> she said every voice is needed
> every voice cries out in its own way –

TRANSLINGUAL POETIC EXPERIMENTS

你教我聆听哭声

you taught me to listen to the cries
(...)

XU 2016, 77

Throughout the poem Proctor-Xu mixes Chinese verses with English ones. Some of them are quotations from others' poems and some are her own translations in one of the two languages. For a lay reader, it is impossible to distinguish between the original and the translation. Furthermore, the poet has rearranged the verses to build her own visual pattern out of poetic lines that change meaning when displaced from their original contexts.

After the opening sections of the poem have described the creation of a harmonious multilingual world, the third and last section again confirm the value of this polyphonic creation:

每一个声音喊出来每一个声音 every voice cries out every voice
以自己的方式盛开 flowers in its own way

XU 2016, 78

Proctor-Xu's poem is more than simply an assemblage of sentences taken from her own poems and her translations of poetry; she has also inserted verses taken from texts by the Chinese poets Zhai Yongming, Shu Cai and Li Li, and by the American poet Brenda Hilman. "Counterpoint" can be read as an original reflection on polyphonic poetic subjectivity, or as an anticipation of a feminine ("she said") act of creation that engenders a world in which every voice is perceived as equally valuable. With the repeating images of flourishing and blooming, it is also a cheerful celebration of the multiplicity of species and speeches.

Proctor-Xu's poetic experiment combines linguistic transgression with an opening toward otherness. It shows, in its own way, that the question of the original text and copy or translation has become irrelevant. Instead of questioning the impure origins of the text, rejecting or enforcing it as a language game, we could rather be celebrating the possibilities that have been created through the inclusion of the experiences and voices of others. In her thorough discussion of Derrida's understanding of monolingualism, Rey Chows speaks of the challenge that his concepts of language pose not only to Postcolonial Studies, but also to certain strains of cosmopolitanism. According to Chow, Derrida's "utopian notion of linguistic egalitarianism" claims that language is fundamentally "plural and multiple" and, furthermore, always already a translation without origin (Chow 2014, 29–33). Proctor-Xu's "Counterpoint" suggests that celebrating the open-ended promise inherent to every language may be the name for a new trajectory of flight in the linguistic domain and beyond it.

4   Translingual Trajectories

Postcolonial discourse often describes language as a fundamental site of struggle (Ashcroft, Griffiths and Tiffin 1995, 261). Consequently, the academic and literary inquiry into imperial oppression through control over language has already provided a rich conceptual framework that helps to understand the power relations inscribed into various linguistic practices at the "center" and "peripheries" of the globalized postcolonial world. The three texts discussed in this chapter show that Sinophone authors of translingual poetry have also been creatively "writing back" (Ashcroft, Griffiths and Tiffin 2002) to the linguistic hegemony of standard Chinese and English. In doing so, they choose artful subversion of the dominant linguistic codes instead of entirely rejecting them.

The poets Amang, Tsai Wan-Shuen and Jami Proctor-Xu apply different translingual strategies in their negotiations with their own and foreign poetic and linguistic traditions. Amang's poem is most explicit in its refusal to use correct English and Chinese syntax as a means of taking revenge on the unilateral imposition of linguistic hegemony through, for example, compulsory education. Tsai picks up this thread in her metatextual commentary on her own creative biography in which unlearning and re-learning her native dialect plays an important role. She incorporated Taiwanese place names into her Chinese poem, which in Chow's words (2014) may be described as "dyeing" (16) the standard language "imposed from without" (14) with new contexts and tonal patterns. Furthermore, Tsai emphasizes the organic connection between the mother tongue and the body in which the language spoken resonates and stirs up certain emotions. This connection between language and the body in Tsai and Proctor-Xu's texts extends further their interrogation of linguistic cultures and their legacies, which they simultaneously embody and inhabit. The utopian "Counterpoint" suggests the possibility of a less anthropocentric exploration of the relationship between language and the world in that it invites other-than-human voices – the flowers and the birds – to cohabit the ecosystem of its linguistic landscape. Tsai retrieves the language of her childhood and, at the same time, the "childhood" of the "island with deer" with its flourishing fauna prior to environmental and linguistic colonization.

Translingual poetry is not simply multilingual but also opens up a new linguistic dimension, which seems to be a suitable means of expression of the current postcolonial experience. The translingual poem can be seen as a palimpsest of layers of enunciations "lost and found," or in Chow's words (2014), as a "kind of prosthetics" (17) in today's unprecedented linguistic traffic.

Works Cited

Amang 阿芒. 2016. *Wo jinjin bao ni de shihou zhe shijie hao duo ren si* 我緊緊抱你的時候這世界好多人死 [When I Hold You Tightly, Many People Die in This World]. Taipei: Hei Yanjing Wenhua.

Amang, and Steve Bradbury. 2020. *Raised by Wolves: Poems and Conversations.* Translated by Steve Bradbury. Dallas, Texas: Phoneme Media, Deep Vellum.

Ashcroft, Bill, Gareth Griffiths, and Helen Tiffin, eds. 1995. *The Post-Colonial Studies Reader.* London and New York: Routledge.

Ashcroft, Bill, Gareth Griffiths, and Helen Tiffin, eds. 2002. *The Empire Writes Back: Theory and Practice in Post-Colonial Literatures.* London and New York: Routledge.

Chang, Sung-sheng Yvonne. 2014. "Introduction: Literary Taiwan – An East Asian Contextual Perspective." In *The Columbia Sourcebook of Literary Taiwan*, edited by Chang, Sung-sheng Yvonne, Michelle Yeh and Ming-ju Fan, 1–36. New York: Columbia University Press.

Chow, Ray. 2014. *Not Like a Native Speaker: On Languaging as a Postcolonial Experience.* New York: Columbia University Press.

Danius, Sara, Stefan Jonsson, and Gayatri Chakravorty Spivak. 1993. "An Interview with Gayatri Chakravorty Spivak." *boundary 2* (2) (Summer): 24–50.

Derrida, Jacques. 1998. *Monolingualism of the Other.* Translated by Patrick Mensah. Stanford: Stanford University Press.

Egan, Charles. 2008. "Recent-Style *Shi* Poetry: Quatrains (*Jueju*)." In *How to Read Chinese Poetry: A Guided Anthology*, edited by Cai, Zong-qi, 199–225. New York: Columbia University Press.

Koo, Hui-Wen. 2011. "Deer Hunting and Preserving the Commons in Dutch Colonial Taiwan." *The Journal of Interdisciplinary History* 2: 186–187.

Lin, Hengtai. 1985. "The Translingual Generation of Poets: Beginning with the Silver Bell Society." Translated by Hayes Moore. In *The Columbia Sourcebook of Literary Taiwan*, edited by Chang, Sung-sheng Yvonne, Michelle Yeh and Ming-ju Fan, 352–353. New York: Columbia University Press.

Loda, Alice, and Antonio Viselli. 2021. "Translingualism and Poetry." In *The Routledge Handbook of Literary Translation*, edited by Kellman, Steven G. and Natasha Lvovich, 18–30. New York: Routledge.

Proctor-Xu, Jami 徐贞敏. 2016. *Turan qiwu* 突然起舞 [Sudden Dance]. Beijing: WingWomenPress [unofficial publication].

Tsai, Wan-Shuen 蔡宛璇 et al. 2020. *Xiaohai yujian shi: xiang he ni yiqi shai taiyang* 小孩遇見詩： 想跟你一起曬太陽 [A Child Encounters Poetry: I Want to Sunbathe with You]. Taipei: Muma wenhua shiye gufen youxian gongsi.

Yeh, Michelle. 2001. "Frontier Taiwan: An Introduction." In *Frontier Taiwan: An Anthology of Modern Chinese Poetry*, edited by Yeh, Michelle and N.G.D. Malmqvist, 1–54. New York: Columbia University Press.

CHAPTER 6

Speaking from "In-Between"

Jennifer Wong and the Translation of the Self

Martina Codeluppi
University of Bologna

1 Introduction

The Sinophone world is hardly a monolithic entity through which different communities across the globe represent a univocal interpretation of "Chineseness." Its first and well-known conceptualization by Shu-mei Shih takes the variety of Sinitic languages into account and emphasizes the multilinguality of the Sinophone in terms of sound and script (Shih 2011, 715). Shih also extends the borders of the concept to the "localization and creolization" taking place in specific areas where a Sinitic language overlaps with a foreign one (2011, 716). In more than a decade of debate, the concept of "Sinophone literature" has been widely discussed from many different perspectives, although it still seems impossible to come up with a final and perfectly satisfactory definition, by specifying exactly what one should include or exclude from this "category." Sinophone literature, as part of the Sinophone, still represents an entanglement of concepts such as that of ethnicity, race, nationality, and language ideologies (A.D. Wong, Su, and Hiramoto 2021), which can be modulated according to the perspective from which a certain study is conducted. Twenty-five years ago, the Lebanese writer and member of the *Académie française* Amin Maalouf stated that a language "has the peculiarity of being at once an identity-defining factor and a tool of communication," representing "the pivot of cultural identity," just as "linguistic diversity" represents "the pivot of any diversity" (Maalouf 1998, 153). Therefore, the use of language can always be traced back to a certain interpretation of one's identity and, in the case of Sinophone authors, it can transcend the borders of Sinitic languages and take the form of a foreign language mixed – at some point – with elements deriving from the individual's mother tongue. The nuances coded in language are particularly relevant when studying literature and, within the study of literature, they are exceptionally noteworthy when shifting the focus from prose to poetry. In this chapter, I will delve into the issue of Sinophone poetry in English by analyzing Jennifer Wong's collection 回家 *Letters Home* (2020b).

© MARTINA CODELUPPI, 2024 | DOI:10.1163/9789004711600_008

The author's composite identity, voiced through her "other" tongue, provides a reflection on language that leads to a unique vision of the in-betweenness characterizing her own experience as a migrant woman from Hong Kong.

2 The Sinophone and Foreign-Language Writing

Although the debate about what can be considered "Sinophone literature" is still far from settled, finding a solution should not be considered a utopian dream. Chinese authors writing in foreign languages have been categorized in different ways, based on their own personal histories and their specific use of language. Scholars from the PRC have mainly analyzed these works from a cultural or a linguistic perspective. On the one hand, foreign-language writing can be considered the quintessence of multiculturalism (Ni 2013) and these writers' peculiar location – at the margins of both their homeland and their adoptive country – is seen as a privileged position from which they are able to open up a channel of communication. On the other hand, their works juggling with linguistic hybridization have been analyzed as products of unique interactions between an individual's "soul language" and his or her "tool language" (Huang 2008, 50–51). The problem of harmonizing the idea of a Chinese literature that can no longer be limited by geographic borders and confined to the use of Sinitic languages has been brought to the forefront by Jing Tsu and David Wang (2010), as well as by Yinde Zhang (2014), who has underlined the need to take into account the real polyphony behind a "global" or "transnational" Chinese literature. Although the task of defining a cartography of such a wide and multifaceted concept seems impossible, one must keep in mind that it is only when it is used as a method – and not as a category – that it can prove most useful (Codeluppi 2020, 21).

Analyzing and comparing different manifestations of Sinophone literature, in Chinese as well as in other languages, is a fundamental practice that enables us to fully grasp its composite character. Sometimes, different languages overlap in a single author's mind, as is the case with writers – usually migrants – who choose to express themselves in their "other tongue": a practice which Steven Kellman has termed "translingualism" (Kellman 2019, 337). As Ha Jin 哈金 (b. 1953) explains in his famous essay "Exiled to English" (2013), the choice of abandoning one's mother tongue for another language is never easy or painless. And when an author's bond with their homeland is particularly strong, they quite frequently choose to let their "mother tongue" show through their foreign-language texts, enriching their literary creativity by means of linguistic hybridization. This phenomenon generates a cross-linguistic text that can be

SPEAKING FROM "IN-BETWEEN"   113

analyzed through a precise framework (Yao 2003), in order to locate the cultural echo of migration as it is expressed in an author's language.

3 Jennifer Wong: a Synthesis of Three Minorities

Jennifer Wong is an interesting example of a bilingual author who experiments with language to represent the complexity behind a migrant's identity. She was born in Hong Kong in 1978 and emigrated to the United Kingdom as a college student. She completed her education with a PhD in creative writing from Oxford Brookes University, where she currently holds a position as Associate Lecturer, combining her academic career with her talent for poetry. She has published three collections of poems (2006, 2013, 2020b) and a pamphlet (2019), all dealing with her experience as a migrant, and conveying her special flair for languages. Her latest work, 回家 *Letters Home* (2020b) – the title itself is a sublimation of her linguistic creativity – earned her the "Wild Card Choice" award by the Poetry Book Society. On her personal website Jennifer Wong herself has clarified that this collection encapsulates the migrant's experience, expressing the ambivalent feelings caused by the overlapping of motherlands and mother tongues with foreign places and languages, as well as by an imaginary journey "back home":

> In 回家 *Letters Home*, one returns to the complexities of being between nations, languages and cultures. Intersecting multiple borders of history and place, these poems examine what it means to return home, and whether it is a return to a location, a country or to a shared dream or language.[1]

One of the most interesting traits of Wong's poetry is her way of playing with language, which is a feature she shares with other authors of similar background, such as Sarah Howe (b. 1983) and Mary Jean Chan (b. 1990). By expressing her message in a language that mixes English with Mandarin, Cantonese, dialects, etc., Jennifer Wong stimulates the reader, who is supposed to find a way around her codifications and put together a translation of his or her own (Huen 2022).

Besides writing poems, Wong also engages in academic research on the theme of identity in Chinese diaspora poetry. She has published a number of

---

1   https://jenniferwong.co.uk.

interviews and studies (J. Wong 2022, 2020a, 2018, 2017), as well as a recent monograph (J. Wong 2023), in which she specifically tackles the issue of home and identity in the context of Chinese migration. Her critical perspective toward these themes makes 回家 *Letters Home* an even more interesting work, a testimony to the reality of "being in-between," not only physically but also – and more importantly – culturally and linguistically. Published in 2020, 回家 *Letters Home* is a collection narrating – across five sections – the experience of a migrant girl, who recounts the beauty and hardship of finding herself in a foreign land, while remaining connected to her homeland. Wong defines herself a poet and a translator and, as it is clearly shown by the title of the collection, her work can be regarded as an example of "translingualism." In Steven Kellman's words,

> [T]ranslingual authors are better equipped than isolinguals to step outside the prison-house of language – or at least of L1 – and to make us aware of the factitiousness of verbal constructions. Translingual texts are often metalingual in their self-consciousness about their own linguistic medium, the way they make language itself strange. (Kellman 2020, 12)

I have chosen to focus on Jennifer Wong because of the intersections between her choice to write in English – which can ultimately be regarded as an act of self-translation – and her personal history, which puts her at the crossroads of three minority categories, namely Hong Kong literature, migrant literature, and foreign-language writing. 回家 *Letters Home* contains the essence of the author's "in-betweenness" and in the following analysis I will explore three main themes through which Wong expresses her experimental creativity: the migrant's condition, the maternity metaphor, and the connection between distance and resistance. I will also apply Yao's taxonomy (Yao 2003) to underline the linguistic devices that embody Wong's hybridity, and eventually bring forward the cultural implications of her translingual practice.

4 The Migrant's Condition

回家 *Letters Home* includes many insightful representations of migration, which provide different examples to voice the complexity and the composite nature of such an experience. The poem "Diary of a Miu Miu Salesgirl" offers an interpretation of the phenomenon seen from the eyes of a young girl that finds herself stuck with a language that has somehow been imposed on her:

SPEAKING FROM "IN-BETWEEN"

> I am wearing a crêpe-de-chine dress
> and suede stilettos that do not belong to me.
>
> I'm carrying nothing but my lies
> and my L'Absolut lipstick, red as a warning.
>
> I am rather good at this smiling game,
> speaking Mandarin to the customers.
>
> The trick is to flatter them, flattered as they
> already are, being wives of the nouveau riche
>
> from a changing China.
> [...]
> In our home country we would never
>
> have met, but here I have touched their waists,
> know their bra sizes and their children's names [...]
>> J. WONG 2020b

This poem is not specifically hybrid, since Wong does not incorporate any language other than English, except for a few loanwords or misspelled names. Nevertheless, the reflection on the use of language is still powerful, as she describes how Mandarin constitutes a bridge to communicate with the social group that represents a specific category of Chinese migrants in Europe. Nonetheless, the lyrical "I"'s mother tongue is presumably Cantonese – like Wong's – therefore, she portrays how the language she speaks puts her in an undesirable position. Although she speaks fluent Mandarin, she does not consider it her mother tongue; the need to hide her true native language and speak Mandarin for the sake of her job feels almost suffered.

In the following poem, "Dimsum at Joy King Lau," Wong describes a rather common experience for a Chinese migrant: eating at a Chinese restaurant abroad, in this case in the United Kingdom.

> As soon as we sat down you said:
> *I'm open to anything*
> *except chicken's feet.*
> *And please none of those slippery cheung fun rolls,*
> *sea cucumber or jellyfish!*

Secretly I *know* what you're
missing out on. As usual
we ordered *Chinese tea*:
a brew unheard of.
You devoured the spring rolls
and crispy squid with gusto, leaving
untouched the divine *xiaolongbao*.
[...]
For dessert,
they gave us sliced oranges:
our red bean soups are too sophisticated
for your palate. In the background
we could see the lit-up eyes
of the golden phoenix, this Chinatown
dotted with lanterns and too many
shops selling iPhone covers.
Nothing is authentic
except what we are missing.

J. WONG 2020b

As it seeps from the poem, the main feature of the meal is its fakeness, and the choice to use the original name in *pinyin* to describe the Shanghainese dumpling feels like an almost desperate attempt to preserve the tiniest bit of authenticity. The words that have seeped from Mandarin and Cantonese into the English text serve as an immediate obstacle – although one rather easy to overcome – for the Anglophone reader but, more importantly, they also constitute an example of "cross fertilization" (Yao 2003, 364). In the context in which they are used, these words are stripped of their original meaning – "Chinese tea" is a brew "unheard of" – and come to symbolize the "translation" of Chinese food into English culture.

Although autobiographical influences seem rather strong, Jennifer Wong in her collection does not limit her focus to her own personal experience, but tells many other stories of migrants – not only from China, but also from other countries, and with a variety of different backgrounds. Yet, all these narratives succeed in portraying the perpetual tension characterizing the migrant's condition and the pressing need for a compromise, which must be achieved in both language and behavior. Nonetheless, the author does not paint a negative picture of migration: as she describes in this excerpt from the poem titled "Anser Anser," her vision remains poetic.

SPEAKING FROM "IN-BETWEEN"

Year after year we'd do this: migration
being so natural to us; we know
we can never give up our strong ties
and memories either here or over
there, that the idea of not returning
is as excruciating as of leaving.
See the V shape we spell in the sky, before we scatter.

J. WONG 2020b

Wong uses the metaphor of the graylag goose to represent migration as a sort of innate condition. This nature generates contrasting feelings that constitute the subject's purest nourishment.

5   The Maternity Metaphor

Another major theme that Jennifer Wong addresses in 回家 *Letters Home* is maternity, which can be considered one of the most authentic human experiences. Being so closely related to the natural, almost animal, part of a human being, maternity pervades every aspect of one's mind and body, including language. In the following poem, "Postpartum Vinegar," the perspective of giving birth leads the lyrical "I" to connect with her cultural background by reviving old Hong Kong traditions:

Elephantine in the ninth month,
I'm the butcher's wife from the Ming dynasty
hunting for fresh pig trotters
in the local Morrisons.

Too busy to chill out in Starbucks
with the NCT yummy mummies,
I'm preparing my ginger recipe:
one portion sweet, two portions sour.

Make it not too early nor too late.
In a house spiced with memories
I indulge in my tribal ways,
singing to my baby in the womb the classic tune

紅雞蛋 豬腳薑 hong gai dan, zhu geuk geung,
八珍甜醋分外香 Pat Zhen Tim Cho fen oi heung!

[...]
Baby daughter, get ready for England!

J. WONG 2020b

The author's connection with her motherland takes the shape of a nursery rhyme she sings in her head in Cantonese. The use of characters associated with the transcription of the Cantonese pronunciation – which however is hybridized with Mandarin *pinyin* – produces a foreignizing effect on the readers, tricking them into believing in the alleged mystical powers of this Chinese custom. Linguistically speaking, the author performs a peculiar act of "code-switching," which is a form of what Yao defines as "transplantation" (Yao 2003, 368). Indeed, Wong inserts elements from her own cultural tradition rather abruptly, and by adding the transcription of the pronunciation, she almost fakes the intention to mediate between the Cantonese nursery rhyme and the English poem, without actually providing any tool to overcome potential incomprehensibility (Yao 2003, 369). What might come as a surprise is the fact that the tune quoted is actually the commercial for a widely known brand of vinegar sold in Hong Kong. Therefore, despite Wong's manifest desire to refer to Hong Kong traditions explicitly, she does not stop at the level of cultural evocation, but recreates a play on language that can fool inexperienced readers. Another linguistic device that reveals Wong's linguistic hybridization is the metaphor of the "butcher's wife from the Ming dynasty." By dropping such a reference, the author evokes a particular image that is strictly related to Chinese tradition in a rather casual way; therefore, she provides an example of "grafting," a device that has the purpose of establishing "the terms of [her] ethnic culture" (Yao 2003, 367).

The second poem which the author devotes to the theme of maternity is titled "Daughter," and is largely autobiographical. This poem is an imaginary dialogue with a newborn, to whom Wong speaks in Cantonese, even though the baby cannot understand her:

You arrive in the year of the ram,
a month after the royal birth.

The kindest thing that has happened
in my side of England.

SPEAKING FROM "IN-BETWEEN" 119

Remember the Chinese proverb:
we are of the same bone and flesh

indebted to each other
since the beginning.

My little bird, do you know
love is where you come from?

If one day you look for
my childhood, you will find

it lies elsewhere, in a country
with no alphabet,

but here and now, what I feel
is the clasp of your tiny fist,

the heave of your small chest.
Ka wai, or hai nei gei ma ma,

gung gung por por dou hou gua ju nei

and I know this undulated speech
makes no sense to you and jars the ears,

but baby, this is what I can give.
The rest is your journey now.

J. WONG 2020b

Here the author once again performs an act of "transplantation," as she chooses to report the Cantonese pronunciation by means of a non-conventional transcription, creating a foreignizing effect and making it challenging to understand even for a native Cantonese speaker. As a result, the bar of language tricks is raised, increasing the cryptic nature of the thoughts that Wong, as a migrant mother, decides to express by means of her personal tongue. Even if the interpretation of these lines was not as important for the poem as the presence of Cantonese itself, Wong still makes the reader perceive a distance which reproduces that which the lyrical "I" feels towards her daughter, with whom she shares some DNA, but not the same nationality or mother tongue.

6   Distance and Resistance

The concept of distance represents another main theme in 回家 *Letters Home*, and is strictly related to that of resistance. As a migrant, the author is likely to perceive the distance separating her from her motherland, but as a Hongkongese, she also feels the urge to resist the increasing influence of Mainland China that has marked the recent history of Hong Kong. In particular, in this poem titled "Metamorphosis" she addresses the changes that Hong Kong has undergone since the handover, starting from the educational and linguistic consequences of the new "cultural re-colonization," namely the appearance (and disappearance) of certain content in children's textbooks and the shift in the cultural connotations of the language one speaks:

> The change is all so subtle we hardly
> notice: at first it is just the colour
> of the pillar box or a missing crown
> on a uniform. We laugh at the promise
> horse-racing will go on forever.
> Slowly the textbooks for our children
> are changing: less on the colony,
> more on 'the Chinese dream'.
>
> On birth: pregnant mothers crossing
> the border in haste before due dates.
> On lifestyle: fewer noodle stalls,
> more shops of gold. And every day,
> in Lo Wu, you hear frustrated voices
> and grating wheels of trolley cases.
> It's more useful to speak Mandarin
> when you shop: and swipe Union Pay.
>
> [...]
> I wonder how a city
> can outgrow the country,
> whether going home is still an option.
> > J. WONG 2020b

Clearly, the author is referring to the cultural transformation that Hong Kong has been experiencing since the handover put an end to its colonial history in 1997. The protests that have shaken this contested territory in recent years have left a deep mark on its people, to the point that even language and its nuances

SPEAKING FROM "IN-BETWEEN"

have gained new meanings. It is interesting to note how changes in language end up affecting one's idea of "home." This is not a new concept in Wong's literary production[2] and in this poem we witness a shift from the feeling of rejection she expressed in *Goldfish* (J. Wong 2013) to a sense of loss, which leads the lyrical "I" to open up to the possibility that her home may already have become unreachable, lost in the linguistic invasion from the mainland. Another poem addressing the fate of Hong Kong is the one titled "Truth 2.0," in which the lyrical "I" openly refers to the "Umbrella Movement" of 2014, expressing how her people's resistance is able to reach her across the distance between her homeland and the country she resides in:

1.
Incoming: *I smell tear gas everywhere.*

2.
Imagine there are no countries.

3.
Once upon a time I lived in a place where the metro was never late.
Everything ran like clockwork, and it was so safe you could walk
to Tsui Wah for a bowl of wonton noodles at midnight.

4.
There's no word in the dictionary for this.

[...]
7.
Since June, my screen time has increased by a hundred and fifty
percent. I go to the news as soon as I wake up and right before
going to sleep, concerned something might break out again when
I am out in the supermarket or picking up my daughter.

[...]
12.
A mosaic of dreamers despite the rain. Despite the heavy rain.

13.
人在做。天在看。

---

2   See Ho (2017).

14.
The world will never forget.

J. WONG 2020b

The description of the increased screen time stresses the anxiety of the migrant, who can only follow the protests from afar. Nevertheless, the distance does not prevent the lyrical "I" from speaking directly to those involved in the riots by addressing them in Chinese – code-switching once again – by quoting the popular saying: "The heavens are watching people's actions." Moreover, the reference to the impossibility of finding an appropriate word in the dictionary is an overt expression of her disappointment at the traumatic events that occurred in those years. In "A Chinese Teapot," Wong extends her reflection to recent Chinese history and compares the impossibility of finding a rationale for what has happened to the bewilderment of not knowing how to use tenses in a language that is not one's own:

> Say we can't find the right tense for certain years in our lives. Say nineteen ninety-seven. And nineteen eighty-nine.
>
> J. WONG 2020B

The references to the handover of Hong Kong in 1997 and to the Tiananmen massacre of 1989 are associated with the different use of tenses in Chinese and English. As stated by Kellman, "different languages orient us differently in space and time" and, as a result, they produce a "very different sense of history" (2019, 343). In this case, linguistic hybridization and translingualism give way to a kind of incommunicability that, despite all efforts, cannot be overcome even in the "in-betweenness" experienced by the migrant.

7   Conclusions

In Steven Kellman's words, "switching languages is a way of inventing a new self" (2019, 341), and Jennifer Wong provides an example of how translingualism can represent a way for a migrant to connect with her homeland by means of actual interaction between her mother tongue and her other tongue. The three minorities she embodies – Hong Kong literature, migrant literature, and literature in foreign languages – are masterfully represented in 回家 Letters Home through her linguistic creativity, which produces poems showing different degrees of linguistic hybridization. In my analysis I have shown how the complexity of being "in-between" is reflected by the many facets of Wong's language and how her polyphonic poetry can be regarded as an adjustable tool of interpretation that stimulates the reader and introduces him or her to the complex condition of being a Hong Kong migrant female author. Depending on what theme she wants to address, Wong conveys a more or less cryptic message, using different languages and transcription methods.

By exploring the themes of migration, maternity, and resistance as they are represented in the collection, I have underlined how the use of specific devices such as "cross-fertilization," "transplantation," and "grafting" enables the recreation of a hybridized self in translation, conveying all the tensions and doubts that fill a migrant's soul. Nonetheless, Wong's reflection on language reaches a deeper level when the use of a certain code becomes a metaphor for the cultural value it represents, and becomes particularly interesting if seen from the perspective of Sinophone literature. The author's mother tongue, Cantonese, symbolizes a sort of heritage which the lyrical "I" is trying to pass on to her baby, despite the difficulties of having to face pregnancy and maternity in a foreign land. On the contrary, the representation of Mandarin is often loaded with negative connotations, as it is depicted more than once as the language of consumerism and oppression. These two languages are both part of Wong's "Chinese self" and they are intertwined with her "foreign self" not only linguistically but also symbolically. They possess a power that, depending on the context, can either strengthen the influence of the author's ethnic background *vis-à-vis* the English culture in which she lives or trigger a clash between her Chinese roots and her Cantonese personal history. In Wong's case, the choice of adopting a foreign language to write poetry and of juxtaposing and hybridizing it with one's own linguistic heritage engenders a creative turmoil that is especially effective in emphasizing the importance of any linguistic choice, no matter how small, and hence in representing language as a perpetual act of resistance.

Works Cited

Codeluppi, Martina. 2020. *Fictional Memories: Contemporary Chinese Literature and Transnationality*. Paris and Turin: L'Harmattan.

Ha Jin. 2013. "Exiled to English." In *Sinophone Studies: A Critical Reader*, edited by Shu-mei Shih, Chien-hsin Tsai, and Brian Bernards, 93–98. New York: Columbia University Press.

Ho, Tammy Lai-Ming 2017. "Something Sets Us Looking for a Place: Poetry of Jennifer Wong and Sarah Howe." *Wasafiri* 32 (3): 41–45.

Huang, Wanhua 黃萬華. 2008. "Huibao muyu ziyang de shengming fangshi——huaren xin shengdai he xin yimin zuojia chuangzuo de yuyan zhuiqiu" 回報母語滋

養的生命方式——華人新生代和新移民作家創作的語言追求 [A lifestyle that replaces the nourishment of the mother tongue: the pursuit of language created by new-generation and new-migrants Chinese authors]. *Zhongshan daxue xuebao (shehui kexue ban)* 48 (1): 47–52.

Huen, Antony. 2022. "Chinese and City Aesthetics: A Conversation with Jennifer Wong." *World Literature Today* 96 (3): 49–53.

Kellman, Steven G. 2019. "Literary Translingualism: What and Why?" *Polylinguality and Transcultural Practices* 16 (3): 337–346.

Kellman, Steven G. 2020. *Nimble Tongues: Studies in Literary Translingualism*. West Lafayette: Purdue University Press.

Maalouf, Amin. 1998. *Les Identités meurtrières* [Murderous identities]. Paris: Grasset.

Ni, Tingting 倪婷婷. 2013. "Jiaru waiji de huaren zuojia fei muyu chuanzuo de guilei wenti" 加入外籍的華人作家非母語創作的歸類問題 [The problem of categorising the creations by Chinese writers with foreign citizenship]. *Jiangsu shehui kexue* (5): 202–207.

Shih, Shu-mei. 2011. "The Concept of the Sinophone." *PMLA/Publications of the Modern Language Association of America* 126 (3): 709–718.

Tsu, Jing, and David Der-wei Wang 王德威. 2010. *Global Chinese Literature*. Edited by Jing Tsu and David Der-wei Wang 王德威. *Critical Essays*. Leiden and Boston: Brill.

Wong, Andrew D., Hsi-yao Su, and Mie Hiramoto. 2021. "Complicating raciolinguistics: Language, Chineseness, and the Sinophone." *Language & Communication* 76: 131–35.

Wong, Jennifer. 2006. *Summer Cicadas*. Hong Kong: Chameleon Press.

Wong, Jennifer. 2013. *Goldfish*. Hong Kong: Chameleon Press.

Wong, Jennifer. 2017. "An Interview with Agnes Lam." *Wasafiri* 32 (1): 11–13.

Wong, Jennifer. 2018. "On Home, Belongingness, and Multicultural Britain: A Conversation with Hannah Lowe." *World Literature Today* 92 (2): 14–17.

Wong, Jennifer. 2019. *Diary of a Miu Miu Salesgirl*. London: Bitter Melon.

Wong, Jennifer. 2020a. "Hannah Lowe and Sarah Howe: Multicultural Heritage and Questions of Identity." *English: Journal of the English Association* 69 (266): 246–269.

Wong, Jennifer. 2020b. 回家 *Letters Home*. e-book ed. Rugby: Nine Arches Press.

Wong, Jennifer. 2022. "Redeeming Desire: A Conversation with Li-Young Lee." *World Literature Today* 92 (1): 13–17.

Wong, Jennifer. 2023. *Identity, Home and Writing Elsewhere in Contemporary Chinese Diaspora Poetry*. London and New York: Bloomsbury.

Yao, Steven G. 2003. "Taxonomizing Hybridity." *Textual Practice* 17 (2): 357–378.

Zhang, Yinde. 2014. "La littérature chinoise transnationale et la sinopolyphonie." Translated by Nicole G. Albert. *Diogène* (2): 222–234.

CHAPTER 7

Saying More by Writing Less

Sinophone Small Poetry from Thailand

Rebecca M. Ehrenwirth
University of Applied Sciences/SDI Munich

Contemporary Sinophone Literature in Thailand (Sino-Thai Lit) mainly consists of three genres: short stories (*duanpian xiaoshuo* 短篇小説), essays (*sanwen* 散文) and poetry or verse (*shici* 詩詞). Since the early 2000s new forms of short stories as well as poetry have developed in the community of Sinophone writers in Thailand, which are much shorter, namely flash fiction (*shan xiaoshuo* 閃小説) and short or small poetry, *xiaoshi* 小詩,[1] and which found their way to the Sino-Thai community via China or Taiwan respectively.[2] By analyzing and translating small poems by Sinophone writers from Thailand, I will address the in-between position of these authors. On the one hand, as Thai citizens, they do not belong to China; their poetry is not included in the national narrative of China; on the other, as Sinophone writers, their works do not belong to Thai literature either. This also raises the question of whether they want to belong to either China or Thailand, whether they feel trapped in their in-betweenness as writers, or whether they in fact see themselves in line with transcultural poetics, therefore questioning traditional ideas of cultures as ethnically closed areas, which are defined by their territory and a single homogeneous language.

Although most contemporary Sinophone Thai writers' mother tongue is Thai, they have chosen to write in the Sinitic script because they want to reach a broad readership in China. However, they do not see themselves as Chinese writers, but as Thai who use the Sinitic script to express the Chinese part of their identity and to connect with their heritage. By writing about Thailand in some of their poems, they reflect their biculturality and introduce their homeland to readers in China. For these authors, writing poetry is a form of miniature self-making expressed in a limited number of characters. While the

---

1 I prefer the term "small" in the context of Chinese literature because the poems are called *xiaoshi* 小詩 in Chinese, *xiao* 小 meaning "small" rather than short (*duan* 短).
2 For a more detailed discussion of contemporary Sino-Thai Lit as well as its development see Ehrenwirth (2018; 2023, 141–157).

© REBECCA M. EHRENWIRTH, 2024 | DOI:10.1163/9789004711600_009

shortness of these poems is an expression of the ephemerality and caducity of modern life, it also draws attention to the meaning(s) of every character. By condensing the language to a minimum, they emphasize the multitude of interpretations and the potential for ambivalent meaning.

Small poetry was already flourishing among the Sinophone poets in 2001, when Lin Huanzhang 林煥彰 – a Taiwanese writer born in 1939 who is part of the Sinophone writing community in Thailand[3] – inspired Sinophone poets in Thailand to share their small poems by printing one a day on the cover of the literary supplement (*wenyi fukan* 文藝副刊) of *Shijie ribao Meinanhe* 世界日報湄南河 (The World Newspaper of Chao Phraya); he was the editor-in-chief of the publication at the time. This marked the first time that poetry had been published in the literary supplement of a Chinese-language newspaper in Thailand. As Zeng Xin 曾心 describes, many writers felt inspired and challenged at the same time by the call and started to write small poems:

> The 'cover poem' (*kan tou shi* 刊頭詩) in the supplement is like a pair of beautiful eyes. It only takes up the space of a piece of dried bean curd, but it makes the whole supplement's spirit rise. The first small poem was like a star in the sky, an oriole in the forest, a coral in the sea. It was so refreshing that it attracted many poets and inspired them to write poems, leading to a craze for reading and writing small poems. (Zeng Xin 2010, 2)[4]

Then, in 2006 there was a small group of poets within the community of Sinophone writers in Thailand, who founded the *Xiaoshi mofang* 小詩磨坊 (Little Poetry Mill), including Zeng Xin[5] and Lin Huanzhang. Since then, small

---

3 For more information on Lin Huanzhang and a comparison between his poems and those of Zeng Xin, see Ehrenwirth (2018, 29–39).

4 This quote is from an interview with Zeng Xin conducted by Ji Hongfang 計紅芳. It was originally published in the journal *Huawen wenxue* 華文文學 (*Sinophone Literature*) in June 2010. I only have a private transcript provided by Zeng Xin; the page numbers included here refer to that copy. Zeng Xin (2006, 167) also wrote a small poem entitled "Cover Poem" (*Kan tou shi*) in 2003, in which he describes the nourishing power of these poems as "a few drops of pureness" (*jidi qingchun* 幾滴清醇, l. 3) for the "craving heart" (*jike de xintian* 飢渴的心田, l. 6).

5 Zeng Xin is one of the most prolific Sinophone poets in Thailand. He was born in 1938 in Bangkok; his ancestors came from Puning in Guangdong Province. He grew up in Bangkok and attended a Thai school without learning any Chinese; since his parents did not speak Cantonese/Teochew with him at home, he learned Mandarin on his own. In 1956 he went to China to attend a school for Overseas Chinese in Shantou (Guangdong). In 1962 he was admitted to study at the Institute for Chinese at Xiamen University. It was then that he

SAYING MORE BY WRITING LESS

poetry has changed and developed, as well as becoming an established form of Sinophone poetry.[6]

By the time that small poetry began to spread within the Sinophone writing community in Thailand, Sinophone literature in Thailand (Sino-Thai Lit) had already undergone several phases with varying success. While Chinese immigration to Thailand, or Siam as it was called then, can be traced back to the thirteenth century, Sino-Thai Lit only began to develop in the twentieth century. Inspired by the May Fourth Movement and the New Culture Movement, intellectuals within the community of Overseas Chinese in Thailand started writing literature. This can be seen as the origin of Sino-Thai Lit, which in its early days was very much oriented towards China. It was only in the 1980s that Sino-Thai Lit began to become independent from the mainland. Nonetheless, Sino-Thai Lit is still strongly influenced by contemporary literary trends, which often find their way via China to the Sinophone writing community in Thailand (*Taiguo huawen wenxue zuojia xiehui* 泰國華文文學作家協會).[7] In this chapter, I want to focus on selected small poems by Sinophone poets in Thailand to show how this poetry stimulated the Sinophone writing community across borders. What unites these writers is not just language, but language reduced to a minimum.

1 Modernity's Brevity

While small poems are central to modernist poetry in the West (Montgomery 2020, 1), small poetry, just like flash fiction, has only gained attention in the twenty-first century among the Sinophone Thai writing community. While literary modernism has its origin in the late nineteenth century in the West, Chinese modern literature (*xiandai wenxue* 現代文學)[8] developed under

---

developed an interest in writing. Upon his return to Thailand in the 1980s, he started working in the family business; he continued writing in the Sinitic script in his free time.

6 *Xin shiji dongnanya huawen xiaoshi jingxuan* 新世紀東南亞華文小詩精選 (Anthology of Sinophone Small Poetry from Southeast Asia from the New Century) edited by Zhu Wenbin 朱文斌 and Zeng Xin 曾心, which was published in 2018 by Zhejiang Gongshang University Press in Hangzhou is one example that small poetry is spreading among Sinophone authors in Southeast Asia.

7 The *Taiguo huawen wenxue zuojia xiehui* (Society of Sinophone Writers in Thailand) was established in 1986 under Fang Siruo. It has currently approx. 100 to 120 members, of which 20 to 25 are active writers who publish regularly in the Society's journal and on their website respectively. See thaisinoliterature.com.

8 In historiography, the term *xiandai* is often used to refer to the period between 1911 and 1949, thereby putting it between *jindai* 近代 (the period from the Opium Wars until the May Fourth Movement, 1840–1911) and *dangdai* 當代 (the time from the founding of the People's

Hu Shi 胡適 and Zhou Zuoren 周作人 in the 1910s with the New Culture Movement. Influenced by ideas from the West, they not only argued for substituting Classical Chinese (*wenyan* 文言) with vernacular (*baihua* 白話), but also demanded a turn from traditional to contemporary literature, therefore laying the groundwork for New Poetry (*xinshi* 新詩). Hu Shi started a literary revolution because he believed that Chinese literature needed to evolve, self-improve and look to the West for inspiration. Small poems, as a new genre of Chinese poetry, began to develop from the early 1920s onwards. Bing Xin and Zhou Zuoren were among the most famous and prolific writers of small poetry.[9] It was also around this time that the first small poems found their way to the Sinophone writers in Thailand and some authors, such as Lin Dieyi 林蝶衣 (1907–2004), began to sporadically write small poems. In 1933 he published the first Sinophone New Poetry collection *Pomeng ji* 破夢集 (Broken Dreams). However, overall, small poetry did not gain much attention at that time.

Despite the efforts of some famous Chinese poets, small poetry also did not gain any ground in China in the early twentieth century, and it was only in the 1980s that it experienced a revival. In particular, in Chongqing small poetry or "miniature poetry" (*weixing shi* 微型詩) became very popular with Wan Longsheng 萬龍生, one of its most famous proponents. It was through Lin Huanzhang's initiative in the early 2000s to write small poems in six lines or less that small poetry also found its way into the community of Sinophone poets in Thailand. The Little Poetry Mill was established in 2006 by Zeng Xin and Lin Huanzhang and became the driving force for Sinophone small poetry in Thailand.[10] Following its establishment, the group grew in its number of members, and it has also published a poetry collection every year ever since. They have been reviewed by writers and critics from the PRC and Taiwan, including Luo Di 落蒂, Gu Yuanqing 古遠清, Long Bide 龍彼德 and Ji Hongfang. Zeng Xin calls this "a surprising anomaly" (*lingrenjingxi de yichangxianxiang* 令人

Republic in 1949). However, in other regions, such as Hong Kong, *jindai* and *xiandai* are also often used to refer to the entire period from 1911 onwards.

9   Bing Xin's 冰心 poetry collection *Fanxing* 繁星 (A Maze of Stars and Spring Water) was written between 1919 and 1921. The poems were originally published in the newspaper *Chenbao* 晨報 (Morning Post).

10   Ling Nanren 嶺南人, Bo Fu 博夫, Jin Shi 今石, Yang Ling 楊玲, Ku Jue 苦覺 and Lan Yan 藍焰 (Mo Fan 莫凡) were among the first members of the Little Poetry Mill. They also called themselves the "7 + 1" because they comprised seven members from Thailand and one (Lin Huanzhang) from Taiwan. They thought of themselves as "The Eight Immortals crossing the sea, each showing his own special talent" (Zeng Xin 2010). The group has grown from the initial eight members to 13 members today (Jing Ying 晶瑩, Wen Xiaoyun 溫小雲, Dan Dan 澹澹, Fan Jun 范軍 and Yang Zhuo 楊楝 joining them later).

驚喜的異常現象) in Sino-Thai Lit (Zeng Xin 2010), referring to the long-lasting popularity and abundance of small poetry in Thailand.

Initially, small poetry became famous in Thailand because poets were eager to accept the challenge of expressing themselves in less than six lines. Yet Zeng Xin confessed that he had doubts about small poetry at the start: "Will this little piece of dried tofu [small poem] allow the imaginative wings of poetry to fly?" he wrote in a short essay called *Xiaoshi lushang de hui mou* 小詩路上的回眸 (Looking Back on the Path of Small Poetry).[11] Nevertheless, he started writing small poems, in part because at the time he was still working and had little time to write.[12] It was therefore not only the challenge that drew poets to write small poems, but also their busy lifestyles, which finds expression in the brevity of the poems. Now, it has become more than that, however; small poetry has gained status within Sinophone literature. In the last couple of years, several Sinophone writing communities in Southeast Asia, such as in Malaysia, Singapore and Indonesia, have established similar poetry groups following Lin Huanzhang's model, all called "Little Poetry Mill."

Sima Gong 司馬攻[13] (2008, 88) describes the "birth" of small poetry in his poem "Small Poem," which consists of just 18 characters (including the title):[14]

小詩

從詩的家族
跳出來

只有背叛
纔有出路

---

11   I only have a personal copy of the essay, which Zeng Xin sent to me in an email (Zeng Xin, email to author, September 2, 2022).

12   Ibid.

13   Sima Gong is probably the most famous Sinophone writer in Thailand. He was not only the president of the Society for Sinophone Writers in Thailand for 20 years (1990–2010), but he also introduced the genre of flash fiction to the Sinophone writers' community in Thailand. Sima Gong was born in 1933 in Bangkok; his ancestors came from Chaoyang (today's Chaonan) in Shantou, Guangdong Province. Due to his family's strong connections to China, he was sent to Shantou when he was only six years old to attend school and live with relatives. It was only when he was 20 years old that he returned to Thailand. Since it was not possible to make a living from writing, he stopped and turned to the family business. In the 1980s he picked up writing again.

14   If not stated otherwise, all the translations are mine.

Small Poem

From the family of poems
It jumps out

Treason
Is the only way out

The implicit lyrical "I" on the one hand emphasizes that small poetry is part of poetry as a whole but also highlights, on the other, that small poems "betray" the genre of poetry by being so short. With this poem, Sima Gong draws attention to the writing process; by using the pattern *zhiyou ... caiyou ...* (lit. only if ...) in the second stanza, he not only creates a parallelism, but also emphasizes that freedom (i.e. that of small poems) comes with a price (i.e. treason). However, the poem also highlights the importance of freedom, especially when it comes to creative expression.

Poetry is a way for the authors to understand their existence and experiences, therefore they need to be free to express themselves. In their poems they often combine what they consider to be the most essential parts of their identities, which are their origin (China), their home (Thailand) and their "occupation"[15] (writing). The Sinophone poets use small poems to reflect on writing itself, as well as their own identity as writers. As well as the aforementioned poem, Sima Gong wrote a series of small poems in which he discusses various literary genres, such as flash fiction, essays and poetry. In "Xin shi" 新詩 (New Poem) (2008, 86), the implicit lyrical "I" compares new poetry to a white cloud floating in the heart (*yi tong baiyun / zai xin zhong piaoguo*, l. 1–2).

新詩

一朵白雲
在心中飄過
空靈 飄逸
志有所託
情有所寄

---

15 I put "occupation" in quotation marks here since most of the writers are not professional authors and do not earn a living with their literature. Before turning to writing completely, many of them worked as businessmen, such as Sima Gong and Zeng Xin, and wrote only as a hobby, which they can pursue in their free time. Since many of the authors are already very advanced in age and have retired from their daily jobs, they can now solely focus on writing and it has therefore become their "occupation" in the sense that it is not just a pastime anymore.

New poem

A white cloud
Floating in the heart
Free and natural   elegant
The aspirations have support
The emotions have a medium

He breaks away from the pattern in the middle of the poem by adding a line that consists of two adjectives (*kongling piaoyi*, l. 3), which are separated by a space in between. The break in the pattern is therefore not only made visible in the content but also in the poem's structure. The last two lines are connected by their parallelism, while the last line draws attention to the poem itself – it is the medium, which enables the poet to convey their feelings and emotions. With this poem, Sima Gong hints at the idea of Hu Shi, the pioneer for new poetry, that new poetry should be written in free verse, thereby freeing itself from the shackles of traditional poetry. Sima Gong's poem connects this freedom with naturalness and elegance (l. 3), which is also expressed in the form of the poem by combining the parallelism of the last two lines with the free form of the first two lines. Once again, the main idea is "freedom," which was also expressed in his poem "Small Poem." These poems could therefore also be read as allegories for writing poetry: a poet needs to be free, not restrained by language or formal aspects. The fact that the poet is "free to talk" is also expressed in Zeng Xin's poem "Xiaoshi mofang ting" 小詩磨坊亭 (The Little Poetry Mill's Pavilion) (2011, 148):

小詩磨坊亭

風兒到這裏
駐了腳
醉——詩人的自由談

鳥兒到這兒
停了歌唱
驚——磨坊裏磨出的詩

The Little Poetry Mill's Pavilion

The wind comes here
It stays for a while
Drunkenness – the poets' free talk

The birds come here
They stop singing
Surprise – the poems ground in the mill

The poem consists of two parallel stanzas in which the implicit lyrical "I" describes the symbiosis of nature and poetry creation. By putting the words "drunkenness" (*zui*, l. 3) and "surprise" (*jing*, l. 6) at the start of the line and at the end of the stanzas, and adding a dash, the two words are not only highlighted by their position, but also by the pause that follows. The two lines can be read as inversions, therefore suggesting that drunkenness is the effect of the poets' free talk, while surprise is the result of the poems that come out of the mill.

Nature in the form of the wind and the birds – both symbols of freedom – comes to linger at the pavilion to witness the creation of the poems. Poetry is thereby intertwined with nature as well as being the subject of that very poem. The pavilion, which is mentioned in the title, is the place where the poets meet regularly. It stands in Zeng Xin's garden next to a mango tree and amidst several bonsai. Amidst the bustle of Bangkok, it is a source of peace and quietness. Zeng Xin uses poetic language to portray reality, a reality that inspires him to write poems.

With metapoetry like this, the writers openly discuss the question of how poems are composed, thereby remind the readers of the constructedness of poetry and "self-consciously and systematically draw [...] attention to its status as an artefact" (Waugh [1984] 2003, 2). Not only can the poems as a whole be seen as artifacts, but the language itself is also an artifact: language is formed by humans, but the language they use also hints at the speaker's cultural background. By using the Sinitic script instead of their mother tongue Thai, the authors point to China and the main culture they identify with.[16] This shows that they – in their identity as writers – see themselves as more rooted in Chinese cultures than Thai, although in some cases Chinese/Mandarin is not their mother tongue.

---

16   I want to highlight here that although the Chinese government likes to convey the image of one homogeneous culture with one unifying language, i.e. Chinese, there are different languages, topolects and cultures in China. As Shu-mei Shih has pointed out: "the Chinese culture mainly refers to the culture of the Han" (2003, 26). Wherever possible, I will therefore use the plural form, also because the writers themselves identify more as being from a specific region in China, e.g. the Chaoshan area, rather than being Chinese in general. In their short stories and flash fiction in particular they express their feeling of belonging to Chaoshan by including characters who speak the Chaozhou topolect or references to special Chaozhou traditions.

2 Chinese Writing as Practice

Chinese[17] became the "writing language" of Sinophone authors in Thailand because most of the authors started writing literature while they lived in China, where they were also introduced to literary works that are traditionally seen as part of the Chinese canon, such as *Honglou meng* 紅樓夢 (The Dream of the Red Chamber) and *Shuihu zhuan* 水滸傳 (Water Margins). Therefore, they feel a stronger literary connection to the Chinese writing culture. However, writing in the Sinitic script also means practicing Chinese. Since Thai is the language they use in an everyday context, Chinese is reserved for writing and communicating with their Sinophone peers. Using the Sinitic script is therefore practice and guarantees that they neither forget their Chinese nor their origin.

The authors reflect their feeling of belonging to China not only by using the Sinitic script but also by including imagery associated with classical Chinese poetry, such as the image of the moon, the longing for home or roots, which often refers to China, or references to Chinese mythology or tradition. In traditional Chinese poetry, such as in the poems of Li Bai 李白 or Su Shi 蘇軾, the moon is usually associated with loneliness and longing for friends and relatives. The moon becomes a medium to convey the lyrical "I"'s feelings: "Chinese poems focus on the moon's ability to express the feelings of longing across space. Regardless of how far away a friend or relative is from the poet, poets share the same moon with them" (Ding Shi and Jing An 2021, 577).

品茗

月下品茗
杯子圓圓如月
滑落
跌碎
濃濃故鄉情

Sipping tea

Sipping tea under the moon
The cup round like the moon

---

17   I am using the term Chinese here because although the writers sometimes include words and expressions from Teochew (*Chaozhou hua* 潮州話) or Cantonese, they mainly write in Mandarin. However, I want to emphasize the previously stated fact that there is indeed not one Chinese language.

Slips
Falls and breaks
A strong hometown feeling

This poem by Ma Fan[18] (2018, 103) starts in Chinese with the moon (*yue*) at the beginning of the first line, and the second line ends with it; the moon elegantly embraces the two lines and unites them. Not only does the implicit lyrical "I" enjoy their tea under the moon, but with the comparison in the second stanza, the lyrical "I" themself also feels very close to the moon by holding the "moon-like" cup. The breaking of the cup can be compared to the destruction of the moon, which evokes a longing for home in the implicit lyrical "I". Without the moon, the implicit lyrical "I" has no means of conveying their feelings to their friends and family.

Besides the moon, drinking tea is also a metaphor for thinking about home. Although it is not mentioned what kind of tea the lyrical "I" is enjoying, drinking tea, or rather drinking Gongfu-tea (*gongfu cha* 功夫茶), is a recurring theme in the oeuvre of Sinophone writers in Thailand.[19] The breaking of the cup in Ma Fan's poem not only leads to the moon being damaged, but also to the loss of the tea. The implicit lyrical "I" therefore suffers a triple sensory loss: deprived of visual contact (cup/moon) with the hometown as well as connection via taste and smell (tea).

Just like the lyrical "I" in Ma Fan's poem, the implicit lyrical "I" in Sima Gong's poem "Pin yue" 品月 (Tasting the moon) (2008, 8) is also "sipping or tasting tea" (*pinming* 品茗), when the moonlight of his hometown (suddenly) "flies into the teapot" (*guxiang de yueguang* / *feiru hu zhong* 故鄉的月光 / 飛入壺中, l. 2–3). In the second stanza, the lyrical "I" describes the tea as "sour sweet bitter spicy" (*suan tian ku la* 酸甜苦辣) Gongfu tea (l. 6). Tea is therefore strongly connected to China, while drinking tea is a metaphor for longing for the land of their ancestors. Zeng Xin compares the tea in his poem "Cha ye" 茶葉 (Tea Leaves), which is poured out of a Zisha teapot[20] with "the hometown's

---

18   Ma Fan (also Ma Qingquan 馬清泉) was born in 1934 in Bangkok. His ancestors came from Chaoyang in Guangdong province.

19   For the meaning of Gongfu tea, see Victor H. Mair 2011. For a discussion of Gongfu tea in the works of Sima Gong and Zeng Xin, see Ehrenwirth (2017, 204–207).

20   *Zisha* 紫砂 (literally "violet sand") is the term for brown or red stoneware, often unglazed, from Yixing in Jiangsu Province. As the clay from this area often has a violet color, it is referred to as "zisha." Zisha pottery was very famous, especially during the late Ming Dynasty. Many teapots were engraved with poems, probably because at that time several literati lived in Jiangsu Province. See Zhan and Du (1982).

landscape / the tea ceremony of our ancestors" (*jiaxiang de shanshui* / *zubei de chadao* 家鄉的山水 / 祖輩的茶道, l. 5–6).

Tea is not only associated with a longing for the "hometown" (*guxiang* 故鄉) or "home" (*jiaxiang* 家鄉), i.e. China, but also with literary productivity. The explicit lyrical "I" in Zeng Xin's poem "Yu zhong pinming" 雨中品茗 (Sipping Tea in the Rain) "tastes" the small poems that come out of the spout (l. 5) (2011, 150). This is expressed even more clearly in Yang Ling's[21] poem (2018, 114–115), in which the two parallel lines in the first stanza directly compare the moonlight to poems:

月光

蘸月光寫詩
月光淡淡　詩也淡淡
月光朦朧　詩也朦朧

月光如水
詩如水上的月光

Moonlight

Writing poetry dipped in moonlight
The moonlight is dim　the poem is also dim
The moonlight is hazy　the poem is also hazy

Moonlight is like water
Poems are like the moonlight on the water

With the simile in the second stanza, the implicit lyrical "I" conveys that the moonlight is the essence (water) and poetry is what makes this water beautiful by being reflected on its surface. By adding the character *zhan* 蘸 (lit. to dip in) in the first line and breaking the four-character pattern (*zhan yueguang xieshi*), emphasis is placed on this first character. The dependency between the poems and the moonlight is established here; they are two components that complement each other, like a brush and ink – the brush needs to be dipped in

---

21　Yang Ling was born in Bangkok. She is the daughter of the Sinophone poet Lao Yang 老羊. Inspired by her father, she started to write in the 1990s and joined the Society of Sinophone Writers in Thailand in 1996. She is also a member of the Little Poetry Mill.

ink to be able to write. The poet uses the moonlight like water (as ink) to write a poem about moonlight.

The poems combine metafiction with a reference to traditional Chinese imagery and nature, while nature serves as the source of inspiration. The writers blur the line between fiction and reality, not only to hint at the poem's creation process, but also to make sense of themselves as writers. By writing about what they do, they can better understand why they do it and what it means to them. As a proponent of small poetry, in poems such as "Shimo feizhuan" 石墨飛轉 (The Millstone Spins Rapidly), Zeng Xin (2011, 148) also refers to the Little Poetry Mill to illustrate the members' importance to the spread of small poetry. They – "the eight volunteers" (*bawei zhiyuanzhe* 八位志願者, l. 1) – create small poems "night and day" (*yeyijiri* 夜以繼日, l. 3). Words such as "spring breeze" (*chunfeng* 春風, l. 4) and "spring" (*chuntian* 春天, l. 6), which frame the second stanza, emphasize once again the involvement of nature in the creation process. The poets are "famous masters" (*mingshi* 名師, l. 4) to them and the creators of "a spring of small poems" (*xiaoshi de chuntian* 小詩的春天, l. 6).

Anne Waldman and Laura Wright (2014, 1–2) describe "language as agent of, and as changed by, globalization" in the introduction to their anthology of transcultural poetics. The authors use the Sinitic script, not only because it enables them to speak to a larger audience since Chinese, including all its associated languages and varieties, is still the most spoken language worldwide, but also because it enables them to show their support for Chinese and the Chinese literary tradition.

3 Bicultural Poets, Transcultural Poetics

"Narrative psychology assumes that individual identity formation is based on a sense of unity and sameness over time. It is exactly this (illusionary and always fluctuating) sense of sameness that is sustained by narratives" (Neumann et al. 2008, 6). Although poems, especially small poems, usually do not count as narratives (excluding narrative poems), through the repetition within the poems and the recurring isotopy of nature in contemporary Sinophone poetry in Thailand, "a sense of unity and sameness" is created for the readers, as well as for the writers. By writing small poems, through the genre they mirror their impression that while Sinophone poetry in Thailand – and they as proponents of such poetry – might be small compared to, for instance, Chinese poetry in China and Chinese poets, by sticking to their roots – which lie in their biculturality – they can contribute to the consolidation of Sinophone poetry in Thailand as an independent literary branch.

SAYING MORE BY WRITING LESS

It is only through and in literature that the authors can express their selves, because in the poems the three parts of the writers' identities can come together. By including Thailand in their poetry, they bridge the gap between the cultures they feel attached to, while introducing and portraying their homeland to their readers. Poems such as Zeng Xin's "Meinanhe" 湄南河 (Chao Phraya River) (2006, 8) and "Zhaopian" 照片 (Photo) (2006, 10) concentrate on one of the two main rivers that flow through Thailand. The Chao Phraya is not only an important traffic artery, but through its many channels it also provides water for rice paddies across the country. The Chao Phraya is more than just key to the country's logistics and supply; it also plays a "vital role [...] in Thai consciousness" (van Beek 1995, xiii). The implicit lyrical I in the poem "Chao Phraya River" calls it "a ceaseless pulse of the nation" (*yi tiao buxi de guomai* 一條不息的國脉, l. 4), which forms the characters of its inhabitants (l. 5). While in the first stanza everything is calm and relaxed, expressed by the adverb "leisurely" (*youyou de* 悠悠的, l.), the second stanza begins with the word "ceaseless" (*buxi de* 不息的, l. 4), indicating a kind of restlessness, since the verb *xi* in Chinese also means "to rest." The two stanzas are diametrically opposed, not only with regard to content, but also in form. The first stanza consists of three lines with eight characters in total: the two adverbs in lines one and two describe the southward flow of the river (l. 3). The second stanza consists of just two lines with 17 characters in total, which, when read together, form a whole sentence. The flow of the water described in the first stanza becomes the flow of the blood, which leads to a pulse (a rhythmic expansion of an artery when the blood is ejected by the heart) and the personification of the river. The Chao Phraya turns into an artisan "casting the characters of Buddha's sons and daughters" (*rongzhu zhe foguo ernü de xingge* 鎔鑄著佛國兒女的性格, l. 5).

In his poem "Ye Mangu" 夜曼谷 (Nightly Bangkok) Ling Nanren 嶺南人[22] elegantly combines nature with the vibrant city of Bangkok. The poem consists of three stanzas with two lines each. In the first stanza a very calm atmosphere is portrayed by the simile in the second line and by turning the rush-hour traffic into images of nature. It is only in line four that the pace suddenly increases, as people start rushing (*congcong ganfu* 匆匆趕赴) to their destinations. It is with the turn to night that the city changes: sex work and partying are implied by the implicit lyrical "I" in the third stanza, in which the people get lost. By putting "night" (*ye* 夜, l. 6) at the start of the last line and separating it with a comma afterwards, it is highlighted that this only happens at night, and it is implied that Bangkok during the day is very different.

---

22   Ling Nanren (also Fu Jizhong 符績忠) was born in 1932 in Hainan. During the 1950s he lived in Hong Kong, before moving to Thailand in the 1960s.

夜曼谷

暮色從歸鳥翅膀滑落
車如流水，把路流成燈的河

多少人在回家的路上
多少人匆匆趕赴燈紅酒綠

霓紅燈閃爍吧女的媚眼
夜，醉倒在玫瑰紅的酒窩裏

《詩外》曼谷是不夜城，是溫柔鄉，燈紅酒綠，酒不醉人人自醉。

Nightly Bangkok

Twilight slides from the wings of returning birds
Cars flow like water, turning the road into a river of lights

How many people are on their way home
How many people are rushing to feasting and revelry

The bewitching eyes of bar girls glimmering like neon lights
Night, drunken in the rose-red dimples

<Note> Bangkok is a city that never sleeps, a land of warmth and tenderness, with red lanterns and green wine [i.e. feasting and revelry], where liquor doesn't make one drunk, yet one gets oneself drunk. (Ling 2016, 16)

In the note to the poem, Ling Nanren calls Bangkok "a land of warmth and tenderness" (*wenrouxiang*), suggesting that men can find solace in feminine charms. He describes Bangkok as "a city that never sleeps," where people go out at night to have fun. In the poem and in his note, he euphemistically hints at sex work and alcohol abuse through phrases such as "red lanterns and green wine" (*denghong jiulü*), "land of warmth and tenderness" (*wenrouxiang*) and "where liquor doesn't make one drunk, yet one gets oneself drunk" (*jiubuzuiren renzizui*). With this, he confirms Bangkok's image as a metropolis with a vivid nightlife, where sex work retains a significant presence.

By writing a small poem about Bangkok's nightlife in which the people's urge for a life of debauchery is expressed, the author further draws attention to the feeling of ephemerality. By using words such as "slide" (*hualuo*, l. 1), "flow" (*liu*, l. 2), "river" (*he*, l. 2) and "rush" (*ganfu*, l. 4), which suggest continuous and uninterrupted movement, he hints at the fleetingness of life. When the pace is suddenly hastened in the second stanza by adding the adjective "hurried" (*congcong*, l. 4) to the verb "to rush" (*ganfu*, l. 4) the urgency with which people live their lives is further highlighted.

As a bicultural poet, Ling Nanren creates a transcultural poem by writing about Bangkok (which he regards as his home) for a Sinophone reader, including idioms – such as "red lanterns and green wine" – his intended readership is most likely familiar with. He is an example of a Sinophone poet in Thailand whose mother tongue is indeed not Thai but Chinese, but since he has lived most of his life in Thailand, he considers himself to be Thai rather than Chinese. In the poem, he creates a kind of intimacy with the readers to acquaint them with the place he regards as home, a country and culture that might be unfamiliar to the readership. By comparing the rush-hour traffic with a river and personifying the twilight, which slides from the birds' wings in the first stanza, he slowly introduces the setting and creates a candy-coated picture of Bangkok's congested roads. In the third stanza, he elegantly describes the red-light district not by mentioning the actual word (*hongdengqu*) but rather by integrating the color red (*hong*) twice into the poem (*denghong jiulü*, l. 4; *meiguihong*, l. 6). The anaphora in the second stanza draws particular attention to the people who live in Bangkok, all of them out on the street and on their way somewhere, attesting to the fact that this city and its inhabitants seem to never sleep.

With their poems, the poets foster transcultural intersections and demonstrate what Brian Bernards has called a "Sino-Thai biculturalism," which he sees as "the formation of two creolized (rather than impenetrable) spheres" (2015, 167).[23] The different generations of writers mirror the development of Sinophone literature in Thailand in their writing: from more dependent on China to more independent. The establishment of the Little Poetry Mill in 2006 marked the beginning of a new high for Sinophone poetry. The poets do not feel like they are in between two countries or cultures; they rather see themselves and their literature as a combination of the two.

---

23   I want to highlight that Bernards is referring here to Sino-Thai narratives of the Cold War
       in particular, but I argue that this very biculturalism is reflected in contemporary small
       poems.

4   Conclusion

> [A]ctually identities are about questions of using the resources of history, language and culture in the process of becoming rather than being: not 'who we are' or 'where we came from', so much as what we might become, how we have been represented and how that bears on how we might represent ourselves. Identities are therefore constituted within, not outside representation. (Hall [1996] 2010, 4)

As Stuart Hall has pointed out, identity is not something "fixed and given," but a thing that is always changing. To introduce and express their Thai identity, the Sinophone authors in Thailand often depict Thailand, or rather Bangkok, in their poems. The isotopy of nature is what unites many of the poems. Not only do nature metaphors help to describe something more euphemistically, but they also create a sense of unity. Every reader, no matter where they are, can relate to natural things such as the moon, rivers, and birds, but by including traditional Chinese imagery, such as the moon, the poets also show their alliance with traditional Chinese poetry. Yet, nature in its very essence is not static but always in flux, which is also expressed in the poems and mirrors the identities of their very creators, the poets themselves. By writing small poems in the Sinitic script about China, Thailand and the writing process, they not only bridge the gap between cultures but also show how for them these three aspects depend on one another.

At the same time, by fostering the establishment of the Little Poetry Mill among Sinophone poets in other countries, they contribute to the formation of transcultural alliances and encourage the spread of transcultural poetics. On the one hand, by using the Sinitic script they draw attention to China, where different languages, topolects and cultures exist alongside each other, although the PRC's cultural politics likes to convey the image of one homogeneous culture with a single unifying language: Chinese. On the other hand, by writing about Thailand, the place they speak from, they also highlight that Chinese is not only used within China but in a wider sphere outside and that these poems written "from the outside" can actually contribute to a more diversified Sinophone small poetry.

Whether Chinese is their mother tongue or not, in their identity as writers they feel more connected to and comfortable with the Sinitic script. However, they also use this "other tongue," which in most cases is not their mother tongue, and cling to their descent, because they consider themselves to be in a position to transcend cultural borders. As Sinophone poets and as advocates for the establishment of the Little Poetry Mill across the world, they want to highlight the unique position of bicultural writers, who are not only able to speak to different (cultural and linguistic) audiences, but who can also speak about cultural and linguistic differences. They not only determine the direction of the conversation (to whom they speak) but also the content (what they speak about). Therefore, they do not experience their situation as in-between, but rather as able to bridge gaps between China and Thailand.

Works Cited

Bernards, Brian. 2015. *Writing the South Seas: Imagining the Nanyang in Chinese and Southeast Asian Postcolonial Literature*. Seattle: University of Washington Press.

Ding, Shi and Jing An. 2021. "A Comparative Study on Moon Imagery in Chinese and Western Classical Poetry." *Advances in Social Science, Education and Humanities Research* 615: 576–582.

Ehrenwirth, Rebecca. 2017. *Zeitgenössische Sinophone Literatur in Thailand* [Contemporary Sinophone Literature in Thailand]. Wiesbaden: Harrassowitz.

Ehrenwirth, Rebecca. 2018. "The Depiction of Countries in T(h)ai-Sinophone Literature: A Comparison of Two Writers from Thailand and Taiwan." In *Peoples and Cultures in Motion: Environment, Space and the Humanities*, edited by Christian Soffel and Ralf Hertel. Taipei: Chengda University Press, 29–39.

Ehrenwirth, Rebecca. 2023. "Journey to a Foreign Land: Imagining Migration in Sinophone Literature from Thailand." In *Words and Visions around/about Chinese Transnational Mobilities*, edited by Valentina Pedone and Miriam Castorina. Firenze: Firenze University Press, 141–157.

Hall, Stuart and Paul du Gay, eds. [1996] 2010. *Questions of Cultural Identity*. London: Sage.

Ling, Nanren 嶺南人. 2016. "Ye Mangu" 夜曼谷 [Nightly Bangkok]. In *Xiaoshi Mofang xiaoshi dianping* 小詩磨坊小詩點評 [Comments on Small Poems by the Little Poetry Mill], edited by Zhao Zhen. Bangkok: Liuzhong daxue chubanshe, 16.

Ma Fan. 2018. "Pinming" 品茗 [Sipping Tea]. In *Xin shiji dongnanya huawen xiaoshi jingxuan* 新世紀東南亞華文小詩精選 [Anthology of Sinophone Small Poetry from Southeast Asia], edited by Zhu Wenbin and Zeng Xin. Hangzhou: Zhejiang Gongshang University Press, 103.

Montgomery, Will. 2020. *Short Form American Poetry: The Modernist Tradition*. Edinburgh: Edinburgh University Press.

Neumann, Birgit, Ansgar Nünning and Bo Pettersson, eds. 2008. *Narrative and Identity: Theoretical Approaches and Critical Analysis*. Trier: WVT.

Shih, Shu-mei, Chien-hsin Tsai, and Brian Bernards, eds. 2013. *Sinophone Studies: A Critical Reader*. New York: Columbia University Press.

Sima, Gong 司馬攻. 2008. *Ting yue* 聽月 [Listening to the Moon]. Bangkok: Taihua wenxue chubanshe.

Van Beek, Steve. 1995. *The Chao Phraya River in Transition*. Kuala Lumpur: Oxford University Press.

Waldman, Anne and Laura Wright, eds. 2014. *Cross Worlds: Transcultural Poetics*. Minneapolis: Coffee House Press.

Waugh, Patricia. [1984] 2003. *Metafiction: The Theory and Practice of Self-Conscious Fiction*. London: Routledge.

Yang, Ling. 2018. "Yueguang" 月光 [Moonlight]. In *Xin shiji dongnanya huawen xiaoshi jingxuan* 新世紀東南亞華文小詩精選 [Anthology of Sinophone Small Poetry from Southeast Asia], edited by Zhu Wenbin 朱文斌 and Zeng Xin 曾心. Hangzhou: Zhejiang Gongshang University Press, 114–15.

Zeng, Xin 曾心. 2006. *Liang ting* 涼亭 [Pavilion]. Bangkok: Liuzhong daxue chubanshe.

Zeng, Xin 曾心. 2011. *Zeng Xin zixuan ji: Xiaoshi sanbai shou* 曾心自選集：小詩三百首 [300 Small Poems by Zeng Xin]. Macao: The Milky Way Publishing Co.

Zhan, Xunhua 詹勳華 and Du Jiexiang 杜潔祥, eds. 1982. *Yixing taoqi tupu* 宜興陶器圖譜 [A Catalogue of Yixing Pottery]. Taipei: Nantian.

Zhu, Wenbin 朱文斌 and Zeng Xin 曾心, eds. 2018. *Xin shiji dongnanya huawen xiaoshi jingxuan* 新世紀東南亞華文小詩精選 [Anthology of Sinophone Small Poetry from Southeast Asia]. Hangzhou: Zhejiang Gongshang University Press.

CHAPTER 8

Poetry in Motion

Transnational Sinophone Poets across Italy and China

Valentina Pedone
University of Florence

1 Introduction

Following the establishment of the Marco Polo program in 2005 and the Turandot Program in 2009, a massive number of Chinese exchange students arrived at Italian universities. Considering the special interest in the arts of this specific flow of students, it is safe to assume that today the largest contribution to the local cultural landscape by the Chinese residing in Italy is constituted by the art produced by these students, who currently arrive in Italy with the specific goal of pursuing their practice by displaying their works in galleries and sometimes even by creating new spaces or groups aimed at promoting their art on Italian soil.[1]

Alongside these lively yet recent visual endeavors, the Chinese and their descendants in Italy have also engaged in written production by creating a literary repertoire that, despite not being as weighty as that left in the arts, still boasts a rather long and stable history. With talented writers across genres and a growing number of works by authors of Chinese origin living in Italy, there is merit for more studies that track not only the literary accomplishments of this new generation, but also the important facets of contemporary Sino-Italian mobility. In this chapter, I adopt a Cultural Studies angle to analyze poetry in particular, looking closely at the lyrical production and language use of the Chinese and their descendants in Italy. By focusing on linguistic choices as part of a larger poetics that includes issues relating to tradition, identity, and exchange, we can see how these younger poets maneuver deftly in an evolving cultural landscape.

A very articulated network of diverse mobilities connects China to Italy. As will be shown in detail in the following pages, various kinds of mobility define very different positionalities and attitudes toward society for Chinese

---

1 It is the case for instance of the art collective WUXU, or the Zhong Art International group for Chinese art promotion, TRAT ART gallery in Rome, or HOAA gallery in Milan.

© VALENTINA PEDONE, 2024 | DOI:10.1163/9789004711600_010

individuals who settle in Italy. These circumstances clearly have an important impact in terms of what language these people choose for their creative writing, whom they choose to address, and for what purpose. While in some respects Chinese voices are marginalized by the mainstream cultural establishment, if not silenced and interpreted as subaltern (in the meaning that Spivak [1988] attributed to the term), at the same time the cultural contact zones created within the China-Italy mobility network are also exposed to other dynamics, most of which are embodied by a strongly essentialist cultural discourse elaborated within the global Sinosphere.

By focusing on the cultural materials that are produced within China-Italy mobility, I adopt a *New Mobility Studies* lens (Sheller and Urry 2006); in particular, I place its emphasis on the intersection of Mobility Studies and the humanities as developed by Merriman and Pearce (2017) to tackle all these different aspects. In fact, while a traditional post-colonial perspective can very well guide a partial analysis of the textual materials produced by the Chinese in Italy, it would tend to focus on the power imbalance between Chinese lower-income labor workers and the host society, thus overlooking the specificities of the social, political, and cultural dynamics of today's China and its influence on the overseas Sinophone communities. Considering the cultural production of *all* components of China-Italy mobility, however, permits the localization of Sino-Italian cultural discourse within the larger sphere of the dominant culture. As we will see, poetry becomes a creative practice to negotiate space and affirm identity.

Elsewhere I have defined Sino-Italian literature as the literary production of Chinese people or their descendants who reside permanently in Italy (Pedone 2013). This corpus of writings is multilingual, as it is mainly expressed in Mandarin and standard Italian, but it additionally presents some forays into dialectal varieties and forms of translanguaging. It is also a transnational literary corpus, meaning that many authors who produce this literature participate in frequent mobility between China and Italy, and publish their work in both countries and online. The corpus is furthermore characterized by the fact that it addresses a very diverse readership, as it might be targeted to Italian readers, Chinese-Italian readers, and Chinese readers outside Italy. In the selection of this corpus, I use a perspective that combines Mobility Studies with Sinophone Studies as defined by Shih Shu-mei (2007), one that foregrounds the mobility experience of those who produce these writings regardless of the language in which they are expressed, thus understanding the Sinophone as "a 'place-based' practice of reading and interpreting literary and other cultural texts" (Bernards 2016, 76–77). Within this perspective Sino-Italian writings are

POETRY IN MOTION   145

not to be framed as expressions of the Chinese diaspora, interpreted as generic
emanations of Chinese literature (substitutable across other contexts), but
must instead be considered as Sinophone texts rooted in the chronotope in
which they are produced (Bernards 2016, 76–77).

A common tendency toward culturalist frames of interpretations perme-
ates most of the Sino-Italian literary production, which revolves around the
representation of Chineseness, a concept that is highly debated in cultural
studies. The idea of Chineseness can be summed up as the belief that there
is a set of tangible qualities that are specific to people of Chinese heritage.
The contours of the concept are blurred, and different people can define it in
various ways. The general belief, however, is that being Chinese is something
inherited through blood and implies an ancestral belonging that entails cer-
tain values and behaviors (Dikötter 2015). This idea matches with the Italian
counterpart that today still promotes a conceptualization of the Italian pop-
ulation as essentially Christian and Caucasian, with public discourse consis-
tently silencing non-white voices or turning to racialization and othering when
referring to them (Bond, Bonsaver, and Faloppa 2015). In short, the two heavily
essentialist discourses of the Chinese and the Italian – often reflecting ongoing
colonial and nationalist ambitions – promote the representation of Chinese in
Italy as "perennial others." For Italians, the Chinese will never be good enough
to be culturally Italian, while for the Chinese, there is no cultural reason to
assimilate, considering that their own heritage boasts a far more ancient and
civilized status. In this contemporary confrontation we can observe legacies of
conflict, occasionally marked by moments of meaningful cultural exchange,
between opposing claims over the origins of civilization. This results in Italian
attitudes of cultural superiority that cannot accept a Chinese population wish-
ing to remain apart from the larger society, and Chinese attitudes that con-
tend with Sinophobia and racism through cultural reification and community
empowerment. As a result, the modes of cultural production explored in this
chapter reflect the unique local conditions, represented in diverse forms of
mobility, which have given rise to a growing movement of Sino-Italian artists
and writers.

2   China-Italy Mobility Patterns and Cultural Production

While the history of cultural contact between China and Europe is many
centuries old, as seen in the fact that Ancient Romans already had indirect
contact with Chinese merchants in the second century BC when they started

purchasing silk produced under the Han empire (Wilkinson 2000), long-term migration of large numbers of people from China to Europe became a numerically significant phenomenon only with the rise of European colonial powers in East Asia in the late nineteenth century and the crisis of the Qing Empire. According to Benton (2011), there is no such thing as a single European Chinese community, but rather there are many, as the history of mass migration from China to Europe is manifold and engendered very different Sinophone multilingual and multicultural communities.

The first Chinese to immigrate to Europe were sailors moving from Canton who settled in the main European port cities (Liverpool, Hamburg, Marseilles, Amsterdam) and created little Chinatowns already in the late nineteenth century. Another small flow of people from China arrived in the early twentieth century on land; this group originated from just two Chinese counties, namely Qingtian, in Zhejiang Province and Tianmen, in Hubei. The Qingtianese were peddlers selling soapstone creations imported from their home country and they spread around Europe in small communities without mingling with the other Sinophone communities. A third group arrived during the First World War; they had been hired in different parts of China by the Allied troops to dig trenches, and many stayed in Europe, especially in France, after the War ended. They did not mix with the other Chinese groups, just like what had happened with the Cantonese and the Qingtianese. Another major flow arrived in France from Indochina during the Vietnam War (1975) and another stream targeted Britain from Hong Kong and the new Territories from the 1950s until the 1970s. These first groups gave origin to distinct Sinophone minorities that still exist today as separate groups (Benton 2011). From the 1980s, following Deng's reform and opening policy, a significant migration flow from Southeast Zhejiang began and saw the fastest-growing number of arrivals in history. Two more flows originating from Fujian and Northeastern Provinces also became prominent in the 1990s. However, most new Chinese migrants in Europe today are from the Southeastern part of Zhejiang Province, especially from the Wenzhou area, and follow the chain migration started with the peddlers that moved from Qingtian about a century ago (Thuno 1996).

Italy is one of the European countries that has been receiving the highest number of immigrants from Southern Zhejiang, and today Chinese people constitute the second nationality of non-European origin in Italy (after Moroccans) with over 300,000 individuals and the fourth in absolute terms (Istat 2022). Among the reasons that made Italy an attractive destination for these migrants, compared with other European countries, there is certainly the fact that Italy had several amnesties for undocumented migrants throughout the 1980s and 1990s, and the fact that a general tolerance toward off-the-book work in some specific niches created virtually infinite demand for low-skilled workers (Li 2002). On these premises, it is easy to understand how the first wave of arrivals could gather the necessary know-how, networks, and small capital to open their own businesses and invite more immigrants from the same areas of origin, with the result that today the Chinese minority in Italy is in fact very homogenous in terms of areas of provenance. This population is mostly involved in catering, manufacturing and retail. While they usually hire other Chinese immigrants and thus tend to function in an almost completely Sinophone network with little interaction with locals on a social level, there is a recent trend of upward mobility on a socio-economic level for many of these self-employed entrepreneurs from Zhejiang. The outcome of the intersection of all these different conditions is that upon reaching Italy, despite originating from a very circumscribed area in China, the main migration flow from China results in a rather layered group in terms of class status, clan lineage of belonging, and linguistic use.

All this complexity seems to go almost completely undetected in the Italian mainstream social and political discourse, where the Chinese Italian population is wrongly represented as very cohesive and homogenous. When other kinds of mobility from China to Europe (not strictly linked to labor) are considered, the one that deserves the most attention for its impact on the Chinese-Italian culture is that of exchange students arriving in Europe from the PRC every year. It is a rather new phenomenon, and it is playing an important role in the creation of a new European image of China and of the construction of Chinese-European local identities. According to the Statistical Office of the Italian Ministry of Education, from 2010 to 2021 a total of 663,506 Chinese students were welcomed into Italian universities. Many of them overstay their period of study and some open their own business or start collaborating with local Zhejiangese entrepreneurs. This group of exchange students is therefore a powerful new actor within the Chinese-Italian dimension, and it plays a key role in Chinese-Italian cultural production. Unlike first-generation working migrants, they come from all over China and usually belong to families with high social and cultural status (Huang 2002). The contribution to the cultural contact between Chinese contemporary urban elites, embodied in these international students, and Italian society at large is often underestimated in Italian public discourse on the Chinese population in Italy.

Besides the types of mobility, another important factor to consider when observing the cultural dynamics of Chinese in Italy is the Chinese government's control on overseas Chinese populations by the PRC's so-called "diaspora governance." In fact, the role of the PRC's government in shaping the cultural discourse within the Chinese population in Italy is rather gripping (Ceccagno and Thuno 2022). Lastly, Italian media and political narratives about the Chinese in Italy have only recently started taking into account the very diverse factors that influence if, when, and how this population achieves incorporation into the local society and in every major dimension of everyday life. Until now, the depictions commonly spread of Chinese in Italy have been very biased and characterized by superficiality, generalizations, cultural essentialism – if not outright orientalism – and racial prejudice (Zhang 2019). The points presented so far contribute to shaping the Sino-Italian cultural production, just like they obviously influence many other aspects of the lives of people of Chinese background in Italy.

3 Language Choice in Poetry

Although not the dominant literary form, poetry is nonetheless well represented in the repertoire in Sino-Italian writings. Besides Li Shuman 李叔蔓 and Heng Zhi 衡之, who have both authored a full collection of poems, other Chinese authors based in Italy have published some poetry on the side of their main production in fiction, namely Mao Wen 毛文 and Hu Lanbo 胡蘭波.

Li Shuman (b. 1969) is the editor-in-chief of the Italian Sinophone newspaper based in Rome, *Xinhua shibao* 新華時報. She graduated from Beijing's Media University in 1991, and in 1997 she published her first collection of poems titled *Chuntan xiaoyue* 春潭簫月 (*Spring Lake and Moonlight Shadow*). In 1998, she moved to Italy and chose Rome as her new home. While in Italy, she published a memoir in China of her Roman life, titled *Binfen Luoma* 繽紛羅馬 (*Colorful Rome*, 2002), which included a few poems drawn from her first collection as well as some originals. In 2021, she published her first book in Italy, which is also her second collection of poems, titled *Hao* 好 (*Good*). The collection was published by Cina in Italia, an Italian publishing house run by another Chinese journalist based in Rome, Hu Lanbo. *Hao*, which does not have an Italian title, includes 35 poems divided into five vaguely thematic sections. In the preface of the book, the author explains that she wrote the poems for her daughter's eighteenth birthday and that her daughter suggested to simply name the book *Hao*, like the Chinese character that depicts a mother and a child together. Li's daughter also provided the illustrations for the book; each section is introduced by a pencil drawing.

The choice of an untranslated Chinese title for the collection shows the author's desire to explicitly perform her Chineseness right from the very first encounter with the reader. The poems span from shorter works of four lines

POETRY IN MOTION 149

of six to seven characters/syllables, to longer two to four stanza compositions, which do not exceed 15 lines. In many poems, the lyrical "I" addresses a lyrical "you" who is said to be her daughter, to whom she reveals her deepest feelings. Although the collection is strongly framed as a tribute to her child and to the maternal experience in general, the poems are for the most part rather indefinite; they often hinge on an inner existential reflection and can also represent other forms of romantic love, as in the following poem titled "Companion" (*Ban* 伴):

> Now close your eyes
> Be my companion
> In this moment that is only ours
> no need for words
> no need for thoughts
>
> Stop this world
> Hold your breath
> Just you and me
> Forgetful of the immensity
> Forgetful of the time
>
> Now close your eyes
> Our souls connected
> In a thousand year-long moment.[2]
>
>   LI 2021, 14

The collection is published with a parallel translation into Italian by Maura Schettino, a professional Italian translator who is not qualified in literary translation. The desire to be translated into Italian makes this product particularly interesting, since the author faces the challenge of addressing two different readerships simultaneously. While this might not be a problem in other contexts, it becomes a sensitive issue when the creative text engages in the representation of Chineseness, which takes different shapes for different readerships.

The peculiar choice of providing the preface first in Chinese and then in Italian, and the fact that the title is a Chinese word make the book fully enjoyable for both Italophone and Sinophone readers. As for specific elements representative of Chineseness, the poems contain a rich presence of

---

2 My translation from Chinese

cross-references to Buddhist concepts, lexicon, and images that for the average Italian, scarcely informed about Buddhism, can go undetected or simply sound cryptic or exotic.[3] Some of this opacity has been valorized by the translator; for instance in the poem "Ding" 定 (fixity), re-titled "Samadhi," the Sanskrit religious term makes the religious reference more explicit while conversely making the meaning more obscure to the general public. Another recurring element that brings out the Chineseness in the collection is the frequent presence of flowers that are common in Chinese literary and artistic heritage (peonies, prune flowers, peach flowers, lotus flowers, and so on) and of typical images of Chinese classical poetry (moon, landscape, wine-induced inebriation, nostalgia for one's homeland). Some of the poems are extremely descriptive, such as the group of 4-line poems dedicated to the four seasons, which provide images of typically Chinese landscapes at different times of the year. The reference to China is strong since this particular set of poems is rich in culturally specific elements, such as the Chinese Spring festival decorations, traditional Chinese architectural elements, and typical literary vegetation once again (Chrysanthemums, prune trees, lotus leaves).

The decision to involve a professional translator suggests that the author is conscious of how different readers will interpret and be touched in disparate ways when accessing the content in Italian or Chinese. Even though she has been living in Italy for over twenty years, the issue of translation is another form of transcultural negotiation that remains in play with her expressions of Chineseness. If we compare these poems with those included in *Binfen Luoma*, we notice that in *Hao* the poems feature many more images normally ascribed to Chinese cultural heritage, whereas the poems in *Binfen Luoma* occasionally refer to elements that, on the contrary, evoke the exoticism of Europe to Chinese readers, such as drinking coffee. Another interesting reflection can be made on the strong nationalistic tone that the author assumes in many parts of her memoir *Binfen Luoma*, which is instead completely absent in *Hao*. Although we cannot assume that avoiding such tones was a strategic move by the author who understood that the poems were directed to an Italian readership as much as to a Chinese one, it is certain that Italian readers would not have appreciated the poems had they been framed as too apologetic of Chinese culture in a nationalist perspective. However, as we observe with the other authors, poetry seems to be a literary form wherein Chineseness is expressed and performed in a more individual and subjective way.

---

3 For instance, references to Karma, reincarnation, detachment and so on.

The next published collection of Sinophone poetry I will present is authored by Heng Zhi, a pseudonym of Yan Jiaqing 嚴家慶. Heng Zhi was born in Canton in 1991 and moved to Italy in 2014 to study business at the University of Florence. After obtaining his degree, he decided to stay and in 2018, while still residing Italy, he published his first poetry collection titled *Feichang mie* 非常滅 (*Eternal Cessation*) in Taiwan. He is currently working on the Italian translation of a selection of poems from this collection, a part of which was read by him in Italian and Chinese during a public event held at the University of Florence in 2018. He has already written a draft translation of some of his compositions, which he plans to polish with the help of an Italian native speaker before submitting the final version to Italian publishers.

Feichang mie is composed of 46 poems of various lengths, some exceeding 200 lines. The compositions are in free verse with stanzas that range in form and number. Unlike *Hao*, the poetry included in *Feichang mie* is rather obscure both in language and meaning. It mixes images of Chinese mythology, Taoism and Buddhism with intertextual references to Tang poetry and pre-Qin philosophical texts. Images of heaven and hell are recurring and create a vivid dreamlike atmosphere. Highly imaginative visions of the natural and the supernatural are often juxtaposed within the same poem. Many compositions have a humoristic tone that stems from the irrational and absurd, very much resembling that of classical Taoist anecdotes or Buddhist meditation stories. Nature as a landscape to contemplate is otherwise completely absent. The following is an example of his style:

> I am the summer who sells refreshment,
> By mistake
> I fluctuated into the middle of the river
> and bumped into Li Bai selling wine.
> I gave him stolen verses
> in exchange for a few *liangs* of wine
> And riding the clouds, drunk,
> I crashed into
> The wing-selling angel.
>
> I offered him three thousand shooting stars
> He refused
> and demanded my refreshment and my wine.[4]

HENG 2018, 153

---

4   My translation from Chinese.

Chineseness in Heng Zhi's poems does not emerge as an element in contraposition with Western values; the poems are directed exclusively to a Sinophone readership, which presumably has access to all the cultural references embedded in the compositions. Even though the author explicitly says in the preface that all the poems were written in the city of Florence, it is the occasional images reminiscent of Christianity and the Greco-Roman cultural tradition along with a few place names (Isola Madre, Isola dei Pescatori, Isola Bella) that signal more effectively the author's situatedness in a transnational Italian-Sinophone dimension. In a WeChat exchange, he wrote: "I have read many poems by Eugenio Montale and Juan Ramón Jiménez and some classic Italian poetry, such as that of Giuseppe Parini, Ugo Foscolo, and Torquato Tasso above all. Although I could not understand every word, their sentiment still reached me. If I had never lived in Italy or Europe, maybe that sentiment could have never reached me. Therefore, I think that those who read my work can feel the sentiment of Western culture in it."[5] It is in the transcultural dimension of his creation, then, that Heng Zhi negotiates his de-localized Chineseness.

Another author that deserves attention is Mao Wen, who was born in Beijing in 1953. He left the PRC in 1988 to study in Italy and has been working at different Italian universities since 1991. He is currently a lecturer at the University of Turin. Mao Wen is very culturally active; besides his writing activity, he also paints and directs short films. He has written several books published in Italy for different publishers, such as a grammar of Chinese co-authored with other professors (Biasco, Mao, and Banfi 2003), two co-authored illustrated books for children on Chinese folklore (Gallo and Mao 2005; Gallo and Mao 2007), and two short novels published with parallel Chinese and Italian texts (Mao 2019a, Mao 2019b). Mao Wen has also published fifteen poems that are featured in two different collections along with the work of other poets (VVAA 2013a; 2013b).

Except for one of the aforementioned poems, in which the Italian translation is credited to Mimmo Alfiero, the rest of the poems are most likely self-translated by the author, as suggested by the presence of slightly ungrammatical elements. It is not clear whether the author is aware of the ungrammaticality, but we should take into consideration that he has lived in Italy for a long time and has been in constant contact with Italians for his work at university. He nonetheless evidently still preferred to exercise his full authorial power to control the language of his poems instead of entrusting an external translator with the task. The effect on the reader of such ungrammaticality can be twofold; on the one side the reader can perceive it as a sign of sloppiness

---

5   Private conversation in Italian on WeChat on September 12, 2022.

POETRY IN MOTION   153

or immaturity and be disturbed by it or, on the other side, the ungrammaticality can also suggest authenticity and spontaneity that build an overall impression of sincerity and urgency. Nine of the poems do not report the original in Chinese while five of them do.

Although his published fiction deals extensively with Chinese folklore and offers a wide array of exotic stories rich in the Chinese tropes that are most familiar to Westerners, such as dragons and other typical Sinophone cultural elements, in his poetry Mao Wen creates a world of de-ethnicized passionate love that at times does not shy away from open sexual references and that is not spoiled by culturalist stereotypes. Among his poems, the one titled "Tu invece" ("But You, Instead") is openly dedicated to the victims of the 1989 Tian'anmen massacre ("to you/ we offered our fiery youth/ but you, instead,/ crushed us with a tank" [Mao 2013, 719]), and constitutes the only one that expresses a patriotic feeling, although critical. The poem presents an explicit lyrical "you," which is the Chinese government, and an implicit lyrical "we," which represents a collectivity, that of a generation of young Chinese in the 1980s. It is interesting to notice how the poem where Chineseness comes out forcefully, through the reference to Chinese history, is the only one narrated from a collective perspective and not on a subjective dimension like his other poems.

The vast majority of the other compositions are romantic love poems dedicated to different women. In them, elements of the Chinese cultural context are referenced as well as others from the Italian and the broader Western cultural context. The one titled "The Love of My Life" contains such an interweaving of references:

> As the Yellow River runs screaming on earth
> Your love runs inside my veins.
> As the Great Wall meanders on the mountains
> Your love twists inside my heart.
> As the spring rain wets the tender grass
> Your love makes the withered tree spurt.
> As a loud roar on a snowy peak
> Your love provokes a terrifying avalanche.
> You have watered love with your life,
> Love
> Will reward you with the fresh flower of my life.[6]
> > MAO 2013, 719

---

6 My translation from Chinese.

Like Li Shuman, Mao Wen seems to reserve poetry to voice more intimate emotions that can be linked to a private sphere. In their novels, on the contrary, they both often turn to the display and performance of their Chineseness, from different angles, to be categorized, studied, offered, explained, and appreciated by the readers as something that transcends the individual to represent all the Chinese that ever existed and that ever will exist. Chineseness intended as a collective set of symbols and shared narratives seems to disappear completely in Mao Wen's poetry to leave space conversely to the description of subjective sentiments. In the Italian self-translations of his poems, the literality of the translations seems to show that the main motivation behind the operation is not creativity but mostly to reach the Italian audience. This is also confirmed by the fact that he does not make an effort to replicate in Italian the symmetry created by verses composed of the same number of characters in Chinese, a formal aspect that gets completely lost in the translations.

The last group of poems I present here are those written by Hu Lanbo and published in the collection titled *La primavera di Pechino* (*Beijing Spring*, 2019). Hu Lanbo is a journalist and businesswoman born in Heilongjiang who moved to Paris in 1984 and then arrived in Italy in 1989, where she has lived ever since. She runs the magazine *Cina in Italia* (*China in Italy*) and the publishing house of the same name mentioned above which specializes in books on Chinese culture. Hu Lanbo has written several memoirs of her life in the three countries which were published both in China (Hu 1993; Hu 2015) and Italy (Hu 2009; Hu 2012). She has also written a novel set in Beijing during the Cultural Revolution (2017), a few short stories (mostly autobiographical), and a handful of books on Chinese folk stories. In 2017, she was invited to the Perugia-based international poetry prize Insula Europea, where she presented her poems in public for the first time.

The collection *La primavera di Pechino* is formed by 31 short narrative texts that span 1–2 pages in length each, presented both in Italian and in Chinese with parallel texts. While the narrative texts are mostly short annotations about her life in China, France, and Italy, themes on which the author had previously published extensively in both languages, the last part of the book includes the poems along with some illustrations by an Italian artist, Bibi Trabucchi, exclusively in Italian. Hu Lanbo is not a native speaker of Italian and she generally resorts to professional translators (though not always specialized in literary translations) for her works. In the case of poetry, however, she chooses exophony; she prefers to use a language that is not her mother tongue. The poems, in fact, do not have a Chinese original and have been composed by the author directly in Italian. In the preface, presented first in Italian and then in Chinese, the author explains her reasons for writing poetry exclusively in Italian:

I have lived almost 30 years in Italy, but I still cannot speak very good Italian. However, in the past two years, when I suddenly felt the urge to write poems, I did so in Italian! I could not dare to write poetry in Chinese, because I knew that if I had written in my mother tongue and the result was bad, I would have felt so ashamed.[7]

Hu Lanbo's poems, unlike the others considered so far, have a rather defined structure, being mostly formed by stanzas composed of the same number of lines. This emphasis on structure could stem from the author's desire to label these compositions (in a not entirely familiar language) as "real" poetry. If absolute control over words cannot be guaranteed, the length of the poem and the number of lines can be mastered in full by Hu Lanbo, and there she can make sure that these writings are unequivocally perceived as "poems." There are many references to both Italian and Chinese culturally specific elements, such as hints to the Italian Renaissance or classical age, as well as the evocation of specific places in China, such as Shanghai or the Huangpu River, or the shopping outlet Florentia Village.

Hu Lanbo's style of narration is quite recognizable, and it is echoed in her poems just as much as in her fiction. With simple language and common vocabulary, she manages to create images that fuse romanticism, sense of humor, and sensuality in a playful and sometimes ironic way. As for the display of Chineseness, in her other writings Hu Lanbo tends to organize the concept by accentuating the culturalist frame, depicting herself as a spokesperson for Chinese modern womanhood at large in the Italian context. Although her engaging style saves her memoirs from being just trite copycat accounts of intercultural marriages so common in overseas Chinese literature, Hu Lanbo's writings always revolve around Chineseness as the main literary theme. In her poems, however, as I have also pointed out for the other authors, a whole set of alternative feelings and emotions that are more individual and subjective manage to find a place.

In the specific case of Hu Lanbo's poetry in Italian, what is surprising is that she refers to facts and contexts that could be completely ignored by the average local reader without showing any particular effort to provide further explanations. Some of these can even be very specific. For instance, she dedicates one poem to how building the large Florentia Village outlet near Shanghai negatively impacted the lives of local peasants, who consequently lost their land just to please the *tuhao*, the Chinese *nouveau riche*. While the trademark of Hu Lanbo's fiction lies exactly in the didactic tone and perspective through

---

7 My translation from Italian.

which she literally explains Chinese and Italians to the readers, in her poems she adopts a rather opposite role, leaving her thoughts be, without the urge of providing any explanations. Despite the fact that she tells stories that are most likely unknown to Italians, they are still accessible thanks to the language in which they are written and to the author's choice to channel them through the emotions that they provoke in her or in other individuals' sensibility, which makes spheres of reality that are distant from those of the typical Italian reader feel nonetheless familiar. Thus, what could appear as yet another epic account of China and Chineseness turns into an original story framed in an inviting and attractive context to the Italian reader, even though (or exactly because) it lacks all the elements of blatant self-orientalization, or the emphasis on the magnitude of cultural differences between China and the West that she usually adopts in her fictional work. For instance, one of the longest poems in the collection is titled "Qinghai tu sei una grande bellezza" ("Qinghai You Are a Great Beauty"), which has a total of 65 lines divided into 5 stanzas. Despite the title and the subject of the poem, which cannot be considered common knowledge for Italians, the composition is actually dedicated to a possibly imaginary person whom the lyrical "I" wants to rejoin. So, it is not the patriotic sentiment that is celebrated in the poem, as one could be led to expect from the title and the many references to Chinese geography, but a fantasy of a mysterious love, maybe a memory from the author's past.

> I had already crossed these grasslands many years ago,
> Qinghai was desolated in memory.
> Today the sun is so hot,
> Its light makes me want to get close to you.
> I would like to hold you in my arms,
> Your body hot as the desert's sun.[8]
>
>> HU 2022, 219

While the personification of specific territories is not uncommon in the tradition of Chinese regional poetry, the erotic possibility of the poem is what would stand out to the average Italian reader. The linguistic choice to write the poem in Italian allows for the *entendre* to function in an especially provocative way also for a Sino-Italian reader who might be familiar with the established genre of regionalist Chinese poetry. This gives such a reader agency to choose how to read the poem, encouraging an interplay between languages

---

8 My translation from Italian.

and perhaps opening new creative avenues for a future Sino-Italian poetics. Indeed, this is precisely how language and art evolve through the playful (and often intimate) process of cultural contact.

The poems in the collection are not even featured in the Chinese language table of contents, as if they really constituted an unforgivable act of hubris on behalf of the author in front of her Chinese audience. In these verses written in the non-mother tongue, the author allows herself the guilty pleasure of discovering a private Chineseness without adherence to a collective standard or preservation of a patriotic heritage. The desert is vast and desolate, but the author is moving from memory toward a potential embrace that gives shape to innermost desire. Where the light is brightest and the sun hottest, she can fashion herself anew.

In diverse ways attesting to the connection between identity and culture, the experience of mobility plays a crucial role in shaping the poetics of all the presented authors. As already observed for Sino-Italian literary production in general, none of these authors belong to the typical path of mobility for the majority of Chinese citizens in Italy – employment as low-skilled workers within Chinese-run activities of various kinds. The authors mentioned here all belong to a privileged type of mobility, whether working in media (Li Shuman and Hu Lanbo) or involved in education (Mao Wen and Heng Zhi). It is very likely that their privileged position as people of culture with a minority ethnic background has provided them with further opportunity to publish their works, as they could rely on an audience of people interested in that aspect (in the case of Heng Zhi, in the fact that he is immersed in a different culture than that of origin). If they never had the experience of mobility, they might never have imagined a writing career in the first place.

More concretely, the mobility of these authors has informed their lyrical production and intentional choices of language and translation, leaving distinct traces in both content and form. In the case of Li Shuman, as we observed, the desire to address an Italian audience enriched the references in her poetry to Chinese classicism and traditional imagery. Conversely, it also helped her writing eschew an emotional patriotism that was common in her other works and that would probably be unwelcome to Italian readers. For Heng Zhi, the experience of mobility ignited new intellectual interests and a deep appreciation for the tradition of modern European poetry, sentiments which are visible in his poems. Similarly, the works of Mao Wen also feature traces of Italian cultural references, although the most significant aspect that marks his personal story of mobility is the will to keep alive the memory of the protests of Tian'anmen in 1989, something that certainly would not be possible if he had not left the PRC. Finally, living in Italy gave Hu Lanbo the confidence to write poetry in a language that was not overburdened with ancestral heritage. As discussed earlier, she does not publish her poems in Chinese, even though they refer to very specific situations taking place in the PRC. For all the writers discussed in this chapter, their works exist in a non-exclusive reality with plenty of room to move.

We should consider this specific repertoire of Sino-Italian writing as poetry in motion: experimenting with translation and self-translation, sometimes opting for exophony and avoiding translation in other instances, while still engaging in transcultural intertextuality. The individual experiences of these authors within the China-Italy mobility network – reading their poems not only through Literary Studies but also through the lens of New Mobility Studies – gives us valuable insight into the current aesthetic trends, socio-political critiques, and academic strategies of Sino-Italian cultural discourse.

4 Conclusions

How do we understand and deal with a theme such as Chineseness in Italian Sinophone cultural production? If we are looking for it, we find it everywhere. If we are suspicious of it, we easily see ways in which Sino-Italian artists and writers are challenging and resisting essentializing discourses and forms of identity politics. Chineseness is always being performed, and at the same time, it is being avoided, erased, and transfigured until it seems conspicuously absent. It has evolved past post-colonial critiques to find new articulations in young generations of Italian born (or raised) Chinese who are keen to embrace a fluid process of self-actualization that represents their own multi-directional forms of mobility – often moving back and forth from the mainland to Europe and Italy.

This can only be partially related to the general trend towards ethnicization (or self-ethnicization) that is found in other writers of foreign origin active in Italy. Many authors of Italian migration literature focus their works on their respective cultures of origin, but they also reflect on how their culture of origin can find its place in Italian society. As this chapter has shown, Sino-Italian writings are distinguished, rather, by the desire to re-establish connections and reinvent forms of cultural expression – dealing mainly with the nostalgia of the ancestral homeland and with the challenge of maintaining and preserving one's Chineseness in a context that incessantly tries to erase it. These are almost opposite stances: one that demands inclusion and the other that aspires to exclusion.

To account for the positioning of authors of Chinese descent with respect to their attachment to Chineseness, the particular socio-cultural background

POETRY IN MOTION   159

of those who publish books, short stories, or poems must be considered. Only a negligible part of Sino-Italian authors, in fact, belong to the same social class of the great majority of Chinese immigrants in Italy. The works published by Chinese authors in Italy today mostly come from people with privileged mobility paths; they are often individuals of medium or high cultural level who are active in the fields of education (Gao Liang, Zhai Ran, Yang Xiaping, Mao Wen, Lala Hu), business, politics, media, and entertainment (Hu Lanbo, Li Shuman, Marco Wong, Shi Yang Shi, Angelo Ou, Zhang Changxiao). The socio-cultural positioning of these authors generates a very different perception of their role in the identity negotiation between author and reader, when compared to migrant writers from more modest socio-cultural backgrounds. Furthermore, China and Italy do not have a historical past that is deeply characterized by the colonial experience that, for example, influences the production of various authors of Italian migration literature with African heritage. Past and present international relations between Italy and China, with the latter being firmly established as a global superpower, also constitute an element that radically affects the position of the writer towards the reader and acts on the power dynamics that define the role of Sino-Italian authors within contemporary Italian society and culture.

The theme of Chineseness in Sino-Italian literature is so central that few texts written by Sino-Italians do not revolve around it, even when the theme is felt as a central absence drawing attention to the lack thereof. Even when analyzing works by the same author, we discover how Chineseness is treated to fit different literary forms. As this chapter has shown, poetry seems to be the literary form wherein the theme of Chineseness is interpreted and expressed on a more personal dimension and sometimes even put temporarily aside to leave room for lyrical and linguistic experiments. The fact that so many fictional Sino-Italian writings claim to be autobiographical to some extent might give the impression that the discourse on Chineseness found in these works actually reflects the authors' subjective perception of the matter. When we take into consideration how Chineseness is expressed in poetry, however, much more nuanced manifestations of the authors' sense of ethnic belonging come to light.

Works Cited

Ang, Ien. 2001. *On Not Speaking Chinese: Living between Asia and the West.* London: Routledge.

Benton, Gregor. 2011. "The Chinese in Europe: Origins and Transformations." *Religions & Christianity in Today's China* 1 (1): 62–70.

Bernards, Brian. 2016. "Sinophone literature." In *The Columbia Companion to Modern Chinese Literature*, edited by Kirk A. Denton, 72–79. New York: Columbia University Press.

Biasco, Margherita, Wen Mao, and Emanuele Banfi. 2003. *Introduzione allo studio della lingua cinese* [Introduction to the Study of Chinese Language]. Rome: Carocci.

Bond, Emma, Guido Bonsaver, and Federico Faloppa. 2015. *Destination Italy: Representing Migration in Contemporary Media and Narrative*. Oxford: Peter Lang.

Ceccagno, Antonella, and Mette Thunø. 2022. "Digitized diaspora governance during the COVID-19 Pandemic: China's diaspora mobilization and Chinese migrant responses in Italy." *Global Networks* 0: 1–16.

Chow, Rey. 1998. "Introduction: On Chineseness As a Theoretical Problem." *Boundary 2* 25 (3) (Autumn): 1–24.

Chun, Allen. 2017. *Forget Chineseness: On the Geopolitics of Cultural Identification*. Albany NY: State University of New York Press.

Dikötter, Frank. 2015. *The Discourse of Race in Modern China*. Oxford: Oxford University Press.

Gallo, Sofia, and Wen Mao. 2005. *Fiume di stelle* [River of Stars]. Rome: Sinnos.

Gallo, Sofia, and Wen Mao. 2007. *Il duca Yè e la passione per i draghi* [The Duke Yè and the Passion for Dragons]).Rome: Sinnos.

Hannam, Kevin, Mimi Sheller and John Urry. 2006. "Editorial: Mobilities Immobilities and Moorings." *Mobilities* 1 (1) (March): 1–22.

Heng, Zhi 衡之. 2018. *Feichang mie* 非常灭 [Eternal Cessation]. Taipei: Bokesi chubanshe.

Hu, Lanbo 胡蘭波. 1993. *Xin silu shang de Zhongguo guniang* 新絲路上的中國姑娘 [A Chinese Girl on the New Silk Road]. Beijing: Beijing lüyou jiaoyu chubanshe.

Hu, Lanbo 胡蘭波. 2009. *La strada per Roma* [The way to Rome]. Rome: Laca.

Hu, Lanbo 胡蘭波. 2012. *Petali d'orchidea* [Orchid's Petals]. Rome: Barbera.

Hu, Lanbo 胡蘭波. 2015. *Shuo zou jiu zou! Cong Beijing dao Luoma* 說走就走！從北京到羅馬 [It's Time to Go. From Beijing to Rome]. Beijing: Zhongguo huaqiao chubanshe.

Hu, Lanbo 胡蘭波. 2017. *Il sole delle otto del mattino* [The Sun of Eight O'Clock in the Morning]. Rome: Cina in Italia.

Hu, Lanbo 胡蘭波. 2022. *La primavera di Pechino* [Beijing's Spring]. Rome: Cina in Italia.

Huang, Hui. 2002. "Overseas Studies and the Rise of Foreign Cultural Capital in Modern China." *International Sociology* 17 (1) (March): 35–55.

Li, Minghuan 李明歡. 2002. *Ouzhou huaqiao huaren shi* 歐洲華僑華人史 [The History of the Chinese in Europe]. Beijing: Zhongguo huaqiao chubanshe.

Li, Shuman. 2021. *Hao*. Rome: Cina in Italia.

Merriman, Peter, and Lynne Pearce. 2017. "Mobility and the Humanities." *Mobilities* 12, no. 4: 493–508.

Mao, Wen. 2013. "Tu invece" [And You, Instead]). In VV.AA., *I Poeti Contemporanei 96* [Contemporary Poets 96], 179. Rome: Pagine.

Mao, Wen. 2019a. *La luna a forma di spada dell'Imperatore Wu* [The Moon Shaped as the Sword of the Emperor Wu]. Milan: CUEM.

Mao, Wen. 2019b. *La storia della grande campana* [The Story of the Big Bell]. Milan: CUEM.

Pedone, Valentina. 2013. *A Journey to the West. Observations on the Chinese Migration to Italy*. Florence: Firenze University Press.

Sheller, Mimi and John Urry. 2006. "The New Mobilities Paradigm." *Environment and Planning A: Economy and Space* 37 (2) (February): 207–226.

CHAPTER 9

Borderless Creation

Ming Di's World of Poetry between Translation, Self-Translation and Co-Translation

Nicoletta Pesaro
Ca' Foscari University of Venice

1   Introduction

What is a Sinophone poet? Someone who writes poems in a Sinitic language, while living in a non-Chinese speaking territory or rather a poet whose cultural background constitutes an array of fundamental resources to which they almost inevitably respond by absorbing and re-interpreting them, or, on the contrary, by contesting and negating them in their own creation. What if the poet's works are written in Chinese and are published in Mainland China, but the author and her main activities are placed in an international context beyond it? The concept of 'Sinophone' as a tool of analysis has been recently questioned and re-thought, in order to embrace a variety of controversial issues, spanning political, cultural, gender and ethnic issues, in the attempt to avoid new hegemonies and new ethnocentrisms. No matter how we define her, a Sinophone poet is often bound to work in a transcultural and polyphonic condition in which Chinese operates as a languaculture,[1] and translation, both as a mental process and a practice, is often entailed in the creative process.

This chapter deals with the fascinating entanglement between poetic creation, self-translation and co-translation, by focusing on the very peculiar case of the Chinese poet Ming Di 明迪 and the process of double or multiple creativity entailed in her work *River Merchant's Wife*, a collection of poems published in English translation in 2012. I will consider her multifaceted role as a poet, translator, editor and poetry critic, and her cross-lingual and cross-cultural identity as a Chinese expat in the United States. Indeed, all these elements play a pivotal role in shaping both the creative process and the intrinsic texture of

---

1 This concept has been developed by the American anthropologist Michael Agar (1994) in order to emphasize the strong interrelation between linguistic and cultural elements in the process of "culture description (i.e. thick description)" or translation.

© NICOLETTA PESARO, 2024 | DOI:10.1163/9789004711600_011

her poems, making her case a very specific one that challenges the definition of Sinophone and its borders.

I will address her figure and work by drawing upon translators' studies and actor-network theory (ANT) in order to analyze her poetry in translation, in an effort to put together her two complementary identities as a poet and translator and her bilingual translation activity.

2   A Versatile and Cosmopolitan Poet

Ming Di (pen name of Mindy Zhang) was born and raised in Wuhan; she earned a Master of Arts degree in Beijing, and later, after her doctoral studies in Boston, settled in Los Angeles where she presently lives and works. She embodies the strange paradigm of the dislocated writers, who – borrowing an expression from Salman Rushdie – have been defined as "translated beings" by Michael Cronin (2006). But in Ming Di's case, I would argue, quoting Cronin again, that "there are different ways of reacting to difference" (2006, 47). Indeed, she does not passively receive the culture and language she is living within, but rather, she actively navigates them, also continuing to work with and write in her mother tongue. Her poems are largely based on intertextuality and translation, insofar as they create a variety of cross-cultural references between Chinese tradition, legends and symbols, and Western literature and culture. Thus, she is neither assimilated within the host culture nor does she resist it; on the contrary, she manages to accommodate herself to cultural diversity, approaching poetry as a language that can accommodate both her home culture and her host culture.

Although she refuses to be geographically defined, she recognizes the fact that living abroad has enhanced her sensitiveness for her mother tongue and culture:

> To me it's not the geographic location that makes the difference. *It's the desire to reinvent poetic forms and syntax* that makes a vital difference. The most courageous poets inside and outside a country share many goals: to constantly try new things, go beyond, or make old things new. *Poets outside China are more exposed to Western literature but at the same time try harder to preserve the old traditions.* In my case I guard Chinese as if it's an extinguishing language among English and Spanish in California. I also guard my identity as a Chinese poet – I never say I'm Chinese American. I'm not hyphenated. I refuse to be assimilated because I know the fifty-five minority nationalities in China are assimilated and losing

their languages. There is a belief that diaspora writers tend to be out of touch with societies (native country or adopted country), but I don't think it's true, especially in the Internet age. With or without Internet, one can choose to deal with social issues directly or in a subtle way. (Ming Di 2016b, italics added)

In a recent article, which questions the "China-dominates-all syndrome" in Sinophone Studies, Flair Donglai Shi criticizes the fact that "Sinophone" writers are "often categorized according to a reductive logic of 'where you come from' rather than *the views and sentiments expressed in their works*" (2021, 320, italics added). In this case, Ming Di can be seen as simultaneously representing a Chinese poet still rooted in her own country and culture, and a dynamic international literary activist, who not only collaborates with American literary circles but also takes part in poetry projects including in Europe and other countries, from her privileged position as an expat. According to Rey Chow (1993), this condition is both a privilege and a risk as the intellectual diaspora have the privilege of living in the West, but risk acting and considering themselves as a minority. I would argue that Ming Di, apparently aware of this risk, acts as a Chinese poet speaking in the world and to the world, which prevents her from being a "truly minor" voice, as she is definitely not "voiceless" (Chow 1993, 112) and her voice is definitely a Chinese one.

As a poet, she has published six collections of poetry in Chinese and a book of poems in English is on the way; many of her works have been published in leading Chinese and international poetry journals. As a translator and an editor, she has put together several anthologies of modern Chinese poetry translated or co-translated into English and other languages, and she has also translated a variety of foreign poems into Chinese. Besides, she is the translator of *Selected Poems of Ha Jin* (*Ha Jin shixuan* 哈金詩選, 2009), and of his essay *The Writer as a Migrant* (*Zai taxiang xiezuo* 在他鄉寫作, 2010) into Chinese, as well as of Liu Xia's 劉霞 collection of poems *Empty Chairs* (*Kong yizi* 空椅子 2015, co-translated with Jennifer Stern) into English. Much of her activity is disseminated through *Poetry East West*, the journal she co-founded and still edits, but also by participating in a variety of literary events, such as conferences, meetings, poetry workshops, readings, etc. Despite claiming she is not a bilingual poet (Ming Di 2016b), she undoubtedly works with and between the two languages of her home country and host country; her creations are therefore often marked by a double linguistic/cultural identity.

In fact, her double identity is continuously affirmed and, to some extent, complicated by her multifaceted activity: by acting as an assertive mediator – not only between different languages but also between a variety of other actors of the networks she weaves together – Ming Di makes an excellent example of Latour's ANT theory, as I will demonstrate later. In her own words,

> Co-translation of my own poetry has become bilingual writing sometimes and independent rendition other times. Why do I translate so much? I'm always curious what a poem would look like or sound like in another language. It's an intuitive reaction, not purposefully. (2022)

In addition, I would argue that, in a wider sense, poets are always translators, as they constantly move from a psychological and cultural universe – both within themselves and in the outside world – that they "translate" into words, images, sounds and rhythm.

Thus, Ming Di represents a meaningful example of modern Chinese poetry conceived and written in a transcultural context. Perhaps this can help us better define Sinophone poetry by avoiding both an overly politicized approach and the narrowness of a purely linguistic or geographic perspective. As an active translator and mediator of modern Chinese poetry, Ming Di locates herself within the literary space of modern Chinese poetry as a "part of 'world literature'"; according to her, "[continuing] this tradition requires generations of poets to keep working for the contributions"; besides, she claims that

> Western modernist poetry was very much influenced by classical Chinese poetry through translations, which in turn influenced the modern Chinese poetry. The literary communication of reciprocal influence has been possible due to cross translation. [...] Although mutually influenced, poetry in a particular region maintains its own characteristics, its own [historical] path and its unique styles due to the individual features of its language(s) and dialect(s). (Ming Di 2022)

Rejecting the connotation of a "hyphenated" identity (Chinese-American), Ming Di considers herself a member of the community of Chinese poets. Her works in Chinese have been published in Mainland China – where she continues to busily interact with local poets, editors and publishers – and in Taiwan. At the same time, she belongs to the multifaceted world of Sinophone writers: I would argue that the definition that best fits her is "cosmopolitan Chinese poet," as she is still closely connected to her mother tongue and homeland, while smoothly navigating the complexity of international literary and cultural exchanges. Strongly believing that modern Chinese poetry is part of world literature, she strives to contribute to it through both her creative and her translation activity.

3   The Sociological Approach

Ming Di's double agency as an individual poet and as an all-round (co-)translator makes her part of a multilingual and multicultural[2] process of poetry creation, translation and dissemination that shapes her peculiar Sinophone identity. Nonetheless, her literary connection with China remains crucial; for all her activism in the United States, she makes no secret of the difficult condition of the migrant writer, mentioning her feelings of isolation and loneliness in her interviews: she feels "artistically very isolated in the US" (Ming Di 2016b). The space she is occupying, thus, seems to fall somewhere between China and the world: she is physically located in the United States and her poetry is probably better known outside China than in the country itself (Ming Di 2014), where she is recognized more for her poetry translations than for her own creative work. Nevertheless, she embodies the concept of Sinophone poet, by situating herself at the center of a vast and articulated network of international collaborations, made easier by her position.

In order to answer some of the questions raised in this book, I will analyze this poet/translator's activity from two perspectives, the sociological and the linguistic one: I will examine her own creative work, which has been only partially translated in cooperation with English mother tongue poets, against the backdrop of her tireless endeavors as an editor and a translator of Chinese poems into English. In particular, I will focus on her collection of translated poems *River Merchant's Wife*.

Ming Di's activity as a poetry creator and translator is suitable to be studied through a sociological approach, but I would argue that her poems and translations should also be scrutinized under the intersectional lens of Sinophone and Gender Studies. Although the text remains central in my analysis, I am drawing inspiration from Latour's "actor-network theory" (ANT), and its application to Translation Studies.[3] The ANT notion of agency suits my case study very well, as it considers the actor as a powerful mediator, whose action produces a transformative process. The concept of actor, compared to that of "agent," is a more abstract and sociological one: "It designates an entity endowed with

---

2   Although this chapter deals mainly with the English translation of her poems, it must be remarked that Ming Di has also produced collaborative translations from and into languages other than English.

3   Buzelin argues that Latour's more scientific-oriented approach is complementary to Bourdieu's more social-oriented one. "ANT-inspired research can reveal more efficiently the existence of translation networks which are not clearly visible at the field or polysystem level, while Bourdieu's approach may direct our attention to institutional factors that still inform, to varying degrees depending on the context, the translation process" (2005, 210).

agency, which is the ability to exert power in an intentional way." Besides, as Buzelin observes,

> [a]dapted to the analysis of the genesis of literary translations, the methodology [Latour] designed could certainly allow us to move one step further in the understanding of the many strategies, negotiations, struggles, conflicts – but also alliances – and consequently the modalities and reasons underlying the importation of foreign literature in a given context. (2005, 208–9)

According to this approach, Ming Di perfectly suits the definition of actors as "proactive 'mediators' rather than passive intermediaries [...] [whose] actions and interactions, propelled by specific motivations, shape the product (here, collections of poems) in sometimes unpredictable ways" (Munday and Blakesley 2016, 6). Something that Latour's theory brings into the analysis of the translation process is, for instance, empirical data:

> data on the multiple mediators potentially involved in the translation process, including the way they make or explain their decisions (when they are still unsure about the outcome of this process), and the strategies by which they negotiate their place in the process, convince others to participate, etc. (Buzelin 2005, 215)

I will examine the multiple modalities of translation adopted by Ming Di to enhance and develop her creativity, and thus I will adopt a mixed research strategy, also including other elements in my analysis such as the different languages encompassed in the translation process, her relationship with translators, poets, scholars and publishers in the translating process. Finally, I will observe the result of such a network of collaboration by taking one translated poem as an example.[4]

---

4 "The observation, recording, and analyses of translational practices locally – be it in a courtroom, translation bureau, translation department of a firm or publishing house – over a sufficient period of time, combined with the study of the various drafts of a translation, will generate data that should enable us to get a better idea of who participates in the translation process, how they negotiate their position, and of how much and where translators, in practice, comply with or contest norms" (Buzelin 2005, 205).

4   Creating a New Tradition

By analyzing Ming Di's prolific production of poetry, one will find that it ranges across a wide variety of themes: gender and the world of women, Chinese mythology re-arranged as a modern expression of both culture and feelings, the author's experience as a migrant, Western music and poetry, and a rich array of interpersonal emotions.

In particular, *River Merchant's Wife* is a free self-selection of 46 poems in Chinese spanning the years from 2003 to 2011, some of which were never published before. The collection was published in 2012 by the small and independent Marick Press, specializing in poets from all over the world and especially under-published women poets. Most of the poems have been co-translated by Ming Di and English mother-tongue poets and translators, such as Toni Barnstone, Neil Aitken, Sylvia Burn, Katie Farris and Aafa Weaver, who are also involved in many other of her projects, including anthologies of Chinese poems. The title of the collection is taken from a poem written by Ming Di in 2009 and has a strong "transcultural" character insofar as it hints at the famous and controversial poem composed by Ezra Pound by "borrowing"[5] from the ancient Chinese poet Li Bai's 李白 *ci* "Changgan xing" 長干行 (The Song of Changgan). This choice is not random, as it puts Ming Di's creation directly in the eye of the storm, namely the endless polemics on Pound's misunderstandings and Orientalizing approach.[6] Ming Di implicitly advocates a method of poetic translation (and creation) based on free inspiration, although she is clearly concerned with the translator's awareness of the cultural background (Ming Di 2015, 35). The ancient poem deals with the feelings of a young woman, and her "transformation from childhood love to marital love" (Tang 2011, 529). According to Jun Tang, what is noteworthy in this ancient *ci* is "its deviation from the traditional representations of complaining merchant wives" (529).

I will not enter the heated debate about the manipulation of the poem carried out by Pound; suffice it to say that, by building on a close-reading and a

---

5   Ezra Pound's collection of Chinese classical poems according to Fenollosa's notes is entitled *Cathay*, the name by which North China was known in medieval Europe. The word resonates with Western culture – especially thanks to Marco Polo's travelogue – and embodies a romantic and highly idealized vision of China. The poem from which Ming Di draws her inspiration, as well as the other included in Ezra Pound's *Cathay*, are often called "translations"; however, the profound transformation and the free interpretation of Li Bai's original poems carried out by Pound have led most scholars to define them at their best as a re-invention, or as "bad" translations.

6   For a most comprehensive and rich analysis of the complex reception of this poem among Chinese and Western critics, see Jun Tang (2011).

solid grasp of the poem's cultural background, Tang demonstrates that many scholars, approaching Pound's work, "tend to ignore the social context of the production of 'Changgan Xing' and fall victim to the misconception of a homogeneous Chineseness" (2011, 528). That said, what I find interesting is the way in which Ming Di consciously walks in the footsteps of the imagist poet, by drawing upon a history of entanglements (and misunderstandings) between Western and Chinese culture, to the point of even disregarding and challenging the claim for a more philological approach to her own tradition. In one of her collected and (co)translated anthologies of Chinese poets (which is significantly entitled *New Cathay*), Ming Di directly addresses themes such as Chineseness and the "new tradition," welcoming "influences and interactions" and stating that "[l]ike the poet-translators from the 1920s and 1940s, many contemporary Chinese poets view translation as part of their own creative writing" (Ming Di 2013b, xxiii). In her mind, the final goal of translating verses both with other poets and scholars is to "ensure the presentation of varied styles" (2013b, xxvii).

Ming Di's *River Merchant's Wife* directly tackles the contradictions embodied in Pound's re-invention of Chinese poetry, questioning her own role as a Sinophone poet. In an interview included in one of her books, while describing her collection of translated poems as partially focused on her own life, Ming Di evokes this specific poem by self-fashioning herself as an imagined re-incarnation of the character: "龐德眼裡的李白筆下的那個步行到長風沙的女子一路走到美國此地…" (Ming Di 2016a, 213) (The woman in Pound's eyes and described by Li Bai as walking to Changfengsha made her way here to the United States ...).[7]

In addition, although aware of the doubts and criticisms raised by Pound's detractors, she believes that "誤讀和誤譯有時會帶來意想不到的奇妙效果" (misreadings and misinterpretations can sometimes have unexpected and wonderful effects) (Ming Di 2015, 37). In confirming this, the poem – although occurring in the final pages of the book – reads like a sort of manifesto of her poetics. Ming Di directly addresses the female character of the poem, giving her life and autonomy against the poets' male-dominated discourse: "Li Po fictionalizes her past, she trusts him; / Pound misspells words, she takes all puns as her hours" (Ming Di 2012a, 78).

In order to examine the way in which Ming Di establishes herself within this self-made new tradition of modern Chinese poetry at the crossroads between

---

7   If not otherwise indicated, all translations are mine.

Western and Chinese culture, I will first analyze the selection of her own poems in the translated anthology and then her translation methods.

In scrutinizing these aspects, it is also useful to consider Ming Di's activities as an editor and translator, in other words as an actor in the network of Chinese poetry translation. I would argue that in both roles, as poet and translator, she empowers herself by following in the steps of Chinese poets-translators from the past century (about whom she often writes in her essays and in the paratexts of her translations), in an effort to establish a new tradition for Chinese poetry.

As the editor and translator of two anthologies of Chinese poems in English translation – *New Cathay: Contemporary Chinese Poetry*, North Adams, Mass.: Tupelo Press (2013) and *New Poetry from China 1917–2017*, Berkeley: Black Square Editions (2018) – Ming Di expresses her desire to emphasize the novelty and the revolutionary role played by modern and contemporary poets in China. She thus implicitly agrees with Michelle Yeh, who – in the context of the debate on the effective importance of new poetry with respect to classical poetry – has stated: "[...] modern poetry has finally walked out from under the shadow of classical poetry and earned a place of its own in world literature" (Yeh 2011, 604).

Ming Di's evaluation of modern poetry is reminiscent of Michelle Yeh's concept of "encounter," which has been explained in the same article, as the main trigger for the creation/translation of Chinese poetry, based on mutual affinities:

> To a significant extent, the newness of modern Chinese poetry lies in the creative ways in which indigenous and foreign resources are melded. [...] These encounters between translators and modern Chinese poetry are also founded on intellectual and aesthetic resonances. (Yeh 2011, 607–608)

Ming Di's creation and her concept of poetry can be located at the intersection between these traditions. She recalls having written poetry from a very young age under the influence first of traditional and then modern Chinese poets.

> I wasn't very young when I moved to the US. I finished college in China. I started writing poetry in middle school in my hometown by the Yangtze River, in classical forms, but soon changed to free verse due to the influence of Western literature in translation. Then I moved to Beijing, Boston, and finally settled in California. Occasionally I write in English, but I'm not a "bilingual poet." Chinese is a more complicated language

and inspires me more visually and emotionally. I started making "visual poems" in recent years. I play with words that are similar in shapes as well as in sound when I explore deeper meanings and associations. (Ming Di 2016b)

Not surprisingly, as Ming Di is a prominent figure in the context of Chinese poetry creation/translation – a context always at the center of fiery debates both in China and abroad – some criticisms have been directed at her activity as a mediator of Chinese poetry in the West. I am especially referring here to some observations made by Maghiel van Crevel on the lack of evidence behind certain assumptions that Ming Di has made in her 2018 anthology regarding modern and contemporary poets' "return to classical poetry" (Ming Di 2018, 15); according to van Crevel, this connection between contemporary Chinese poetry and its classical forebears is established without enabling the foreign reader to be more aware of the internal debate on the matter (2019, 342).[8]

Despite his critical observations, van Crevel – just like Yeh in her 2011 article – points out the importance of this kind of engagement in the translation of Chinese poetry, by utilizing the word "encounter" himself: "Contemporary Chinese-English translation anthologies embody the encounter of outside narratives and inside stories, and the complexity of that encounter" (2019, 348). The desire to disseminate Chinese culture is sometimes stronger than the philological accuracy of such an endeavor. Ming Di herself seems quite aware of this complicated weaving of influences and makes no secret of her dissemination policies in the wake of modernism.

I would argue here that, beyond the controversial debate on Chinese classicism and modern poetry, Ming Di so far has significantly contributed to the spread of Chinese poetry, in a very creative way, by opening up a new space for translation and co-translation: as it emerges from the way she performs her agency, poetry translation is also a social act, which involves a variety of subjects.

5 The Status of the Translator and Her Working Processes

I take *The River Merchant's Wife* as an example and the main object of my analysis, aiming to describe the relationship between the individual and the

---

8 "[…] New Cathay takes domestic debate on contemporary poetry's relation to classical poetry straight to the foreign audience, but it does so in a claim that comes across as wishful, and less substantiated than might be required in Chinese-language discourse" (van Crevel 2019, 343).

collective in the creation of Sinophone poetry; the sociological approach to translation provides useful tools to develop this kind of analysis. Ming Di is an actual agent of translation, but I would also define her as an "actor," considering translation as an "event" that is not merely the product of socio-cultural constraints, but that also displays a certain potential for "action." Hence

> "translation 'acts' in a partial and relational (i.e. dialectical) kind of autonomy (Agorni 2002, 2): it is subject to socio-systemic pressures, and yet, at the same time, it is also capable of creating new cultural meanings and social relations and/or transforming existing ones" (Agorni 2007, 131–132).

Ming Di has proved to possess a high degree of both autonomy and relational skills in her practice of translation and publication of poetry. In her tireless activity, she regularly deals with a range of actors, including poets, scholars, editors, publishers and especially translators. If we analyze her interplay with these different actors, we can state that she is often at the center of a working network (or indeed constitutes a network herself, as suggested by Gonne 2018, 268),[9] in which she cooperates with both the Chinese and the foreign side, as an essential mediator. In Latour's words: "mediators transform, translate, distort, and modify the meaning or the elements they are supposed to carry" (2005, 39). Indeed, when it comes to analyzing the "behavior of the translator as individuals or groups or institutions", what matters is to observe their "social networks, status and working processes", and "their relations with other groups [...]" (Chesterman 2009, 19).

Latour's concept becomes particularly valuable in this case, when considering poetry translation not only as an entirely personal artistic act but also as a professional practice. Indeed, the act of translation is seen by Ming Di not only as a creative performance, but also as a professional task, where intuition and inspiration blend with rigorous linguistic and cultural analysis, in order to grasp, for instance,

> 如何在中西文學傳統中進行取捨并探索新路的實驗，這些除了通過介紹來傳遞之外，譯文本身也可以傳遞大量的信息，而且讓文本說話更直接。(Ming Di 2013b)

---

9 "[...] analyzing networks of mediators and, at the same time, mediators *as* networks promises to open up new ways of thinking about both the modalities of exchange, and the individual and collective objectives (pecuniary, aesthetic, professional, ideological political etc.), that configure cultural transfers" (Gonne 2018, 268).

how to choose within Chinese and Western literary traditions and explore new ways of experimenting. In addition to transmitting these elements through an introduction, the translation itself can also convey a lot of information, and make the text speak more directly.

Even before the act of translation, that of selection is highly significant for the main "translation policy" adopted by the translator. This phase belongs to the so-called "preliminary norms" as defined by Toury (1995): indeed, the selection of Ming Di's own poems for her first collection in English might provide some interesting hints about her poetics and her attitude towards her implied non-Chinese reader. The book is divided into five sections, each of which gathers poems that are somehow connected: 1. the general themes of female identity, love, and fragility; 2. a selection of 11 poems dedicated to famous Western musicians, but actually dealing with personal emotions and everyday thoughts; 3. poems based on quite traditional symbolic images, such as the moon or snow; 4. poems on sexuality and gender; 5. the final section deals with the themes of distance, migration, barriers and home-sickness.

In her activity of creating and translating poetry, Ming Di makes the most of her being both an insider and an outsider with respect to Chinese society (a condition that might actually be seen to define the Sinophone poet in general). Her own poems harmoniously blend her Western experience and her perspective on Western culture with her own traditional heritage (such as Chinese folklore and legends). In addition, I would argue that she plays the role of the translator in two senses: 1) in the conventional sense of the word, as she actually translates or co-translates her own poems and other poets' works;[10] and 2) according to the special meaning provided by Latour in the ANT theory, according to which a "translator" plays a performative role, inducing others to do things; in this case, it refers to Ming Di's action of recruiting other poets and scholars as co-translators,[11] but also of appropriating her own culture and (im- or pro-)posing her views on Chinese poetry.

---

10 As I wrote before, she is also deeply involved in the translation and dissemination of modern and contemporary Chinese poetry: she has already published two English anthologies of Chinese poets and is the editor of similar works in several other languages and countries.

11 It is interesting to note that this specific meaning of the word "translator" in ANT theory has been recently analyzed by Gisela Silva, whose interpretation reinforces the idea of a powerful mediator who not only performs her translations but also makes the whole process possible: "it is up to the translator-spokesman to set the balance between, on the one hand, the requirements necessary for the network to function properly and, on the

On the one hand, Ming Di plays a fully individual role as a poet and a translator; on the other, her "social" or "collective" interpretation of the translating act makes her deal with a range of agents of translation, including poets, scholars, editors, publishers, and translators, both in China and abroad. As an actor, or a mediator, – in Latour's sense – she performs a full-blown social function, fostering cross-cultural interactions and collaborative translation.

The very choice of a direct reference to a problematic "model" such as Ezra Pound's "translations" of Chinese poems sheds light on the provocative role she plays within the field of Chinese poetry translation and dissemination. As John Williams shows in his essay, reading the Chinese poetic tradition through the lens of Pound's "scandalous" (mis)interpretation of Chinese ancient poetry "closes our eyes to the simple fact that Chinese poetry is much more than the imagistic expressionism that Pound attributed to it" and "glosses over the contemporary realities that Pound ignored" (Williams 2009, 160). However, in this case, I would argue that what Ming Di draws from this disputable cultural re-invention is neither Pound's imagined Chinese poetry nor his imagined and "entirely misunderstood" Chinese language – both detached from any actual reality – but mainly the idea of re-appropriating her own legacy, as a migrant poet, in order to freely express a modern sensitivity, as though she wanted to free herself from cultural and linguistic shackles, overcoming language and space barriers.

Consider for instance her poem "Qiangbi zhi jian" 墙壁之间 (Between walls): "Through the language walls I sense / your hopelessness so many new words pelt me like grit" (Ming Di 2012a, 63) (隔著語言的牆壁，感知/你的走投無路—那些生詞，灰塵一樣朝我襲來, Ming Di 2010a, 73): "Poetry was my cage/ now it's my universe, with a little shake, the physics of *distance* shifts" (Ming Di 2012a, 67) (詩，曾經是我的籠子，現在是我的天空/不許打破，稍一搖動，距離就發生物理變化, Ming Di 2010a, 73), she states in another poem from the same collection. Being an "in-betweener," like many Sinophone poets, Ming Di seems to feel a sense of *distance* (in space and time, between human beings and between words). Indeed, distance and the ways to fill it or to cope with it seem to be the guiding thread linking the 12 poems included in the last section of *River Merchant's Wife*. One may also refer to "Bici zhijian" 彼此之間 (Between here and there) which hints at cultural difference and identity through the elements of food and taste; or to the sense of remoteness evoked, as in ancient poetry, by simple weather events: "It's warm here, but it's snowing

---

other, the actors – formerly entities existing independently of any networks of relationships – needed for mobilisation" (2019, 403).

in China" (Ming Di 2012a, 73). Another articulation of the theme of distance is interpersonal relations in "Yiwai" 意外 (Unexpected): "the distance between you and me, so hard to arrange, / to get close to you seem so desperate, like a verse from Tang / dynasty," (Ming Di 2012a, 75) (你我的距離也是這樣/難以擺弄，怎麼隨意都顯得刻意，怎麼刻意都顯得零亂, Ming Di 2010a, 108). With regard to this stanza, one may note that in the English translation, carried out by the author with Sylvia Burn, a reference has been added to ancient Chinese poetry, a culture-specific element, as if to enhance the idea of distance in the eyes of the Anglophone reader.

In all the above-mentioned poems, the themes of distance and difference, lack of communication and the effort of mutual understanding play an important role. Therefore, I would argue that questions of gender and migration intersect with Ming Di's views on poetry creation and translation. As a woman she pro-actively takes the responsibility for leading translation projects, often involving male poets and translators (gender dislocation); as a foreign poet (geo-culturally dislocated), she involves – and cooperates with – Western poets/translators to allow her poetic voice to be heard outside China and promote her idea of modern Chinese poetry. Indeed, such a complicated and culturally challenging task is not without risks and potential misunderstandings: "[...] dislocation creates distance between languages and mindsets and enacts an economy of loss"; besides, "the juxtaposition of languages and discourses suggests the incomplete nature of cultural exchange, the lack of total reciprocity between signifying systems" (Simon 1996, 158). Building on these losses and gaps, the female editor/poet/translator embraces a new and sometimes ambiguous perspective on the translation and transmission of Chinese poetry. It might be interesting to ascertain whether this mediating role taken up by the poet is connected to her Sinophone identity – in other words, to what extent Ming Di re-builds her own tradition, reinventing it for both Chinese and Western readers.

Alongside the status of the translator, another important element to be considered when analyzing translation as a social act is the working process. Regarding the methods of collaboration and the status of the actors involved in the translation process, I will draw upon Ming Di's own statements about her translations and upon my reading of the anthology of her translated poems.

Based on the variety of collaborations and translations carried out by Ming Di, I would describe her role as both proactive and inclusive. Not only for her own poems, but also for her translations of other poets' works, Ming Di usually seeks the collaboration of mother-tongue poets and translators. This practice of co-translation is by no means a new thing in the translation of modern Chinese poetry: for instance, as recalled by Michelle Yeh,

> [t]he earliest collection of [modern Chinese poetry in English] appeared in 1936 and was edited and translated by Harold Acton (1904–1994) and Shih-hsiang Chen 陈世骧 (1912–1971). [Robert] Payne also collaborated with a Chinese colleague, in this case, the prominent poet and scholar Wen Yiduo. (Yeh 2011, 601)

A later translation of modern Chinese poetry is somehow also connected to the poet Wen Yiduo 闻一多, as the editor and translator of an anthology published in 1963, Kai-yu Hsu, was also a former student of his. In the 1980s, there was a great flowering of poetic translations, but these anthologies were mainly edited by Western Sinologists, such as for instance Michael Duke, and scholars of Chinese literature, such as Julia Lin.

Many of the editors of poetic anthologies analyzed by van Crevel (2019), including Ming Di herself, possess a double identity (if not bilingual, they have been trained both in China and in anglophone countries) and a double role or multiple roles as professors, editors, poets, and translators.

Regarding her choice of mostly producing collaborative translations, in cooperation with other poets or translators, in a recent interview, Ming Di stated:

> I think co-translation can bring out more interesting translations. Even if one can be bilingual and fluent in both the source language and target language, "native intuition" is very important in the process of translation. Co-translation can also reach more readers (the literary circles of the co-translators as well as general readers). (Ming Di 2022)

6   Creating and Translating Sinophone Poetry

In order to examine the concrete manifestation of Ming Di's attitude as a Sinophone poet and translator, I have scrutinized her first collection of translated poems, *River Merchant's Wife*.[12] First, I will provide an overview of her own ideas on poetry creation and translation in this respect, then, I will comment on a few examples from two renditions of one of her poems: one co-translated by the author and one translated by another poet.

---

12   A second collection of self-translated poems was published in 2010: "I actually started writing poetry in English in 2002 and published a bilingual collection *Fenshenshu* 分身 术 [The Art of Split] (New World Poetry, 2010)" (Ming Di 2022).

BORDERLESS CREATION

When speaking of her own creations, Ming Di emphasizes that self-translation is a method that allows an author to either take a step back from themselves or, on the contrary, to expand their creative universe:

> There are two kinds of self-translation, one is to translate your own work as if translating a stranger's work, the other is to re-create while translating. I usually automatically take the second route. I always end up writing a different poem when I translate myself, unless I force myself to follow the original lines when I'm asked to present bilingual versions of a poem. Sometimes I co-translate myself with another poet, sometimes I do it by myself. I find it interesting either way. Sometimes I write in English first and then the Chinese version. Most of the time I write Chinese versions first. (Ming Di 2022)

On the one hand, Ming Di's translation practice is somewhat typical of Sinophone poets, as she navigates between the two languages of her homeland and host country with considerable ease. On the other hand, besides choosing what language to use depending on her creative impulse, Ming Di argues that while her mother tongue and acquired one are increasingly overlapping, something is lost in this process; therefore, in her view, poetry creation and poetry translation could both be a way to make up for this loss. In an interview with an Italian poet back in 2016 she stated:

> After so many years of traveling back and forth, I'm beginning to lose the sense of "difference" between Chinese and English. I write in both languages every day, but English is only a tool – Chinese is the source of inspiration. In translating poetry, what gets lost are the linguistic subtleties and cultural references. What to sacrifice? Translators are making choices every day as to how to make up for what's lost and where to find alternative ways. One has to be more creative and more resourceful. And it takes time. (Ming Di 2016b)

Spivak's concept of translation as reparation resonates in Ming Di's words here.[13] Her engagement as a poet and a translator from her mother tongue

---

13   "When a translator translates from a constituted language, whose system of inscription, and permissible narratives are 'her own', this secondary act, translation in the narrow sense, as it were, is also a peculiar act of reparation – toward the language of the inside, a language in which we are 'responsible', the guilt of seeing it as one language among many.

into English often appears aimed at restoring or newly presenting her own language and culture.

The Sinophone poet can usually be referred to as someone in between (center and periphery, Chineseness and cosmopolitanism, the Chinese language and the host language, etc.): poetic language can therefore spring from one's own mother tongue but also from its translation into a foreign language, or, from contamination between the two. In Ming Di's case she mainly (co)translates her poems into English, but occasionally she also writes in English. Based on my reading of her English collection of poems *The River Merchant's Wife*, I would argue that Ming Di's creation of poetry, in some sense, has always been entangled with translation or, at least, affected by her contact with another language.

In a previous study (Pesaro 2019) I did on a Chinese writer living in the United States and writing only in English, Yiyun Li, I elaborated on the concept of "erasing" one's mother tongue as a liberating act as well as the result of trauma. In Yiyun Li's case, she has completely assimilated herself into the other tongue, as a reaction to her own troubled relationship with both her mother and her motherland. Moreover, she even rejects her linguistic roots through the "rejection of translation" (108), as she refuses her novels to be translated into Chinese.

In Ming Di's case, she operates in a different way, as she herself admits. She rejects *assimilation*, but she sometimes *accommodates* (to adopt Cronin's categories) her creation into the host language, as she easily shifts to English, when she deems it appropriate, often by building symbolic and logical associations between words and images. Moreover, she adopts rewriting and collaborative translation as two additional forms of poetry creation.

Beyond the questions of identity, I would like here to describe some elements of her translation strategies. Being a Sinophone author has somehow oriented her creation towards self-translation and co-translation, but she describes how many Chinese poets feel a sort of "pressure" nowadays:

> 越來越多的中國詩人都出英譯詩集。　我翻譯別人的詩，　慢慢就自然而然地想到，　哎，　是不是自己也出一本書啊。《長干行》英譯本是從我不同詩集來的挑選出來的詩，有些甚至還沒有發表過[⋯]。(Ming Di 2016a, 213)

Translation in the narrow sense is thus a reparation. I translate from my mother tongue" (Spivak 2000, 15).

> More and more Chinese poets are publishing English language collections. Translating other people's poems, I have naturally come to think: have you published a book yourself? The English translation of "Chang Gan Xing" is a selection of poems from different collections of my poetry, some of which had never been published [...].

Whereas one can find some notable examples of research on self-translation in modern and contemporary Chinese fiction – for instance on Zhang Ailing's self-translations and, more recently, on Guo Xiaolu – the practice and aesthetics of self-translation are rarely analyzed in the field of Chinese poetry.[14]

My study thus touches upon an almost unexplored territory, in which Ming Di seems to have been moving over the past ten years, by both reflecting and experimenting on the hybrid process of creation and translation, which has been defined by some scholars as *transcreation* (Spinzi et al. 2019).

By Ming Di's own admission,[15] she started translating and co-translating Chinese poetry into English in 2009, before translating her own poems into English. Dickinson College invited her to give a reading of her poems in 2011 and they published a chapbook, which was the prelude of her *River Merchant's Wife*. However, she continued translating other poets' works more than her own, in her capacity as an editor of poetry journals. Self-translation is thus a frequent choice for Ming Di, but it often blends or overlaps with collaborative translation. In this sense, I would argue that her creation and translation activities are closely interconnected and that translation is often only the first step for the creation of a brand-new work. Ming Di herself defines self-translation as "a creative process, more so than translating other people's work" through which she "usually end[s] up with a new poem." To her English and Chinese obey "different logics in the linguistic flow of [her] mind," as she "think[s] differently in two languages." She then states that "[s]ometimes a poem [comes] to me in English first, sometimes in Chinese first. Sometimes I keep two different versions, sometimes I try to stay with the original thoughts" (Ming Di 2022).

---

14   Just to provide a few additional examples, I can mention the following cases: Mu Dan 穆旦 and his self-translations; a study focusing on the Taiwanese poet Yu Kwang-chung's self-translations (Chen and Wu 2011; Gallo, 2022); Leon Burnett's recent analysis of the relationship between poetry-writing and translation in Wang Jiaxin (Burnett 2019).

15   I am referring here especially to my correspondence with the poet, carried out via email (Ming Di 2022).

This process of poetry translation can be defined as a "transcreative process". Shifting from self-translation to co-translation means adding an outside voice and letting it overlap with one's own. But both methods – self- and co-translation – imply the creation of something new. Let us just think of another Sinophone poet, Ouyang Yu, who has mostly engaged himself in self-translation (the very title of one of his collections of poems is precisely *Self-Translation*). His self-translated poems, according to Yulia Dreyzis (2021), appear to be based on a deliberate clumsiness, by which the poet challenges his own position and status as an allegedly bilingual or migrant poet.

As for Ming Di, she rather tends to adopt co-translation in order to avoid misunderstandings or clumsiness in the target language. Answering a question in an interview included in one of her collections, Ming Di talks about self- and co-translation, pointing to language games, invisible relationships, the use of ancient myths and the musicality of sentences ("语言游戏，隐身关系，古代神话的借用，句子的音乐性") as the most difficult elements to be translated:

> 我覺得理解原作需要來源語的母語詩人，翻譯成另一種的詩需要目標語的母語詩人，一首詩要兩個寫作者，共同完成，否者只是翻譯而不是詩。這本詩集有几首我自譯，其餘大部分是合譯。中文理解上我自己把關，但如果沒有合譯者在另一頭把關就沒有最後的英語詩。所以我強烈建議與英譯母語詩人合作，英語再好也不要自譯。(Ming Di 2016a, 215)

> I think that understanding the original text requires a poet who is a native speaker of the source language, while a poem translated into another language requires a poet who is a native speaker of the target language. A poem requires two writers, to complete it together, otherwise it is only a translation rather than a poem. I have translated a few poems in this collection myself, and most of the rest are co-translated. I can personally vouch for the quality of the Chinese language, but if there is no co-translator on the other side, there will be no final check on the English language. Therefore, I strongly recommend cooperating with English native-speaking poets: no matter how good one's English is, it is best not to self-translate.

In this passage she takes a precise stand on the never-ending question of poetry translated by poets or by translators. It seems as though, no matter what form it takes, poetry translation always ends up with collaborative practices or can be seen as the result of a plurality of subjects. In this sense, I would argue that Ming Di's self-translation can be described as a form of transcreation in which not only her poetry but she herself is transformed into something different. She is the author of both versions, but as a result of the self-translation, like in a performance, her poems acquire a different identity, as if endowed with an autonomous (with respect to its author) nature. Borrowing Hennion's words: "it is a performance, with unforeseeable effects." According to him, artworks are "objects you make, but in return make you; [...] they have their agency, their capacity to act." (Hennion 2020).

Another well-known poet-translator, Wang Jiaxin 王家新, "sees translation as an act of completion, which acknowledges the unfinished state of a poem that exists in another language" (Burnett 2019, 48). As already mentioned, from self-translation, Ming Di often shifts to co-translation: "Co-translation of my own poetry has sometimes become *bilingual writing* and other times *independent rendition*" (2022, Italics added).

To apply ANT theory to the practice of co-translation is somehow quite natural, as this process entails a continuous and entangled flow of actions or "movement" (in Latour's words) between the components of the network. In order to analyze the artworks created, one needs to track this back-and-forth movement of creation, interpretation and manipulation. In the interview she gave me, Ming Di describes co-translation as a multifaceted activity spanning from more formal team-work and collective readings to occasional email exchange and friendly conversations.

This oscillation between the two poles of bilingual writing and independent rendition into "a new poem" is also, in my opinion, one of the many ways in which Sinophone poetry takes shape, one of the many possible creative methods adopted by poets. In the last part of this chapter, I will illustrate this sort of "split" between authorship and translatorship that is reflected in Ming Di's transcreative practice.

In order to highlight some features of Ming Di's creative translation, I would like to analyze one of Ming Di's best-known poems, published in 2010. It is also a fundamental poem in terms of defining her poetic identity and points of reference. "Nüren de fangjian" 女人的房間 was composed in a "translational" way, as the title clearly hints at Virginia Woolf's seminal essay *A Room of One's Own*. The theme of female identity and literary creation is often discussed in Ming Di's poems and other texts (as can be seen from many of her interviews).

The case discussed in this chapter concerns the original Chinese text along with two translations (one into English and the other into German), which have been carried out respectively by the author herself in collaboration with Sylvia Burn and Kate Ferris (as a reviser), and by the German poet Jan Wagner.

It is interesting to note that while the American version is freer and takes more liberties, the German one is sometimes closer to Ming Di's original poem, as he translated the poem not via the American rendition but from a different version. Wagner, who does not speak or read Chinese, wrote his rendition based on Ming Di's self-translation into English.

女人的房間

她從沒有想到愛會使她這麼孤獨。
冬天太冷，她為自己畫一個房間，
然後躲進去，看書，聽音樂。
痛已蔓延到手臂，琴上結了一層蜘蛛網。
每天她用鄧肯的步子來回走，從一角
走到另一角，房間似乎一天比一天大起來。
有時陽光照進來，有時月光照進來，
她將這些光吸進身體，痛從手臂上退落。
她畫牆，畫了抹掉，抹掉又畫，又抹。
牆，自己長了起來，如同孤獨上開出的
冬青樹葉。她想在牆外畫一個欄杆，
柵住記憶的細節，然後種花，種草，種鳥，
種春天，夏天，秋天，種山，種海——
海水漲潮，如一圈花環襲上來，套住她。

我在窗外，看自己掙扎，想拉"她"，又想
推"她"一把，也許另一個窗口通向一片天。

MING DI 2010b

A Room of Her Own
She never knew love made for such cold winters.
She hides in the room she painted for herself,
tuning, listening, as music spreads pain
like spiderwebs down her legs
She walks from one corner to another,
the room grows bright with sunlight, or moon,
stabbing her with needles.
She paints a wall. Erases. Paints again.
Erases.
A wall grows like leaves emerging in winter.
She wants to paint a wall around the wall
to guard a memory, then
paint flowers and birds, mountains and oceans – a wave
swirls around like a wreath, circling up,
entangling her.

BORDERLESS CREATION

I see myself in that room, struggling. "Paint a window,"
I tell her, a window that leads to the sky.
Paint a sky. (trans. with Sylvia Burn and Kate Ferris, Ming Di 2012a, 15)

Ein Zimmer nur für Sie
Der Winter ist kalt, sie malt ein Zimmer, nur für sich allein,
und versteckt sich darin, liest und hört Musik.
Schmerz dringt in die Arme, die Guzheng ist voller
Spinnweben. Sie geht im zwanglosen Stil Isidora Duncans
von einer Ecke zur andern, und das Zimmer wirkt manchmal
größer und heller, wenn Sonne hineinscheint, der Mond.
Ihr Körper nimmt Licht auf, der Schmerz strömt in die Beine.
Sie malt eine Wand, streicht aus, malt und streicht
erneut. Eine Wand wächst ganz von allein, als wüchsen Winterblätter
aus der Einsamkeit. Sie will einen Zaun um die Wand malen,
die Erinnerung einhegen, Blumen pflanzen, Gras und Vögel,
will Frühling pflanzen, Sommer, Herbst, die Berge
und Meere – ein Wellenstrudel, ein Wellenkranz umschließt sie,
umschlingt sie.
Ich stehe vorm Fenster, beobachte meinen eigenen
Kampf. Ich will „sie" ziehen, schubsen – vorm anderen Fenster
kann ein weiterer Himmel sein. (trans. by Yan Wagner, Ming Di 2010c)

According to the small group of poets/translators who adopted this method for a workshop on modern Japanese poetry translation, the process of co-translation is characterized by "scrupulous freedoms, tempered by a meticulous attention to the original work and a sense of the places from which that work emerged" (Atherton et al. 2021, 14).

It is this kind of "scrupulous freedom" that we detect in the co-translated version of Ming Di's poem. In particular, in the English poem we may note that: some words are omitted or changed in order to re-create the same poetic atmosphere, but by different means – for instance the word "*gudu*" 孤獨 (solitude) (which appears twice in the Chinese version, once in the German one, "Einsamkeit"), is omitted in the English one, and rendered only through the image of "winter"; the co-translation reinforces the symbolic concept of "cold" and "winter";[16] finally "*kan shu*" 看書 (reading) ("liest" in the German

---

16   Ming Di explained in our email exchange that, while working with Sylvia Burn on this poem, she did not like the word "lonely," as it sounded plain and too straightforward, and preferred to omit it.

translation) is replaced in English by the verb "tuning" (which hints at the stringed instrument, the "*qin*" 琴 in the Chinese poem).

In the third stanza there are two juxtaposed scenes: the "pain" spreading from "her" arms, and the "spiderwebs" wrapping the musical instrument: they are blended into a similitude, where "legs" replace the arm (*shoubi* 手臂) of the original poem. Generally speaking, compared to the original and to the German translation, the English version seems more implicit and tends to avoid culture-specific elements, which are on the contrary emphasized by Wagner: this is the case with the Chinese instrument (the term *qin* 琴, which is also a general term for chord instrument, is more specified in the German translation, where it occurs as *guzheng*) and Isadora Duncan, the famous dancer and a recurring figure in Ming Di's poems. The woman in the poem "將這些光吸進身體" (absorbs the light into her body) "nimmt Licht auf" in German, while in the English co-translation she is "stabbed by needles" (a violent action inflicted to her rather than a subjective act of reception), which encapsulates the pain descending from her arms (only in the Chinese version and in the German one). Again, the word "solitude" is omitted in the English version. Also, in the co-translated version of the poem one can notice the repetition of the word "*qiang*" 牆 (wall), as if to reinforce the idea of enclosure; the verb "*zhong*" 種 (to plant) ("pflanzen") is replaced by the more abstract action of "painting"; seasons are omitted in the English translation, which provides, again, a more abstract, less detailed, and implicit rendition of the original poem.

In the last couplet Ming Di offers a change of perspective, realizing the split identity of the self: "*ta*" 她 (she) sees herself from outside (out of the window) in Chinese, while in the English version, she sees herself inside the room. The same scene is viewed from two different perspectives, as though the poet were hinting at how different languages can show different points of view.

In the final couplet, again, the two action verbs "*la*" 拉 (pull) and "*tui*" 推(push) (respectively "ziehen" and "schubsen" in the German version) are replaced by a single performative verb – "tell" – in the English rendition. The act of painting (of creating from scratch) replaces the original "也許另一個窗口通向一片天" (perhaps another window opens up leading towards the sky) which in German sounds like "vorm anderen Fenster/ kann ein weiterer Himmel sein" (outside the other window there can be another sky).

In the ending, as often happens in Ming Di's poems, there is a shift in the pronouns from the third to the first person (sometimes the shift is from the first to the second). "*ta*" 她 (she) becomes "*wo*" 我 (I), and the protagonist of the poem is eventually doubled or split in two.

As explained by Ming Di herself "[...] '我' 與 '她' 的對視，是一種嘗試，" (Me and her looking at each other is a kind of experiment). Talking about this doubling or splitting of the pronouns, she reveals that "[...] 第一人稱 '我' 有時候並非自己，而是一個設定的戲劇人物，但最終是另一個我的化身" (2012b) (the first person 'I' is sometimes not myself, but rather a set dramatic character, but in the end it is another incarnation of myself).

I consider this poem a particularly revealing one, a sort of self-portrait of the poet herself: the poem describes Ming Di's most intimate space: the poet herself engrossed in her favorite activities (playing the *guzheng*, dancing, reading), as well as her projection outside of this intimate room, a window opened towards the sky as if to point at her being engaged in a larger social space, interacting with the outside world through her creative activity.

To conclude, I would argue that Ming Di represents an interesting case of a Sinophone poet who continuously blends poetry creation and translation. Her role as a cosmopolitan Chinese poet is constantly intertwined with her role as a "mediator" of poetry. One of the preferred types of translation performed by Ming Di is co-translation, often involving poets who work with her through another tongue. As in the poem analyzed above, poetry creation is at the same time intimately individual and profoundly social: it seems to me that this method allows the poet, who is also a co-translator, to feel free to re-create and re-shape her own poems.

Indeed, one of the activities promoted by Ming Di through the journal she has co-founded, *Poetry East West*, is the hosting of a recurring column titled "Poets translating other poets," where creation and translation merge in a seamless blend.

A first conclusion to my preliminary study is that there is an apparent connection between the multiple voices that interact in Ming Di's creative work – as she tries to see herself from a distance or at least by letting her multiple identities emerge in her poetry writing – and in her poetry translations through a collaborative practice which is a form of self-othering: the poets she cooperates with are also other voices that not only help her to check on the target language but also contribute to the re-creation or trans-creation of her own poems. Ming Di herself offers a psychological explanation for the process of both creation and translation, a process also reflected in the way she plays with identity in her poems through the device of shifting pronouns. This explanation is found in the concept of the defamiliarization of the author:

> 陌生感 and 距離感 feel better than familiarity, at least to me. It's the strangeness in poetry that attracts me as a reader. It's the sense of distance that makes a writer more objective, even though lyric poetry sounds very subjective on the surface level. Translation should bring out

the strangeness in poetry, although not necessarily the sense of distance. (Ming Di 2022)

Moreover, thanks to the analysis conducted on her practices of self-translation and co-translation, based on ANT theory, Ming Di's case is particularly meaningful as it can explain or at least describe in a more subtle way how Sinophone poetry is constituted. Indeed, this case study allows us to shed light on textual and social practices shaping the very essence of Sinophone poetry as a product of continuous interactions and movements within complex networks. In these networks, the poet-translator is at the center as one of the key mediators, but other actors such as co-translators, poets, scholars, and the texts themselves – whether they be the original poems, different versions, or other influential poetic texts – play a prominent role.

Works Cited

Agar, Michael. 1994. *Language Shock. Understanding the Culture of Conversation*. New York: Morrow.

Agorni, Mirella. 2007. "Locating Systems and Individuals in Translation Studies." In *Constructing a Sociology of Translation*, edited by Michaela Wolf and Alexandra Fukari, 123–34. London: John Benjamins Publishing Company.

Atherton, Cassandra, Paul Hetherington, and Rina Kikuchi. 2021. "Poetry Co-translation and an Attentive Cosmopolitanism: Internationalising Contemporary Japanese poetry." *Coolabah* 30: 4–22.

Burnett, Leon. 2019. "The Eye of the Scorpion: Wang Jiaxin as Translator-Poet." In *Translation or Transcreation? Discourses, Texts and Visuals*, edited by Cinzia Spinzi, Alessandra Rizzo, and Marianna Lya Zummo, 39–50. Newcastle upon Tyne: Cambridge Scholars Publishing.

Buzelin, Hélène. 2005. "Unexpected Allies: How Latour's Network Theory Could Complement Bourdieusian Analyses in Translation Studies." *The Translator* 11 (2): 193–218.

Chen, Li-yin and Wu, Yi-ping. 2011. "Self-Translation and Identity in Yu Kwang-chung's *The Night Watchman.*" *Journal of Applied Foreign Languages/Yingyong waiyu xuebao* 16: 35–56.

Chesterman, Andrew. 2009. "The Name and Nature of Translator Studies." *HERMES – Journal of Language and Communication in Business* 22 (42): 13–22.

Chow, Rey. 1993. *Writing Diaspora. Tactics of Intervention in Contemporary Cultural Studies*. Bloomington and Indianapolis: Indiana University Press.

Crevel, Maghiel van. 2019. "A Noble Art, and a Tricky Business. Translation Anthologies of Chinese Poetry." In *Chinese Poetry and Translation Rights and Wrongs*, edited by

BORDERLESS CREATION

Maghiel van Crevel and Lucas Klein, 331–50. Amsterdam: Amsterdam University Press.

Cronin, Michael. 2006. *Translation and Identity*. London and New York: Routledge.

Dreyzis, Yulia. 2021. "The Quest for Bilingual Chinese Poetry: Poetic Tradition and Modernity." In *Literary Translation, Reception, and Transfer*, edited by Norbert Bachleitner, 491–501. Berlin and Boston: De Gruyter.

Gallo, Simona. 2022. "The Prism of Self-Translation: *Poiesis* and Poetics of Yu Guangzhong's Bilingual Poetry." *The Translator* (December): 1–16. https://doi.org/10.1080/13556509.2022.2140623.

Gonne, Maud. 2018. "From Binarity to Complexity. A Latourian Perspective on Cultural Mediators: the case of Georges Eekhoud's Intra-National Activities." In *Literary Translation and Cultural Mediators in 'Peripheral' Cultures: Customs Officers or Smugglers?*, edited by Diana Roig-Sanz and Reine Meylaerts, 263–290. London: Palgrave Macmillan. E-book.

Hennion, Antoine. 2020. "From ANT to pragmatism. A Journey with Bruno Latour at the CSI." In Latour and the Humanities, edited by Rita Felski and Stephen Muecke. Baltimore. Johns Hopkins University Press. Kindle ed.

Latour, Bruno. 2005. *Reassembling the Social. An Introduction to Actor-Network-Theory*. Oxford: Oxford University Press.

Ming, Di 明迪. 2010a. *Ming Di shixuan* 明迪詩選 [Ming Di's selected works]. Wuhan: Changjiang wenyi chubanshe.

Ming, Di 明迪. 2010b. "Xingbie wenti (13 shou)" 性別問題（13首）[Questions of Gender. 13 poems]. Available online: https://www.poemlife.com/index.php?mod=transhow&id=58401&str=1682. Accessed June 21, 2022.

Ming, Di 明迪. 2010c. "Ein Zimmer nur für sie." *Poetry East & West* 1 詩東西雜志創刊號 12: 109. Available online: https://poetryeastwest.files.wordpress.com/2012/08/poetry-east-west-1.pdf. Accessed June 21, 2022.

Ming, Di 明迪. 2012a. *River Merchant's Wife*. Translated from Chinese by Tony Barnstone, Neil Aitken, Afaa M. Weaver, Katie Ferris, Sylvia Burn with the author. Grosse Pointe Farms: Marick Press.

Ming, Di 明迪. 2012b. "Ming Di fangtan: Shi shi chongxin ganzhi de guocheng" 明迪訪談：詩是重新感知的過程 [Interview with Ming Di: Poetry is a process of re-perception], interview by Mu Duo 木朵, *Nanfang yishu*, 2012-09-28. Available online: https://www.zgnfys.com/a/nfpl-7913.shtml Accessed June 21, 2022.

Ming, Di 明迪, ed. 2013a. *New Cathay. Contemporary Chinese Poetry*. North Adams Massachusetts: Tupelo Press.

Ming, Di 明迪. 2013b. "Dangdai hanyu shi de ying yi kunjing" 当代汉语诗的英译困境 [Difficulties in translating contemporary Chinese poetry into English]. In *Shi jianshe*, 8, edited by Quanzi, 214–219. Beijing: Zuojia chubanshe. Available Online: https://www.poemlife.com/index.php?mod=libshow&id=2776. Accessed May 18, 2022.

Ming, Di 明迪. 2014. "Ming Di fangtan: cong mosheng dao mosheng" 明迪訪談:從陌生到陌生 [Interview to Ming Di: from estrangement to estrangement], interview by Zhang Shuguang 張曙光. *Shige yuekan* 5: 12–15.

Ming, Di 明迪. 2015. "Yingxiang yu jiaolü: Zhongguo dangdai shi zai Meiguo yijie de zhuangkuang" 影響與焦慮:中國當代詩在美國的譯介狀況 [Influence and anxiety: the introduction and translation of Chinese poetry in America]. In *Tazhe yanguang yu haiwai shijiao: Shijie shiye Zhong de Zhongguo dangdai wenxue* 他者眼光與海外視角:世界視野中的中國當代文學 [The gaze of the Other and foreign perspectives: contemporary Chinese literature in the eyes of the world], edited by Zhang Qinghua 張清華, 34–74. Beijing: Beijing daxue chubanshe.

Ming, Di 明迪. 2016a. *Jihu meige tianshi dou you chipang yiji yixie qiguai de chihao* 幾乎每個天使都有翅膀以及一些奇怪的嗜好 [Almost every angel has got wings and some strange hobby]. Taiyuan: Beiyue wenyi chubanshe.

Ming, Di 明迪. 2016b. "'I Was Born Out of the Chrysanthemums': An Interview with Ming Di," by Franca Mancinelli. *World literature today*. https://www.worldliterature today.org/blog/interviews/i-was-born-out-chrysanthemums-interview-ming-di. Accessed April 20, 2022.

Ming, Di 明迪, ed. 2018. *New Poetry from China 1917–2017*. Berkeley: Black Square Editions.

Ming, Di 明迪. 2022. Unpublished interview.

Munday, Jeremy S. and Jacob Blakesley. 2016. "Introduction. Poetry Translation: Agents, Actors, Networks, Context." *Translation and Literature* 25 (1): 1–9.

Pesaro, Nicoletta. 2019. "The Death of the Mother Tongue: Language's Inadequacy and Body Representation in Chinese-American Writer Yiyun Li." In *Viajes y escrituras: migraciones y cartografías de la violencia*, edited by Nicoletta Pesaro and Alice Favaro, 8, 107–23, Paris: Eduardo Ramos-Izquierdo.

Shi, Flair Donglai. 2021. "Reconsidering Sinophone Studies: The Chinese Cold War, Multiple Sinocentrisms, and Theoretical Generalisation." *International Journal of Taiwan Studies* 4: 311–44.

Silva, Gisele. 2019. "Traduttore-Traditore All Over Again? The Concept of Translation in the Actor-Network Theory." In *Traducción y sostenibilidad cultural: sustrato, fundamentos y aplicaciones*, edited by Cristina Carrasco, María Cantarero Muñoz, and Coral Díez Carbajo, 401–06. Salamanca: Ediciones Universidad de Salamanca.

Simon, Sherry. 1996. *Gender in Translation. Cultural Identity and the Politics of Transmission*. London and New York: Routledge.

Spinzi, Cinzia, Alessandra Rizzo, and Marianna Lya Zummo, eds. 2019. *Translation or Transcreation? Discourses, Texts and Visuals*. Newcastle upon Tyne: Cambridge Scholars Publishing.

Spivak, Gayatri Chakravorty. 2000. "Translation as Culture." *Parallax* 6 (1): 13–24.

Tang, Jun. 2011. "Ezra Pound's *The River Merchant's Wife*: Representations of a Decontextualized 'Chineseness.'" *Meta* 56 (3) (September): 526–37.

Toury, Gideon. 1995. "The Nature and Role of Norms in Translation." In *Descriptive Translation Studies and Beyond*, 53–69. Amsterdam-Philadelphia: John Benjamins.

Williams, R. John. 2009. "Modernist Scandals: Ezra Pound's Translations of 'the' Chinese Poem." In *Orient and Orientalism in US-American Poetry and Poetics*, edited by Sabine Sielke and Christian Kloeckner, 145–165. Frankfurt: Peter Lang.

Yeh, Michelle. 2011. "Modern Chinese Poetry: Translation and Translatability." *Frontiers of Literary Studies in China* 5 (4): 600–09.

CHAPTER 10

Epistolary Translation

Daryl Lim Wei Jie's Correspondence with Bai Juyi

Joanna Krenz
Adam Mickiewicz University

1   Introduction: an Unlikely Encounter

Dear Mr. Bai,

Honestly, I didn't know about your poetry until my trip to Xi'an with my good friend H ––. For years I had been taught and instructed that the masters of Tang poetry were names like Li Bai, Du Fu, Wang Wei and Meng Haoran. Perhaps even more pertinently, my Chinese wasn't and still isn't all that good. I did decently enough at Higher Chinese, in a school where failing Chinese was often seen as a badge of honor. But certainly not good enough to fluently read and interpret Tang poetry, though I am pretty adept at ordering from the caifan stall. (Lim 2021a)

With disarming unceremoniousness, the modern Singaporean poet Daryl Lim Wei Jie thus begins one of his five letters to the Tang dynasty Chinese poet Bai Juyi 白居易 (772–846). The letters accompany a selection of nine poems by Bai in Lim's experimental translation as part of the project titled *White Spaces: Encounters with Bai Juyi*, published in the spring issue of *Exchanges: Journal of Literary Translation* in 2021: *Hua fei hua* 花非花 (DLWJ: "Flower Yet Not"), *Baiyunquan* 白雲泉 (DLWJ: "In White Cloud Spring"), *Yexue* 夜雪 (DLWJ: "Night Snow"), *Weiyu ye xing* 微雨夜行 (DLWJ: "Night Walk in the Light Rain"), *Fu de guyuancao songbie* 賦得古原草送別 (DLWJ: "Grass"), *Pu zhong ye bo* 浦中夜泊 (DLWJ: "Moored at Night"), 白鷺 *Bailu* (DLWJ: "Egrets"), *Yeyu* 夜雨 (DLWJ: "Night Rain"), *Xi mudanhua* 惜牡丹花 (DLWJ: "Feeling Sorry about the Peonies"). From the – not entirely one-directional, as we shall soon see – correspondence between the poets, we learn, among other things, that as a descendant of Chinese immigrants, during a trip to the land of his ancestors, Lim came across Bai's *Song of Everlasting Sorrow* (*Changhen ge* 長恨歌), which enchanted him and prompted him to find out more about its ingenious author. As the curious poet-tourist started to read more widely and dig more deeply, particularly in available translations and scholarship on Bai, he also

© JOANNA KRENZ, 2024 | DOI:10.1163/9789004711600_012

kept discovering intriguing correspondences between the complicated history of Bai's career and reception in China and beyond, on the one hand, and his own fate as a poet and as a human, on the other. Born and raised in Singapore to a family with mainland-Chinese roots, educated first in a Methodist school in his home country and later as a student of History and Political Thought at Oxford and Intellectual History at Cambridge, Lim, too, has experienced the turbulence of local and global cultural and sociopolitical currents and has been forced to carefully navigate between them.

Having liberated himself, as he notes in one of the later letters, from the burden of cultural ambassadorship, which is what many people still expect from members of various diasporas, Lim approaches his task as translator in a very personal and subjective way. At the same time, however, he tries to avoid self-serving appropriation and to do justice to the poems' "gravity and grace," to use Simone Weil's famous antithesis. With regard to specific language choices, his renditions are, by and large, faithful to the originals in the conventional sense of the word, implying first and foremost a literality of translation. Yet, as far as form is concerned, the poet-translator introduces significant modifications: large breaks between words and unconventional line divisions and visual arrangement. As a result, the originally two- or four-line poems in translation each occupy an entire page. This, as will be discussed more extensively later, is meant to slow down the reading and produce the effect of estrangement, which, in turn, is intended to inspire a more profound reflection.

In the letters, Daryl Lim tells Bai Juyi about the contemporary world, explaining phenomena such as the internet or the Covid-19 pandemic, he introduces modern Sinophone poets, and – perhaps most interestingly – informs Bai Juyi about the afterlife of his poetry since the late ninth century: in particular, its popularity in Japan, where some of Bai's works were even misattributed to local authors. Lim also undertakes a more general literary-philosophical reflection on translation, and seeks Bai's approval of his decisions, innovations, and motivations as a translator. One of these, which appears to be of particular importance, is rearticulated in his "Translator's Note" in the following way:

> In his short poems, Bai seems to me to prefigure certain aspects of Japanese aesthetics, especially in poetry. Looking back, I think perhaps one of my subconscious aims as a member of the Chinese diaspora was to destabilize the rigid conception of Tang poetry as a cultural product only of China, and the increasing tendency to think of cultures as the exclusive property of one group or another. (Lim 2021a)

Toh Wen Li, commenting on Lim's renditions, says that they would be a good match for Joshua Ip's provocative *Translations to the Tanglish* (Li 2022). In his collection, Ip recreates moods, concepts, and concerns from classical Tang- and Song-dynasty poems using elements of the modern imaginarium, in the center of which is the smartphone screen as a counterpart to moonlight in ancient verse. This association between Ip and Lim is justified if one takes into account what is at stake in both projects in cultural-political terms: the identity of the poet-translator, bridging remote spatiotemporal realities, and the dehegemonization and dehomogenization of the Chinese-language cultural heritage. On the other hand, nothing could be more different than the respective approaches of the two authors. Ip finds theoretical backup for his experiments in the work of Haroldo de Campos (1986) and his discussion of the postcolonial idea of transcreation as modern cannibalism – that is, the ingestion and metabolic processing of the literary heritage of the culture of the oppressor. He argues that:

> when applied to this project, the source text is not the domain of a colonial master, but to a distant ancestor who still wields a unique and significant source of cultural and historical power, relative to a displaced ethnically Chinese Singaporean who thinks and dreams in English rather than their government-mandated "mother tongue." (Ip 2021)

Daryl Lim's more subtle and pensive take, rather than as ingestion, could be defined as inspiration in the etymological sense of the word. He "inhales" Bai's poetics in order to inject new life in his own writing. Perhaps we should even speak of "transmutation" – the word Lim himself uses when referring to Malaysian poet Wong Phui Nam's renditions of Tang verses (Lim 2021a) as a process analogous to that of "inner alchemy" (or *neidan* 內丹 in Chinese) that allows for self-cultivation in harmony with the world, textual and nontextual alike.

This transmutation and circulation of Bai's lyrical energy in Lim's work can be observed in his 2021 poetry collection *Anything but Human*. In its second part, titled "great reset," which comes after the escape from the eponymous Baudrillardian "desert of the real" in part one, he includes his translations of Bai, this time without the accompanying letters or any other commentary. They are scattered among his own texts and contribute to a roughly consistent, albeit anything but smooth and unambiguous narrative of rebirth through re-cycling, in the lit(t)eral sense of the term, with waste being one of the leitmotifs of the collection, as well as in a quasi-religious sense, as in the great cycle of constantly renewed life. In some cases, Bai's work seems to create a counterpoint, or perhaps counterweight, to what the modern world mirrored in Lim's intense and sometimes perverse verse has to offer. Elsewhere, it looks as if Lim's poems were a direct, natural extension of Bai's work, incubated in its lyrical cradle. Reveling or rebelling, at some point, however, they always start rocking themselves in it so energetically that they sooner or later fall out of it, often crying loudly to attract attention – not to themselves but to the problems that they hopelessly but persistently try to address.

In the following two main sections of the present chapter, I will first take a closer look at what I tentatively deem Lim's epistolary translation. I will approach it as an alternative form of cross-epochal and cross-cultural communication in the world after the postmodern decomposition of "the postal principle" portrayed in Jacques Derrida's *Post Card* (2020) first published in 1980 – a pitiless satire on epistolary literature, on the one hand, and a criticism of the logocentric tradition, on the other. I will try to establish the (spectral) address of the sender, who is compelled to maneuver between different force fields, and localize the addressee on the dynamic map of cultural production following the hints included in the letters' content, for the envelopes with the addresses and postal stamps are, unfortunately, what is first lost in translation ...

I will also reflect upon readers' status in this peculiar exchange, as receivers of carbon copies, or, precisely, blind carbon copies (bcc), of letters addressed to someone else. As readers, what is our presumed role in this enterprise? Are we supposed to support the author and, if a need arises, testify to his attempts to establish contact with the sender in (an almost certain) case of failed communication in order to confirm his best intention to authorize his renditions? Or, perhaps, our part is that of archivists, whose function in Lim's poetry goes far beyond keeping track and preserving the textual documents but also entails codetermining the documents' meaning? Like in quantum-physical experiments – wherein the eye of the measurer determines the outcome of the measurement – in the short "quantum" poem from *Anything but Human* titled "Narrative (IX)," we are told: "This poem is behaving as it should because you're reading it. / Otherwise, it is usually all over the place" (Lim 2021b: 80). Or, yet differently, may it be that we are actually the proper addressees of this poetic correspondence? Does the author simply prefer for us not to know our actual role or, alternatively, wishes to fool someone or something else – for example, some form of censorship that might potentially disrupt or distort intercultural communication? I am thinking here mostly of ideological, rather than institutional censorship, to which we voluntarily, if not always entirely consciously, subject ourselves in the name be it of some kind of political correctness, or an ethical self-image, or a yet different incarnation of what in religious societies used to be known as conscience. It is as if the sender wishes to tell us: forget your current circumstances and personal interest, and focus, as much as you can, on the texts before your eyes. Perhaps he hopes to remind us of an obvious truth that we have forgotten in our narcissistic era: not all texts on earth are about you, even if you happen to read them! In a little phenomenological experiment that Lim, as the author of "A Phenomenological Cookbook", included in *Anything but Human* (Lim 2021b, 24), would hopefully approve of, bracket yourself out, as Husserl would say, and try to see what the poems wish to show and not just what you would like to see in them or how you would like to see yourself in them.

Only by fully realizing this obvious but strangely forgotten truth, can one be transformed – and not just have one's views reconfirmed or one's ego augmented – by what one is reading. By analyzing in part two how his translations of Bai Juyi interact with Daryl Lim's own poetry, I will try to demonstrate how what I tentatively term the "post-postal principle" works in lyrical practice and how the internalized epistolary dialog with Bai shapes Lim's collection as such and guides its reception amongst various worldwide audiences.

2 Translation in Letters: toward the Post-Postal Principle

Before setting out to investigate the identity and actual locations of all the parties involved: the sender, the addressee, and the recipients of carbon copies, let us – for the purpose of customs control on transnational borders – determine the actual content, dimensions, and proper poetico-political weight of this peculiar shipment. A thorough examination of this correspondence's properties will be followed by some cultural-detective work in the second half of this section aimed at reconstructing the network of connections between different agents and its philosophical implications.

2.1 *Scanning the Shipment*

The correspondence between Daryl Lim and Bai Juyi in *White Spaces* begins, curiously enough, with an excerpt from a text written by a third party. Before turning to the addressee, Lim quotes a description of an unusual encounter between Japanese authors Takashina no Moriyoshi and Ōe no Asatsuna and Bai in the dreams of the first two. Takashina no Moriyoshi dreamt of encountering Bai during his journey to China and perpetuated this encounter in verses. Asatsuna, in turn, was visited by Bai at his own residence. His vision is as memorable as it is ephemeral, for, overjoyed by the encounter, Asatsuna asks the Chinese poet if he came from heaven. Bai Juyi reveals he has come to tell Asatsuna something. At that very moment, Asatsuna awakes from his dream[1] (Lim 2021a).

As if the dreamy source were not blurred enough, the anecdote is not from a firsthand account of the dreamer but cited from an academic book: Leo Shingchi Yip's *China Reinterpreted: Staging the Other in Muromachi Noh Theater*, where the oneiric scene is used to illustrate the profound impact Bai Juyi had on Japanese poetry. Thus, the reader immediately gets the idea of how many mediators and fluky coincidences were needed to establish communication and how many unobvious channels mobilized, including as different ones as poetic dreams and scholarly monographs, to get in touch with the addressee.

The excerpt is followed by the first of Lim's translations: the poem "Flower Yet Not". The short and seemingly simple text gives us the foretaste of the confusing ambiguity and undecidability of the reality that emerges from the entire epistolary exchange.

> Flower
>   yet not
> mist
>   yet not
>
>   arrives midnight departs daybreak
>
>   like a   spring dream   how long can this
>   last?
>
>   vanishes   :
>
>   a spectre
>
>   never
>
>   to be found

It is almost impossible not to think in this place of the famous *quid pro quo* from Zhuangzi's dream about a butterfly and the porous boundaries between the human subject and nature, the objective and subjective realities the story

---

1   All quotes in this section, unless otherwise indicated, come from this source. Online source, no page numbers.

illuminates. Who talks to whom, then? Is it Daryl Lim addressing a projection of Bai Juyi in his mind, or, maybe, the other way around: Bai Juyi speaking to a projection of Daryl Lim and all his future readers whom he could not know but whose existence he must have tacitly assumed and tentatively inscribed into his poems, hoping they would respond in due time? Or both?

The next text we encounter is finally a proper letter, the one quoted in the introduction to the present chapter, from which we learn about Lim's and H's trip to Xi'an and their reading of *The Song of Everlasting Sorrow* in a modern hotel with a bottle of cheap Chinese beer, a performance they recorded and posted on Instagram – another notion that needs to be explained to Bai ("Instagram's going to be difficult to explain to you, along with the whole concept of the internet, but imagine being able to let your friends see what you're doing right now, in an instant"). Briefly recapitulating the *Song*'s content, Lim recalls how "the Emperor remains haunted by the memory of his favorite consort, and eventually contacts her in the afterlife with the help of a Taoist priest." Another memory within a memory, epiphany within an epiphany. And another boundary blurred: that between life and death.

And then, as frustration gradually upsurges in some readers, many of whom will probably start looking for some sharp and decisive interpretive tool to cut the Gordian knot of dreams, hallucinations, texts, and facts, the next portion of correspondence offers a soothing image: Bai's poem "In White Cloud Spring". While the opening lines read peacefully, the poem's second stanza sounds like an admonition for our impatience and a warning against the desire to "rush down" and "bring more ferment" rather than contemplate and let oneself be immersed in, and transformed by, beauty.

> clouds float   free
> and waters
>
> idle
>
> why rush down the mountain
> and bring more ferment
> to the world below?

The translation of "In White Cloud Spring" is then supplemented with another cross-cultural reference: a scene from the Japanese classic *The Pillow Book of Sei Shōnagon* (枕草子) invoked in Ivan Morris's rendition. On a snowy day, sitting by a fireplace, the Japanese Empress alludes to a yet different landscape poem by Bai Juyi, *Xianglu feng xia* 香爐峰下 (At the Foot of Xianglu Mountain), asking: "how is the snow on Hsiang-lu peak?". She is advised by one of her

EPISTOLARY TRANSLATION

interlocutors, Sei, who instantly identifies the allusion, to roll up the window blinds and see, as in Bai's poem (cf. Li 2012, 38–39). This leisurely lyrical conversation from Japanese literature subsequently leads us through visual-linguistic links – pillow and snow – back to China, as depicted in Bai's "Night Snow". Preceded by the fragment from *The Pillow Book*, Bai's "pillow poem" reads like a response to the text that was actually a response to his work.

Stunned
          by cold   pillow &
                           quilt

          the window flashes

          white   again

dark night   but I know

          the snow falls heavy

     as   the bamboo   snaps

                     and

                           snaps

After this transcultural journey through dreamy lands, we are unexpectedly brought down to earth by "Night Walk in Light Rain", invoked directly after "Night Snow" without any narrative interruptions. There, Bai Juyi dramatically shifts his attention from the mystical landscape to his soaked clothes and the unpleasant feeling they impart:

Out of the mistsrise

                     autumn clouds

     but

          by
               bit

                     the night's chill grows

> All I feel are
>
> My damp clothes
>
> Not the raindrops &
>
> not a sound

This is also where Daryl Lim shakes off the dreamy mood and tries to critically re-examine what he has been doing for the last several pages as if in a trance (shall we call it 'trance-lation', perhaps?). In his second letter to Bai, he starts from a question that is both theoretical-methodological and deeply personal, on which he elaborates in the subsequent paragraphs:

> What is it that draws so many of us to translation? To that space between the languages, and that seductive and impossible task of converting the hard, glittering gems of Tang poetry into the promiscuous, easy and endlessly evolving language that is English. Writers like myself, with Chinese ancestry, seem particularly drawn.

Further on, we read about Wong Phui Nam's "transmutations," which Lim illustrates with a brief analysis of Wong's rendition of Du Fu 杜甫, where "instead of trying to preserve the brevity of Chinese, he commits fully to exploiting the verbosity of English, to fill in what Du Fu left to the imagination." Lim wonders what Bai would have said about this method of translation, as well as about his own, which – at first glance – is ideally opposite to Wong's, although it aims at a similar effect: recreating the thoughtful (Chinese) silence in the thoughtless (English) language. He makes an observation that is crucial for our understanding of his approach to translation and to writing at large, and to which we will return in the ongoing discussion of *Anything but Human*:

> In modern English, words flow too easily into each other, and we are too quick to fit ourselves into that flow and ease, consuming each word and moving on to the next. The world we live in, with that internet I spoke of, encourages this. Language is cheap, grubby and easily processed, and we seem less and less concerned with language and more with images and graphics. This is why I have tried to put space between characters, to let the reader feel the gravity and significance of each word, and to let the significance sink in more fully.

This reflection on the difference between languages is followed by the translation of Bai's "Grass". In the poem, "wild / grows grass on the plain." In the

EPISTOLARY TRANSLATION

context of the preceding letter, this image might indeed be read as a prefigurative metaphor of the "cheap, grubby and easily processed" English: its lack of elegant dignity that Lim tries to remedy by planting more silence between the leaves of grass so that they can breathe, and to create space for bigger concepts and concerns. The image of "the grey city" in the translated poem will perhaps lead a modern poetry reader toward Lu Xun's 魯迅 prose poetry collection *Ye cao* 野草 (Wild Grass), the cornerstone of Chinese literary modernity, and further across time and space toward Walt Whitman's pathbreaking *Leaves of Grass*, with its celebration of vitality and of the self. These associations will be particularly justified in the reading of *Anything but Human*, where Bai's poems are scattered between vivid and provoking images of life in the contemporary transnational metropolis that is Singapore. Here, however, Lim's thought takes a slightly different route and instead of modern cities, the author decides to visit ancient Chang'an, together with Bashō:

> After nine years, growing weary of living in the city, I moved my dwelling to the vicinity of the Fukagawa River. "Chang'an was, since ancient times, a place for fame and profit, a place difficult for those who are empty-handed and penniless to live." I found the person who said this to be very wise, and I wondered if this was because I myself was poor. (Bashō)

This person was, obviously, Bai Juyi, and the quoted poem is titled "Song Zhang shanren gui Songyang" 送張山人歸嵩陽 (Farewell to Hermit Zhang on His Return to Songyang) (Qiu 2005, 47). The reflection on relocation from the countryside to the city, and the other way around, prompts Lim to dwell on the topic of exile, which in classical poetry is often intertwined with the course of the author's career as an official. Lim empathetically reconstructs Bai's biographical circumstances and expresses his desire to understand his addressee's intentions:

> I mentioned Du Fu in my last letter: I know you admired Du Fu's work. Like you, he was deeply concerned with social problems: the corruption of the court and officials, and the suffering of the people, the lao bai xing. A whole new style, called the *xin yuefu*, arose from your satirical and political writings, which you developed with your friend, Yuan Zhen. In your exile in Xunyang, in a letter you wrote to Yuan Zhen, you poured your heart out, and told him that despite your banishment you were content: after all, Du Fu was an official of low rank, and was destitute to the very end. Meng Haoran and Li Bai didn't even manage to get official posts

or keep them for long. What you wished for then was for your poetry to benefit the country and its people.

In the second part of the letter, for a change, Lim offers an account of what Bai Juyi cannot know: that is, how Bai's wish came true, and his poems reached broader audiences in the country:

> During the Tang dynasty, it was believed the *yuefu*, the Music Bureau in Chinese bureaucracy, descended from institutions that collected popular songs so that the emperors could learn of social ills and the abuses of their officials. And it seems your poems were truly popular. The Tang magistrate Li Kan complained that your poems had spread among the common people and were written on screens and walls. Your "lewd words and indecent talk are like winter's cold and summer's heat. They enter into men's flesh and bone and cannot be expelled". I think you wouldn't have thought this an insult at all.

Then, after two nostalgic poems, "Moored at Night" and "Egrets", he hastens to complement this account with the long and detailed story of Bai's work's presence in Japan, including names of authors and titles of literary works inspired by his poetry. It is as if Japan provided an asylum to his verse when it became increasingly unwelcome in its homeland, and Bai went through a sort of banishment in the afterlife, which Lim sums up as follows:

> Though you had never been to Japan nor met any Japanese person in your life, you became a spectre hanging over Japanese literature. Meanwhile, some Chinese critics had decided that your poetry was too su: too common, too vulgar. As your star rose in Japan, it fell in China.

The entire reflection is framed in the dream narrative again. This time, it is Lim's own dream, although tellingly, mediated by Japanese culture. Dreams, the children of anything but an idle mind, as Shakespeare's Mercutio would have it, are here mostly second-hand and inspired by the dreams of others: in particular, Takashina no Moriyoshi and Ōe no Asatsuna. Profoundly absorbed and processed, they are displayed before Lim's mind's eye as described below:

> Last night I think I dreamt of you, but you were Japanese. I had seen a Japanese woodblock print of you from the Edo period, where you are on a cliff, surrounded by attendants who are unfurling a piece of Chinese

calligraphy; it appears to be a couplet, though I can't make out the words. You are looking into the blue and oddly calm sea. Behind you is a ship. Yet further behind are some pillar-like rocks, reminiscent of karst formations. The proportions and spatial arrangements are certainly off.

Aside from the vicariousness of this recycled dream, the oneiric convention allows the poet-translator a less strict logic, underlaid by purely personal readerly experience and vague, intuitive linkages that are difficult for others to grasp. From the recapitulation of Bai's reception in Japan, he makes a sudden leap to contemporary Singapore, and – through an unexpected association with Arthur Yap – proceeds to a reflection on his own writing:

> The Japanese connection reminds me of a Singaporean poet, the late Arthur Yap, who took inspiration from Japan in his poetry, especially in the collection man snake apple. Some of your poems and some of his have that remarkable and restrained stillness I find difficult to achieve in my own poetry, and perhaps actively avoid.

Along the way, reflecting on Yap's homosexuality as a possible reason for his incredible restraint, he also digresses about the social perception of homosexuality in Singapore in the 1970s and 1980s, and even tries to probe into what Bai might have thought about homosexuality. And here, another turn of events takes place. The letter closes with a rather strained attempt to redirect the attention to the addressee, followed by a surprising and rather unclear response:

> Arthur is certainly someone I wish I'd met. You too, of course, and I am glad I have.
> In the dream, you tell me: I have said enough.

Is "I have said enough" Bai's reaction to the question about homosexuality, encouraging Lim to read more carefully and draw conclusions from his poetry, which contains the answers? Or, perhaps, "I have said enough" refers to Lim himself (as in: you tell me *that* I have said enough), and it is Bai's subtle indictment as he observes his young pen pal's associations become increasingly loosened and idiosyncratic, straying too far from actual poems and the essence of the things they wish to convey …

What makes me more inclined toward the latter interpretation is the fact that in the next step, Lim indeed lets Bai finally return to China and sends his poems back to their native place. But, again – as in his first attempts to establish a connection – he does so using a Japanese vehicle fueled by English-language academic discourse. As the means for this exchange, he reaches for a theatrical play titled after its main hero, Bai Juyi, whose name in Japanese reads *Hakurakuten*. In the play, in LeRon James Harrison's summary from *Staging Poetic Balance: A New Introduction to and Translation of the Noh Play Hakurakuten* (2019) invoked by Lim, Bai/Hakurakuten encounters the deity Sumiyoshi, the patron of Japanese *waka* poetry, dressed as a fisherman, and he enters into a conversation with the god. Later on, Sumiyoshi "summons other deities to play music for him and as he dances, he summons a wind that blows Hakurakuten back to China, bringing the play to an end." Bai's symbolic return to China is additionally reconfirmed by the inclusion of the poem *Night Rain*, long misattributed to Basho, as Lim stresses more than once.

Then, when Lim's mental journey in Bai Juyi's footsteps comes full circle, Bai finally responds, having received justice and regained his proper voice, not just in dreams but on paper. Perhaps his response is addressed not to Lim but to his contemporaneous friend, Yuan Zhen, yet Lim assumes that, just like he has "bcc'd" all his current and future readers in his correspondence with Bai, certainly Bai had done so in the past and he, Lim, is one of those hidden addressees. The letter he cites recapitulates the story of Bai's life: his career from zero to hero and back again. In its final words, Bai ascribes all his successes and failures to his literary activity:

> Outside of the Imperial Court I was in correspondence with other worthy and noble gentlemen. Within the Court I was in service to the Emperor. It was in the beginning that I made a name for myself through writing; and it was in the end that I was incriminated by my works, as well I should be.

Lim does not explicitly comment on these words, but he takes up the thread of the reflection on the relationship between poetry and politics, beginning his final letter to Bai with a remark on the possible misinterpretations of the intentions behind this epistolary translation:

> It would be easy for someone reading these letters to read it as a tale of rediscovering roots, of retrieving supposedly ancient wisdom, or even as making claims of Chinese chauvinism.

Instead of exploiting the safe and politically rewarding narratives of victimhood into which non-mainland Sinophone literature falls all too often, he proposes another strategy – namely, to demystify the image of China as a monocultural empire, to begin with. Thus, he can, in a sense, both destabilize and rehumanize the hegemon by showing the inherent fragmentation of its mammoth body. He tries to bring out the wonderful cultural potential that the hegemon itself has buried and which may actually benefit Mainland China, if it is willing to acknowledge it, as well as smaller nations that share its language and part of its cultural heritage. That is indeed what Lim has been doing implicitly from the start: showing the fluidity of Chineseness and how it has shaped the process of constant interaction with Japan and other cultures, as illustrated by the reception of Bai Juyi. Now, he wants to make it more self-evident not only to lovers of literature but to a broader audience. Therefore, he reaches for what is conceivably his second favorite topic after literature: namely, food, making a case for the cultural heterogeneity of China based on the diversity of its cuisines. This is not very surprising if we recall, for instance, that in 2020, Lim co-edited a collection of Singapore poetry and prose titled *Food Republic: A Singapore Literary Banquet*, which showed the creative and conceptual potential of combining his two passions.

One of the snacks discussed in the letter, called *hubing* but known more widely as *shaobing*, by means of etymological reflection, finally leads him back to the discussion of spiritual heritage and to the context of Bai's life:

> After all, hu is the Chinese word for foreigner or barbarian. I read a paper that claimed your family had Central Asian roots, originating from Kucha, which is also in Xinjiang. Kucha was actually an ancient Buddhist kingdom, and you were a fervent Buddhist. You would have known that Buddhism, though it was at its zenith under the Emperor Daizong, never lost the taint of being a foreign religion. In the last years of your life, the Emperor Wuzong began a campaign to purge China of supposedly foreign influences, destroying thousands of Buddhist temples and shrines and defrocking monks. This happened in 845. You died in 846, in a monastery in Longmen, famous for its Buddhist statues carved out of rock. Did you die of a broken heart, as your brethren were ruthlessly suppressed? H –– and I visited Longmen, two hours away, using China's incredible high-speed rail network. Dwarfed by a giant and awe-inducing statue of the Buddha, we were thankful that Wuzong didn't completely have his way.

Again, Bai doesn't reply directly, but his poetry offers an answer. One that is melancholy and deeply aware of the passing of time and the ephemerality of life, yet simultaneously incredibly far from self-pity, instead shifting its attention from the self toward the world:

Feeling Sorry about the Peonies

feeling sorry
            about the red peonies

                        before the steps

by evening   : just two   dying branches

                                left

morning's winds   will surely

                  blow them

                          bare

holding a light
            I cherish

        the   ebbing

                  red

2.2 *Localizing Senders, Addressees, and Recipients*

If we read Bai Juyi's gesture of withdrawal, or – as Daryl Lim puts it – his "restrained stillness" in light of modern hermeneutics with its deep indebtedness to postal vocabulary as an endless source of self-suggestive metaphors, we might see it as the purest and most radical act of *sending* (German *Sendung*). In Martin Heidegger's definition: "A giving which gives only its gift, but in the giving holds itself back and withdraws, such a giving we call sending" (quoted in Bass 2020). Although in the preserved letters, it is Lim who technically works as the (only possible) sender, it is Bai who is the *actual* sender in the most fundamental and ontological sense of the notion: as the one who gave himself but erased his presence, leaving no more than shallow and fading fingerprints on the present, which are his perfectly crafted, moderate, and self-restrained poems.

Lim is attracted by this radicality of writing as gift/withdrawal, but he is not convinced of its applicability in his own work. As a poet of complicated identity who is continuously exposed to the impact of various global and local sociopolitical forces but also as a translator who works for a transcultural and trans-epochal "postal system," he is all too aware of the many extratextual factors that impact the circulation of texts, as well as of the many inherent imperfections and traps of the system that stem from the very nature of linguistic communication. These turbulences were thoroughly reconstructed by Alan Bass in the foreword that precedes his translation of Derrida's *Post Card*, a polemic with Heidegger's communicational idealism, and, at the same time, its most extreme embodiment. Alluding to Freud's study of the Rat Man (Paul Lorenz) invoked by Derrida, in which Lorenz expresses his absurd wish for the letter "L" in his surname to be moved before the letter "K" in the alphabet, Bass explains:

> One of the major concerns of *The Post Card* is the possible subversion of what is usually taken as a fixed sequence – e.g. Socrates before Plato, the passing of an inheritance from a prior generation to a succeeding one, the death of the old before the young. What if the usual and seemingly fixed sequence were reversible? What if each term of the sequence contained within itself the principle that subverts the usual progression? What could there be between each term and itself that would operate this subversion? [...]
>
> A question that runs throughout *The Post Card* is, Why this inconceivable union, why the one always in back of the other (like Plato in back of Socrates on the carte)? Another paraphrase of Derrida: if Being is sent, then there must be a system that sorts, routes, and delivers it. What if this system necessarily contained a kink, so that despite the absolute authority of its usual sequences (like the absolute authority of alphabetical order), somewhere it contained the subversion and reversal of its own progression (L before K)? What would happen to the thought of *es gibt* as sending? To the destiny of Being? (Bass 2020).

As the history of Bai's reception throughout the centuries shows, there have been many letters rushing and crowding before his "B" that ignored the rule of progression, among them, well, another "B" – that of the more famous Bashō whose indebtedness to Bai was long underacknowledged. At the same time, Bai himself – one could say, tongue-in-cheek – was relegated to an even more distant place and rebaptized in Japanese as Hakurakuten, although, of course, applying alphabetic considerations to Asian languages is a tremendously problematic operation. In any event, Lim is certainly not a person who would like to smuggle his "L" before Bai's "B." On the contrary, he consistently emphasizes his appreciation of Bai, as well as of translators and scholars who had brought his work closer to English-language audiences and on whose work he builds. Knowing that he cannot fix the inherently flawed postal system but also cannot do without it (yet), he at least wants to make its mechanisms transparent. All his letters are in fact meta-letters. They are communications designed to reveal the very mechanisms of communication in the first place, and to make all of the "bcc'd" parties across the world and centuries aware of the complex paths Bai's generous gift of self has traveled to reach them, as well as of the many hands through which it has passed that have left a palimpsest of fingerprints on it, including the most visible ones – that is, his own.

Unlike many contemporary translators who prefer to emphasize their agency or co-authorship, Lim acknowledges that he is but a mediator between the presence that offered and withdrew itself and the present recipients to whom that presence entrusted itself without even knowing them. Still, as a postman by vocation and not only by profession, he is determined to localize the original sender and establish personal contact. He also hopes to share this finding with others so as to make sure that they will appreciate the value of the shipment. That said, he knows that he cannot do it in an ostentatious way, by explicitly instructing people on how to read with piety; he must act shrewdly to outsmart their big egos: allow them to "overhear" his correspondence and feel like detectives and discoverers who arrive at certain conclusions on their own.

On top of that, the choice of what I deemed epistolary translation as translation strategy is, as we read in the "Translator's Note," itself a homage to the presence behind the present, as the form of communication that Bai himself would have used:

> After fully realizing and embracing this, I tried a much more subjective approach to translation, which focused on my particular encounter with Bai Juyi and my attempt to bridge vast distances of space and (especially) time. The letters to him allowed me to do this, and I felt that a man like Bai Juyi would not have minded receiving letters from an admirer: he seemed to have been a generous, open-minded and kindly sort of person. And letters would have been the main form of communication he had with his friends and fellow poets across China. (In these pandemic-stricken times, this mode of communication seemed entirely apt, as I kept up with friends around the world with texts and emails.)

There is some deep yearning in Lim's words and translational choices for this long-dismissed presence, shamefully stifled by the modern hyperawareness of

EPISTOLARY TRANSLATION

the discursivity of everything and of the trickiness and metaphysicality of the mechanisms of discourse. Like a barefoot courier, the poet-translator traverses the ruins of the dismantled postal infrastructure, in search of real persons. On the one hand, he seems to have "realized and embraced" deconstruction of the old postal principle on which human written communication has been built with its hazardous and self-contradictory nature, explained perhaps most comprehensibly by Martin Hägglund in his *Dying for Time*. Hägglund describes sending a letter as binding oneself "both to the material support of the letter and to the other who receives it," and thus making oneself dependent on both past and future, which translates well into the epistolary-translational situation in which Lim founds himself:

> On the one hand, the letter establishes a relation to what has been: the Latin word *post* means after and reminds us that a letter never arrives without delay. On the other hand, the letter is by definition written for a reader to come. Both the sender and the addressee must, from the beginning, calculate with an interval of time that separates them from each other. When writing a letter, one knows that the message will belong to the past when it is read. In this transition from one time to another, there is both a chance and a threat. By corresponding, one can establish connections across spatial and temporal distance, but at the same time one is dependent on a sending that cannot finally be controlled. The letter may be destroyed or end up in the wrong hands. And even if it arrives safely, the interval between sender and addressee is a source of disquietude in itself. When the letter arrives, the sender may already be dead or no longer subscribe to the meaning of the letter. This is a necessary possibility, which is latent even when the correspondence apparently works smoothly. To send a letter is by definition to inscribe a trace of the past that is addressed to a future that may erase it. (Hägglund 2012)

Simultaneously, with all that modern hyperawareness, a sort of post-postal principle appears to be taking shape in Lim's mind: what about teasing the future (addressees) to make an active step toward the past (sender) and to invest the skills and effort in "intercepting" the letter? Send what you find relevant wherever, to a random address on the other end of the world, the farther the better, for it to travel as long a way as possible; and inconspicuously "bcc" all people through whose hands it may pass, putting them in the role of observers and external analysts of the situation. Unlike on social media, where posted news can immediately be commented on and thus provoke havoc rather than reflection, in such a way, all parties could consider themselves the sole "interceptor" of the correspondence, read it independently and with a genuine endeavor to make the best of it, instead of mobilizing what is most effective, eye-catching, popular, politically correct, etc. This would minimize the risk of erasure but also of rhetorical-political distortion, or appropriation, that goes beyond the common-sense freedom of well-meaning interpretation.

Would Lim himself have appreciated Bai Juyi had he been taught about him at High Chinese classes rather than having discovered him on his own? Presumably, not. Loyalty to one's discovery is a form of loyalty to self: not by self-affirmation and self-confirmation but by means of a voluntary commitment, a free choice, a sincere reciprocation of the present of presence which skeptical (post)modern hermeneuts seem to have ruled out from the get-go – that is, giving oneself as a thank-you gift, and, likewise, withdrawing to let the gift travel faster and farther than the senders could themselves. And, needless to say, the very act of giving-and-withdrawing, with its liberating power, sometimes can change us much more significantly, and in a much more desirable way, than getting. Lim's poetry, arguably, in many ways perfectly showcases this point.

3 Inspiration: Unpacking the Gift of Self

Anything but Human is Daryl Lim's second individual collection. It came out five years after the debut volume *A Book of Changes* (2016), which the publisher's blurb aptly describes as "a young poet's attempt to make sense of the impossible ebb and flow of time" (Lim 2016, back cover). Through "de-familiarization of the otherwise recognizable images of the country," in Wong Yang's words, it "not only deconstructs official narratives of the past but also invites readers to question their own position in the ever-changing present" (Wong Yang 2021). In a nutshell, the book offers an intelligent, witty portrayal and contestation of the construct of modern identity (Singaporean and otherwise), yet without offering any positive, if only tentative, proposal, as a way out of its tiring in-betweenness.

Likewise, from the very first page, *Anything but Human* (un)welcomes the reader with a motto from Wang Xiaoni's 王小妮 poem *Yi kuai bu de beipan* 塊布的背叛 ("A Rag's Betrayal"): "now I'd like to pass myself off / as anything but human" (Lim 2021b, 11).[2] The lyrical persona consistently, if teasingly, presents himself as a misanthropic prophet of the doomsday of humankind. Having spent thirty years of his life in the stomach of a capitalist whale, like the Biblical

---

2   All quotes from *Anything but Human* come from this edition, pages indicated in brackets.

Jonas, the author sets out to the *desert of the real,* as the title of the first part of the volume suggests. With deeply ingrained poststructural suspiciousness and "memories of betrayal" fermenting in his frustrated mind, as in "The Prophet's Day Out", he announces a garbage apocalypse to modern Ninevites, intoning his lyrical "Junkspace Rhapsodies":

> We've lost count of the subsidiaries we have
> Money, they say, is its own reward
> Your girlfriend would appreciate a new succulent
> We've recently reached new heights of customer feedback
> Money, they say, is its own reward
> 42

And yet, as he walks through the "land of perpetual discounts" (88), which sells itself so cheaply as if sensing its own expiration date approaching, tenderness wells up in his heart. Thus, gradually, instead of impatiently awaiting a flood of trash, he implements his inconspicuous world-saving mission through lyricism and humor, which is meant to lead to the *great reset* in the second part of the volume. The "I"-speaker's task is, at first glance, a Sisyphean one. In an overwhelming reality that is perhaps best described by the title of the Daniel Kwan and Daniel Scheinert film *Everything Everywhere All at Once* (2022), he tirelessly collects whatever is still usable from the muddy blind alleys of civilizational development and buys out the almost expired products from the lowest shelves of supermarkets; he packs his findings in the seemingly provisional but in fact very finely woven and surprisingly capacious and durable bags of his poems. In this secret stash, tellingly, poetry lies "next to the alternative history of dry-cleaning" (Lim 2021b, 29). Among the scavenger's trophies, one can identify pitiful caricatures of history, such as a "snowglobe of the Vietnam War" or one "of the Watergate Scandal" (30), remnants of great architecture, including "makeshift Corinthian columns" (34), and great human values – for instance, "truth beauty beauty truth" chanted obsessively out of the tune in "Cloisters" in the "face of an unknown god" (36). There are also shards of religious rituals and texts: for example, in "The Librarian", where, lingering in the modern scriptorium, with an Oreo wrapper as a bookmark, the "I"-speaker wonders, "What sets my announcements apart / from the Lord's command to Abraham?" (29). Or a line from a Christian hymn "Our Lord, Our Help", which the author learned as a child in a Methodist school, that serves as the title of a series of seven poems: "Fly Forgotten, as a Dream". The liberated words that were falling into oblivion with dust gathering on their feathers, indeed, start flying again, on deplumed, emaciated wings, closer to earth, more like chickens than like angels that deliver human prayers to the throne of God, but still – they fly.

This is where his old pen-friend Bai Juyi comes to the rescue, to save the self-appointed savior from an existential and communicational collapse that he is constantly facing, having accepted a mission that is clearly beyond his powers. In part two, hand-in-hand, they undertake a "great reset" of the postal system, with its "outdated technology", which in the final poem, "Age of Miracles" (90), is humorously blamed for all failures:

> Terror ate
> our gut flora   while the post office suspended
>
> habeas corpus
>
> I have waited fifty years   for running water
> and aerosol cheese
>
> before our lord I deigned
> to perspire   the clouds bubbled
> with chlorine
>
> the angels spoke   of bulk discounts
>
> the light shaved ten pounds
> off my wrist
>
> I came back to earth
> with a new calendar   the months named after
> nerve agents
>
> sorry?   I tried to reach you
> with outdated technology
>
> forgive me

In this and several other poems from the second part, we can see, on the formal plane alone, in the internal scattering of the texts, how Lim's occasional verbosity is flavored with silence, to paraphrase "Narrative (IV)", which he had let "well up for years" (71) before releasing it, conceivably, under the influence of Bai Juyi, whose verse inspired him deeply and thoroughly – although not

EPISTOLARY TRANSLATION

without certain immunological reactions from his hypermodern mind. While there is no room here to analyze the entire collection in detail, which I do elsewhere, reconstructing the dynamic interplay between Lim and Bai,[3] let me just say that what happens in the book can be perceived as an interesting disintegration, or indeed a disproval, of the combined concepts of "the metaphysics of presence" which many people today recite in one breath, and the criticism that has become the taken-for-granted deconstructionist foundation of various forms of constructivism, including social constructivism. Lim's activity as a translator and as a poet may be seen as a rediscovery of the purely physical sovereignty of presence and its fundamental innocence, or at least neutrality, in metaphysical terms. When he invites the flesh-and-blood Bai Juyi into his world via letters, accepts Bai's gift-of-self or present-of-presence in the form of poetry, and finally unpacks it in his own re-cycled poetic universe, we constantly observe the various frictions, little explosions, or refractions of meaning in places where the content of Bai's correspondence encounters the elements of Lim's own poetics, imagery, and sensibility, with some revealing if rare moments of temporary alignment or resonance. In all cases, however, one can sense an actual mutual interaction and experience its transformative power – constructive and destructive alike – that shapes the track of the development of the overall narrative trajectory in *Anything but Human*.

Moreover, in Lim's poetry, Bai's presence does not imply any kind of depreciation of absence, as in the deconstructionist theory of binary oppositions, which claims the existence of a dangerous frame from which the human mind – or, minimally, the Western mind – can never liberate itself; nor does it feed the monster of logocentrism. On the contrary, this presence comes *as* absence, in a twofold way. First, it is preceded by an act of *self-sending*, which requires voluntary withdrawal of the self and initiates the voluntary process of the restitution of presence on the part of the recipient. Second, it carries both an explicit and implicit message about the importance of absence as part of, not *counter*-part to, existence.

One may obviously argue that this reconciliation of presence and absence reflects the transplantation of a pre-modern Eastern worldview into a contemporary Westernized one – that is, that the supposedly logos-free philosophy, sensibility, and mindset that inform Bai Juyi's classical Chinese poetry transform the context of a modern cosmopolitan metropolis like Singapore or the underlying matrix of the English language. Nevertheless, I am inclined to think

---

3   The paper "Resetting the Broken World: A Dialogue Between Tradition and Modernity in Daryl Lim Wei Jie's 'Anything but Human'" is under preparation intended for submission in *CLCWeb*.

that, while the encounter between East and West in Lim's work may catalyze the reader's reflection on this fundamental reconciliation, the latter is not, strictly speaking, caused by the former. If only because, from the very beginning, there was probably nothing to reconcile.

The resolution of such putative binary tensions, in general, I venture, stems first and foremost from a common human desire for intellectual and spiritual intimacy, and largely, if not utterly, an intuitive grasp of all levels of proximity, ranging from presence to absence and including everything in between, as well as the ability to flexibly adjust our reactions to those levels of proximity. We have been tricked into believing that we are prisoners of dualisms and need special effort to overcome them. But perhaps we actually are not, and the only thing we need to do is listen to each other with attention and care? Considering the naturalness with which Daryl Lim enters into a deep translingual, transcultural, and trans-epochal correspondence with Bai Juyi, and how, for all his modern hyperawareness – including a lifetime of exposure to a critically-minded society and the even more critically-minded Western academic world – he responds without excessive calculation, putting at stake the future of his poetic universe, one is prompted to revisit the vision of the world as an interplay of differences fueled by the restless engine of *différance*. This conception might have been intellectually productive for some time and ethically beneficial in that it has contributed to a more evolved understanding of Otherness and subsequently to the enrichment of postcolonial reflection or development of fields such as Gender Studies and other discourses on diversity. But, on the other hand, it has also collectively incapacitated us by programming learned helplessness into our system of thinking and reinforcing the habit of constant hair-splitting and micro-judgments, the existence of which we are not supposed to publicly admit. As they accumulate, however, they tend to explode with a doubly destructive power – as uncontrollable convulsions of distorted social justice, one of its manifestations being the phenomenon broadly known as cancel culture.

We have been, in a sense, collectively fooled into one of Zeno's old paradoxes: that the arrow will never reach the target because it first has to make it halfway and then halfway again, or, by dint of a similar logic, why Achilles will never catch up with the turtle. The distance between you and someone else (whether individually or collectively) may look small, but it is conceptually infinite, so do not even try to cover it, and instead simply accept the brutal reality of eternal alienation, we have been told. In fact, this is exactly the overemphasis on difference that Western – and Chinese – imperialism and colonialism have always built upon: the irreconcilable "us" and "them," the civilized people and the barbarians, the enlightened and the ignorant, the

EPISTOLARY TRANSLATION 213

aware and the naïve, etc. The only thing that has notably changed thanks to postmodern deconstructionist interventions was a de-axiologization of this difference, which nonetheless proved to be rather transient and has been followed in recent years by its gradual re-axiologization in a way that opposes the initial configuration but is no less harmful. This overcorrection also goes hand-in-hand with further erosion of the idea of community (in a solid singular, not the increasingly fragmented plural), to be replaced with the notion of solidarity, which is noble but insufficient. Solidarity between the solitary. Or more than solitary: alienated not just from other humans but from ourselves, constantly falling prey to more and more sophisticated paradoxes that make us doubt if we are internally coherent or self-same at all. One of the most playful and thoughtful poems in Lim's collection, "The Futility of Lists" (28), where the "I"-speaker cites Russell's antinomy, sheds doubt on whether we can, for example, become both subjects and objects of our own actions:

> 11. I tell you about Russell's paradox, and the example of the
> barber who only shaves men who don't shave themselves.
> Would the barber then shave himself? Your answer, as always:
> "they should have got a woman."

The barber, of course, cannot shave himself, but if he does not, then he would be a man who does not shave himself, so thereby he must. The logical answer is that such a barber cannot exist at all. Nor can a person – or a culture or a species – that is trapped for too long in such questions. The narrator in the first part of *Anything but Human* seems to be exhausted with the constant intellectual-ethical maneuvers he feels obliged to perform at every step, and, eventually, he decides to brutally stop all the annoying "background applications" that slow down the system by pressing the reset button. This allows him to finally move on even at the cost of – or perhaps with a conscious intention of – losing some unsaved changes before they get automatically saved for good by the system.

Reading the second part of the collection, which effectively bridges the spatial, temporal, and cultural distances that we have repeatedly been told are impossible to traverse, an open question imposes itself: is it really not high time for a great collective "reset" before we get stuck in a self-perpetuating loop, with our minds burning themselves out in futile, ever more listless efforts? Even if the producer's warranty period has not expired yet, due to consistent misuse of the product, as one of Lim's titles, "Against the Natural Order of the Things", has it, I am afraid we may not get a refund or free replacement. I shall spare the reader the naturalistic descriptions of destruction the said poem contains and skip directly to the last line, which I quote here as, first and almost, a note to self (noncommittally "bcc'd" to everyone else, to avoid being seen as an obnoxious moralist): "Be careful, just be careful, will you, just be" (53).

Works Cited

Bass, Alan. 2020. "Translator's Introduction: L Before K." In Jacques Derrida, *The Post Card*, translated by Alan Bass. Chicago and London: University of Chicago Press. Perlego Library. E-book.

Campos, Haroldo de. 1986. "The Rule of Anthropophagy: Europe under the Sign of Devoration." *Latin American Literary Review*, translated by María Tai Wolff, 14 (27):42–60.

Derrida, Jacques. 2020, *The Post Card*, translated by Alan Bass. Chicago and London: University of Chicago Press. Perlego Library. E-book.

Hägglund, Martin. 2012. *Dying for Time: Proust, Woolf, Nabokov*. Cambridge MA and London: Harvard University Press. Perlego Library. E-book.

Ip, Joshua. 2021. "Kidnapping a Beloved Ancestor from Their Home Timeline: On Translating Chinese Poets from the Tang and Song Dynasties." *Cha: An Asian Literary Journal*, 6 February 2021, https://chajournal.blog/2021/02/06/tang-and-song-dynasties/. Accessed March 22, 2023.

Li, Toh Wen. 2022. "Book Review: Daryl Lim's Poems Are a Kaleidoscopic Twist on the Familiar." *The Straits Times*, 5 February 2022, https://www.straitstimes.com/life/arts/book-review-daryl-lims-poems-are-a-kaleidoscopic-twist-on-the-familiar. Accessed March 22, 2023.

Lim, Daryl Wei Jie. 2016. *A Book of Changes*. Singapore: Math Paper Press.

Lim, Daryl Wei Jie. 2021a. "White Space: Encounters with Bai Juyi." *Exchanges*, Spring 2021, https://exchanges.uiowa.edu/issues/without/white-space-encounters-with-bai-juyi/. Accessed March 22, 2023.

Lim, Daryl Wei Jie. 2021b. *Anything but Human*. Singapore: Landmark Books.

Lin, Che-Wen Cindy. 2012. *Bai Juyi's Poetry as a Common Culture in Pre-modern East Asia*. MA Thesis. University of Toronto. *Tspace* https://tspace.library.utoronto.ca/bitstream/1807/33668/1/Lin_Cindy_CW_201211_MA_Thesis.pdf. Accessed March 22, 2023.

Qiu Peipei. 2005. *Basho and the Dao: The Zhuangzi and the Transformation of Haikai*. Honolulu: University of Hawaii Press.

Wong, Yang. 2021. "No Absolutes: A Review of Daryl Lim Wei Jie's *A Book of Changes*." *Cha: An Asian Literary Journal*, 15 May 2021, https://chajournal.blog/2021/05/15/daryl-lim-book-of-changes/. Accessed March 22, 2023.

PART 3

Experiences from the Sinophone

∵

CHAPTER 11

A Matter of Survival

Ying Chen 应晨

I started to build the website "Isola Poetry" (www.yingchen365.com) in 2019, initially launched thanks to the participation of a group of young people from various Chinese backgrounds living in BC, Canada and knowing very minimally the Chinese language and culture. Within the piece of a "cultural mosaic" dedicated to Chinese ethnic groups, very rare are the first generation of immigrants from Hong Kong able to read and write Chinese except keeping Cantonese dialect. Rarer are the second or even the half-second generation of Chinese descendants from the mainland who could carry a real conversation in their mother tongue, and reading and writing would be impossible. For about a decade, the community has been further torn apart in terms of dialects and regions of origin, as it was never before. For example, those without a British first name can be singled out as typical Mainland people, during some crises, for instance to be targets to scrutinize for house flipping. If I participate in a social linguistic survey, to answer the question about the language in which I was born, I must scroll down a whole list of world languages, that includes Cantonese dialect, but excludes my mother tongue, then I must check the box "Other" to specify. The Chinese language being named "Mandarin" as something opposite to Cantonese dialect is also troublesome, because this language has not been one for feudal "Mandarins" for ages, and has been used as "common Chinese" (*putonghua* 普通話).

One would not be surprised by the fast erosion of Chinese heritage in these young people, by how little interest and incentive among Chinese immigrant youth, if not avoidance and sometimes shame, to learn and maintain their cultural heritage. If one noticed on a school playground the unspoken ethnic and linguistic hierarchy often echoing geopolitical tumults occurring in the world, throw a glance to less than thin materials taught, from primary to secondary schools about Chinese culture, attend a "multicultural heritage event" reduced mainly to foods and to a dragon dance, or count the scarce number of schools providing Chinese language courses in the region, proportionally to the given population. The phenomenon is not exclusive to Chinese immigrants, but it is rendered certainly more acute both by the historical tension in the region towards Chinese immigrants, materialized by the famous "Head Tax" targeting at that time Cantonese speaking workers, and by the recent resurfacing of that secular unease due to various layers of new circumstances.

So, in "Isola Poetry," the group of young fellows are encouraged to write poems of only four verses, following approximately the rules of shortened form of *Qing Ping Yue* 清平樂 (Clear and Even Music). Here is what such a poem looks like in English:

1) Shivers below
   A slight spark within
   Far too many moons ago
   Uncertainty sets in

2) Through buzzing beach
   Screaming children play
   As the hot golden sand bleach
   A classic summer day
   by Lee Chen, "Isola Poetry" summer 2019

I myself make one meditative poem every month, honoring Mother Nature only, like the following:

林間新菇
lin jian xin gu
黯然秋雨中
an ran zai yu zhong
幾處殘缺一朝榮
ji chu can que yi zao rong
敢與落葉爭寵
gan yu luo ye zheng cong

Après la pluie
Des bolets tendres
Surgissent ça et là
Couleurs des feuilles mortes

After the rain
Tender mushrooms
Suddenly appear here and there
Colours of fallen leaves

October 2021

A MATTER OF SURVIVAL

Through this exercise, and especially by regularly sending to young readers my translation of selected ancient Chinese poems in chronological order, I would wish to see mutual solidarity in them, no matter where they come from, gathered onto one common ground which is our Ancestors' poetry that we all love. To expose them to some of the unique characteristics of the Chinese language, to its poetry mirroring a spirit that is obviously universal, to its unspeakable beauty.

The use of the Qing Ping form here is a way to express my concern about the necessity to point out the diversity of East Asian poetical forms. The much-promoted Haiku is far from being the only one of those forms that deserve attention. There are in fact a great deal of minimalist poetical forms practiced over several thousand years.

I extended my invitation to authors from other cultural and linguistic backgrounds, especially to bilingual or even multilingual individuals who sympathize with our approach, to participate in our poetry writing game, using Qing Ping form. Languages and cultures are not ranked here. As living beings with their own scent and flavor, they contribute each in their way to the colorful garden of human expressions. In parallel with the ancient poems, I plan to show and to translate some magnificent contemporary songs chanted in Cantonese dialect. Instead of being exploited to divide or dominate, languages and dialects were created, and continuously so, to facilitate communication, understanding, cultural transmission, and to record distinguished existences.

"Isola Poetry" is also a utopia where I fancy the region, always having been a land of migrants, it has the potential to become cosmopolitan, maybe many centuries after me, under the condition that an already cracking mosaic eventually yields to a flowing river, truly inclusive and tolerant, and all joined currents carry and bring its real substances, and are able to become larger than itself but not less, to maybe invent something new that almost always ought to stand on the shoulders of the old.

It is important for me to explain here the purpose of such a website, designed not for a pass-time nor as an integrated part of my literary explorations, but as an existential cry, inspired by the acknowledgment of the cruel fact that languages are extinguishable living beings together with the cultures they carry, and the linguistic ecosystem is a complicated and sometimes disastrous one for many.

In practice, although I feel distressed by the translations of Chinese ancient poetry done by some western translators that tend to turn, in my view, a glass of old, heavy and condensed wine into a glass of common sugary drink – it is not the case for modern Chinese poetry translation because the modern Chinese syntax is very similar to Western languages, I am still full of gratitude for any efforts and time allocated to this poetry. After all, translators are free to interpret and to let their work reflect more or less their own understanding of the *Other*. They are the ones who would step out of the hard lines of a mosaic.

On the website, with my shaky knowledge of both English and French, I try to indicate the ancient Chinese language sometimes have a flexibility that a western language might not have in poetry writing: all words could be verbs, verses do not always need to have a subject, the "I" could be less important than objects, past and present can cross without signal, descriptions could be allusive, the stylistic concerns could be placed above the meaning and, in some occasions, become largely the *raison d'être* of a poem. In this sense, this very ancient art sometimes is also post-modern. I would not accept to translate those poems by giving up the original syntaxes where, in my view, their very essence resides. And yet, how to make "sense" in the eyes of western readers, regarding a poem which may or may not always have a need to make much sense, especially not to deliver any important discourse, content of only building a tiny but complex structure of words that stands on a brief moment of life without much significance? That challenge, I think I share it with all translators.

From the *Shijing* 詩經 (The Classic of Poetry) to the *Li Sao* 離騷 (Encountering Sorrow), from the *Yuefu geci* 樂府歌辭 (Yue Fu songs) to the *Gu shi shijiu shou* 古詩十九首 (The Nineteen Old Poems), and so on, I wish to cover the Chinese classical poetry from antiquity till the end of Song era, by translating selected extracts, accompanied with a brief presentation of the related historical background. I would eventually give more emphasis to poets of Song epoch, where Qing Ping form as well as other forms of *Ci* 詞 poetry were frequently used. Not only do I hope to fill a little the gap in the less than poor chapter of Canadian local textbooks about Chinese culture for immigrant youth from East Asia, to soothe their wonders if there were any, to spare them from psychologically unhealthy heritage denial, I realize the project is also a wonderful occasion for myself to revise old lessons, as if to caress a distant intangible statue, or to try to feel and to transfer some warmth by filtering ancestors' fine ash though my unskilled fingers.

I am currently working on *The Nineteen Old Poems*, a collection of anonymous poems written probably near the end of the second century CE. They already manifested some of the basic characteristics that would appear in later centuries. Here is how I tentatively translated poem number 6 (*She jiang cai furong* 涉江采芙蓉), followed by notes:

涉江采芙蓉，蘭澤多芳草。
采之欲遺誰？所思在遠道。

A MATTER OF SURVIVAL

還顧望舊鄉，長路漫浩浩。
同心而離居，憂傷以終老。

Harvesting lotus
A lake of sweetgrass
For whom are the flowers?
The one far away
Looking back to old town[1]
Oh endless journey
Hearts were teared apart[2]
Aging in sorrow[3]

It is to be noted that, in this "five-syllable poem" (*wu yan shi* 五言詩), almost every verse is of different syntax, but the last group of two verses shares a similar pattern:

同心而離居，

Adjective made of combined words *tong xin* 同心 / coordinative adverb *er* 而 / combined word *li* 離 used as adverb / *ju* 居, verb.

憂傷以終老

Adjective made of combined words *youshang* 憂傷 / coordinative adverb *yi* 以 / combined word *zhong* 終 used as adverb / *lao* 老, verb.

Here appears the early sign of a tendency for parallelism. The rule would develop in the following decades and centuries. In the above group, the two verses follow an identical grammatical pattern, but diversify themselves in tones.

Also of note is that, within the community, there are many debates around which dialect is more beautiful, about whether the creation of modern Chinese at the turn of the twentieth century with less tones is a gain or a loss. The same sort of arguments also frequently happens concerning the simplified or

---

1 Change of subject here: a man on exile thinking about his hometown.

2 Ancient poetry was chanted. There were many tones for each and different word. Today left four tones in modern Chinese language remain: -, /, v, ` (about eight tones in Canton region dialect, about ten tones in Delta region dialects). The first two tones are commonly labeled as *ping* 平, the last two tones as *ze* 仄. The pattern of tones here is therefore: *ping ping ze ping ping / ping ping ze ping ze* 平平仄平平/平平仄平仄. The variation of such tones will be more and more codified in subsequent epochs.

3 The rhyme is applied to the second verse of each group: *cao* 草, *dao* 道, *hao* 浩, *lao* 老.

traditional characters. I think when it sacrifices a number of beautifully musical tones, invented in ancient times to differentiate meanings of a limited vocabulary, the Modern Chinese reduces the number of tones (we all know the tones are the most difficult part for learners of this language, not just for foreigners), but at the same time it has added and keeps adding new words to adapt to new concepts in the new era. The simplified Chinese characters, on the other hand, were invented to combat the illiteracy problem affecting a vast population, at a time when handwriting was still the only option. Even in today's digitalized world, even when writing with traditional characters is no longer a challenge for many, the characters continue to be simplified, words continue to change, the language is still constantly reshaping itself, slowly transforming, indifferent to any querulous comparisons.

When translating this poem, I tried to preserve the original rhythm, its briefness, its reserve, and its jumps in time and space, to give up complete sentences so that the poem would not become too narrative. And yet, I still feel far from capable of presenting faithfully in English, or in French, what the original poem expressed in its quite visual structure that stands alone with concrete words and bare meaning but also beyond, so I indulged myself in providing a few notes to complement the translation.

I nevertheless feel that translating Chinese classical poetry into Western languages might be an illusionary task, that no translation could replace the actual learning of the original language, nor could it eliminate the necessity of linguistic immersion, in order to truly widen one's vision of the world.

Otherwise, I imagine it may become more universally appreciable, and one would probably render more justice to this poetry by chanting it, and by calligraphing it, instead of translating it into a Western language that might not be compatible to it.

Finally, what probably makes me most different from translators having the target language as mother tongue is indeed something beyond literary or technical issues. It has much to do with my own living condition described above. Under the cheerful endeavor of this stretching website, I have to confess, lies a profound disillusion and sense of fatality, when contemplating the vicissitudes of languages and cultures, feelings that match the state of mind of most ancient poets I have been translating. Today, when I look back, as a "Sinophone," wandering on the other side of the Pacific Ocean, on the other side of the river of life, experiencing the vertigo of time difference, those pages of Chinese ancient poetry in which I grew up become, to me, floating leaves on the permanently agitated currents formed with past dreams, present realities and the uncertainty of the future. Each of those pages, those fallen leaves, constitutes

A MATTER OF SURVIVAL

an extraordinary inner monument that is truly unique in human history, but difficult to exhibit, and when translated, by others and also by myself, it often becomes a disturbed reflection in the water. I realize that my fear of loss, of this sublime fruit of mankind to be unknown, forgotten or misinterpreted, is nothing else than the unwise fear of my own passing. Moreover, that fear is nothing compared to the dreadful prospect for me and for this poetry of becoming a living corpse. The potential fate of this crystal-like poetry broken into a handful of perfectly correct sentences with conventional make-ups would be worse than death. Just as I would rather prefer to see the piece of mosaic mentioned earlier, into which my ethnicity would be designated with polite correctness in this part of the world, simply dissolve, disappear, instead become air, merge into the cosmos, so that no earthly force could arrange it into some empty shell.

This should have been the aspiration of the Chinese poets of all time.

Vancouver, August 2022[4]

---

4   Grammatical revision by Paul Matthew St Pierre.

CHAPTER 12

The Other Mother Tongues and Minority Writing in China

Ming Di 明迪

In an effort to document the mother tongue writing and bilingual writing in the ethnic minority[1] communities in China at a critical time of language policy changes,[2] I have interviewed and/or collected videos of Mother Tongue Reading from over eighty ethnic bilingual poets from all corners of China. This is a very preliminary report of this project in progress. While previous studies of ethnic minority poetry tend to mix Chinese speaking and ethnic languages speaking poets together,[3] as if ethnicity were something bonded by blood, I look at the work of linguistic minority poets who can speak and/or write in their ethnic languages[4] because, without language, ethnicity might be just a political label.

1   Sinophone Poetry Redefined

In the one-hundred-year history of Chinese modern poetry, there have been many efforts made for a new breakthrough, such as using vernacular language, new formal writing, avant-garde writing, dialect writing, new nature poetry, etc.,

---

1 Indigenous people (non-Han) have been categorized as "ethnic minorities" (*Shaoshu Minzu* 少數民族) in China since 1954. I used "Indigenous-Minority" in the video project, but here I use "ethnic minority" in a neutral tone.

2 China's new language policy was issued in 2020, implemented from region to region, by the State Council in the publication entitled *Guowuyuan Bangongting Guanyu Quanmian Jiaqiang Xinshidai Yuyanwenzigongzuode Yijian* 國務院辦公廳關於全面加強新時代語言文字工作的意見 [Opinions by the State Council on Strengthening Languages and Writing Systems in the New Age]. Available online, URL: https://www.gov.cn/zhengce/content/2021-11/30/content_5654985.htm (accessed September 20, 2023). The goal of the policy is to reach 85% Mandarinization nationwide by 2025, implying a gradual cut down of the education of ethnic minority languages.

3 For example, Bender (2012).

4 The criteria I have used in selecting poets: having written poems in an ethnic minority language or translated poems from or into an ethnic minority language; having demonstrated the ability to speak the ethnic mother tongue more than just saying a phew simple phrases such as hello and thank you.

© MING DI, 2024 | DOI:10.1163/9789004711600_014

THE OTHER MOTHER TONGUES AND MINORITY WRITING IN CHINA

but nothing has been more successful (as a breakthrough) than mother tongue writing and bilingual writing by linguistic minority poets in recent decades. It embodies regional poetry (*difang shige* 地方詩歌) *vs.* official poetry (*guanfang shige* 官方詩歌), periphery *vs.* center, oral *vs.* written literature, local writing *vs.* Western influences, long narratives *vs.* short lyrical poems, eco-poetry *vs.* nature poetry, among many other literary and aesthetic dualities and conflicts. Bukun Ismahasan Islituan 卜袞·伊斯瑪哈單·伊斯立端wrote the first ballad in Bunun in 1977 and started bilingual writing in Bunun and Chinese in 1987; Alu Siji 阿魯斯基 was the first contemporary Yi poet writing in Nuosu Yi 諾蘇彝, who launched *Liangshan Wenxue* 涼山文學 (Cold Mountain Literature) in 1980 and as its chief editor published many young poets including Aku Wuwu 阿庫烏霧; Aku Wuwu is the most well-known Yi poet writing in Nuosu Yi since 1984 who has transformed the classical Yi rhyming epics into modern free verse; Sadet Jamal 薩黛特·加馬力is the first Kyrgyz poet of modernist poetry (she has been publishing free verse since 1985); Gebu哥布, the first Hani哈尼poet ever, has been publishing Chinese poetry since 1985 and modern Hani epics in Hani since 1989; Pan Nianying 潘年英, poet-anthropologist, has been promoting Dong 侗 writing since the 1980s; A Su 阿蘇, one of the few bilingual Xibe 錫伯poets, has blended avant-garde elements into folk poetry; Kongno 坤努is one of the very few bilingual women poets in the Jingpho 景頗 (Zaiwa 載瓦) community; Li Hui 李輝 has identified his ethnicity and mother tongue as Dônđäc 傣傣(not one of the 56 officially identified ethnic groups in China) through field investigation and research work; and there are many others who recite their poems in their ethnic mother tongues such as Luruo Diji 魯若迪基in Pumi 普米, Nie Le 聶勒in Wa 佤, Wolfman 人狼格in Naxi 納西, to name just a few outstanding ones[5] as they have, together, redefined the scope of Sinophone poetry.

2 Last Generations of Bilingual Poets in China

But all this will possibly end soon due to the new policy of Mandarinization. Assimilation has already been serious, especially in Bai 白and Buyi 布依communities and even in certain Yi communities:

---

5 There are less than ten poets reciting their poems in ethnic minority languages publicly in China, therefore they are very prominent as compared to the poets who do not recite ethnic poems publicly. The majority of the poets in this project read, upon my invitations, and recorded their reading in their ethnic languages for the first time, but were happy about doing it – they said it's good to have a video recording of their ethnic languages to be shared internationally.

漢字進山 (excerpt)
從古甲骨片上紛紛而下
漢字 匯成河流
歷經千年滄桑
抵達異族山寨

漢字 魚貫而入
衝破寨子古老的籬笆牆
淹沒寨子
載自異域的水生物和陌生的垃圾
漂浮在上面

漢字紛紛爬上岸
首先佔領我們的舌頭
再順勢進入我們的體內
爭噬五臟
等到飯飽酒足
便塗脂抹粉
從我們的口齒間轉世
成為山寨的聲音

Into the Mountains, the Chinese Characters Came
Falling from the ancient oracle bones, fragmented
Chinese characters converge into a river
After a thousand years of vicissitudes
They reach the mountain village of an alien tribe

Chinese characters break in like fish
Through the aged fence of the village
They flood the village
Their exotic aquatic creatures and strange garbage
Float on top

Chinese characters climb ashore one after another
First they take over our tongues
Then into our bodies
Fighting for our internal organs
After they have had enough to eat and drink
They put on make-up

THE OTHER MOTHER TONGUES AND MINORITY WRITING IN CHINA 227

> Reincarnated between our lips and teeth
> Becoming the voice of copycats
> OXDDI XUOFO 俄狄小丰[6]

Yet they fight for their own voices. 310 poets writing in Nuosu Yi, from Alu Sijito young poets born in the 1990s, are gathered in the *Grand Anthology of Contemporary Yi Mother Tongue Poetry in China*.[7] In the same year of 2017, an anthology of nine ethnic Mongolian poets was published, in Chinese translation, entitled *Moving Mountains*.[8] The year before, *The Burning Ears of Wheat – Selected Poems of Young Uyghur Avant-Garde Poets* (Salam 2016) showcased thirty-three poets from Xinjiang, the most astonishing anthology out of China in recent decades. There was also a collection of poetry written in Tibetan published in 2005.[9] Today, there are many bilingual poets writing in Tibetan and Chinese such as Samer Darkpa 沙冒智化 and Yungdrung Gyurmè 永中久美. But all this will possibly end soon. The ethnic mother tongue writing that has changed the landscape of Sinophone poetry will no longer be possible when China is promoting the *Putonghua* 普通話 and *gongtongti* 共同體 (lit. unified community).

> 大梦 (excerpt)
> 我幻想馬克思幻想一座翠柏似的小島，
> 空無一物，海浪將他遣返。
> 從養殖場回來，換掉污穢的衣裳，
> 沒有翅膀的生活，我心依然，
> 夢見馬克思主義者夢見無物的群島，
> 我的心分作窗外的微風和草。

---

6 All the poems cited are translated from Chinese by myself. *Shanzhai* 山寨 means "fake" (not original) in Chinese. Here the poet plays on the words as a pun: *shanzhai* "mountain village" vs. "copycat." Another pun (with different tones) in the poem: *Yizu* 異族 ("alien people") implies *Yizu* 彝族 ("Yi people").

7 *Zhongguo Yizu Dangdai Muyu Shige Daxi* 中國彝族當代母語詩歌大系 [Grand Anthology of Contemporary Yi Mother Tongue Poetry in China] edited by Latyip Atshop and Mathxie Chytjip (2017) is a two-volume anthology of poems written in the reformed Nuosu Yi.

8 *Youdongde Qiongshan* 游動的群山 [Moving Mountains], edited by Chen Ganglong, et al. (2017) was translated from Mongolian to Chinese by Ha Sen 哈森 and various hands.

9 *Xinchao* 心潮 [The Tides of the Heart] edited by Bsod Nam Dar Rgyas (2005), is a collection of Tibetan poetry from the 1980s to 1990s written in Tibetan.

The Big Dream
I imagine Marx imagining a cypress-like island.
Empty. Waves pushing him back.
I return from the farm, take off the filthy clothes.
Life without wings, I tuck my heart that remains.
I dream of Marxists dreaming of the empty archipelago,
My heart splits into the breeze and grass outside the window.
by LAN DINGGUAN 藍定官

Can different ethnic groups build an imagined community by learning to speak one official language? Or is it an empty dream? Ethnic Yao 瑤 poet Lan Dingguan 藍定官 asks the question but has splitting answers.

The fifty-five officially recognized minority groups of 125 million people today account for less than 9% of the total population in China, but they are indigenous to 64% of the land (mostly in the peripheral regions). 117 out of the 129 minority languages are classified as endangered languages (Sun 2007). It was because of the awareness of the endangered status that many poets such as Pan Nianying, Gebu, A Su, Aku Wuwu, Luruo Diji, Nie Le and Kongno started Mother Tongue Recitation to save their ethnic languages and maintain ethnic identities. Many other poets have made various efforts to promote their literature and cultures: Sadet Jamal has compiled an anthology of literature from Kyrgyz and translated authors of several languages such as Kyrgyz, Kazakh and Uyghur into Chinese; Samarkand 撒瑪爾罕 has compiled an anthology of poetry from Salar ethnic group; Ha Sen 哈森 has translated many ethnic Mongolian poets into Chinese and Aynur Mawltbek 阿依努爾·毛吾力提 from Kazakh into Chinese; Wolfman as a popular singer sings bilingual songs to promote Naxi; Li Hui, as a molecular anthropologist and linguist, has written enthusiastically about Dônđäc as an ethnic minority speech rather than a Shanghai dialect; Bukun Ismahasan Islituanfrom Taiwan has been tirelessly promoting indigenous Bunun by writing and performing his poetry in Bunun; Puchi Daling 普馳達嶺, poet and scholar of Yi from Yunnan, has created a website to promote Yi literature.

3   Cultural-Linguistic Corridors

With so many languages in the border regions and especially some languages such as Tibetan and Yi spreading to multiple regions, organizing even a limited sample can be a problem. In a transdisciplinary approach, I use a

THE OTHER MOTHER TONGUES AND MINORITY WRITING IN CHINA   229

FIGURE 12.1   Administrative Map of China. Public domain
Note: This map of China is from the public domain, showing 23 provinces, five minority autonomous regions, four municipalities and two special districts. It is reprinted here to help readers find the provinces in each Cultural-linguistic Corridor. It should not be taken as linguistic mapping because, for instance, in Gansu province, Eastern Yugur belongs to Mongolic, but Western Yugur belongs to Turkic.

framework of Cultural-Linguistic Corridors based on the three "ethnic migration corridors" (Fei 1979; 1982) proposed by anthropologist Fei Xiaotong 費孝通 (1910–2005) plus two of my own, as his model has shed light on my study of linguistic overlapping and interconnections of various ethnic groups. I look at the poetry by ethnic-linguistic minority poets based on where they were born (i.e. where they acquired their mother tongues) and group them along five corridors (and within each corridor in the order of geographical locations and languages; see Fig. 12.1).

3.1 Hexi Corridor

Geographically, Hexi Corridor in the northwest used to be part of the Bronze Road and Silk Road connecting ancient China to the West. It is where the Loulan Kingdom was as well as where Zhang Qian exited and Marco Polo entered China. For this essay, it covers Gansu, Ningxia, Qingai and Xinjiang.

He Zhong 賀中(b. 1964) from Gansu: Yugur 裕固

Samer Darkpa 沙冒智化 (b. 1989) from Gansu: Amdo Tibetan安多藏

Na Sa那薩(b. 1977) from Qinghai: Kham Tibetan 康藏

Chakdor Gyal 吉多加, aka Dongbu 東布 (b. 1985), from Qinghai: Amdo Tibetan 安多藏

Dilmurat Talat 狄力木拉提 · 泰來提 (b. 1963) from Xinjiang: Uyghur 維吾爾

Aliye Rusol 阿麗耶·如蘇力 (b. 1992) from Xinjiang: Uyghur 維吾爾

Anaer 阿娜爾 (b. 1963) from Xinjiang: Oirat 衛拉特

Sadet Jamal 薩黛特·加馬力 (b. 1968) from Xinjiang: Kyrgyz 柯爾克孜

Aynur Mawltbek 阿依努爾·毛吾力提 (b. 1974) from Xinjiang: Kazakh 哈薩克

A Su 阿蘇(b. 1962) from Xinjiang: Xibe 錫伯

3.2 Tibet-Qiang-Yi Corridor

This refers to the complicated valleys formed by the six rivers in southwest China in current Tibet, Sichuan and Yunnan provinces.

Tenzin Pelmo 旦增白姆(b. 2000) from Lhasa: Ü Tibetan 衛藏

Yungdrung Gyurmè 永中久美(b. 1985) from Back Tibet: Tsang Tibetan 後藏

Chengxu Erdan 成緒爾聃(b. 1972) from Sichuan: Qiang 羌

Aku Wuwu 阿庫烏霧 (b. 1964) from Sichuan: Nuosu Yi 諾蘇彝

Yi Wu 依烏(b. 1969) from Sichuan: Nuosu Yi 諾蘇彝

Jike Bu 吉克布(b. 1986) from Sichuan: Nuosu Yi 諾蘇彝

Puchi Daling 普馳達嶺(b. 1970) from Yunnan: Nasu Yi 纳苏彝

Luo Yu 羅鈺 (b. 1983) from Guizhou: Eastern Yi 東彝

Gebu哥布 (b. 1964) from Yunnan: Hani 哈尼

Wolfman 人狼格(b. 1965) from Yunnan: Naxi 納西

Banamu 芭納木(b. 1974), from Yunnan: Mosuo 摩梭

Luruo Diji 鲁若迪基(b. 1967) from Yunnan: Pumi 普米

Nie Le 聶勒(b. 1968) from Yunnan: Wa 佤

Kongno 坤努(b. 1968) from Yunnan: Jingpho 景頗

THE OTHER MOTHER TONGUES AND MINORITY WRITING IN CHINA   231

3.3   *Southern Mountains Corridor*

A range of five traveling routes along the five Southern Mountain Ranges (*Nanling* 南岭) bordering the provinces of Guangdong, Guangxi, Guizhou, Hunan and Jiangxi, dividing Central China and South China.

> Zhong Xiuhua 鍾秀華 (b. 1980) from Jiangxi: She 畬(Shanha)
> Pan Liwen 潘利文(b. 1975) from Guizhou: Shui 水
> Pan Nianying 潘年英 (b. 1963) from Guizhou: Dong 侗
> Xi Chu 西楚(b. 1976) from Guizhou: Miao 苗/Hmong
> Lan Dingguan 藍定官(b. 1996) from Guangxi: Yao 瑤
> Qin Shuxia 覃淑霞(b. 2000) from Guangxi: Zhuang 壯

3.4   *Southeast Coast Corridor*

I propose this coastal corridor to connect the coastal regions such as Shandong, Shanghai, Zhejiang, Fujian and Taiwan:

> Li Hui 李輝 (b. 1978) from Shanghai: Dônđăc 傷僗
> Lan Chaojin 藍金朝 (b. 1976) from Fujian: She 畬(Shanha)
> Tung Shuming 董恕明 (b. 1971) from Taiwan: Puyuma 卑南
> Bukun Ismahasan Islituan 卜袞·伊斯瑪哈單·伊斯立端(b. 1956) from Taiwan: Bunun 布農

3.5   *Northeast Corridor*

Mongolic-Tungusic corridor: Mongolian, Manchu, Xibe, Ewenki, Oroqen and Hezhe.[10]

> Sun Junmei 孫俊梅 (b. 1984) from Heilongjiang: Hezhe 赫哲
> Wu Yingli 吳穎麗(b. 1967) from Inner Mongolia: Daur 達斡爾
> Ha Sen 哈森 (b. 1971) from Inner Mongolia: Mongol 蒙古
> Naren Tuoya 娜仁圖雅(b. 1981) from Inner Mongolia: Ewenki 鄂溫克; Oroqen 鄂倫春

---

10   The cultural-linguistic corridors are not dividing lines of language families, for example, Bonan 保安 and Dongxiang 東鄉 languages in Gansu province belong to the Mongolic language family. A large number of Xibe people migrated to Xinjiang in the 18th century. The historical migration explains why Xibe people in Xinjiang use a writing system based on Manchu from the northeast. A Su from Xinjiang writing in Xibe to revive the language is listed in the first corridor.

The five Cultural-Linguistic Corridors circle the central land of the Han Chinese who historically developed commercial routes to reach the south, assimilating the communities along the way and, as a result, some ethnic minority people have lost their languages, some are even classified as Han Chinese and their languages are becoming "dialects" of Chinese. There have also been contacts between and among minority groups. Naxi folklore speaks of three brothers becoming Tibetan, Naxi and Bai who worship the same ancestors.

From the languages in each corridor, we see that the historical migrations have been multi-directional. Zhong Xiuhua from Jiangxi talks about her mother tongue, She, originating from the South. Samarkand (Chinese name Han Wende 韩文德) from Qinghai writes about his ancestral tribe coming from the West, Central Asia. Li Hui has identified his mother tongue in the Fengxian District of southern Shanghai as Dônđăc related to Tai in southwest China, but he classified it as a creole of Daic and Wu Chinese just to be politically safe as ethnicity has always been a sensitive topic in China (a double-edged sword as it goes).

Parallel to the one-hundred-year history of modernist poetry in China is the one-hundred-year history of archaeology in China. More and more discoveries of archaeological sites dated 6000–7000 BCE indicate that civilizations rose in the South earlier than in the central land. Over the past twenty years, molecular anthropological studies have been extremely dynamic in China. Li Hui proposes that modern humans migrated to China from Africa via India and South Asia to Yunnan and Guangxi (Li 2008 and Li 2020), while Fu Qiaomei proposes that multiple waves of human migration in Southeast Asia differentiated Northern and Southern settlers in China (Fu 2021). My mapping of the languages and poets along the migration corridors that formed ethnic groups linguistically and culturally do not contradict their findings, but I only consider the recent 9,000 years, i.e. from the Neolithic age when the rise of agriculture led to settlements which eventually "froze" the languages and the subsequent migrations (due to famine or catastrophes or wars) caused an interaction of the languages which gave birth to new languages.

I have divided the poets of study into three groups:[11]

---

11   I have also interviewed and/or collected videos from many other bilingual poets such as A Marjen 瑪爾簡 (b. 1968), Western Yugar 西部裕固 from Gansu; Ma Xuewu 馬學武 (b.1972), Bonan 保安 from Gansu; Ha Mo 哈默 (b. 1973), Dongxiang from Gansu; Kulaxihan Muhamaitihan 庫拉西漢·木哈買提漢 (b. 1974), Kazakh from Gansu; Dong Yongxue 東永學 (b. 1965), Tu 土 from Qinghai; Mu Xue 牧雪 (b. 1965), Salar 撒拉 from Qinghai; Chakdor Gyal 吉多加(b. 1985), Amdo Tibetan from Qinghai; three more Uyghur poets from Xinjiang: Turahan Tohuti 圖拉汗·托乎提 (b. 1964), Aynur Abdukerim 阿依

THE OTHER MOTHER TONGUES AND MINORITY WRITING IN CHINA   233

Group I: Bilingual and biliterate poets writing in Chinese and/or an ethnic language: Bukun Ismahasan Islituan, A Su, Pan Nianying , Aku Wuwu, Gebu, Sadet Jamal, Kongno, Ha Sen, Li Hui, Chakdor Gyal, Yungdrung Gyurmè, Samer Darkpa, Aliye Rusol, Tenzin Pelmo;

Group II: Bilingual poets writing primarily in Chinese: Dilmurat Talat, Yi Wu, Puchi Daling, Aynur Mawltbek, Na Sa, Luo Yu, Jike Bu, Lan Dingguan, Qin Shuxia;

Group III: Bilingual poets of endangered languages or languages without a writing system who have to write in Chinese: Anaer, He Zhong, Wolfman, Luruo Diji, Nie Le, Tung Shuming, Chengxu Erdan, Banamu, Lan Chaojin, Zhong Xiuhua, Pan Liwen, Xi Chu, Sun Junmei, Wu Yingli, Naren Tuoya.

4   Bilingual Writing and the Other Mother Tongues

All the above-mentioned poets learned to speak their ethnic mother tongues as children and later acquired Chinese in school.[12] It is the education of minority languages in some school systems since the 1980s that enabled some of

---

努尔·阿不都克力木 (b. 1975), Mohammedyehya Tusunbaki 麥麥提亞合亞·吐孫巴克 (b. 2001); Hazhibek Aidarhan 哈志別克·艾達爾汗 (b. 1979), Kazakh from Xinjiang; Abiba Yiminjan 艾比拜·依明江 (b. 1975) Tajik from Xinjiang; Pema Yangchen 白馬央金 (b. 1974, Tibetan); Chungkyi 瓊吉 (b. 1978, Tibetan); Suolang Ciren 索朗次仁 (b.1992, Lhopa); Yomqung Sangmo 永瓊桑姆 (b. 1998) from Ngari; Norzin Dolma 郎澤卓瑪 (b. 1999), Amdo Tibetan from Sichuan; four poets of Nuosu Yi from Sichuan: Lama Itzot 拉瑪伊佐 (b.1987), Jibu Riluo 吉布日洛 (b. 1994), Sugasela 蘇呷色拉 (b. 1996), Abu Masen 阿布馬森 (b. 1997); Azhe Luchouzhi 阿哲魯仇直 (b. 1967), Yi from Guizhou; Tong Qi 童七 (b. 1993), Yi from Yunnan; Yi Wei 一葦 (b. 1971), Bai from Yunnan; two Naxi poets from Yunnan: Nimei Nami 妮美納蜜 (b. 1974), He Fukai 和富開 (b. 1976); two Jino 基諾 poets from Yunnan: Zhang Yun 張雲(b. 1970), Abu Jino 阿布基諾 (b. 1984); Aili Munuo 艾傈木諾 (b. 1970), De'ang 德昂 from Yunnan; Feng Maojun 豐茂軍 (b. 1974), Lisu 傈僳 from Yunnan; Liu Wenqing 劉文青 (b. 1984) Nu 怒 from Yunnan; Gao Qiongxian 高瓊仙 (b. 1986), Derung 獨龍 from Yunnan; Lal Vet 臘維(b. 1988) Lahu 拉祜 from Yunnan; Sun Baoting 孫寶廷 (b. 1965), Achang 阿昌 from Yunnan; two poets of Tai 傣 from Yunnan: Ye Zheng-guang 葉正光 (b. 1963), Wang Mei 王玫 (b.1973); Zhan Jiayu 詹家雨 (b.1982), Southern Dong 南侗 from Guizhou; two poets of Buyi from Guizhou: Pan Mei 潘梅 (b. 1987), Wu Tianwei 吳天威 (b. 1991); Tong Yu 桐雨 (b. 1978) Mulao 仫佬 from Guangxi; Huang Xiufeng 黃秀鳳 (b. 1974), Pan Yao 盤瑤 from Guangxi; Li Xingqing 李星青 (b.1993), Li 黎 from Hainan Island; Quan Chunmei 全春梅 (b. 1970), ethnic Korean from Jilin; Bayin Hehe 八音赫赫 (b. 1985), Manchu 滿語 from Jilin; Solongod Todgerel 蘇倫嘎德·陶德格日勒 (b. 1980, Mongolian), Dai Lin 戴琳 (b. 1994, Ewenki), etc., but have not included them in this essay due to limited space.

12   Among the eighty-four bilingual poets so far in this project, all speak their ethnic language as the first mother tongue except three poets who spoke the local dialect of Chinese first and then learned their ethnic languages.

them to write in their native languages. Some had formal bilingual education while others had formal education in Chinese first and then had training in the writing scripts of their ethnic languages. Most of them have become so proficient in Chinese that Chinese has become their primary language, and their ethnic languages have become the "other mother tongues."

"Other" also refers to their status. History of China's literature has been the history of Han Chinese literature. There has been a separate history of ethnic minority literature in China. The thirty volumes of *The One Hundred Year Canon of New Poetry in China*[13] included less than ten minority poets who write in Chinese except Aku Wuwu. Poets such as Gebu, Nie Le and Luruo Diji who have received the highest award for minority writers in China, the Junma (Gallant Horse) Literature Awards, feel neglected by "mainstream" poetry circles (Ming and Gebu 2022). Aku Wuwu, the most recognized bilingual Yi poet, states in the interview that he has been ignored by the minority world as well as the Han world. While indigenous poetry, such as Sami and Inuit poetry, and poetry of minority languages such as Basque and Galician, rose internationally in the 1970s and have received recognition in their home countries as well as internationally, minority poetry in China has been severely underestimated.

Ethnic minority poets emerged in the 1980s at the same time as the Third Generation in the Post-Misty age. While Zhou Lunyou 周倫佑 launched the *Not Not* Movement in 1986 in Xichang, capital of the Big Cold Mountains, Aku Wuwu (from the same region) started publishing poems in Nuosu Yi in 1984 and in bilingual versions in 1986. *Not Not* has been frequently talked about but there was hardly any mention of the rise of Yi poetry until much later (and on a small scale).

Geographically, Misty poets emerged in Beijing in the North (with Shu Ting from Fujian as the only exception), Third Generation emerged in the South such as *Macho Men*, *Not Not* and *Wholistic Writing* in Sichuan, *Coquetry*[14] and *On the Sea* in Shanghai, *Them* in Nanjing, *Tropic of Cancer* in Zhejiang, and *Ugly Stones* in Fujian. Most of them became well known as groups of poets around an independent magazine and in large cities. But most of the ethnic minority poets have been writing individually in remote and isolated regions.

---

13   *Zhongguo Xinshi Bainian Dadian* 中國新詩百年大典, published in Wuhan in 2013. Over thirty prominent poetry critics from all over China gathered at Beijing University to vote on whom to include in each of the 30 volumes prior to the publication. Minority poets included are Shen Congwen, Niu Han, Xi Murong, Jidi Majia, Aku Wuwu, He Xiaozhu, Na Ye, etc.

14   I used to use Sa Jia 撒嬌 with a footnote, but here I am adopting the term "Coquetry" from van Crevel (2008).

THE OTHER MOTHER TONGUES AND MINORITY WRITING IN CHINA 235

Some of them got to publish in major journals[15] but were outshined by the Third Generation in the 1980s and 1990s, except for two minority poets, both speaking and writing in Chinese only, who joined the *Not Not* group.

Liangshan Wenxue (Cold Mountain Literature), launched by Alu Sijiin 1980, was never mentioned along with the *Not Not* journal. Aku Wuwu published his first Yi poem in *Liangshan Wenxue* in 1984 but later criticized Alu Siji for writing new poetry in old forms. He himself is labeled as a performing poet by Mark Bender (2012), a term not taken seriously inside China, especially when the "performing" is associated with long traditional poems (Ming and Yi Wu 2022). Aku Wuwu, nevertheless, writes avant-garde poems in Chinese, but he himself always prefers to perform traditional poems. He is one of the two exceptions among the poets I have interviewed who state that their Chinese is the weaker language. The other one is Gebu who only studied Chinese for one week. Aku says his Yi is much stronger and he sometimes translates in his mind from Yi to Chinese. But his poetry written in Chinese is very interesting and thought-provoking.

While Aku has a Ph.D. in Yi, Gebu (Hani from Yunnan) only has a high school education. Gebu became an elementary school teacher after gradua-tion from high school, with one week of special training. He then used a small dictionary to learn standard Chinese and started writing short poems in 1984 as a way to practice Chinese. In 1989 he started writing in Hani to preserve his ethnic identity and became the very first poet of Hani in history. Same with Nie Le, the first Wa poet, and Aili Munuo, the first poet of De'ang. But Gebu's "bilingual" writing is very different. His bilingual poems are Hani poems and Chinese translations. He translates the sound of Hani places and certain names that only exist in Hani and then uses footnotes to explain what they are, so the flow of the poems is not interrupted. The use of Chinese as phonetic words in the poems is very peculiar, almost his signature style. After he started writing in Hani (Romanized script), he became more proficient in Hani. He could fin-ish a book-length poem in Hani in three months but would spend five years translating it into Chinese.

Luruo Diji writes in Chinese first and writes it again in Pumi (Latin script) for the purpose of reciting it in Pumi. He acquired Pumi first, then a small dia-lect of Yi, and then Chinese in school. Nie Le graduated from Yunnan Minzu

---

15   For instance, Gebu was published in *Dianchi* 滇池 and *Shikan* 詩刊 (Poetry Monthly) in 1984–88, the same journals that published Misty and Post-Misty poets at that time. I asked him if he knew about the 1986 Exhibition of avant-garde poetry. He said that he had read about it but had not been invited to that exhibition.

University in 1991 and started publishing poetry in Wa (Latin script) in 1996. "Someone has to write in Wa," as he says. But he writes more in Chinese for the sake of communicating with poets in other parts of China and beyond. Kongno is fluent in all dialects of Jingpho and writes in Zaiwa (Latin script). She says she does not have bilingual versions of each poem because some of her poems only exist in Jingpho and some only in Chinese.

Samer Darkpa spent only two years in school learning Chinese before becoming a monk at age nine. He has published five books of poetry, three in Tibetan and two in Chinese. He translates himself both ways and finds it interesting to do so as if it were a mental game. He says they are two completely separate kinds of logical thinking when he switches back and forth, into and out of each language. He finds it fascinating. He says poetry comes to him in a mother tongue that is above Tibetan and Chinese and he tries to capture it in both languages.

A Su, original name Asu Sumur, who has been publishing poetry since 1984 under the name A Su, says he thinks in Xibe when he writes poems in Xibe, but when he writes in Chinese he thinks in Xibe first and then transforms the lines in his mind into Chinese. He translates himself to publish in Chinese journals so he can connect with other poets.

Luruo Diji and Wolfman have both mentioned that it was extremely difficult for them to learn standard Chinese (spoken and written). The younger generation of bilingual poets such as Yungdrung Gyurmè (Tibetan), Aliye Rusol (Uyghur), and Tenzin Pelmo (Tibetan) are more fluent in Chinese and write in Chinese independently without relying on their first language.

Pan Nianying from Guizhou borrows Chinese characters to record Dong poetry, reviving a traditional Dong script from the Tang dynasty. He says: "Of the three million Dong people in China, twenty thousand understand the Dong script." There was a Latin script implemented in 1958, but it was not accepted by the Dong people, whereas the government-administered Nuosu Yi script was welcomed by Nuosu Yi intellectuals.[16]

---

16   China implemented Latin scripts for several ethnic groups back in the 1950s. Those with a traditional way of writing resist the Latin scripts. The reformed Nuosu Yi was designed in 1974 by Han Chinese scholar Chen Shilin representing the central government who, after his Romanized Yi System failed three times since the 1950s, selected 819 symbols from the classical Yi characters to represent syllables and rotated them by 90 degrees. It was approved by the Sichuan provincial government in 1975 and by the State Council in 1980. This new script, i.e. Romanization in disguise, representing sound rather than meaning, has changed the Yi writing system fundamentally. Yi people in Yunnan, Guizhou and Guangxi provinces use Chinese or the classical Yi, refusing to adopt the Nuosu Yi as the standard Yi (Ming 2023c).

Chinese:

我的傷口泣不成聲
從來處來的溫暖
又到去處去了

一聲巨響
世界被一陣沉默粉碎

悲傷鋪天蓋地
傷口泣不成聲

Dong script:

堯裡傷心呃國麻水大
多傻耨麻里宋飄噶
又轉多麻里薩噶拜了

像岜樣雷雷里空喲
得悶當時薩秀

傷心像悶樣雷，像地樣寬
我額國麻水大

A rough English version goes like this:

My Wound Weeps
the warmth from where it should've come
has gone to where it should've gone

bang, a loud sound, then
the world is shattered by a moment of silence

sadness overflows from sky to earth
soundlessly sobbing from within the wound

Pan says it is much more difficult to write in Dong because Dong poetry requires alliteration, end rhyming and internal rhyming. He says the mainstream only recognizes minority poets who write in standard Chinese and ignores the real beauty of ethnic poetry.

Tung Shumin (Puyuma) from Taiwan likes to mix Pinuyumayan and Chinese characters in her poetry to preserve her indigenous identity without losing touch with other people. Bukun Ismahasan Islituan writes poems in Bunun first and translates them into Chinese to be published together in order to let more people know about Bunun culture. He grew up in a monolingual village in Taiwan speaking Bunun only and did not speak Chinese until the third grade. He says writing in Bunun is his way of connecting to the universe directly and through Bunun he can explore deeper meanings of language and write more meaningful poems. Li Hui from Shanghai learned the special script of his mother tongue Dônđăc from his great-grandmother but it is very difficult to write it with a pen. So he has adopted Chinese and Tai script.

5 Second Mother Tongue and Second Chinese

For various reasons, poets in Group II prefer to write in Chinese. Dilmurat Talat (Uyghur) translates poetry and fiction from Uyghur, Uzbek, Kyrgyz and Tajik into Chinese as a professional translator for a Xinjiang-based journal. He says "90% of the minority poets of my generation in Xinjiang write in the ethnic mother tongues, I don't need to increase that number." He chooses Chinese as his poetic language, but he writes about life in southern Xinjiang including Pamir Mountains.

Yi Wu (Yi), original name Ashuo Yiwu, is also fully bilingual, but he refuses to write poetry in Yi as a rebellious act against his predecessor Aku Wuwu (Ming and Yi Wu 2022). Aku Wuwu is one of the High Lofty Poets (*Gaodaopai* 高蹈派) related to the Intellectual Writing, while Yi Wu is one of the Down-to-Earth (*Jiediqi* 接地氣), successor of the Spoken Language Poetry but without neglecting craftsmanship.

Pan Liwen (Shui) speaks Shui as his mother tongue at home but has been educated in Chinese. He struggled in the first few years in school but managed to communicate in Chinese in the fifth grade. His hometown, Sandu County of Guizhou, is the core region for Shui. He says there are about 400 words in modern Shui, enough for daily conversation but insufficient for literary work. He has to write poetry and poetry reviews in Chinese.

He Zhong was born in the Yugur Autonomous County of Gansu Province at the foot of the Qinghai-Tibet Plateau, from a mixed family with Yugur, Mongolian and Ü Tibetan on his father's side, and Ando Tibetan and Chinese on his mother's side. He learned to speak Eastern Yugur first and soon became fluent in all the languages from both sides of his family. His grandfather taught him Tibetan script for a few years, but he lost it eventually. He never learned Mongolian or Tibetan in school. Chinese was the only language taught in school at that time in Gansu. He moved to Lhasa in 1984 and has been publishing poetry in Chinese ever since. He read Gabriel García Márquez translated into Chinese in 1984, whose magic realism changed him completely. He is not sure whether he is writing authentic Chinese or a foreign Chinese in his Márquez style of poetry (Ming 2020). He says that he usually has an idea in Yugur, his first language, before writing it down in Chinese. He says that many poets and writers in China have been deprived of the right to write in their native languages because of the institutionalized educational system where minority languages were not taught in schools in certain regions until recent years. He feels like a cultural refugee belonging nowhere.

Na Sa (Kham Tibetan from Qinghai), original name Nasa Suoyang, started learning Chinese and Tibetan at the same time in the first grade of school but found it difficult to keep up with the Tibetan script. She writes poetry in Chinese but speaks fluent Tibetan, which is her stronger language. She is a typical minority poet in China: speaking the ethnic mother tongue, adopting Chinese as "second mother tongue" for writing. She usually formulates a poem in her first mother tongue Kham Tibetan, then writes in Chinese through mental translation.

你在我的晨光裡
你在我的晨光裡
塵埃落定
在你的身後
除了影子的凹凸
光陰的附和
還有
雙目里陷落的城池
和落滿城池的歲月
我都一一拾起
成為暮年裡的
一座白塔
潛心修持

You Are in My Morning Light
you are in my morning light
dust settles
behind you
behind the rising and falling shadows
and all the accessories of time
remains
a sunken city in your eyes

and the years fallen inside the city
I pick them up one by one
and transform them into a white pagoda
of old age
where I meditate to cultivate my twilight

Both He Zhong and Na Sa write beautiful Chinese poems: "strangeness" is manifested in the wild imagination in He Zhong's poetry, while in Na Sa's poetry it can be found in its syntax and vocabulary. Her elegant, almost archaic vocabulary sounds strange and fresh at the same time. Her language reminds me of Yungdrung Gyurmè who has a collection of poems entitled "Weibizhichuang" 微閉之窗 (Slightly Closed Window). They are both influenced by Tsangyang Gyatso (1683–1706). It is precisely the "strangeness" in their poetry that has added something new to their Chinese, or a Second Chinese, making it more prominent as if Chinese were revived through minority writing. Many poets from Groups I–III have such characteristics in their writings. They have not only enriched Sinophone poetry in general but also enriched the Chinese language.

Aku Wuwu (aka Luo Qingchun 羅慶春) was the first in China to theorize the concepts of the Second Mother Tongue and Second Chinese when he praised the work of minority novelists from Sichuan province in the 1980s for writing in Chinese as "Second Mother Tongue," a term referring to the first culture and second culture well acculturated and merged. He found those novelists writing Chinese through thinking in ethnic language to reflect their heritage and ethnic culture (Luo and Wang 2008). He did not define Second Chinese. I use these two terms too but with a different notion of Second Mother Tongue. Aku places the Sichuan novelists in the context of the national reinforcement of Chinese as the official language, in which the writers become motivated to merge into the mainstream culture. But to me, the cultural decoration in their writings is the very worst thing in mainstream literature in China. To me, Second Mother Tongue is a linguistic term. The poets in Group I–III acquired Chinese between the age of five and ten, all within the critical period of second language acquisition. I see "Second Mother Tongue" as possible, or "Double Mother Tongues" as Lama Itzot 拉瑪伊佐 and other poets have put it, when one is fluent in two languages and can switch back and forth easily and can speak the second language like a native speaker. This ideal model of "Second Mother Tongue" is very common among young bilingual poets in China such as Tenzin Pelmo, Aliye Rusol, Qin Shuxia, Yungdrung Gyurmè and Samer Darkpa. I will discuss "Second Chinese" more in the next section.

THE OTHER MOTHER TONGUES AND MINORITY WRITING IN CHINA   241

Wolfman (aka Li Chenghan 李承翰) grew up speaking Naxi in a Naxi village in Lijiang, Yunnan and was not able to speak Chinese until the age of ten. It was like learning a foreign language and he eventually became fully competent in Chinese. When writing poetry in Chinese, he thinks in Chinese, not translating from Naxi unless a poem comes to him in Naxi. But he has not had an opportunity to learn either the syllabic Geba or the pictographic Dongba script. He does not use the Romanized new Naxi either. He uses Chinese characters as a phonetic system to transcribe and write his Naxi poems. This has been a popular way to transcribe English in China, for instance, *si da di* 撕大地 (tear-big-earth) for "study." But to see him write Naxi this way is a total surprise for me, yet at the same time reminds me of how humans create a writing script using another script that they already know. Wolfman innately knows how to transcribe his oral Naxi poetry by creating a personal writing system through borrowed characters, a practice by Dong people for centuries. A younger Naxi poet, Nimei Nami, uses a combination of Dongba, Chinese and Latin script of Naxi.

6   Language Loss, Resistance to Mother Tongues, and Cultural Translation

I started the project by sending out a survey questionnaire to carefully selected minority poets to find out what language was learned first and how, any exposure to other languages in childhood, when and how other languages were acquired, and proficiency levels in each language in terms of listening comprehension, speaking, reading and writing. In reality, most of the minority writers in China write in Chinese, the official language of the country (except in Tibet, Xinjiang, and Inner Mongolia where many poets write in their native languages exclusively). From the surveys and subsequent interviews, I found various reasons behind that phenomenon: one has to make extra efforts to write in a different writing system.

I have interviewed a few poets who have lost their mother tongues or have missed the opportunity to learn to speak their ethnic languages. Narenqiqige 娜仁琪琪格, born and raised in Liaoning, used to be fluent in Mongolian but after moving to Beijing, she gradually lost it. When I talked to her a few years ago, she was able to write a few words in Mongolian and sent a picture to me, but now she says she is no longer able to speak or write. Feng Na 冯娜 grew up in a mixed region in Yunnan. She was exposed to Bai and Naxi at home and also picked up Tibetan from her childhood friends in the neighboring village. But she ended up speaking Baizu Tongyong Yu 白族通用語 (the regulated Common Speech of Bai), which is similar to Yunnan Guanhua 雲南官話 (Yunnan Official Dialect of Chinese), a *lingua franca* in the multi-ethnic Yunnan.

Meng Yifei 梦亦非, born and raised in the Buyi-Hmong Autonomous County in southern Guizhou, has never had a chance to learn to speak Buyi. His village was assimilated by Han Chinese long before he was born. Buyi was actually first assimilated by Shui, a smaller ethnic group with a writing script, and then both Shui and Buyi were assimilated by Han. Buyi has had several writing scripts, but none has become a unified standard one for the Buyi language. Meng Yifei adopted Chinese as his functional language but was never happy about it. He tries to write in English and then gives up, which seems to indicate that he has thought about the situation of the Romanized scripts such as Hani, Wa, and Jingpho and the fate of minority writing.

Xi Chu speaks Eastern Hmong, aka Hnu, as his mother tongue and started learning Chinese at the age of five in school. The first year of education in school was learning Chinese through Hmong. The second year was total immersion in Chinese. Later on, he learned how to write Hmong through his uncle but found it easy because it is similar to *pinyin* for Chinese. He writes poems in Chinese and translates some into Hmong where he has to make small changes to adapt to Hmong. He frequently writes about La'er Mountain, which is the primary land of Miao/Hmong people where historical uprisings took place against the central government.

I have sensed a rebellious spirit in the poems by Xi Chu and many other minority poets in various degrees of subtlety. Meng Yifei says that most of the minority poets in China have been so institutionalized that they follow the taste of the mainstream journals. He himself was promoting "regional poetry" with Fa Xing but departed from him. He did not see anything good in the *Grand Exhibition of China's Marginalized Ethnic Poetry* (compiled by Fa Xing in 2009, in Chinese.) He said that if you write in Chinese, you are no longer a "marginalized minority," you are merely imitating the Han Chinese and therefore worthless.

Yi Wu from Group II, fully bilingual and even teaching Yi and Yi literature at Southwest Minzu University, writes poetry in Chinese. While Meng Yifei and He Zhong resent being labeled as minority poets and yet at the same time are not happy about writing in Chinese, the forced official language, Yi Wu chooses to write in Chinese but, similarly, resists being labeled as a Yi poet because of the stereotype of Yi.[17] He makes fun of the "cultural writing" of Aku

---

17   Nuosu Yi dialects are named after the costumes men wear in each area. The dialect of the area where Yi men wear pleated pants with big bottoms is called Big Pants Speech. The

THE OTHER MOTHER TONGUES AND MINORITY WRITING IN CHINA 243

Wuwu (Ming and Yi Wu 2022). He makes fun of the Yi language and tradition, but not in a harsh way:

大褲腳 (excerpt)
很奇怪
穿上大褲腳的時候我變成了另一個人
這條用三十尺藍布做成的大褲子
一下就讓我的下半身寬廣起來
不論從左到右還是從右到左
兩條褲管一氣呵成
山風自由進出
人也大氣了許多
感覺可以包容一座山
一條河
一頭野豬
甚至一個女人

My Big-Bottom Pants
very strange
when I put on big-bottom pants
I become another person
the big pants, thirty feet long, of blue cotton
make my lower body bigger
from left to right or right to left
blown up in just one blow of breath
mountain breeze goes in and out
freely
I become big-minded as well
I can take a mountain
a river
a wild boar
or even a woman

It seems that Meng Yifei and Yi Wu write in a major language out of a deep reflection on the culture and language that they try to escape from. But somehow there seems to be a sort of unavoidable or subconscious cultural translation in their poetry. Other poets such as Gebu and Luruo Diji write about their

---

dialect where Yi men wear pleated pants with medium-sized bottoms, i.e. the regional dialect Shyp Nra Hxop 聖乍土語, is called Medium Pants Speech 中褲腳話 which is the dialect that the modern standard Nuosu Yi is based on.

hometowns almost all the time as a way to promote their ethnic cultures. But Nie Le says ethnicity is deep, there is no need to show off. Zhong Xiuhua does not seem to have any ethnic identity anxiety. She writes about private feelings or social issues not related to a specific ethnic group.

In the interviews, I asked when and how they became aware of their "minority" status and the answers varied. It happened either in childhood or in the first grade. He Zhong was called a bastard (hybrid) and Yi Wu a Manzi (savage) by Han students in school. Aku Wuwu noticed the different clothing of Han children. Meng Yifei noticed the different customs of the Shui people and Han people. Li Hui noticed the difference in burial customs: Han Chinese bury the dead underground while his Dônđäc folks always burn the dead with fire. Many were labeled minorities by others, for instance, Aliye Rusol was labeled a Uyghur when she went to a Han school. The self-identifying as a minority poet occurs much later, either out of love-hatred such as Meng Yifei and Yi Wu, or with a wish to carry on the cultural tradition such as Luruo Diji and Kongno or a determination to revive a minority language such as Aku Wuwu and Gebu. It appears that the cultural translation in their writings, from different directions, and for completely different reasons, has been motivated by a kind of identity complex from childhood and a desire to write a different kind of poetry.

Chengxu Erdan is one of the very few people who still speak Qiang, an ancient language that only exists in the spoken form today. The script has been long lost. He says that Qiang people live in clusters speaking different dialects that are not mutually intelligible. As a result, most Qiang people are bilingual, speaking Chinese as a second language for communication, and are gradually losing Qiang as their mother tongue. Chengxu Erdan speaks several dialects of Qiang but writes poetry and lyrics in Chinese to reach more readers. He writes about sheep and sheepskin drums as Qiang people worship sheep, which may sound like culturally decorated writing, but many other poets in this project write ethnic themes with profound thoughts: for instance, the way He Zhong dwells on the ancient Imperial City in Gansu where he grew up, Dilmurat Talat on southern Xinjiang, Gebu on Red River of the Hani-Yi autonomous region, A Su on Honduk Tala, the grassland in his hometown that has disappeared on the map, Luruo Diji on his hometown Small Cold Mountain in Yunnan, and Yungdrung Gyurmè on Shigatse, the Back Tibet where he was born and is spiritually rooted (Ming 2020). There is a fine line between the "cultural writing" that Yi Wu and Meng Yifei resent and the "cultural translation" that happens subconsciously in the poetry of many poets, including Yi Wu and Meng Yifei themselves. Cultural translation happens when one writes about something deep in his mind related to his minority identity from early childhood. Yi Wu writes "I hold on to my skin color" and his name Yi Wu means "still black." Aku Wuwu claims to be a "cultural hybrid" and juxtaposes Yi cultures in his Chinese poems. Feng Na very subtly writes about the complicated situation that a minority poet has to face, so does Meng Yifei, the two poets that do not have a "mother tongue." They speak and write a Second Chinese as they see it, a *lingua franca*, or a creole as He Zhong feels about his Chinese (even though I find their Chinese exquisite and fresh, adding another dimension to the language). On the other hand, they feel they have mastered Chinese so well that they have to free themselves from it in order to be themselves. The complexity of their state of mind brings depth to their poetry. To Meng Yifei and Yi Wu and the like, ethnicity has given minority poets too much illusion that it is, perhaps, just a left-over of cultural encountering and incomplete assimilation. And this is why I have incorporated genetic findings from molecular anthropology into the study of ethnic poetry – we all come from the same ancestors (Li 2020), it is the languages that make us think that there are separate ethnicities, imagined ones, associated with each language.

7 Alternative History of Feminism as Seen in Minority Writings

Western feminism was introduced to China by Zhu Hong 朱紅 in 1982 as a theoretical approach to reanalyzing women's writing in China. Self-conscious feminist poetry was started in the mid-1980s by the Post-Misty generation who were influenced by the American Confessional poets such as Sylvia Plath and Anne Sexton through translation in Chinese. What has been shadowed is the long history of women's writing in ethnic-linguistic minority communities. The re-discovery in 1982 of the folk poetry in *Nüshu* 女書 (Women's Script), a writing system exclusively for women, of women and by women in southern Hunan, has broadened the view of what women's writing in China is.

The new generation of women poets in the Twenty-first century sometimes respond to the earlier generations, and are sometimes more concerned about their ethnic identities. Ha Sen writes about women in her hometown in the Horqin grassland:

科爾沁女人 (excerpt)
若把她們比做風，沒有比她們更自由的風
若把她們比作火，沒有比她們更烈烈的火
草原最嬌美的花，科爾沁女人
北方最明亮的月，科爾沁女人
傳說最潔白的雪，科爾沁女人

Horqin Women

not even wind moves more freely than them
nor fire more fiercely than them
Horqin women, the most beautiful flowers in the prairie
Horqin women, the brightest moon in the north
Horqin women, the purest snow from the legend

Banamu 芭納木writes about Mosuo 摩梭people in Yunnan,[18] the last matriarchal tribe in China where "walking marriage" is a typical lifestyle – a woman is not tied to a man even after giving birth to a child. Aliye Rusol writes about Uyghur women feeling free only when they go to a bazaar. Tenzin Pelmo writes about how Tibetan women give names to their children to change their lives. Kongno, Aynur Mawltbek, Na Sa, and Gao Qiongxian often write about women's lives in minority communities. Jike Bu 吉克布prefers to write in Chinese in order to keep up her linguistic skills in Chinese as she teaches art at Xichang College, which is a common concern for many minority people when they try to pursue a career in the Chinese-dominant society. But writing in Chinese or not never stops them from writing about their ethnicity.

就叫她索瑪 (excerpt)
但她擁有自己的花園和舊夢
還有清澈透亮名字——
就叫她索瑪，像是呼喊自己

Call Her *Suoma*
She has her own garden, her old dream
and her clearly sounding name –
Call her Suoma out loud
like calling yourself.

Suoma 索瑪 means "azalea flower" in Yi. It is also the most common name for women in the Yi region.

---

18   Mosuo people were classified in the 1950s as a subgroup of Naxi people in Yunnan and a subgroup of Mongolian in Sichuan due to different policies in two separate provinces. But they speak Mosuo, a different language from Naxi and hardly related to Mongolian. Mosuo people have a very old writing system, Daba script, simpler than the well-known Dongba script of Naxi people. Another interesting thing is that Mosuo priests have bilingual ritual texts in Daba and old Tibetan (hieroglyphics).

[…] 無損她的美：冰清玉潔
不是誰的小鳥依人的紅顏。 鏗鏘之情
來自逆行的空氣，以及逆行的水土
也將懷抱它們荒老，像天地、萬物

Nothing distains her beauty: she is pure
like ice jade
but she is not just pretty and frail.
Her sonorous voice comes from the air,
the revolving stream, the soil.
Love her.
And embrace her barren body
like heaven and earth
and everything that grows on earth

Jike Bu is weaving a feminist thread in her ethnic fabrics, or vice versa. Call it cultural translation or something else, she is blending Virginia Woolf's "A Room of One's Own" into her garden of "suomas," or vice versa. She seems to be following the tradition of Bamo Qubumo 巴莫曲布嫫 (b. 1964, Yi), one of the pioneer women poets writing about Yi women and Yi mythologies, but at the same time she tries to stay away from the Yi tradition in order to become an independent woman in all possible ways:

姑娘，姑娘 (excerpt)
你赤足，你散發
你丟掉束縛腰肢的古老銀飾
你臨水照鏡
開成自由行走的藍月亮

A Young Woman
barefooted, you let your hair down casually
and throw away the ancient silver belt that binds your waist
you look into the water as a mirror and see yourself
blooming into a blue moon that walks freely

Nüshu was rediscovered in Yongjiang county of Hunan bordering Guangxi, a mixed region of 63% of Yao and 37% of Han, Miao, Dong, Zhuang, etc., bordered by three Yao Autonomous counties and the birthplace of Yao – Thousand Household Cave. It is a slanted writing script embroidered on handkerchiefs or weaved on ribbons, passing on from generation to generation among women only, in the form of poems and letters, as wedding gifts or worshiping lines, chanted in the local speech of Pingdi Yao 平地瑶 (the ethnic Yao language in the non-mountain area) at women's gatherings or in temples. The slant Nüshu reminds me of Emily Dickinson's line, "Tell all the truth but tell it slant." There must be a need for women to have a secret language in that region.

Is *Nüshu* a variant of Chinese or the Yao script? There has been a debate for decades because Pingdi Yao is believed to be a creole of Yao and Xiang Chinese. Another woman script recently discovered on Floral Belts in southern Shanghai is more fortunate as Li Hui has already determined the local speech to be different from Shanghai dialect. He calls it Dônđăc dialect, I call it Dônđăc language. From the symbols on his great grandmother's apron floral belt that he has translated into Chinese, I can see distinguishable patterns weaved on fabrics, bearing meanings in a systematic way, with a combination of pictographs and abstract symbols, similar to the formation of Chinese characters (See Fig. 12.2).

Floral Belts of Dônđăc and *Nüshu* of Yao remind me of early graphic-writing systems related to symbols on pottery or carvings on stones. Floral Belts seem to be related to Liangzhu pottery symbols while *Nüshu* to Yao petroglyphs. *Nüshu*, on paper or fabrics, is a deviation from Chinese. It is syllabic, each symbol corresponds to a word in Pingdi Yao 平地瑶 speech. It has been used in the borderline zone of Chu culture and Yao-Miao. Chu Kingdom was arguably

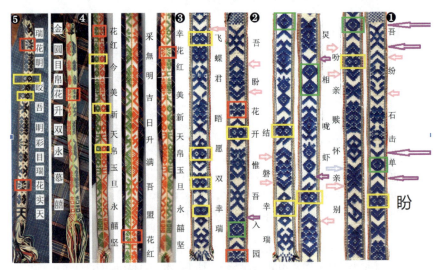

FIGURE 12.2   Recurring symbols and compounds on Dônđăc Floral Belts
Note: The floral belts are provided by Li Hui, with my annotations of recurring symbols and compound words to confirm it is a writing system. My analysis and discussion will be in a separate essay.

THE OTHER MOTHER TONGUES AND MINORITY WRITING IN CHINA   249

founded by either Han or Miao. The latest DNA findings show that Daxi culture and Gaomiao culture were built by Miao-Yao people (Xu 2017) which explains why Qu Yuan's poetry has many elements of Miao-Yao cultures.[19] My argument for *Nüshu* being a script of Yao language is supported by several observations: Yao communities have maintained many features of a matriarchal society; Yao shamans are female; the ancient symbols discovered on stones in the same region are believed to be Yao; historically petroglyphs were carved for worshiping ceremonies in many indigenous communities globally and *Nüshu* was used for worshiping in Yao temples; the borrowed Chinese characters are limited the slanted shape may have been formed in the process of embroidering.[20]

Many ethnic communities have a long tradition of weaving and/or embroidering colorful patterns, such as Tibetan, Tujia, Dong, Tai, Zhuang, Li, besides Miao and Yao. Where and when exactly weaving turned into making a patterned script needs to be explored further. But *Nüshu* is clearly related to or is a result of women's weaving/embroidering in the South. Li Hui thinks that Dong-Tai people migrated from the east coast to southern China and Southeast Asia, spreading to the Pacific Ocean. I have noted patterns of weaving among indigenous women in the Americas and Asia – flowers, plants, animals, geometric symbols and celestial signs – similar to rock engravings and simpler marks on pottery relics, early sources of writing systems, which are all inspiring for the study of indigenous-minority languages and the study of women's role in creating writing systems.

Floral belts of Dôndäc women on the east coast of China carry three-word verses. Xu Xiaomei 徐曉梅 (1896–1997), Li Hui's great-grandmother, was one of the authors. In southern Hunan, *Nüshu* is usually written in the form of rhymed verses, seven or five syllables for each line. He Yanxin 何豔新 (b. 1940), the last natural inheritor of *Nüshu*, acquired *Nüshu* from her grandmother when she was ten years old. She graduated from the local middle school and is fully bilingual and biliterate in *Nüshu* and Chinese, but she worked hard in the fields to raise her family. In the 1990s she was invited to Japan and the United States

---

19   Miao and Yao have the same origins in that Miao, Yao and She are descendants of a branch of Miao (Xu 2017).

20   Archaeological findings of the Chengtoushan site dated 6,800 years ago, the first ancient city in China, is believed to have been built by the Yao people. The proximity of the site and where Yao symbols and women's script *Nüshu* were found suggest that *Nüshu* belongs to the Yao language. The nearby Pengtoushan archaeological site dated 9,000 years ago was also built by the Yao People where the oldest fossil of rice was found (Pei 1998). There are continuous archaeological sites in the mid-stream Yangtze River that belong to Miao-Yao (Wu 2007).

to read her poems in *Nüshu* and thus became known outside her hometown. Here is my translation (through Chinese) of a very short poem by her:

月亮
春天不下壟
四季不開花
一時結香蕉
一時結西瓜

Moon
it doesn't go down the fields in spring
nor bloom in any of the four seasons
yet out of it a banana grows
and sometimes even a watermelon

The Moon has been the subject of poetry for centuries in China from Li Bai 李白 (arguably a minority too) to contemporary poets. What stands out in He Yanxin's modern quatrain is her wit, unusual metaphors and reference to women's stages of life as reflected in the shape of the Moon, from a young skinny banana to a round body watermelon. The Moon gives birth to women who in turn give birth to moons from crescent to full moons. In various cultures in China, it is common to see the Sun representing the masculine and Moon the feminine, but in the *Nüshu* community, the Moon is not passive in taking light from the Sun. Instead, the Moon is productive and shines its own light. It is through the writings of *Nüshu* that embodied Yao-Miao culture and that were self-translated into Chinese by bilingual women that we see a new feminist trend in China.

8 Non-conclusion and Problems

Along the five cultural-linguistic corridors, we see five clusters of languages and dialects that interact with each other. Some poets speak several ethnic languages, for instance, Naren Tuoya speaks Ewenki, Oroqen, Mongolian and Dagur. He Zhong speaks Yugur, Tibetan and Mongolian. Sadet Jamal is fluent in Kyrgyz, Kazakh and Uyghur. Luruo Diji speaks Pumi and Yi. Gao Qiongxian speaks Derung and Nu. Chengxu Erdan speaks several dialects of Qiang. Kongno speaks Zaiwa and all the Jingpho dialects. There has also been linguistic contact across the corridors, for instance, Li Hui has discovered that Dôndäc in Shanghai is related to Tai in southwest China and Southeast Asia.

Several poets talk about how their children do not want to speak their ethnic languages. Languages are time and space, crystallized during historical migration and settlement, and disappear due to the cultural integration of different ethnic groups.

The limited case studies presented in this shortened essay suggest that the choice of writing in a given language is personal as well as social; if a poet is more proficient in one language than the other, translation tends to take place; when there is equal competence in both languages, the double creative process kicks in. Bilingual writing depends on proficiency in Chinese and the literacy level of the ethnic mother tongues, the latter of which depends on the opportunities to learn the writing systems of minority languages. Some poets translate into or rewrite their poems in the ethnic languages to promote minority cultures such as Luruo Diji, Li Hui and Xi Chu; some translate into or re-write in Chinese for wider readership such as Gebu, Kongno and Bukun Ismahasan Islituan. Besides this type of self-translation, there is also the reported "mental translation" or internal translation by He Zhong, A Su and Na Sa, and "cultural translation" as observed in the work of multiple poets.

On the one hand, I find that the poets writing in one language write more cutting-edge poetry, on the other hand, the bilingual poets have brought their unique literary traditions and cultures into Chinese poetry, rewriting the history of contemporary Sinophone poetry, and all of them, regardless of whether they are bilingual or not, seem to be frequently translating their cultural identities into their writing, whether through the "other" mother tongues of minority nationalities or their second mother tongue, Chinese.

The limited samples already show how closely related each language is to the other languages, as if on a continuum spectrum when I listen to their recordings again and again. It is the writing systems that separate the languages and divide them into "strangers" of each other.[21] But as long as the languages and variants exist, it will always be a fascinating subject for study and comparison.

Some of these minority poets have become a vital part of the contemporary poetry scene in China or Taiwan. Bukun Ismahasan Islituan has been a prominent voice of indigenous poetry in Taiwan. He Zhong has been a member of the important Lhasa School of Literature since the 1980s. Meng Yifei is

---

21   First, according to the DNA analysis by Li Hui (2020), Han and Tibetan separated only 5,300 years ago. Despite the different writing systems, I can identify the link of the two languages by listening to the video recordings from these poets, for instance, from Amdo Tibetan to Yi and Pumi, etc. and from Zaiwa (descendant of Tibetan) to Southwestern Dialect of Chinese. Secondly, Southern minority languages are closer to archaic Chinese in vocabulary and phonology. One way to approach them is through Southern dialects of Chinese such as Xiang, Yue and Wu.

a representative of the post-70s generation and a major promoter of regional poetry as opposed to the central official poetry. Feng Na and Zhong Xiuhua are prominent new voices of women's writing in China. But many others have been sheltered or underestimated, such as Pan Nianying, Gebu, A Su, Dilmurat Talat, Aynur Mawltbek, Na Sa, Xi Chu, Yungdrung Gyurmè, Jike Bu and Tenzin Pelmo, which is part of the reason why I have done this project.

Last but not least, the rise of ethnic minorities and minority poetry has brought out so many literary treasures since the early 1980s – the Tibetan *Epic of King Gesar* that used to circulate in minority regions of Tibetan, Mongolian, Monguor (Tu), Yugur, Naxi, Bai, Pumi, Mosuo, etc., the Oirat Mongolian *Epic of Jangar* that circulated in the Uyghur region, the *Epic of Manas* by the Kyrgyz people, the creation epic of *Sart* by Yugur people, the creation Epic *Mauna Jaiwa* by the Jingpho people, *Baeuqloegdoz* by Zhuang people, to name a few and of course the various mythologies of Yi – which have complemented the lack of epics in the history of Han Chinese literature. Some of the creation epics look familiar as they have been incorporated into the Han mythologies, such as Pangu and Fuxi. It is interesting to see that the circulation route of Gesar epic coincides with the Tibet-Qiang-Yi Corridor (which supports the concept of Tibet-Qiang-Yi Corridor and shows the interaction among the ethnic groups along the corridor) but Yi has its own epics, so does Jingpho, which suggests a correlation between having maintained a linguistic system and having one's own epics even though the epics have been orally transmitted, which further suggests that ethnic minority groups historically isolated by mountains tend to have their culture, language, and oral literature less influenced by others. It would be interesting to explore the relationships between the cultural corridors and epic circulations with language extinction due to acculturation and assimilation.

It is not only the oral literature of epics but also the contemporary poetry of ethnic-linguistic minorities that have emerged and surged. But I have been frustrated about not being able to reach several authors in Xinjiang whose writings are astonishingly beautiful and profoundly meaningful, allowing readers to see a new poetry scene in the wild West as never seen before. This is a sensitive topic at this very moment, or rather always is, as the ethnic policy in China constantly changes. I have, nevertheless, attempted to document the process of creation and self-translation of some of the brilliant bilingual poets from many ethnic minority communities around the edges of the central Han land, in light of genetic and archaeological findings on ethnicities, before total Mandarinization.

THE OTHER MOTHER TONGUES AND MINORITY WRITING IN CHINA 253

Works Cited

Aku, Wuwu and Mark Bender, eds. 2006. *Tiger Traces: Selected Nuosu and Chinese Poetry by Aku Wuwu*. Columbus: Foreign Language Publishers of the Ohio State University.

Bender, Mark. 2012. "Ethnographic Poetry in North-East India and Southwest China." *Rocky Mountain Review*. Special Issue 2012: 106–129.

Crevel, Maghiel van. 2008. *Chinese Poetry in Times of Mind, Mayhem and Money*. Leiden & Boston: Brill.

Fei, Xiaotong. 1980. "On Identification of Ethnic Nationalities in Our Country." *China's Social Science* 1: 147–162.

Fei, Xiaotong. 1982. "On Thorough Investigation of the Ethnic Nationalities." *Journal of South Central China Ethnicity* 3: 2–6.

Fu, Qiaomei et al. 2020. "Ancient DNA Indicates Human Population Shifts and Admixture in Northern and Southern China." *Science* 369: 282–288.

Fu, Qiaomei et al. 2021. "Human Population History at the Crossroads of East and Southeast Asia since 11,000 Years Ago." *Cell* 14: 3829–3841.

Gao, Qiongxian, 2023. "Prophet" and "Seven Color Lone-Dragon Blanket." Translated by Ming Di. *World Literature Today*, Nov–Dec: 30.

Gong, Zhebing. 2018. "My Discovery and Rescue of *Nüshu*." *Wuhan Literature and History Archive* 7: 32–39.

Li, Hui et al. 2007. "Y chromosomes of prehistoric people along the Yangtze River." *Human Genetics* 122: 383–388.

Li, Hui and Jin Li. 2008. "Reconstructing the Genealogy of East Asian Humans." *Scientific Men* 78: 35–39.

Li, Hui and Jin Wenli. 2020. *Human Origin and Migration*. Shanghai: Shanghai Science Education Press.

Li, Jen-kuei. 2019. "Following the Footsteps of Fang Kuei Li's Fieldwork on the Minority Languages in Southwestern China." *Bulletin of Chinese Linguistics* 12: 3–12.

Luo, Qingchun and Wang Ju. 2008. "Poetic Creation of Second Mother Tongue: Creative Writing in Chinese by Ethnic Minority Novelists in Sichuan." *Fiction Reviews* 3: 57–62.

Ming, Di. 2020. "God is plural in China – Poetry travels in the time of quarantine," part 6. *Poetry International*, December 19, 2020. Available online, URL: https://www.poetryinternational.com/en/poets-poems/article/104-30316_god-is-plural-in-china-poetry-travels-in-the-time-of-quarantine-6# (accessed August 9, 2023).

Ming, Di, and Gebu. 2022. "'Rooted in my homeland by the Red River': An Interview with ethnic Hani poet Gebu by Ming Di." *Tupelo Quarterly* 28. Available online, URL:

https://www.tupeloquarterly.com/editors-feature/rooted-in-my-homeland-by-the-red-river-an-interview-with-ethnic-hani-poet-gebu-curated-by-ming-di/ (accessed on 20 April 2023).

Ming, Di, and Yi Wu. 2022. "'I resist tradition. I don't want to be labeled as a Yi poet': An Interview with 'Still Black' Yi Wu by Ming Di." *Tupelo Quarterly* 28. Available online, URL: https://www.tupeloquarterly.com/editors-feature/i-resist-tradition-i-dont-want-to-be-labeled-as-a-yi-poet-an-interview-with-still-black-yi-wu-curated-by-ming-di/ (accessed on 20 April 2023).

Ming, Di, and Bukun Ismahasan Islituan. 2023. "'My tribal language is my window to see the world' – Interview with Indigenous Bunun poet Bukun Ismahasan Islituan by Ming Di." *Tupelo Quarterly* 30. Available online, URL: https://www.tupeloquarterly.com/editors-feature/my-tribal-language-is-my-window-to-see-the-world-interview-with-indigenous-bunun-poet-bukun-ismahasan-islituan-curated-by-ming-di/ (accessed on July 31, 2023).

Ming, Di, et al. 2023a. "'My ancestors fought with arms ... I fight with words' – A survey interview with four Indigenous-minority poets – by Ming Di." *Tupelo Quarterly* 30. Available online, URL: https://www.tupeloquarterly.com/editors-feature/my-ancestors-fought-with-arms-i-fight-with-words-a-survey-interview-with-four-indigenous-minority-poets-curated-by-ming-di/ (accessed on July 31, 2023).

Ming, Di, et al. 2023b. "'Injecting new blood into native literature' – Interviews with four indigenous poets from Xinjiang by Ming Di." *Tupelo Quarterly* 30. Available online, URL: https://www.tupeloquarterly.com/editors-feature/injecting-new-blood-into-native-literature-interviews-with-four-indigenous-poets-from-xinjiang-curated-by-ming-di/ (accessed on July 31, 2023).

Ming, Di, et al. 2023c. "Yiwen Qianjing Kanyou" 彝文前景堪憂 [The future of the Yi writing system causes worries?]" *Southern Poetry*. Available online, URL: https://m.booea.com/news/s_3302533.html (accessed on September 11, 2023).

Ming, Di. 2023. "Indigenous-Minority Poets from China." *World Literature Today*. Available online, URL: https://www.worldliteraturetoday.org/blog/audio-poetry/indigenous-minority-poets-china-15-recordings-international-day-worlds-indigenous (accessed on August 9, 2023).

Nisuruo, Axiong, 2019. *Lun Yiwen he 819* 試論彝文和819 [On Yi Script and 819]. *Kknews*, August 27, 2019. Available online, URL: https://kknews.cc/news/ply6gxe.html (accessed August 24, 2023).

Pei, Anping. 1998. "On the Rice Fossils from Pengtoushan Culture and Rice Farming in Prehistoric China." *Agricultural Archaeology* 1: 1–12.

Salam, Shayip, ed. 2016. *Ranshaode Maisui* 燃燒的麥穗 [Burning Ears of Wheat]. Wuhan: Yangtze River Literature and Arts Publishing House.

Sun, Hongkai, et al. 2007. *Languages in China*. Beijing: Shangwu Press.

Wang, Chuanchao, Ding Qiliang, Tao Huan and Li Hui. 2012. "Comment on 'Phonemic Diversity Supports a Serial Founder Effect Model of Language Expansion from Africa.'" *Science* 335: 657c.

Wu, Rongzhen, ed. 2007. *History of Miao Nationality*. Beijing: Publishing House of Minority Nationalities.

Xu, Jieshun and Li Hui. 2014. The Origin of the Lingnan Peoples. Kunming: Yunnan People's Press.

Xu, Jieshun and Li Hui. 2017. "From the Perspective of Molecular Anthropology: A New Theory on the Origin of the Indigenous People in Guangxi." *Journal of Guangxi Normal University* 4: 29–36.

CHAPTER 13

Why Do I Translate Myself?

Mai Mang 麥芒

I sometimes call myself a poet writing in both Chinese and English. But perhaps a more accurate description is this: I am a poet writing in Chinese and, from time to time, translating myself into English. Why do I translate myself, then, instead of leaving the job to translators for whom English is their native tongue?

For that question I can come up with different answers. Here, however, I will choose to present one explanation that is at once personal and metaphysical: I translate myself to discover or excavate the unknown selves or others within myself. I translate myself to assert the rootedness of silence or foreign and excluded voices in my own poetry, and to demonstrate that true poetry often exists beyond the borders of the literary establishment, in the East or in the West, dominated by a hegemonic *lingua franca* or disguised as a self-centered "world literature" or "the world republic of letters."

1

French scholar Pascale Casanova in her academic bestseller *The World Republic of Letters* very confidently charted an uncontested empire and institution of "the world republic of letters." She claims:

> This world republic of letters has its own mode of operation: its own economy, which produces hierarchies and various forms of violence; and above all, its own history [...]. Its geography is based upon the opposition between a capital, on the one hand, and peripheral dependencies whose relationship to this center is defined by their aesthetic distance from it. (2004, 11–12)

And,

> This improbable combination of qualities lastingly established Paris, both in France and throughout the world, as the capital of a republic having neither borders nor boundaries, a universal homeland exempt from

all professions of patriotism, a kingdom of literature set up in opposition to the ordinary laws of state, a transnational realm whose sole imperatives are those of art and literature: the universal republic of letters. (29)

It is with this Eurocentric or Western-centric mapping of "the world republic of letters," with Paris or London serving as its capital, that Casanova designates translation as "a form of literary recognition," "the principal means of access to the literary world for all writers outside the center," and "the major prize and weapon in international literary competition" (133). She further elaborates on the role of translation with regard to cementing the Western hegemony:

> Translation therefore stands revealed as an ambiguous enterprise as well: on the one hand, it is a means of obtaining official entry to the republic of letters; and, on the other, it is a way of systematically imposing the categories of the center upon works from the periphery, even of unilaterally deciding the meaning of such works. In this sense the notion of universality is one of the most diabolical inventions of the center, for in denying the antagonistic and hierarchical structure of the world, and proclaiming the equality of all the citizens of the republic of letters, the monopolists of universality command others to submit to their law. (154)

On her map, Casanova leaves little space for the non-Western languages and literatures owing to their peripheral positions and distances from the self-titled center or capital: "Finally, there are languages of broad diffusion such as Arabic, Chinese, and Hindi that have great internal literary traditions but nonetheless are little known and largely unrecognized in the international marketplace" (256–257).

Casanova's "world republic of letters" is, as accommodating at times as it might seem, actually, nothing new or original at all. In fact, it is simply another later rehearsal of the enterprise of "world literature" imagined and imposed from a Western-centric vantage point, affirming Western hegemony and its colonial and imperialist legacy. To give another example of how such a self-centered and ultimately self-serving "world literature" has been taken as a given, in 1990, American sinologist Stephen Owen put it bluntly in his controversial book review "What Is World Poetry?":

> American poets have the provincial's sweet gift of needing to dream no further than an eternity of English-speaking audiences. To write in the dominant language of the age is to have the luxury of writing with unshaken faith in the permanence of a culture's hegemony. But poets in

many other countries and languages must, as their imaginary audiences swell, dream of being translated. And thus they must write envisaging audiences who will read their work in translation. (1990, 28)

Back in 1928, in his introduction to Ezra Pound's *Selected Poems*, T.S. Eliot also famously said: "As for *Cathay*, it must be pointed out that Pound is the inventor of Chinese poetry for our time" (1928, xvi). Eliot further qualified his ambivalent appraisal in the same and next paragraph:

I predict that in three hundred years Pound's *Cathay* will be a 'Windsor Translation' as Chapman and North are now 'Tudor Translations': it will be called (and justly) a 'magnificent specimen of XXth Century poetry' rather than a 'translation'. [...]
This is as much as to say that Chinese poetry, as we know it to-day, is something invented by Ezra Pound. It is not to say that there is a Chinese poetry-in-itself, waiting for some ideal translator who shall be only translator; but that Pound has enriched modern English poetry as Fitzgerald enriched it. [...] People of to-day who like Chinese poetry are really no more liking Chinese poetry than the people who like Willow pottery and Chinesische-Turms in Munich and Kew like Chinese Art. (xvii)

Whether a "Windsor Translation" or simply a "magnificent specimen of XXth Century poetry," in Eliot's eyes, Pound's *Cathay* had nothing to do with the actual China or Chinese poetry at all, but rather a new acquisition and conquest of the seemingly permanent British Empire. As for "Chinese poetry-in-itself," it was the mere raw material for Western appropriation and "invention" and did not possess any of its own agency: it is passive, decorative, and irrelevant.

All of these could not but make me think of what Lu Xun, father of modern Chinese literature, had to say in his public lecture "Silent China" (*Wusheng de Zhongguo* 無聲的中國) delivered in Hong Kong in 1927, one year prior to Eliot's calculated assessment of Pound:

Yet others urge that since foreigners have translated our classics, thus proving their worth, we ought to read them ourselves. But, as everyone knows, foreigners have also translated the hieroglyphic texts of the Egyptians and the myths of the African Negroes. They do so from ulterior motives, and to be translated by them is no great honour. (Lu Xun 1973, 166)

"They do so from ulterior motives, and to be translated by them is no great honour," Lu Xun summed it all up. I myself had the following to say on the issue of translating Chinese poetry back in 2011:

WHY DO I TRANSLATE MYSELF?

In an age of globalization when translation activities have intensified, when authors and translators have expressed a strong wish to connect to more readers and kindred spirits, I am, nevertheless, a pessimist above all: a poem cannot be translated, and to be translated means to be misunderstood. It is like contemporary American poets who have translated and borrowed from classical Chinese poets such as Li Bai, Du Fu, Wang Wei, and Han Shan. Who knows if these classical poets really came back to life again, would they approve or even care about the attention and acclaim they have received in English-language poetry? (Mai Mang 2011, 228)[1]

Can one translate poetry with purposes other than purely "obtaining official entry to the republic of letters," or gaining an imaginary seat in a fictive pantheon of a Western-centric "world poetry" or "world literature"? Have scholars like Casanova ever considered the possibility that "world literature" might actually exist in a different form, not disguised as "the world republic of letters," outside and beyond the bounds of such a literary map monopolized by Western hegemony and biases?

2

I had a chance to visit the Pilgrim Hall Museum in historic downtown Plymouth, Massachusetts, in spring 2018. What most impressed me was this particular fact: all the names of the 102 original *Mayflower* passengers in 1620 were carefully recorded, preserved, and weaved into the foundation myth of America. What about Angel Island on the West Coast, in San Francisco Bay, and the Chinese immigrants who were once detained on it? Where are their names?

> 埃崙此地爲仙島，
> 山野原來是監牢。
>
> In LAI, LIM, YUNG 1991, 61

These are two lines from one of the Angel Island poems, inscribed anonymously on the wooden walls of the detention barracks on Angel Island that served as a US immigration station between 1910 and 1940. Now we can read some of them in English translations:

---

1 Here I am using my own translation.

This place is called an island of immortals,
When, in fact, this mountain wilderness is a prison.

60

Angel Island poetry, locked in its Chinese original, was essentially a body of "foreign" poetry kept away from mainland America, a poetry of "exclusion" and "imprisonment," and not a poetry like "Song of the Open Road" as Walt Whitman had envisioned. But can it not be seen as American, too? Does it have to be translated into English first in order to be accepted as American? Or, should it be regarded as an indispensable part of American poetry anyway, as long as it exists, regardless of in its Chinese original or in English translation, a poetry that has challenged and disrupted the boundaries of American poetry, as it narrates a different and complex America, and, to a great extent, a more real America?

Angel Island poetry is a good example of how a body of anonymous poetry was written out of necessity, not of vanity, across boundaries. In a more fundamental sense, for me, the Angel Island poets, precisely because of their "foreignness" and anonymity, and precisely because of their existence in silence and exclusion, were the true "inventor[s] of Chinese poetry for our time," not Ezra Pound of *Cathay* or the other white mandarins of Anglo-American modernism, in the broad context of American poetry. In that sense, when I write and translate my own poems, the Angel Island poets are my imaginary audience and my personal role model.

3

I wrote "Stone Turtle" (*Shigui* 石龜) on June 25, 2000 in Los Angeles. I wrote it first in Chinese, which begins with:

六月
炎熱的一天
我們循著
乾涸的洛杉磯河谷
尋找合適的
岩石
河水早已逝去
不再有
粼粼的波光
有如熟悉

WHY DO I TRANSLATE MYSELF?

的指紋
而假想的魚則從
我們腳底溜走
進入史前

MAI MANG [2005] 2011, 171

Shortly after that, I translated it into English myself. The same stanza now reads as:

> June
> A day in the heat
> We follow
> The dried-out L.A. River bank
> Looking for the right
> Rocks
> The river water has long gone
> No more
> Shining of the ripples
> Like once familiar
> Fingerprints
> While the imagined fish
> Slip through under our feet
> Entering pre-history
>
> 173

My purpose in writing this poem and then translating it into English was not at all to gain acceptance into some imagined capital of "the world republic of letters." On the contrary, I wanted to translate myself out of my comfort zone, to enter the unfamiliar and unknown, until I recognized myself and my others in an entirely new light:

> At this polluted
> Deserted
> Site
> All of a sudden, we find
> A
> Turtle-like rock
> Or rather
> A stone turtle
> Slowly carrying

Its body
As if trying to
Pull itself
(On the verge of annihilation)
Out of the flowing sand

> 173

In addition, this moment of recognition was marked by myriad questions arising from the lyrical protagonist addressing the stone turtle that had existed here long before his own arrival:

Recalling
Ancient sacred spirit
Stone turtle
We meet you
Faraway in a foreign land
Do you remember still
Your once noble origin
And language
How have you
Managed not to confuse yourself entirely
With the other rocks around
Have you ever expected
One day
Such recognition and salvation

> 173–174

The dedicatee of the poem, Chinese American poet Russell Leong noted: "The stone turtle, it seems, found voice in a Chinese poet who traveled thousands of miles from Hunan to create a poem from sunlight, dirty water and the littered banks of the L.A. River" (Leong [2001] 2011, 176). After having lived in America for seven years back then, through discovering that stone turtle, I finally broke the long-held silence as if breaking a spell.

Furthermore, I finally began to hear my own voice emerging in a foreign tongue, which was becoming my adopted tongue, that is, regardless of how strange this might sound, my own tongue nevertheless. Actually, only after I translated it into English, did it dawn on me that "Stone Turtle" is a poem that has already translated itself. "Stone Turtle" is not only my "first poem about living in America" (176), as Leong called it, but more importantly, my first Chinese American poem, or, simply, my first American poem. It is in "Stone Turtle" that

WHY DO I TRANSLATE MYSELF? 263

I first recognized myself as not just a Chinese poet, but a Chinese American poet. I came to the realization that I must discover, or rediscover, "America" by asserting myself in America, just as the Angel Island poets did. I must have my own voice, whether in my suppressed mother tongue, or in a new adopted tongue, or in writing in silence, just as those Angel Island poets already demonstrated: silence, once written down or inscribed on the wooden walls, is a voice that can find and grow its own roots, and will not be easily erased or eradicated.

4

Such visions or epiphanic encounters by the banks of a river or a lake have happened before in American poetry. Whitman's "By Blue Ontario's Shore," for instance, has left a longstanding impact on me ever since my first reading it in English, describing his encounter with a "Phantom gigantic superb" on the shore of Lake Ontario:

> By blue Ontario's shore,
> As I mused of these warlike days and of peace return'd, and the dead that
>   return no more,
> A Phantom gigantic superb, with stern visage accosted me,
> *Chant me the poem*, it said, *that comes from the soul of America, chant me*
>   *the carol of victory,*
> *And strike up the marches of Libertad, marches more powerful yet,*
> *And sing me before you go the song of the throes of Democracy.*
>   WHITMAN 2004, 362

Unlike my mute "stone turtle," the "phantom" speaks in a lofty tone, as "the voice arising demanding bards" (368), dictating the social role of the new American poet that it would approve of. In section 12, especially, the "phantom" starts by asking: "Are you he who would assume a place to teach or be a poet here in the States?" And then, it warns: "He shall surely be question'd beforehand by me with many and stern questions" (370). These "many and stern questions" include:

> Who are you indeed who would talk or sing to America?
> Have you studied out the land, its idioms and men?
> Have you learn'd the physiology, phrenology, politics, geography, pride,
>   freedom, friendship of the land? its substratums and objects?

Have you consider'd the organic compact of the first day of the first year of
  Independence, sign'd by the Commissioners, ratified by the States, and
  read by Washington at the head of the army?
Have you possess'd yourself of the Federal Constitution?
  370

Most importantly,

What is this you bring my America?
Is it uniform with my country?
Is it not something that has been better told or done before?
Have you not imported this or the spirit of it in some ship?
  371

And so on and so forth. I could almost picture Whitman's "phantom," in the
guise of an immigration officer or judge, dutifully and diligently interrogating
those tongue-tied new immigrants detained on Angel Island, as you can feel
the aggressiveness and weight of this pointed question:

Is it uniform with my country?

In fact, this question, among others, was the very same that Whitman asked in
his 1855 preface to *Leaves of Grass*: "Whether or no the sign appears from the
mouths of the people, it throbs a live interrogation in every freeman's and free-
woman's heart after that which passes by or this built to remain. Is it uniform
with my country?" (761).

Nearly one hundred years later, Allen Ginsberg wrote his "Sunflower
Sutra" (1955), recounting his own encounter with a sunflower "on the banks
of the tincan banana dock" and "under the huge shade of a Southern Pacific
locomotive":

I walked on the banks of the tincan banana dock and sat down under the
  huge shade of a Southern Pacific locomotive to look at the sunset over
  the box house hills and cry.
[...]
The oily water on the river mirrored the red sky, sun sank on top of final
  Frisco peaks, no fish in that stream, no hermit in those mounts, just
  ourselves rheumy-eyed and hung-over like old bums on the riverbank,
  tired and wily.

WHY DO I TRANSLATE MYSELF? 265

> Look at the Sunflower, he said, there was a dead gray shadow against the
> sky, big as a man, sitting dry on top of a pile of ancient sawdust –
> – I rushed up enchanted – it was my first sunflower, memories of Blake –
> my visions – Harlem
> and Hells of the Eastern rivers, bridges clanking Joes Greasy Sandwiches,
> dead baby carriages, black treadless tires forgotten and unretreaded, the
> poem of the riverbank, condoms & pots, steel knives, nothing stainless,
> only the dank muck and the razor-sharp artifacts passing into the past –
>> GINSBERG 1988, 138

Ginsberg, too, asks, almost impulsively, a string of questions about the sun-
flower's origins and identity:

> How many flies buzzed round you innocent of your grime, while you
> cursed the heavens of the railroad and your flower soul?
> Poor dead flower? when did you forget you were a flower? when did you
> look at your skin and decide you were an impotent dirty old locomo-
> tive? the ghost of a locomotive? the specter and shade of a once pow-
> erful mad American locomotive?
>> 139

Please compare this part with "By the Blue Ontario's Shore," and also with what
Whitman had to sing of a locomotive in "To a Locomotive in Winter" (1876):

> Type of the modern – emblem of motion and power – pulse of the
> continent
>> 2004, 483

> Fierce-throated beauty!
> Roll through my chant with all thy lawless music, thy swinging lamps at
> night,
> Thy madly-whistled laughter, echoing, rumbling like an earthquake, rous-
> ing all
>> 483

Ginsberg, however, identifies himself with the "sunflower" and not with the
"once powerful mad American locomotive." He turns with his back against the
"locomotive" and, instead, directly addresses the "sunflower" with a resound-
ing reminder:

> You were never no locomotive, Sunflower, you were a sunflower!
> GINSBERG 1988, 139

In other words, whereas Whitman demands a national bard with a sublime, all-encompassing mission of American democracy who must pass the high bar of his citizenship test, Ginsberg questions "America" and argues the opposite: perhaps what is truly uniform with America needs to be debated or dissented, whose idealistic vision might find its true incarnation in the "sunflower," not in "an impotent dirty old locomotive" or "the specter and shade of a once powerful mad American locomotive."

I find many unexpected similarities between Ginsberg's "sunflower" and my own "stone turtle." Mute, buried, struggling "on the verge of annihilation," does not my "stone turtle," just like Ginsberg's "sunflower," despite their silence and neglected presence, also belong to America and represent America?

> Is it uniform with my country?

I wonder how my mute "stone turtle" would have responded to Whitman's aggressive and discriminatory "interrogation." Should it follow the example of Ginsberg and loudly assert its own voice, like Whitman's "fierce-throated" "locomotive" itself, by "Howls"? Or, should it chant sutras? Or, to what extent should my "stone turtle" choose to exercise its Fifth Amendment rights: "You have the right to remain silent"?

As a matter of fact, I was in no way influenced by Whitman or Ginsberg at all while writing or translating my own "Stone Turtle." But, after I translated it into English, some of those previously hidden or obscured connections slowly revealed themselves. As mentioned above, I consider my "Stone Turtle," first of all, a continuation of the Angel Island poetry tradition and lineage. As now I see it, "Stone Turtle" is not just a Chinese or "foreign" poem in translation, but, more quintessentially, it is a poem about "America," a poem claiming "America," and an American poem. It is as American as Whitman's "By the Blue Ontario's Shore" and Ginsberg's "Sunflower Sutra" are, and as American as Angel Island poetry is.

Like Langston Hughes once declared in his 1924 poem "I, Too," I, too, want to use my "Stone Turtle" to firmly assert that "I, too, sing America" and "I, too, am America." Perhaps, by putting "America" back into its own historical context, by scrutinizing and redefining "America," a true American poem should be not just a "Song of the Open Road," but also of Angel Island and other immigration detention centers, not just a "Song of Myself," but also a "Song of Others," and, sometimes, more fundamentally, simply "silence" itself. "Stone Turtle," along with its "foreignness," its exclusion, its muteness, its silence, in its translated or bilingual format, just like Angel Island poetry, is perfectly "uniform with my country."

5

Come back to Ginsberg's reaction to "a once powerful mad American locomotive," which was drastically different from what Whitman had seen in the latter: "Type of the modern – emblem of motion and power – pulse of the continent," and, "Thy madly-whistled laughter, echoing, rumbling like an earthquake, rousing all." In fact, Whitman not only sang the hymn to the "locomotive," but, more importantly, sang praise to the newly completed transcontinental railroad, and hailed it as a great modern achievement in "Passage to India" (1871):

> Singing my days,
> Singing the great achievements of the present,
> Singing the strong light works of engineers,
> Our modern wonders, (the antique ponderous Seven outvied,)
> In the Old World the east the Suez canal,
> The New by its mighty railroad spann'd
>> WHITMAN 2004, 428

And,

> I see over my own continent the Pacific railroad surmounting every barrier,
> [...]
> I hear the locomotives rushing and roaring, and the shrill steam-whistle,
> I hear the echoes reverberate through the grandest scenery in the world,
> [...]
> Bridging the three or four thousand miles of land travel,
> Tying the Eastern to the Western sea,
> The road between Europe and Asia.
>> 430

Is this the true and only hymn to internationalism or cosmopolitanism bridging East and West? What happened to the anonymous and unrecognized Chinese railway workers whose blood was spilled and whose bones were buried underneath the tracks of the transcontinental railroad? Moreover, what happened to the Native American tribes whose lands were grabbed for building the transcontinental railroad and for the "great achievements" of Manifest Destiny and Westward Expansion? Where were their voices? Were they doomed to being "on the verge of annihilation" as stated in my "Stone Turtle" and drowned by Whitman's "full-lung'd" singing of the imperialist expansion of the US in the name of progress and democracy?

Here, my "Stone Turtle" partakes in an ever-larger conversation that goes beyond merely Chinese or English languages, beyond narrowly defined Chinese or American poetry or a self-celebratory and boastful cosmopolitanism, and reaches into a wordless, vast silence which is ever more meaningful, enduring and universal.

6

I wrote "Copper" on the night of January 10, 2013, in Peru. It was the second and last night of my two-day trip visiting Mina Tintaya, an open-pit copper mine located at an elevation of about 4,100 meters or 13,400 feet, in Espinar, Cusco. I witnessed how the copper mine was like a gigantic open wound borne out of the depths of the earth and learned the controversial impacts of the copper mine upon the environment and the local community, consisting mostly of the indigenous population. My mind was overwhelmed with impressions and thoughts, yet for which I could not find adequate expression.

On that night, upon listening to the silence on the Andean high plateau with no one else in my sight, I jotted down a few lines in Chinese, simply to make a mark on the vastness of that space, night, and time:

> 我夢見很多我不認識但與我相似的人，
> 像銅一樣被挖出來，
> 又重新被埋進去，
> 埋進地球黑暗的深處。
>
> MAI MANG [2013–2014] 2017, 137

I later titled this short poem "Tong" 銅 and translated it into English, "Copper," to further grope for its invisible connections:

> I dreamt of those whom I did not know
> but who looked just like me,

dug out like copper,
and buried again,
back into the source of the earth.

137

"Copper" is a poem about silence, an expansive, infinite silence buried underground, on a high plateau, deep down in the earth, a silence traversing borders of languages and peoples, a different and more ancient universal bond beyond languages and words. I had this feeling: the silence that I wrote in "Copper" must have been written by others who came prior to me. Different, various silences of the others converged into my own life and became my own silence.

I had long known the richness of copper resources in the Andes in South America, including Chile and Peru. However, my first knowledge of copper mining in this part of the world was more directly owing to my reading of the great Chilean poet Pablo Neruda in Chinese translations in China in the 1980s. Particularly, I read his "Ode to Copper" in Chinese translation, "Tong de songge" 銅的頌歌:

> 黃色的銅
> 從古以來就睡在山頂。
> 這是赤裸裸的北方的
> 偏僻的丘陵，
> 這是儲滿銅的懸崖峭壁，
> 時間火熱的呼吸在上面留下了溝痕，
> 這是被無數傷疤割裂了的
> 淺藍色小山的圓頂……
>
> 在我這兒的腳下
> 是礦井的有毒的礦藏。
> 但是要知道是人
> 挖掘了這些礦井！
> 礦石不是來自
> 大地的深處，
> 礦石是來自人的胸膛。

NERUDA 1983a, 270

Copper lies
asleep there.

There are the hills
of the desolate North.
From above
the summits
of copper,
disdainful scars,
green mantles,
cupolas in decay
a result of the burning
impetus of time,
near
us
the mine:
the mine is only man,
the mineral
doesn't emerge
from the earth,
it leaves
the human chest

NERUDA 2013, 168

I always felt this intrinsic affinity with Neruda. Many of Neruda's lines had long etched into my memories, across the language barriers between Chinese and Spanish. I even brought my original copy of Neruda's *Canto General* in Chinese translation along with me to Peru, to the Andes, to Cuzco, and to Machu Picchu, as if to fulfill the dreams of my youth.

But, on that particular night, instead of thinking of Neruda, I was recalling more immediately some other nights I once spent on the Qinghai-Tibet Plateau that was more than ten thousand miles away back in China, at the same or even higher altitudes, and recalling the following lines by the Chinese poet Hai Zi 海子 (1964–1989):

亞洲銅，亞洲銅
祖父死在這裡，父親死在這裡，我也將死在這裡
你是唯一的一塊埋人的地方

1997, 3

Asian copper, Asian copper
Grandfather died here, father died here, I shall also die here

WHY DO I TRANSLATE MYSELF? 271

You are the only ground for burial[2]

I responded to this poem, "Asian Copper" (*Yazhou tong* 亞洲銅), in a very personal way. Partly it is because I was probably among the poem's earliest readers shortly after the young Hai Zi wrote it in 1984. Back then, Hai Zi's use of the very word "copper" sounded magical to me, as it instantly invoked a powerful association with roots, ancestry, death, burial, history, silence, and anonymity, and offered a new dimension to my understanding of what an inexhaustible mine of possibilities Chinese poetry tradition could be.

In that sense, I wrote and translated my "Copper" as my tribute to and appreciation of the connections of more than the vast space and time between the Andes Mountains and the Qinghai-Tibet Plateau, between Neruda's "Ode to Copper" and Hai Zi's "Asian Copper," between the aboveground and the underground, and between myself and my other unknown identities, origins, languages, pasts and futures. I did not particularly care whether I had said anything supposedly original or ingenious, or anything that had never been said before by anyone else, such as "Make It New." On the contrary, I wished my poem to echo what my ancestors, my predecessors had said, or, had not yet said, in Chinese poetry or in other languages and on other continents. My obligation was to listen attentively, to recognize these buried voices, and to excavate "those whom I did not know / but who looked just like me." If my "Copper," in its Chinese original and in my own English translation, could somehow serve as a link as such, even if in its minutest way, I would consider it has fulfilled its mission.

Ultimately, "Copper" comes down to the following questions: Can a poem translate itself? Can silence translate itself? Can I translate that vast, expansive silence across continents? Can we decipher and comprehend that silence in a simple and unadorned fashion? Can we envision ourselves living in the same reality, the same silence? I believe the answer to all these questions should be "yes." We share the same silence, which is a universal human language and can and should be able to translate itself.

7

Any truly worthy poetry, by definition, is universal. But who defines "universality"? Is it those who feel entitled to define themselves as the "center" of the

---

2   My own translation. For a full translation of this poem, see Dan Murphy's version (2010, 19).

world simply because they are from the supposedly cosmopolitan centers across the globe?

On that night when I wrote "Copper," facing and surrounded by the silence at the high altitude in the Andes, I had another feeling: I was not at some remote periphery or forgotten corner of the world; on the contrary, where I stood, under my feet, was the very center of a boundless ancient world whose language was silence itself. The center of the world is not in Paris, not in London, not in New York, not in Beijing, but right here, right where I stand in the Andes, on the high plateau, where copper is buried deep down in the earth, where it is dug out and buried down again, in my dreams, that is, where my dreams are.

Two days after I wrote "Copper," I had my own opportunity to ascend Machu Picchu, like Neruda had done seventy years before. Neruda described his own awakening while facing the ancient ruins in his memoirs:

> I felt infinitely small in the center of that navel of rocks, the navel of a deserted world, proud, towering high, to which I somehow belonged. I felt that my own hands had labored there at some remote point in time, digging furrows, polishing the rocks.
>
> I felt Chilean, Peruvian, American. On those difficult heights, among those glorious, scattered ruins, I had found the principles of faith I needed to continue my poetry.
>
> 1977, 165–166

"Sube conmigo, amor americano" (美洲的愛，同我一起攀登[3]/Rise up with me, American love[4]), Neruda proclaimed in "The Heights of Macchu Picchu." Similarly, with his invocation of "Asian Copper," Hai Zi was one of the main pioneers of what became known as the "modern epic" (*xiandai shishi* 現代史詩) movement in China in the 1980s. One way or another, Hai Zi's grand vision was informed by a different conception of "world literature" or cosmopolitanism. I found many similarities between Neruda and Hai Zi, both of whom spoke an epic language, grieved the lost pasts, harbored grand dreams of the bonds of humanity, and gave voices to the excluded, suppressed, and buried futures across barriers: Asian, Chinese, Peruvian, Chilean, American and Indigenous. This is, indeed, an alternative cosmopolitanism. Not everything has to be *en route* to or from Paris or London or New York: the so-called

---

3 Translated by Lin Yi'an and Cai Qijiao (Neruda 1983b, 65).
4 Translated by Jack Schmitt (Neruda 1991, 36).

WHY DO I TRANSLATE MYSELF?

"capital" or "capitals" of the world are not necessarily the real center of the world. In fact, the center of the world may be, as Neruda put it, "the navel of a deserted world." There is a much larger world – Asia, Africa, the Americas – out there, a non-Western world, a third or fourth world, far larger and more diverse than a well-charted and self-centered Western world, even though for some the former might appear to have been plagued or dominated by silences.

When I translate myself, I need to translate all these silences surrounding the center of the world, the navel of the world, as Hai Zi had felt in his "Asian Copper," or as Neruda had called for through, say, his "Ode to Copper" and many other poems. They belong to a collective silence that in turn belongs to and speaks of the majority of humankind, just as Neruda also said in "The Heights of Macchu Picchu":

> I've come to speak through your dead mouths.
> Throughout the earth join all
> the silent scattered lips
> and from the depths speak to me all night long,
> as if I were anchored with you,
> tell me everything, chain by chain,
> link by link, and step by step
> > NERUDA 1991, 41

Or, in his Spanish original:

> Yo vengo a hablar por vuestra boca muerta.
> A través de la tierra juntad todos
> los silenciosos labios derramados
> y desde el fondo habladme toda esta larga noche
> como si yo estuviera con vosotros anclado,
> contadme todo, cadena a cadena,
> eslabón a eslabón, y paso a paso
> > NERUDA 1980, 236, 238

I felt I said just the same, even if in silence, as if my silence was anchored, too, and reverberating with Neruda's passionate incantations, "cadena a cadena, / eslabón a eslabón, y paso a paso," "chain by chain, / link by link, and step by step":

> I dreamt of those whom I did not know
> but who looked just like me

In many ways, "Copper" shares the same quality as my other poem "Stone Turtle." Again, as Russell Leong wrote in his preface to my *Stone Turtle*:

> In closing, the poet pays homage to the "ancient sacred spirit" of "noble origin" whom he has recognized in a foreign land (America). It is a recognition of a shared unofficial memory – unconnected to bureaucrats, academics, history books, or granite monuments – that the poet finds in a turtle-like rock, as large and heavy as a small human head, along the banks of a polluted river. That turtle-like rock, much like the poet, exists beyond the borders of national identity, East or West, and in fact, is a product of fire, water, air, and the shifting of the earth itself. (Leong 2005, 3)

There are two competing and contested cosmopolitanisms: "the world republic of letters" and the excluded, buried global silence. I, for one, translate myself for the latter, for the affinity I have always felt for Neruda and Hai Zi, for the excluded "stone turtle," and for the buried "copper." The silence embedded by "stone turtle" and "copper" is universal and elemental, a wordless silence overriding the confines of any *lingua franca* of a Western-centric, pompous, imperialistic "world literature" along with its parochial "capital[s]."

8

Back in 2006, September 27, on my last night in Venice, near midnight, I was sitting alone on the steps outside Stazione di Venezia Santa Lucia, facing the Grand Canal and waiting for my overnight train bound for Naples. To my left, not far, a young Asian-looking man, more or less my own look-alike, was chatting with two white girls whom he had just met. They were giggling and having a good time. Soon enough two policemen showed up and interrogated him – in fact, harassed him – for apparently no reason. Eventually the policemen found nothing and left. Having witnessed this incident and wanting to show some sort of support or solidarity, I stood up and approached him, trying to strike up a conversation: "Bro, where are you from?"

To my surprise, he looked at me – another Asian-looking man, a mirror image of himself, but that might be just my own assumption – with distrust. Showing little interest, clearly also with pride, he brushed me off, in a deliberately slow yet defiant tone: "Where am I from? I'm from this planet, I'm from the universe."

I stepped back. It is hard to pin down my exact thoughts at that moment. I did not, nor do I now, completely agree with him, or with that answer.

Nevertheless, it stuck in my mind. I have never forgotten that answer, or his refusal to answer, ever since. To this day, I can still hear it ringing with a universal resonance against the backdrop of the night sky in Venice.

9

Many of my peers in contemporary Chinese poetry yearned for a recognition of "universality" beyond their Chineseness, yet oftentimes it is the same poets who had to set their hopes on their Western translators to help them attain that illusory "universality" in non-native languages. However, as I see it,

> Writing for the universe, and not for the Chinese
> Yet still having to rely upon others to translate and promote your works
> This is not freedom
>> MAI MANG 2016

When I wrote my poem "About Freedom" (*Guanyu ziyou* 關於自由) in 2014, I knew that the encounter I experienced at Venezia Santa Lucia in 2006 was somehow embedded in this stanza above.

So, self-translation, at an existential and metaphysical level, is also my way of taking risks and exploring what "universality" and "freedom" truly are, or are not. I want to reach out on my own and make connections with all those whom I do not know but who I know are always out there, in the dark,

> dug out like copper,
> and buried again,
> back into the source of the earth.

By writing and translating my own "Stone Turtle" and "Copper," I invoke myself and selves, my other and others, who are anonymous and have long existed in this world, in this universe. That means he or she or they, in turn, will have to excavate my "stone turtle" and "copper" from silence, from dried-up riverbeds, from underground, from the deep source of the earth, and also let them go, say "farewell," and let them return "back into the source of the earth."

New London, Connecticut
August–November, 2022

Works Cited

Casanova, Pascale. 2004. *The World Republic of Letters*, translated by M.B. DeBevoise. Cambridge: Harvard University Press.

Eliot, T.S. 1928. "Introduction." In *Selected Poems,* by Ezra Pound, edited by T.S. Eliot, vii–xxv. London: Faber & Gwyer.

Ginsberg, Allen. 1988. *Collected Poems: 1947–1980*. New York: HarperPerennial.

Hai Zi 海子. 1997. *Hai Zi shi quanbian* 海子詩全編 [The Complete Poems of Hai Zi], edited by Xi Chuan 西川. Shanghai: Shanghai sanlian shudian.

Hai Zi 海子. 2010. *Over Autumn Rooftops: Poems by Hai Zi*, translated by Dan Murphy. Austin: Host Publications.

Lai, Him Mark, Genny Lim, and Judy Yung, eds. [1980] 1991. *Island: Poetry and History of Chinese Immigrants on Angel Island, 1910–1940*. Seattle and London: University of Washington Press.

Leong, Russell C. 2005. "Mai Mang: Writing as Recognition." In *Stone Turtle: Poems: 1987–2000*, by Mai Mang, 1–5. Des Moines: Godavaya.

Leong, Russell C. [2001] 2011. "Along L.A. River, Poetic Inspiration." *Amerasia Journal* 37 (1): 174–176.

Lu Xun. 1973. "Silent China." In *Silent China: Selected Writings of Lu Xun*, edited and translated by Gladys Yang, 163–167. London, Oxford, New York: Oxford University Press.

Mai Mang 麥芒. 2005. "Stone Turtle"/"Shigui" 石龜. In *Stone Turtle: Poems: 1987–2000*, by Mai Mang, 150–153. Des Moines: Godavaya; reprinted in *Amerasia Journal* 37 (1), 2011: 171–174.

Mai Mang 麥芒. 2011. "Zhuiqiu juedui mangmu de xiangyu" 追求絕對盲目的相遇 [In Search of an Absolutely Blind Encounter]. In *Shige wuxian de keneng: di san jie Qinghai hu guoji shige jie shiren zuopin ji* 詩歌無限的可能：第三屆青海湖國際詩歌節詩人作品集/*Poetry as an Access to Endless Possibilities: An Anthology of Poems Collected for the Third Edition of Qinghai Lake Poetry Festival*, edited by Jidi Majia 吉狄馬加, 228–229. Xining: Qinghai renmin chubanshe.

Mai Mang 麥芒. 2016. "About Freedom." *World Literature Today*, June 1. Available online: https://www.worldliteraturetoday.org/blog/poetry/two-poems-27-years-after-tia nanmen. Accessed April 20, 2023.

Mai Mang 麥芒. [2013–2014] 2017. "Copper"/"Tong" 銅. In *Asian American Matters: A New York Anthology*, edited by Russell C. Leong, 137. New York: Asian American and Asian Research Institute, The City University of New York.

Neruda, Pablo. 1977. *Memoirs*, translated by Hardie St. Martin. New York: Farrar, Straus and Giroux.

Neruda, Pablo. 1980. "Alturas de Macchu Picchu"/"Heights of Macchu Picchu." In *Translating Neruda: The Way to Macchu Picchu*, by John Felstiner, 202–239. Stanford: Stanford University Press.

Neruda, Pablo. 1983a. "Tong de songge" 銅的頌歌 [Ode to Copper], translated by Zou Jiang 鄒絳. In *Nieluda shixuan* 聶魯達詩選 [Selected Poems of Pablo Neruda], translated by Zou Jiang, Cai Qijiao, et al., 270–277. Chengdu: Sichuan renmin chubanshe.

Neruda, Pablo. 1983b. "Machu Bichu gaofeng" 馬楚·比楚高峰 [The Heights of Macchu Picchu], translated by Lin Yi'an 林一安 and Cai Qijiao 蔡其矯. In *Nieluda shixuan* 聶魯達詩選 [Selected Poems of Pablo Neruda], translated by Zou Jiang, Cai Qijiao, et al., 55–76. Chengdu: Sichuan renmin chubanshe.

Neruda, Pablo. 1991. *Canto General*, translated by Jack Schmitt. Berkeley: University of California Press.

Neruda, Pablo. 2013. "Ode to Copper," translated by Ilan Stavans. In *All the Odes*, by Pablo Neruda, edited by Ilan Stavans, 168–173. New York: Farrar, Straus and Giroux.

Owen, Stephen. 1990. "What Is World Poetry? The Anxiety of Global Influence." *The New Republic*. 203 (21): 28–32.

Whitman, Walt. 2004. *The Complete Poems*, edited by Francis Murphy. London: Penguin Books.

Index

Acculturation 252

Actor-network theory 163, 166

Aesthetics 3, 26, 50, 52, 56, 61, 69, 76, 179, 191

Aku Wuwu 阿庫烏霧 (Luo, Qingchun 羅慶春) 84, 86, 89, 225, 228, 230, 233–235, 238, 240, 243–245, 253

Alai 阿來 83, 91

Amang 阿芒 4, 95–100, 106, 108–109

Angel Island poems 13, 259

Anglophone 4, 11–12, 14, 18, 20, 23–25, 28–29, 41, 65, 84, 86, 116, 175

ANT. *See* actor-network theory

Apter, Emily 56, 64, 75, 89

Assimilation 56*n*6, 178, 245, 252

Australia 14*n*6, 33, 42, 44, 70

Avant-garde 75, 224, 235

Bachner, Andrea 28*n*14, 29, 71*n*9, 87, 89

Bai Juyi 白居易 5, 190–215

Bei Dao 北島 14

Bender, Mark 84–85, 89, 224*n*3, 235, 253

Berman, Antoine 52*n*1, 62, 64

Bernards, Brian 1, 7, 13*n*4, 67–68, 89, 139, 141, 144–145, 160

Bhabha, Homi 23, 29, 68–69, 89

Bicultural 23, 139, 141

Biculturality 125, 136

Bilingual x, 3–4, 15–16, 23, 30–32, 35, 38, 41, 44, 52, 62*n*11, 64, 71, 79, 83, 90–91, 106, 113, 163–165, 170, 176–177, 180–181, 187, 219, 224–225, 227–228, 232*n*11, 233–236, 238, 240, 242, 244, 246*n*18, 249–252, 267

Bilingualism 15, 67, 71, 84

Bilinguality 5, 67, 88

Biliteracy 41

Biliterate 3, 35, 41, 44, 46, 233, 249

Bing Xin 冰心 128*n*9

Blommaert, Jan 50–51, 58, 64

Borders 2–3, 6, 12, 69, 76, 111–113, 127, 140, 163, 194, 256, 269, 274

Border-crossing 6, 58, 69

Bordering 3, 52, 68, 231, 247

Borderland 13, 19, 87

Borges, Jorge Luis 59–60

Borrowing 55, 168

Bradbury, Steve vii, ix, 78*n*16, 79, 89–90, 95, 100, 109

Campos, Haroldo de 23, 32, 70*n*5, 83, 89, 92, 192, 214

Cantonese 12–13, 19–20, 54*n*4, 58–59, 63, 113, 115–116, 118–119, 123, 126*n*5, 133*n*17, 146, 217–219

Casanova, Pascale 256–257, 259, 276

Center 6, 28, 102, 108, 166, 171–172, 178, 186, 192, 225, 256–257, 271–273

Centerless 12

Centric 6, 29, 34, 257, 259, 274

Decenter 11–12

Decentering 24

Decentralized 12

English-centred 28

Recenter 12

Centrism 12*n*2, 13–14, 24, 28

Anglocentric 29

Anglocentrism 23, 28

ethnocentrism 1, 62, 162

Logocentrism 211

Sinocentric 28–29, 71, 87, 103

Sinocentrism 31, 188

Chan, Chi-tak 陳智德 44

Chan, Kwan-po 陳君葆 39, 46

Chan, Mary Jean 44, 46, 50, 56–59, 64, 113

Chan, Wai 陳慧 44

Chang, Kuei-hsing 張貴興 13

Chen, Li 陳黎 71*n*9

Cheng, Tim Tim 44

Cheung, Martha 15, 31

China-Italy mobility network 144, 158

Chinese classical poetry 15, 23, 27, 38, 133, 150, 165, 170–171, 199, 211, 220, 222, 259

Changhen ge 長恨歌 (Song of Everlasting Sorrow) 190, 196

Ci 詞 220

Gu shi shijiu shou 古詩十九首 (The Nineteen Old Poems) 220

Li Sao 離騷 (Encountering Sorrow) 220

Shijing 詩經 (The Classic of Poetry) 220

Xin yuefu 新樂府 199

Yuefu geci 樂府歌辭 (Yue Fu songs) 220

Yuefu 樂府 200

Chineseness 1, 14, 18, 23–24, 35, 43, 46, 52, 91, 111, 124, 145, 148–150, 152–160, 169, 178, 189, 203, 275
Chow, Rey 13, 15, 29, 43, 47, 52, 95, 104–109, 160, 164, 186
Classical Chinese (*wenyan* 文言) 128
Code-mixing 55, 83
Code-switching 23, 55, 67, 118, 122
Cold Mountain Literature (*Liangshan wenxue* 涼山文學) 225, 235
Creativity 1–2, 6, 67–68, 70, 75, 88, 112–114, 122, 154, 162, 167
 Invent 81, 219
 Invention 258
 Reinvent 71, 158, 163, 175
 Re-invention 168n5, 169, 174
 Trans-semiotic creativity 76
Creolization 6, 111
 Creolized 139
Crevel, Maghiel van 30, 32, 69, 171, 176, 187, 189, 234n14
Cross-cultural 17, 21–22, 163, 174, 193, 196
Cross-cultural 16
 Cross-culturality 2, 162
Cross-cultural Studies 15
Cross-epochal 193
Cross-fertilization 123
Cultural-Linguistic Corridors 228–229, 231–232
 Hexi Corridor 230
 Mongolic-Tungusic corridor 231
 Northeast Corridor 231
 Southeast Coast Corridor 231
 Southern Mountains Corridor 231
 Tibet-Qiang-Yi Corridor 230, 252
Cultural-linguistic ecosystem 5, 103, 108, 219
Cultural mosaic 5, 217
Cultural re-colonization 120
Cultural Studies xi, 47, 66, 143, 145, 186

Derrida, Jacques 104–105, 107, 109, 193, 205, 214
Descendants 143–144, 217, 249n19
Dialect 28, 54, 60, 84, 100, 103, 105, 108, 113, 165, 217, 219, 221, 224, 228, 232, 233n12, 235–236, 242n17, 244, 248, 250, 251n21

Diaspora 3, 11, 13–14, 18, 20, 28, 31, 34–35, 83, 147, 160, 164
 Chinese diaspora 7, 41–46, 48, 113, 124, 145, 191
 Diasporic 4, 11, 18–19, 24–25, 28–29, 34–35, 42–44, 46, 87
 Hong Kong diaspora 41–48
 Sinophone diaspora 4
Diglossia 6
 Diglossic 83
Dislocation 175
Displacement 6, 11, 43–44, 76
 Displaced 24, 104, 107, 192
Dominant language 62, 67n1, 99, 105, 257
Dreyzis, Yulia 52, 64, 180, 187
Du Fu 杜甫 190, 198–199, 259

Eliot, T.S. 258, 276
Epistolary Translation 190–215
 Post-postal principle 194, 207
Estrangement 88
Ethnic groups. *See* ethnic minority
Ethnic minority 12, 83, 88, 224, 225n5, 228, 232, 234, 252
 Bai 白 225, 232, 233n11, 241–242, 252
 Bonan 保安 231n10, 232n11
 Bunun 布農 225, 228, 231, 238, 254
 Buyi 布依 225, 233n11, 242
 Dagur/Daur 達斡爾 231, 250
 Dônđăc 傷傣 ix, 225, 228, 231–232, 238, 244, 248–250
 Dong 侗 225, 231, 233n11, 236–237, 241, 247, 249
 Dongxiang 東鄉 231n10, 232n11
 Ewenki 鄂溫克 231, 233n11, 250
 Hani 哈尼 225, 230, 235, 242, 244, 253
 Hezhe 赫哲 231
 Hmong. *See* Miao 苗
 Jingpho 景頗 225, 230, 236, 242, 250, 252
 Kazakh 哈薩克 228, 230, 232n11, 233n11, 250
 Kyrgyz 柯爾克孜 225, 228, 230, 238, 250, 252
 Manchu 滿語 231, 233n11
 Miao 苗 231, 242, 247–250, 255
 Minority languages 224n2, 225n5, 228, 233–234, 239, 249, 251
 Mongol. *See* Mongolian 蒙古

INDEX

Ethnic minority (*cont.*)
 Mongolian 蒙古 227–228, 231, 233*n*11, 238, 241, 246*n*18, 250, 252
 Mosuo 摩梭 230, 246, 252
 Naxi 納西 84, 91, 225, 228, 230, 232, 233*n*11, 241, 246*n*18, 252
 Oirat 衛拉特 230, 252
 Oroqen 鄂倫春 231, 250
 Pumi 普米 225, 230, 235, 250, 251*n*21, 252
 Puyuma 卑南 231, 238
 Qiang 羌 230, 244, 250, 252
 Salar 撒拉 228, 232*n*11
 She 畲 231–232, 249*n*19
 Shui 水 231, 238, 242, 244
 Uyghur 維吾爾 227–228, 230, 232*n*11, 236, 238, 244, 246, 250, 252
 Uzbek 烏孜別克 238
 Wa 佤 225, 230, 235–236, 242
 Xibe 錫伯 225, 230–231, 236
 Yao 瑤 228, 231, 247–250
 Yi 彝 84, 87*n*22, 89, 225, 227–228, 230, 233*n*11, 234, 236*n*16, 238, 242–247, 250, 251*n*21, 252, 254
  Eastern Yi 東彝 230
  Nasu Yi 纳苏彝 230
  Nuosu Yi 諾蘇彝 225, 227, 230, 233*n*11, 234, 236, 243*n*17
 Yugur 裕固 230, 238–239, 250, 252
 Zhuang 壯 231, 247, 249, 252
Ethnic minority poetry 82–87
 A Marjen 瑪爾簡 232*n*11
 A Su 阿蘇 225, 228, 230, 231*n*10, 233, 236, 244, 251–252
 Abiba Yiminjan 艾比拜·依明江 233*n*11
 Abu Jino 阿布基諾 233*n*11
 Abu Masen 阿布馬森 233*n*11
 Achang 阿昌 233*n*11
 Aili Munuo 艾傈木諾 233*n*11, 235
 Aliye Rusol 阿麗耶·如蘇力 230, 233, 236, 240, 244, 246
 Alu Siji 阿魯斯基 225, 227, 235
 Anaer 阿娜爾 230, 233
 Aynur Abdukerim 阿依努尔·阿不都克力木 233*n*11
 Aynur Mawltbek 阿依努爾·毛吾力提 228, 230, 233, 246, 252
 Azhe Luchouzhi 阿哲魯仇直 233*n*11

Bamo Qubumo 巴莫曲布嫫 247
Banamu 芭納木 230, 233, 246
Bayin Hehe 八音赫赫 233*n*11
Bukun Ismahasan Islituan 卜袞·伊斯瑪哈單·伊斯立端 225, 228, 231, 233, 238, 251, 254
Chakdor Gyal 吉多加 230, 232*n*11, 233
Chengxu Erdan 成緒爾聃 230, 233, 244, 250
Chungkyi 瓊吉 233*n*11
Dai Lin 戴琳 233*n*11
Dilmurat Talat 狄力木拉提·泰來提 230, 233, 238, 244, 252
Dong Yongxue 東永學 232*n*11
Feng Maojun 豐茂軍 233*n*11
Feng Na 冯娜 241, 245, 252
Gao Qiongxian 高瓊仙 233*n*11, 246, 250, 253
Gebu 哥布 225, 228, 230, 233–235, 243–244, 251–253
Ha Mo 哈默 232*n*11
Ha Sen 哈森 227*n*8, 228, 231, 233, 245
He Fukai 和富開 233*n*11
He Xiaozhu 何小竹 234*n*13
He Yanxin 何豔新 249–250
He Zhong 賀中 230, 233, 238, 240, 242, 244–245, 250–251
Huang Xiufeng 黃秀鳳 233*n*11
Jibu Riluo 吉布日洛 233*n*11
Jidi Majia 吉狄馬加 234*n*13, 276
Jike Bu 吉克布 230, 233, 246–247, 252
Jjinuo Dazzi 86
Kongno 坤努 225, 228, 230, 233, 236, 244, 246, 250–251
Kulaxihan Muhamaitihan 庫拉西漢·木哈買提漢 232*n*11
Lal Vet 臘維 233*n*11
Lama Itzot 拉瑪伊佐 86–87, 233*n*11, 240
Lan Chaojin 藍金朝 231, 233
Lan Dingguan 藍定官 228, 231, 233
Li Hui 李輝 vii, 225, 228, 231–233, 238, 244, 248–251, 255
Liu Wenqing 劉文青 233*n*11
Li Xingqing 李星青 233*n*11
Luo Yu 羅鈺 230, 233
Luruo Diji 魯若迪基 225, 228, 230, 233–236, 243–244, 250–251
Ma Xuewu 馬學武 232*n*11

Ethnic minority poetry (*cont.*)

Meng Yifei 梦亦非　242–245, 251

Mohammedyehya Tusunbaki 麥麥提亞合亞·吐孫巴克　233*n*11

Mu Xue 牧雪　232*n*11

Na Sa 那薩　230, 233, 239–240, 246, 251–252

Na Ye 娜夜　234*n*13

Narenqiqige 娜仁琪琪格　241

Naren Tuoya 娜仁圖雅　231, 233, 250

Nie Le 聶勒　225, 228, 230, 233–235, 244

Nimei Nami 妮美納蜜　233*n*11

Niu Han 牛漢　234*n*13

Norzin Dolma 郎澤卓瑪　233*n*11

Pan Liwen 潘利文　231, 233, 238

Pan Mei 潘梅　233*n*11

Pan Nianying 潘年英　225, 228, 231, 233, 236, 252

Pema Yangchen 白馬央金　233*n*11

Puchi Daling 普馳達嶺　228, 230, 233

Qin Shuxia 覃淑霞　231, 233, 240

Quan Chunmei 全春梅　233*n*11

Sadet Jamal 薩黛特·加馬力　225, 228, 230, 233, 250

Samarkand 撒瑪爾罕 (Han, Wende 韓文德)　228, 232

Samer Darkpa 沙冒智化　227, 230, 233, 236, 240

Sha Li 沙蠡　84

Shen Congwen 沈從文　234*n*13

Solongod Todgerel 蘇倫嘎德·陶德格日勒　233*n*11

Sugasela 蘇呷色拉　233*n*11

Sun Baoting 孫寶廷　233*n*11

Sun Junmei 孫俊梅　231, 233

Suolang Ciren 索朗次仁　233*n*11

Tenzin Pelmo 旦增白姆　230, 233, 236, 240, 246, 252

Tong Qi 童七　233*n*11

Tong Yu 桐雨　233*n*11

Tung Shuming 董恕明　231, 233

Turahan Tohuti 圖拉汗·托乎提　232*n*11

Wang Mei 王玫　233*n*11

Wolfman 人狼格 (Li Chenghan 李承翰)　225, 228, 230, 233, 236, 241

Wu Tianwei 吳天威　233*n*11

Wu Yingli 吳穎麗　231, 233

Xi Chu 西楚　231, 233, 242, 251–252

Xi Murong 席慕鋥　234*n*13

Ye Zheng-guang 葉正光　233*n*11

Yi Wei 一葦　233*n*11

Yi Wu 依烏　230, 233, 235, 238, 242–245, 254

Yungdrung Gyurmè 永中久美　227, 230, 233, 236, 240, 244, 252

Zhang Yun 張雲　233*n*11

Zhan Jiayu 詹家雨　233*n*11

Zhong Xiuhua 鍾秀華　231–233, 244, 252

Ethnicity　5–6, 111, 223–225, 232, 244–246

European　xi, 23, 25, 51, 146–147, 157

Evangelista, Elin-Maria　70, 90

Exile　13, 199, 221*n*1

Exiled　30, 67

Feeley, Jennifer　15, 31

Fei Xiaotong 費孝通　229

Feminism　xi, 245

Feminist　76, 245, 247, 250

Folk poetry　225, 245

Foreignizing　53, 118–119

Foreignness　6, 56, 260, 267

Gao, Jay　50, 53, 61, 64

Ginsberg, Allen　264–267, 276

Global English　11, 13, 18, 25, 28–29

Grafting　118, 123

Gramling, David　69, 70*n*5, 90

Grutman, Rainier　67, 83, 90

Guangzhou　14, 35*n*1, 37–38, 41–42, 46–47

Gu Cheng 顧城　13*n*5

Ha Jin 哈金　13, 30, 67*n*2, 90, 112, 164

Hai Zi 海子　269–274, 276

Hakka 客家　20, 54, 104

Han Shan 寒山　259

Han 漢　85, 132*n*16, 146, 224*n*1, 232, 234, 236*n*16, 242, 244, 247, 249, 251*n*21, 252

He Da 何達　39, 47

Hegemony　1, 62, 73, 83, 100, 106, 108, 257, 259

Counterhegemonic　103

Dehegemonization　5, 192

Hegemonic　6, 104, 256

Heidegger, Martin　204–205

INDEX

Heritage 5, 14*n*6, 123, 125, 145, 150, 157–159, 173, 192, 203, 217, 220, 240

Ho, Tammy Lai-Ming 何麗明 3, 12, 14, 18–20, 29–30, 32, 41, 44, 121*n*2, 123

Hokkien 54, 63, 100, 102*n*4, 104–105

Holton, Brian 15, 31

Homeland 5, 34, 36, 41–42, 44, 112, 114, 121–122, 125, 137, 150, 158, 165, 177, 200, 253, 256

Hong Kong xiii, 4, 7, 13–15, 18–20, 29–32, 34–35, 37–38, 41–44, 46–49, 52, 54, 56*n*7, 57, 59nn8, 9, 65, 67, 76, 89, 112–113, 117–118, 120, 122, 128*n*8, 137*n*22, 146, 217, 258

    Anti-Extradition 18–19, 42, 47

    Handover 18, 42, 120, 122

    Hong Kong literature 3, 34, 41, 43, 47–48, 114, 122

    Hong Kong poetry 3, 15, 34–50

    Occupy Central 19

    Umbrella Movement 18–19, 42, 121

Hongkongeseness 46

Honglou meng 紅樓夢 (The Dream of the Red Chamber) 133

Howe, Sarah 50, 56*n*7, 59–60, 65, 113, 123–124

Hsia Yü 夏宇 vii, ix, 75–82, 88–90, 92

Hu Shi 胡適 92, 128, 131

Hybrid 2, 12, 51*n*1, 87–88, 115, 179, 244–245

    Cultural hybrid (*wenhua hunxue* 文化混血) 84

Hybridity 1, 3, 14, 41, 65, 69, 83–84, 88, 114

Hybridization 112, 118, 122

    Hybridized 4–5, 118, 123

Identity 5–6, 39, 50, 55, 57, 63, 67, 75, 96, 98, 104, 111, 113, 125, 130, 132, 136, 140, 143–144, 157–159, 163–166, 173–176, 178, 181, 184–185, 192, 194, 205, 208, 238, 244, 265

    Cross-cultural identity 162

    Cultural identity 3, 13, 18, 25, 41, 44, 46, 51, 71, 111, 164

    Ethnic identity 235, 244

    Linguistic identity 60, 164

    Literary identity 34

    National identity 51*n*1, 60, 274

    Postmonolingual identity 2

Imagery 81, 133, 136, 140, 157, 211

In-between 2, 18, 70, 87, 114, 122, 125, 141

In-betweenness 4, 6, 65, 69–70, 78*n*17, 86–88, 112, 114, 122, 125, 208

Indonesia 13, 32, 129

Interference 55

Intertextuality xi, 158, 163

Ip, Joshua 小葉子 3, 12, 14, 20–24, 29–30, 192, 214

June Fourth 42

Kellman, Steven 1, 2*n*1, 7, 52, 65–66, 90, 109, 112, 114, 122, 124

Kwek, Theophilus 50, 55, 61, 65

Lee, Laura Jane 50, 54–55, 61, 65

Leftist 38–39

Leung, Ping-kwan 梁秉鈞 13–16, 21, 29, 31, 41

Li Bai 李白 30, 133, 151, 168–169, 190, 199, 250, 259

Li Shangyin 李商隱 27*n*12

Li Yung-p'ing 李永平 13

Liang, Qichao 梁啟超 40, 48

Lim, Daryl Wei Jie 林偉傑 5, 190–215

Lingua franca 98, 242, 245, 256, 274

Little Poetry Mill

    Bo Fu 博夫 128*n*10

    Dan Dan 澹澹 128*n*10

    Fan Jun 范軍 128*n*10

    Jing Ying 晶瑩 128*n*10

    Jin Shi 今石 128*n*10

    Ku Jue 苦覺 128*n*10

    Lan Yan 藍焰 128*n*10

    Ling Nanren 嶺南人 128*n*10, 141

    Wen Xiaoyun 溫小雲 128*n*10

    Yang Ling 楊玲 128*n*10

    Yang Zhuo 楊棟 128*n*10

Liu Wai-tong 廖偉棠 30, 44

Liu Xia 劉霞 xii, 164

Local 11, 18, 24, 34, 38, 44, 54, 83, 100, 103–105, 117, 143, 145, 147–148, 155, 165, 191, 205, 220, 225, 233*n*12, 248–249, 268

Localization 6, 11, 18, 43–44, 111, 144

    Locality 3

    Localized 11, 43, 152

INDEX

Lok Fung 洛楓 15*n*7, 31
Lu Xun 魯迅 xiii, 199, 258, 276

Mainland China 2, 12–13, 34, 38, 41–42, 95, 101, 120, 162, 165, 203
   Mainlandization 18
Malaysia 13, 52, 129
   Malay 24, 53*n*3, 54
   Malaysian 71*n*9, 192
Mandarin 12–13, 20, 24, 51*n*1, 54, 59*n*8, 63, 103, 105–106, 113, 115–116, 118, 120, 123, 126*n*5, 132, 133*n*17, 144, 217
   Standard Chinese. *See* Mandarin
Mandarinization 224*n*2, 225, 252
Manipulation 72, 96, 168, 181
Mao Zedong 毛澤東 38, 47
Maoism 38
Margins 1–2, 6, 77, 112
   De-marginalizing 1
   Marginalized 144, 242
May Fourth Movement 40, 127
Meng Haoran 孟浩然 190, 199
Metalanguage 76
Migrant x, 3, 52, 58, 67, 69, 112–116, 119–120, 122–123, 159–160, 166, 168, 174, 180
   Immigrants 5, 11, 43, 146–147, 159, 190, 217, 259, 264
   Migrant literature x, 114, 122
   Migrants 5, 11, 43, 46, 63, 112, 115–116, 124, 146–147, 219
Migration 3, 6, 22, 34–35, 41–42, 52, 55*n*5, 58, 64, 113–114, 116–117, 123, 146–147, 158–159, 173, 175, 229, 231*n*10, 232, 251
Miller, Cynthia 50, 53–54, 61, 65
Ming Di 明迪 162–190
Minor literature 83*n*20, 89
Minority literature (*shaoshu minzu wenxue* 少數民族文學). *See* ethnic minority
Misty poets 234, 235*n*15
   Post-Misty poets 235*n*15, 245
Mobility Studies 4, 144, 158
Monolingual 3, 6, 21, 23, 50, 54, 57–59, 61–63, 81, 86, 99–100, 104, 106, 238
   Postmonolingual 4, 51, 58, 95
Monolingualism 14, 51, 67*n*2, 73, 88, 90, 104–105, 107
Mother tongue 3–4, 6, 24, 44, 46, 55, 57–58, 82*n*19, 96, 100, 104–105, 108, 111–112,

115, 119, 122–125, 132, 139–140, 154–155, 157, 163, 165–166, 177–178, 192, 217, 222, 224–225, 227, 232, 233*n*12, 236, 238–239, 242, 244, 251, 263
   First mother tongue 84, 239
   Second mother tongue 84, 239
Multilingual 1–4, 12, 19–20, 41, 50, 52–54, 56–58, 60–64, 67–68, 75–76, 78, 82, 87–88, 90, 95, 106–108, 144, 146, 166, 219
Multilingualism 3, 15, 51–53, 55–57, 59–60, 63, 66, 67*n*2, 68, 71*n*9, 88, 99
Multilinguality 111
Muyu 母語. *See* mother tongue

Native 2, 13–14, 50, 58–59, 84, 95, 98, 100–102, 105–106, 108, 115, 119, 151, 154, 164, 176, 180, 202, 234, 239–241, 254, 256, 275
Neruda, Pablo 269–274, 276–277
New Culture Movement 127–128
New Poetry xii, 128, 170, 188, 234
Ng, Florence 吳智欣 41, 44
Ng, Kim-chew 黃錦樹 13
Ng, Mei-kwan 吳美筠 44
Nontranslation 56
Nostalgia 3, 5, 11, 18, 25, 34, 43–44, 150, 158
Not Not (group/journal/ Movement) 234–235
Nüshu 女書 (Women's Script) 245, 253

Oral literature 252
Othering 68, 71–72, 145, 185
   Thirding-as-Othering 69, 84, 86, 88
Otherness 5–6, 65, 69, 88, 107
   Alterity 56, 58–59, 74
Outer Out 鷗外鷗 42
Ouyang Yu 歐陽昱 70–75, 88, 90–91, 180
Overseas 41, 144, 147, 155

Periphery 178, 225, 257, 272
Philippines 13
Pinyin viii, 20, 53–54, 63, 74, 116, 118, 242
Place-based 1, 4, 11, 44, 144
Plurilingual 62*n*11
Poetics 3–4, 14, 17, 26*n*11, 66–67, 69, 72, 75–76, 81, 84, 86, 88, 90, 104, 125, 136, 140, 143, 157, 169, 173, 192, 211
Poetry East West 164, 185

INDEX

Polyphony   17, 29, 78, 84, 112
   Polyphonic   1–2, 12, 23, 82–83, 88, 107,
      123, 162
Polyscriptic   1, 83, 86, 88
Postcolonial   11, 23–24, 57, 99, 104–105,
      107–109, 141, 192, 212
Postcolonial Studies   15, 95, 99, 107
Pound, Ezra   15, 26n11, 55–56, 60, 65,
      168–169, 174, 189, 258, 260, 276
Proctor-Xu, Jami 徐贞敏   4, 95, 106–109
Putonghua 普通話. *See* Mandarin

Qing Ping 清平 form   219–220

Refugees   27, 42
Regional poetry   156, 225, 242, 252
Resistance   48, 120, 241
Rhythm   22, 79, 165, 222
Ricoeur, Paul   63n12, 65
Rojas, Carlos.   91
Roots   4, 6, 34, 88, 123, 133, 136, 178, 191,
      202–203, 263, 271
Routes   6, 35, 42, 88, 205, 231–232
Rushdie, Salman   20, 31, 163

Sakai, Naoki   50–51, 56, 63, 65
Sense of distance   174, 185
Shih, Shu-mei   1, 3, 7, 11–13, 18, 24–25, 35, 41,
      43–44, 48, 68, 111, 124, 132n16, 144
Shu, Hong-sing 舒巷城   15n8, 41
Shuihu zhuan 水滸傳 (Water Margins)   133
Singapore   5, 21–24, 28, 52, 54n4, 55n5, 129,
      191, 199, 201, 203, 211
Sinitic
   Sinitic language   1, 11–12, 28, 41, 67, 84,
      111–112, 162
   Sinitic script   125, 127n5, 132–133, 136, 140
Sino-Italian Literature   143–162
   Heng Zhi 衡之   148, 151–152, 157, 160
   Hu Lanbo 胡蘭波   148, 154–157,
      159–160
   Li Shuman 李叔蔓   148, 154, 157, 159
   Mao Wen 毛文   148, 152–154, 157,
      159–161
Sinophone Literature   1–2, 4, 13, 66, 67n1, 68,
      111–112, 123, 160, 202
Sinophone Studies   3–4, 11–13, 18, 28–29, 31,
      70, 144, 164, 188

Sinophone Studies: A Critical Reader, edited
      by Shu-mei Shih, Chien-hsin Tsai, and
      Brian Bernards   7, 29–31, 90–91, 123,
      141
Sinosphere   1–4, 34, 44, 66–67, 88, 144
Sino-Thai Literature   125–143
   Ling Nanren 嶺南人   137–138
   Lin Huanzhang 林煥彰   126, 128
   Ma Fan 馬凡 (Ma, Qingquan
      馬清泉)   134, 141
   Miniature poetry   128
   Sima Gong 司馬攻   129–131, 134, 142
   Zeng Xin 曾心   126, 127n6, 128, 130n15,
      131–137, 141–142
Small poems. *See* small poetry   136
Small poetry   4, 125–143
Soja, Edward   69, 88, 91
Song, Chris (Song Zijiang 宋子江)   3, 12,
      14–18, 29, 31–32, 41, 44, 64
Southbound writers   3, 34, 42–43
Spivak, Gayatri Chakravorty   99, 109, 144,
      177, 178n13, 188
Su Shi 蘇軾   133
Subaltern   88, 144
Subjectivity   6, 69, 87, 95, 99, 106–107

Taiwan   4, 13, 44, 67, 75, 91–92, 95, 100,
      102nn5–6, 103–104, 109–110, 125, 128,
      141, 151, 165, 188, 228, 231, 238, 251
   Taiwanese   71n9, 75, 91, 95, 100, 102n4,
      103–105, 108, 126, 179n14
Tang 唐   5, 21–22, 24–25, 27–28, 30, 32, 102,
      151, 168–169, 175, 190–192, 198, 200, 214,
      236
Teochew   126n5, 133n17
Thirdlanguaging   3, 66–92
   Thirdlanguaged   70, 83–84, 87
Thirdspace   69, 76, 82–83, 87–88, 91
Tibetan   227–228, 232, 236, 241, 246, 249,
      251n21, 252
   Amdo Tibetan 安多藏   230233n11,
      232n11, 251n21
   Kham Tibetan 康藏   230, 239
   Tsang Tibetan 後藏   230
   Ü Tibetan 衛藏   230, 238
Tones   45, 99, 150, 221, 227n6
Transcreation   23, 70n5, 179–180, 192
   Transcreative   180

Transcultural 1, 4–6, 102, 125, 136, 139–140, 150, 152, 158, 162, 165, 168, 197, 205, 212
Translatability 6, 62, 90
   Untranslatability 53, 74–75
      Untranslatable 58, 74, 84
Translation
   Agents of translation 172, 174
   Antitranslation 50
   Co-translation 86, 162, 165, 171, 175–176, 178, 180–181, 183–186
   Cross-translation 165
   Cultural translation xi, 241–245
   Fidelity 16–17, 21–22
   Mental translation 251
   Nontranslation 50
   Self-translation x, xi, 3, 5–6, 16–17, 30, 50, 67, 83, 90, 114, 154, 158, 162, 177–182, 186, 251–252, 256–277
      Rewriting 67, 178, 251
   Translation policy 173
   Translation strategy 102, 206
   Translation Studies x, xi, xiii, 21, 25, 31, 61n10, 65–66, 166, 186, 189
Translational 1–2, 6, 12, 14–15, 21, 23, 29, 41, 46, 59, 64, 66, 68, 167n4, 181, 206
Translationality 3, 29
Translingual 1–6, 12, 58, 63, 66–69, 81, 83, 87–88, 95, 98–100, 102–106, 108–109, 114, 212
Translingualism 2, 4, 12, 52, 66–68, 76, 78, 82, 95–96, 103, 109, 112, 114, 122, 124
   Translanguaging 67, 144
Transliteration 40, 54–55
Transmutation 192
Transnational xi, 4, 42, 112, 144, 152, 194, 199, 257
Transplantation 118–119, 123, 211
Tsai, Chien-hsin 7, 68, 89
Tsai, Wan-Shuen 蔡宛璇 4, 95, 100–106, 108, 110
Tsu, Jing 1, 7, 13n4, 29–30, 32, 48, 91–92, 112, 124
Tymoczko, Maria 65

Wan, Kin-lau 溫健騮 41
Wang Jiaxin 王家新 179n14, 181, 186
Wang Tao Mode (*Wang Tao moshi* 王韜模式) 34–50
Wang Wei 王維 21–22, 24, 26, 32, 103, 190, 259
Wang Xiaoni 王小妮 208
Wang, David Der-wei 1, 7, 12–13, 29–30, 32, 48, 91–92, 112, 124
Weinberger, Eliot 22, 24–26, 32
Wen Wei Po 文匯報 38, 47, 49
Wen Yiduo 聞一多 176
Whitman, Walt 199, 260, 263–268, 277
Wong, Jennifer 4, 44, 111–124
Wong Man 黃雯 3, 15n8, 35–50
Wong, May 黃梅 3, 12, 14, 24–29, 32
Wong, Phui Nam 黃佩南 192, 198
World language 13
World literature 2n1, 5–6, 165, 170, 256–257, 259, 272, 274
World poetry 92, 176n12, 257, 277
World Republic of Letters 256–257, 259, 261, 274

Xi Chuan 西川 xi, 28n13, 30, 32, 276
Xu Zhimo 徐志摩 40, 49

Yang Lian 楊煉 x, 13n5, 67n2
Yeh, Michelle 13, 15, 31, 33, 75–76, 78, 92, 104, 109–110, 170–171, 175–176, 189
Yesi 也斯. *See* Leung, Ping-kwan 梁秉鈞
Yijing 易經 53
Yildiz, Yasemin 2, 7, 50–51, 58, 65
Ying Chen 應晨 67n2
Yip, Eric 44, 59, 65
Yip, Victor 50
Yu Kwang-chung (Yu Guangzhong 余光中) 30, 90, 179n14, 186–187

Zhang Huan 張洹 ix, vii
Zhang, Yinde 7, 12n3, 33, 112, 124
Zhou Zuoren 周作人 128